Oxford Practice Grammar

With answers

John Eastwood

Oxford University Press

Oxford University Press
Great Clarendon Street, Oxford OX2 6DP

Oxford New York
Athens Auckland Bangkok Bogota Bombay Buenos Aires
Calcutta Cape Town Dar es Salaam Delhi Florence Hong Kong
Istanbul Karachi Kuala Lumpur Madras Madrid Melbourne
Mexico City Nairobi Paris Singapore Taipei Tokyo Toronto Warsaw

and associated companies in
Berlin Ibadan

Oxford and *Oxford English*
are trade marks of Oxford University Press

ISBN 0 19 431352 2 (with answers)
ISBN 0 19 431353 0 (without answers)

© Oxford University Press 1992

First published 1992
Ninth impression 1997

No unauthorized photocopying.

All rights reserved. No part of this publication may be
reproduced, stored in a retrieval system, or transmitted,
in any form or by any means, electronic, mechanical,
photocopying, recording, or otherwise, without the
prior written permission of Oxford University Press.

This book is sold subject to the condition that it shall
not, by way of trade or otherwise, be lent, resold,
hired out, or otherwise circulated without the
publisher's prior consent in any form of binding or
cover other than that in which it is published and
without a similar condition including this condition
being imposed on the subsequent purchaser.

Illustrated by Margaret Heath

Typeset by Tradespools Ltd., Frome, Somerset
Printed in Hong Kong

Contents

Thanks & key to symbols

Introduction

Main verb forms

1 Present continuous and present simple: **I am doing** and **I do**
2 Present continuous or simple? **I am doing** or **I do**?
3 State verb or action verb? **I think** or **I am thinking**?
4 The present perfect: **I have done**
5 The past simple: **I did**
6 Present perfect or past simple? **I have done** or **I did**?
7 Past continuous or simple? **I was doing** or **I did**?
8 Present perfect continuous: **I have been doing**
9 **I have been doing** or **I have done**?
10 Past perfect: **I had done**
11 Past perfect continuous: **I had been doing**
12 Review of present and past tenses
13 **be going to** and **will**
14 **be going to** or **will**?
15 Present tenses for the future
16 **will be doing** and **will have done**
17 Review of the future
18 **have** and **have got**
19 The action verb **have**
20 Short forms, e.g. **'s, 've**

Negatives, questions and answers

21 Negative statements
22 Questions
23 Subject/object questions, e.g. **Who saw you?** / **Who did you see?**
24 **who, what** or **which**?
25 Short answers, e.g. **Yes, it is.**
26 Question tags, e.g. It's nice, **isn't it?**
27 The patterns **So/Neither do I** and **I hope so/not**

Modal verbs

28 **can, could** and **be able to**
29 **can, may, could** and **be allowed to**
30 Saying something is possible or certain: **may, could, must** etc.
31 **must** and **have to**
32 **mustn't** or **needn't / don't have to**?
33 Requests, offers and suggestions: **Would you...? Shall I...?** etc.
34 **should, ought to, had better** and **be supposed to**
35 It **may/could/must have been** etc.
36 Review of **will, would, shall** and **should**

Contents

The passive

37 Passive verb forms
38 Active or passive? **I did it** or **It was done**?
39 Special passive patterns: **I was given . . .**, **It is said . . .** and **He is said to . . .**
40 **have/get something done**
41 **to be done** and **being done**

Infinitive and ing-form

42 Verb + to-infinitive or verb + ing-form? (want **to play** / enjoy **playing**)
43 **start, like** etc. + to-infinitive/ing-form
44 Verb + object + to-infinitive, e.g. **invite a friend to stay**
45 Infinitive with and without **to**
46 Question word + to-infinitive, e.g. I know **what to do**
47 **for** with the to-infinitive, e.g. wait **for you to finish**
48 Verb/Adjective + preposition + ing-form, e.g. **think of going**
49 **afraid to do** or **afraid of doing**?
50 **used to do** or **used to doing**?
51 Preposition or linking word + ing-form, e.g. **before leaving**
52 **go shopping** and **do the shopping**
53 **see it happen** or **see it happening**?
54 Some patterns with the ing-form, e.g. I lay in bed **reading**

Talking about grammar

55 Word classes: noun, adjective etc.
56 The parts of a sentence: subject, object etc.

Nouns and articles (**a/an** and **the**)

57 Count nouns (e.g. **a cup**) and mass nouns (e.g. **milk**)
58 Count or mass? e.g. **a cake** or **cake**?
59 Agreement, e.g. **My foot hurts / My feet hurt**
60 Singular or plural: **clothes, news, means** etc.
61 Pair nouns (e.g. **trousers**) and group nouns (e.g. **team**)
62 **a/an** or **the**?
63 General statements, e.g. **cars** or **the cars**, **money** or **the money**?
64 **go to school, stay in bed** etc.
65 **on Thursday, for lunch, by car** etc.
66 **quite, such** and **what** with **a/an**
67 Place names and **the**
68 Direct and indirect objects, e.g. give **me the money**

Demonstratives, possessives and quantifiers

- 69 **this, that, these** and **those**
- 70 **my, your** etc; **mine, yours** etc.
- 71 **the boy's name** or **the name of the boy**?
- 72 **some** and **any**
- 73 **a lot of, many, much, a few** and **a little**
- 74 **all, most, some, every, each, both** and **none**

Pronouns

- 75 Personal pronouns, e.g. **I, you**
- 76 **there** and **it**
- 77 Reflexive and emphatic pronouns, e.g. **myself, yourself**
- 78 Review of pronouns and possessives
- 79 The pronoun **one/ones**
- 80 **everyone, something** etc.

Adjectives and adverbs

- 81 Adjectives and word order, e.g. a **cold** day
- 82 **exciting** or **excited**?
- 83 Adjective + preposition, e.g. **full of** water
- 84 Adjective + to-infinitive, e.g. **ready to go**
- 85 Adjective or adverb? **nice** or **nicely**?
- 86 Comparative and superlative forms, e.g. **taller, tallest**
- 87 Comparative and superlative patterns, e.g. **taller than, as tall as**
- 88 **much faster, faster and faster** etc.
- 89 Adverbs and word order
- 90 **yet, still** and **already**
- 91 Adverbs of degree, e.g. **very, quite**
- 92 **quite** and **rather**
- 93 **too** and **enough**

Prepositions

- 94 Prepositions of place, e.g. **to, off, near**
- 95 **in, on** and **at** (place)
- 96 **in, on** and **at** (time)
- 97 **for, since, ago** and **before**
- 98 **during** or **while**? **by** or **until**? **as** or **like**?
- 99 Preposition + noun, e.g. **on holiday**
- 100 Noun + preposition, e.g. the **answer to** the question

Contents

Verbs with prepositions and adverbs

101 Prepositional verbs, e.g. **wait for**
102 Verb + object + preposition, e.g. **thank them for** their help
103 Phrasal verbs, e.g. **go out**, **turn round**
104 Verb + adverb + preposition, e.g. **catch up with**

Reported speech

105 Direct and reported speech
106 Changes in reported speech
107 Reported questions
108 Reported requests, offers etc.

Relative clauses

109 Relative clauses with **who**, **which** and **that**
110 The relative pronoun as object, e.g. the letter **that** I wrote
111 Prepositions in relative clauses, e.g. the letter I was looking **for**
112 Relative patterns with **whose**, **what** and **it**
113 The use of relative clauses
114 **people arriving early, people left behind** and **the first people to arrive**

if-clauses

115 Patterns with **if**
116 **if**, **when**, **unless** and **in case**
117 **wish** and **if only**

Other linking words

118 **but**, **although**, and **in spite of**
119 **to**, **in order to**, **so that** and **for**
120 Review of linking words

American English   p 288

Irregular verbs   p 292

Key to the exercises   p 294

Index   p 326

Thanks

The author and publisher would like to thank:

all the teachers in the United Kingdom and Italy who discussed this book in the early stages of its development;

Thomas Lavelle for his work on the American English appendix;

the teachers and students of the following schools who used and commented on the pilot units of this book:
  The Bell School of Languages, Bowthorpe Hall, Norwich
  The Eckersley School of English, Oxford
  Eurocentre, Brighton
  Eurocentre, London Victoria
  King's School of English, Bournemouth
  Academia Lacunza – International House, San Sebastian, Spain

Rod Bolitho

Sheila Eastwood

Key to symbols

Phonetic symbols

iː	tea	ɜː	bird	p	put	f	first	h	house
ɪ	sit	ə	away	b	best	v	van	m	must
e	ten	eɪ	pay	t	tell	θ	three	n	next
æ	had	əʊ	so	d	day	ð	this	ŋ	song
ɑː	car	aɪ	cry	k	cat	s	sell	l	love
ɒ	dog	aʊ	now	g	good	z	zoo	r	rest
ɔː	ball	ɔɪ	boy	tʃ	cheese	ʃ	ship	j	you
ʊ	book	ɪə	dear	dʒ	just	ʒ	pleasure	w	will
uː	fool	eə	chair						
ʌ	cup	ʊə	sure						

' = stress follows, e.g. **about** [əˈbaʊt]
↘ = falling intonation
↗ = rising intonation

Other symbols

The symbol / (oblique stroke) between two words means that either word is possible. *I **may** / **might** go* means that *I may go* and *I might go* are both possible.

Brackets ( ) around a word or phrase mean that it can be left out. *There's **(some)** milk in the fridge* means that there are two possible sentences: *There's **some** milk in the fridge* and *There's milk in the fridge*.

The symbol ~ means that there is a change of speaker.
The symbol □ in an exercise means an example.

Introduction

Who is this book for?

The *Oxford Practice Grammar* is for students of English at a middle or 'intermediate' level. This means students who are no longer beginners but are not yet expert in English. The book is suitable for those studying for the Cambridge First Certificate in English. It can be used by students attending classes or by someone working alone.

What does the book consist of?

The book consists of 120 units, each on a grammatical topic. The units cover the main areas of English grammar. Special attention is given to those points which are often a problem for learners, such as the meaning of the different verb forms, the use of the passive, if-clauses, prepositions and so on.

Many units contrast two or more different patterns such as the present perfect and past simple. The emphasis is on the meaning and use of the forms in context.

Each unit consists of explanations and examples followed by a number of exercises. In most units the explanations are on the left-hand page and the exercises on the right-hand page. There are also some special four-page units on major grammatical topics, with two pages of explanation and two pages of exercises.

The examples are in everyday conversational English, except for the few patterns which are more typical of a formal style.

There is also an appendix on American English (p 288) and a list of irregular verbs (p 292).

How should a student use the book?

The book is not intended as material that a student should work through from beginning to end. Students should use the book to get help with any point of grammar which they need to learn more about or which is giving them problems.

The method of use is as follows.
1. Consult the contents list (p 3) or the index (pp 326–334) to find the relevant unit.
2. Study the explanations and examples.
3. Do the exercises. (Learning will usually be more effective if you do the exercises.) The letter at the beginning of each exercise (A, B etc.) tells you which part of the explanation it relates to. You can write your answers in the book or on a separate sheet of paper.
4. Check your answers with the key (pp 294–325). If you have made mistakes, look back at the explanation.

Oxford Practice Grammar

1 Present continuous and present simple

A The present continuous

The present continuous is the present tense of **be** + the ing-form:
  I'm getting the lunch ready.   *Sarah isn't working today.*
  We're playing cards.   *What are you looking at?*

I **am playing**	OR	**I'm playing**
you/we/they **are playing**	OR	**you're playing**
he/she/it **is playing**	OR	**he's playing**
I'm not playing		**am** I **playing?**
you/we/they **aren't playing**		**are** you **playing?**
he/she/it **isn't playing**		**is** he **playing?**

We use the present continuous to say that we are in the middle of an action. For more details about use see Unit 2.

B The present simple

In the present simple we use the verb without an ending:
  *I **get** the lunch ready at one o'clock, usually.*
  *We **play** tennis most weekends.*
  *Most children **like** ice-cream.*

But in the third person singular (after **he**, **she**, **it**, **your friend** etc), the verb ends in **s** or **es**:
  *He **wants** some help.*
  *My sister **catches** the early train.*

| I/you/we/they **play** |
| he/she/it **plays** |

We use a form of **do** in negatives and questions. We use **do** and **don't** except in the third person singular, where we use **does** and **doesn't**.
Negatives: *We **don't play** tennis in winter.*   *He **doesn't want** any help.*
Questions: ***Do** you **play** tennis?*   *What **does** he **want**?*

| I/you/we/they **do not play** OR **don't play** | **do** I/you/we/they **play?** |
| he/she/it **does not play** OR **doesn't play** | **does** he/she/it **play?** |

We do not add **s** to the verb in negatives and questions.
  NOT *He doesn't plays* or *Does he plays?*

We use the present simple for repeated actions and for thoughts, feelings and states. For more details about use see Unit 2.

1 Exercises

1.1 The present continuous (A)

Complete the conversation. Put in a present continuous form of the verbs.

A: What □ _are you doing_ ?   □ you do
B: I □ _'m writing_ a letter. We ¹_____ to organize a   □ write 1 try
disco.
A: ²_____ time for all your other work too?   2 you find
B: Oh yes. Julie ³_____ me with the disco.   3 help
We ⁴_____ on fine. And there isn't much to do.   4 get
It ⁵_____ too much of my time. Oh, sorry.   5 not take
⁶_____ for the typewriter?   6 you wait
A: Yes, but there's no hurry.
B: I ⁷_____ the last bit of the letter. I've nearly   7 type
finished.

1.2 The present simple (B)

Put in the verb. Use the present simple. You have to decide if the verb is positive or negative.

□ Jerry is very sociable. He _knows_ lots of people.   □ know
□ We've got plenty of chairs. We _don't want_ any more.   □ want
1 Richard is finding life in Paris a bit difficult. He _____   1 speak
French.
2 We live quite close to the school, so the children _____   2 walk
there.
3 I've got my sports kit a bit dirty. This shirt _____ a good   3 need
wash.
4 I've got four cats and two dogs. I _____ animals.   4 love
5 What's the matter? You _____ very happy.   5 look
6 Don't try to use that lamp. It _____ .   6 work
7 I hate telephone answering machines. I _____ talking to   7 like
them.
8 Pamela is good at badminton. She _____ every game.   8 win

1.3 The present continuous and present simple (A, B)

Put in these words: **are, aren't, is, isn't, do, don't, does** and **doesn't**.

A: Who ¹_____ Michelle talking to?
B: I can't see Michelle.
A: You ²_____ looking in the right place. She's over there.
B: Oh, that's Adrian. He's new here.
A: Really? Where ³_____ he live? ⁴_____ you know?
B: No, I ⁵_____ .
A: What ⁶_____ they talking about, I wonder?
B: Well, he ⁷_____ look very interested. He's got a very bored expression. And he
⁸_____ saying anything.

2 Present continuous or simple?

A Now or sometimes?

Look at these examples:

Now compare:

PRESENT CONTINUOUS	PRESENT SIMPLE
We use the present continuous for something happening now. *I'm painting a picture* means that I am in the middle of doing it.	We use the present simple for repeated actions. *I paint pictures* means that I do it again and again.

Here are some more examples:

It**'s raining** at the moment.	It always **rains** at the weekend.
Don't switch off the TV. I**'m watching** it.	I **watch** television most evenings.
Look. That man **is taking** a photo of you.	Jeremy is a photographer. He **takes** photos for a newspaper.

B Thoughts, feelings and states

We normally use the present simple with verbs of thinking and feeling:

    I **think** you're right.   Julia **likes** her job.   He **wants** a new bike.

We also use it to talk about states and permanent facts (see Unit 3):

    I **know** Jane quite well.   Paris **lies** on the River Seine.

C Temporary or permanent?

Compare:

PRESENT CONTINUOUS	PRESENT SIMPLE

We use the present continuous for a routine or situation that we see as temporary, for a short period:
    I**'m working** at a sports shop for six weeks.
    At the moment they**'re living** in a very small flat.
	We use the present simple for a routine or situation that we see as permanent:
	    I **work** at a sports shop. It's a permanent job.
	    They **live** in a very nice flat.

D The present continuous with **always**

In this special pattern **always** means 'very often' or 'too often':

    Peter **is always inviting** friends here. (= He very often invites them.)
    I**'m always making** silly mistakes. (= I make silly mistakes too often.)

Always with the present simple means 'every time':

    Peter **always invites** his parents to stay at Christmas.
    I **always make** silly mistakes when I'm taking an exam.

2 Exercises

2.1 Present continuous or simple? (A, B)

Complete the conversation between two students called Duncan and Paul. Put in the present continuous or simple of the verbs.

Duncan:	▢ _Are you waiting_ for someone?	▢ you wait
Paul:	Yes – for Neil. We ▢ _walk_ home together most days. We ¹_____ in the same street.	▢ walk 1 live
Duncan:	I'm not sure, but I ²_____ he ³_____ to Mr Davis about something.	2 think 3 talk
Paul:	Yes, I ⁴_____ . He told me. What about you? What ⁵_____ here?	4 know 5 you do
Duncan:	I ⁶_____ for the secretary. I can't find her anywhere.	6 look
Paul:	She isn't here today. She only ⁷_____ two days a week.	7 work
Duncan:	Oh, of course. I ⁸_____ my time then.	8 waste

2.2 Present continuous or simple? (A–C)

Complete the sentences. Put in the verbs on the right.

▢ I _'m writing_ to my parents. I _write_ to them every weekend.   ▢ write, write

1. It _____ outside. It _____ down quite hard, look.   1 snow, come
2. Normally I _____ work at eight o'clock, but I _____ at seven this week. We're very busy just now.   2 start / start
3. Usually I _____ two newspapers, but not the same ones every day. On Sundays I _____ four or five.   3 read / buy
4. We _____ a garage next to our house. We _____ somewhere to put the car.   4 build / want
5. I haven't got a car at the moment, so I _____ to work on the bus this week. Usually I _____ to work.   5 go / drive
6. The sun _____ in the east, remember. It's behind us, so we _____ west.   6 rise / travel
7. We _____ camping every year. It's a good cheap holiday. Hotels _____ too much.   7 go / cost

2.3 Present continuous or simple with always (D)

Write the sentences with **always**.

▢ That boy talks too much. _He's always talking_.
▢ You slam the door after you every time. _You always slam the door after you_.

1. Mrs James leaves early every day. _____
2. You very often lose your keys. _____
3. You take time off work too often. _____
4. I go the wrong way here every time. _____
5. Liz thanks me politely every time. _____
6. The Bensons argue so much. _____

3 State verb or action verb?

A States and actions

Compare:

A state means something staying the same.	An action means something happening.
STATES	ACTIONS
*The door **is** blue.*	*I'm painting the door.*
*The farmer **owns** the land.*	*The farmer **is buying** the land.*
*The box **contains** old magazines.*	*He **puts** the magazines in the box.*
State verbs cannot usually be continuous.	Action verbs can be either simple or continuous, e.g. *He **puts** everything away* OR *He **is putting** everything away.*
NOT *The farmer is owning the land.*	

Other state verbs are: **seem**, **consist of**, **exist**, **belong**, **depend on**, **deserve**, **matter**, **mean**, **know**, **understand**, **remember**, **love**, **like**.

B Verbs with different meanings

Sometimes one meaning of a verb is a state and the other is an action. Compare:

STATES	ACTIONS
*I **think** you're right.* (= believe)	*I'm thinking about the problem.*
*We **have** three cars.* (= own)	*We're having lunch.* (= eating)
*Jeff **is** an idiot.*	*Jeff **is being** an idiot.* (= behaving)
*I **come** from Sweden.* (= live in, was born in)	*I'm coming from Sweden.* (= travelling from)

We use simple tenses for these states. With actions, we can use either the simple or the continuous. Here are some more examples to compare:

STATES	ACTIONS
*I **see** your problem.* (= I understand . . .)	*James **is seeing** a doctor.*
	*I **see** Simon quite often.*
*This picture **looks** nice.*	*I'm **looking** at this picture.*
	*I always **look** at the sports news first.*
*She **appears** very nervous.*	*She **appeared/was appearing** in a film.*
*The bag **weighed** five kilos.*	*They **weighed/were weighing** my bag.*
*The milk **smelt** strange.*	*He **smelt/was smelling** the milk.*
*The coat **fits** all right.*	*I'm **fitting** a lock to the window.*

C State verbs in the continuous

But we can use some state verbs in the continuous when we talk about a short period of time. Compare:

SIMPLE (a permanent state)	CONTINUOUS (a short period of time)
*I **love/enjoy** parties.*	*I'm **loving/enjoying** this party.*
*I **like** school.*	*I'm **liking** school a lot better now.*
*Holidays **cost** a lot of money.*	*This trip **is costing** me a lot of money.*

But in these examples we can use either the simple or continuous with little difference in meaning:
*You **look** well.* OR *You're **looking** well.*   *We **feel** a bit sad.* OR *We're **feeling** a bit sad.*
*This tooth **hurts/aches**.* OR *This tooth **is hurting/aching**.*

3 Exercises

3.1 States and actions (A)

Say which verbs express states and which express actions.

☐ I <u>spoke</u> to our new neighbours.   <u>action</u>

1. They <u>seem</u> very nice.   _____
2. The husband <u>builds</u> houses.   _____
3. Our old house doesn't <u>exist</u> any more.   _____
4. I have to <u>go</u> to the dentist.   _____
5. What does 'dentist' <u>mean</u>?   _____

3.2 Verbs with different meanings (B)

Gavin is visiting Judy and baby Emma. Put in the correct form of the verb.

Gavin: Hello, Judy. I rang at about ten, but there was no reply.
Judy: Oh, that was probably when I ☐ <u>was seeing</u> the doctor.   ☐ saw/was seeing
Gavin: Where's little Emma?
Judy: She's asleep. She ¹_____ a very good girl at the moment. I ²_____ at these photos of her.   1 's/'s being
     2 look/'m looking
Gavin: Oh, she's lovely. I ³_____ she ⁴_____ beautiful.   3 think/'m thinking
     4 looks/'s looking
Judy: That jacket was too big then. It ⁵_____ properly.   5 didn't fit/wasn't fitting
Gavin: In this one she ⁶_____ her tea.   6 has/'s having
Judy: And in this one she ⁷_____ about something. I'm not sure what.   7 thinks/'s thinking
Gavin: You ⁸_____ lots of photos of her already.   8 have/'re having
Judy: Mark took this one, look. She cried all the time the nurse ⁹_____ her. When she was born, she ¹⁰_____ four kilos, you know.   9 weighed/was weighing
     10 weighed/was weighing
Gavin: I ¹¹_____. A big strong girl.   11 see/'m seeing

3.3 State verbs in the continuous (C)

Write a sentence which follows on. Choose from these sentences.

I think it's going to suit me.   And I've still got a chance to win it.
I've never wanted to change it.   It uses a lot of petrol.
It's too expensive to buy.   I play it every weekend. ✓

☐ I enjoy the game. <u>I play it every weekend.</u>
1. I'm enjoying the game. _____
2. The car costs a lot of money. _____
3. The car is costing a lot of money. _____
4. I'm liking my new job. _____
5. I like my job. _____

4 The present perfect

A Form

The present perfect is the present tense of **have** + a past participle:
We've washed the dishes.
The aircraft has just landed.
Our neighbours haven't lived here long.
Have you opened your letter?
How many points has Mandy scored?

I/you/we/they **have washed** OR	I've **washed**
he/she/it **has washed** OR	he's **washed**
I/you/we/they **haven't washed**	**have** they **washed?**
he/she/it **hasn't washed**	**has** he **washed?**

Regular past participles end in **ed**, e.g. **washed**, **landed**, **lived**.

We do not use **be** as an auxiliary in the present perfect:
The parcel has arrived. NOT *The parcel is arrived.*

B Irregular forms

Some participles are irregular. They do not end in **ed**:
I've made a shopping list.   *Our guest tonight has written five novels.*
We haven't sold our house yet.   *Have you seen this programme before?*
For a list of irregular verbs see p 292.

There is a present perfect of **be** and of **have**:
That car has been there all afternoon.
I've had these shoes for years.

C Use

The present perfect tells us about the past and the present:
We've washed the dishes.
(They're clean **now**.)
The aircraft has landed.
(It's on the ground **now**.)
Our guest tonight is a writer. So far he has written five novels.
I've just phoned Ben.
(**just** = a short time before **now**)

For details about the use of the present perfect and past simple see Unit 6.

D gone to or been to ?

Compare:

Mike has gone to Corfu. He's having a lovely holiday.	*Mike has been to Corfu. He went there last summer.*
Gone there means that he is still there.	**Been there** means that the visit is over.

4 Exercises

4.1 Form (A)

Put in the verbs. Use the present perfect.

Karen: How is the painting going? □ *Have you started* on the front door yet?   □ you start
Jean: No, the paintbrush □ *has disappeared*.   □ disappear
Karen: ¹_____ for it?   1 you look
Jean: Of course I ²_____ for it. Can I borrow yours?   2 look
Karen: Well, I ³_____ with it. But there's one here. Adrian ⁴_____ it to paint a window. I don't know if he ⁵_____ it.   3 not finish / 4 use / 5 clean
Jean: Yes, it's clean. I'll do the other window.
Karen: Linda ⁶_____ to do that one.   6 promise
Jean: Well, she ⁷_____ yet. She can do the front door. I ⁸_____ to do the window.   7 not start / 8 decide

4.2 Irregular forms (B and p 292)

Put in a verb in the present perfect. Sometimes the verb is negative.

□ When are you going to write to your uncle? You *haven't written* to him yet.
1 Tim buys lots of clothes. I expect he _____ some in town today.
2 Are you going to have a bath? ~ No, I _____ one already today.
3 Mr Smith doesn't often cut the grass. He _____ it for ages now.
4 When did you last see Lisa? ~ Oh, ages ago. I _____ her since Christmas.
5 Bob rings every hour. He _____ five times already today.

4.3 The present perfect (A–C)

Add a sentence with the present perfect and **just**. Use these past participles:
checked, cleaned, made, repaired, spent, tidied.

□ Nicola's car is clean now. She *'s just cleaned it*.
1 The children's room is tidy now. They _____
2 My tea is on the table now. I _____
3 Marilyn's radio is working now. She _____
4 Our money has all gone now. We _____
5 Henrietta's answers are correct. She _____

4.4 gone to and been to (D)

Complete the conversation. Put in **gone** or **been**.

Richard: Hello. Where's Martin?
Angela: He's ¹_____ to the supermarket. We need some sugar.
Richard: It's very busy there. I've just ²_____ there on my way here. Did you know there's a new store outside town? We haven't ³_____ there yet.
Angela: We haven't either. By the way, where's Linda?
Richard: Oh, she's ⁴_____ to London. She'll be back tonight.

5 The past simple

A Positive forms

A regular past form ends in **ed**:
    We **played** basketball yesterday.   I **arrived** ten minutes late.
    Julie **phoned** earlier.   We once **owned** a caravan.
    Harold and Vera **stayed** at the camp site for a week.

Some verbs have an irregular past form. They do not end in **ed**:
    We **won** the game easily.   I **came** ten minutes late.
    Julie **rang** earlier.   We **had** a caravan years ago.
    They **left** the camp site on Friday morning.
For a list of irregular forms see p 292.

The past simple is the same in all persons (e.g. I/you/he/she/it/we/they **played**). The only exception is the past tense of **be**:

    I **was** ill last week.
    Those cakes **were** nice.

| I/he/she/it **was** |
| you/we/they **were** |

B Negatives and questions

We use **did** in negatives and questions:
Negatives: We **did not win** the game.   I **didn't arrive** on time.
Questions: Where **did** you **stay**?   **Did** she **leave** a message?

We use **did** in all persons:

| I/you/he/she/it/we/they **did not win** OR I **didn't win** |
| **Did** I/you/he/she/it/we/they **win**? |

We do not add **ed** to the verb in negatives and questions.
    NOT ~~I didn't arrived on time~~ or ~~Did she left a message?~~

C Use

We use the past simple for something in the past, something which is finished:
    I **passed** the exam **last year**.
    I **told** you **five minutes ago**.
    Debbie **was** a very unhappy child.
    John Lennon **died in 1980**.

For details about the use of the past simple and present perfect see Unit 6.

5 Exercises

5.1 Positive forms (A and p 292)

Complete the newspaper story. Put in the simple past forms of the verbs on the right.

Fire tragedy

Two people □ _died_ in a fire in Ellis Street, Oldport yesterday morning. They ¹_____ Herbert and Molly Paynter, a couple in their seventies. The fire ²_____ at 3.20 am. A neighbour, Mr Aziz, ³_____ the flames and ⁴_____ the fire brigade. He also ⁵_____ to get into the house to get the couple out, but the heat ⁶_____ too great. The fire brigade ⁷_____ in five minutes. Twenty firemen ⁸_____ the fire and ⁹_____ it under control. Two firemen ¹⁰_____ the burning building but ¹¹_____ the couple dead. 'It's a tragedy,' the Fire Officer ¹²_____ .

□ die
1 be
2 start
3 see   4 call
5 try
6 be   7 arrive
8 fight   9 bring
10 enter
11 find
12 say

5.2 Positive and negative forms (A, B)

Put in the past simple of these verbs: **answer, come, eat, enjoy, have, know, leave, play, sleep, stay**. Decide if the verb is positive or negative.

- □ The concert was great. I really _enjoyed_ it.
- □ There was too much food. We _didn't eat_ it all.
1. My watch was broken. I _____ the time.
2. Clive couldn't pay the bill. He _____ his credit card.
3. The party wasn't very good. We _____ after only half an hour.
4. I had a bad night. I _____ very well.
5. Sophie was ill yesterday. She _____ in bed all day.
6. You weren't in very good form. You _____ very well in that match.
7. The driver didn't look. He _____ straight out of a side street.
8. The questions were easy. I hope you _____ them correctly.

5.3 Negatives and questions (B)

Put in the past simple negatives and questions.

Steve: □ _Did you have_ a nice weekend in London?
Brian: Yes, thanks. It was good. We looked round a museum and saw a show. We ¹_____ to do too much.
Steve: Which museum ²_____ to?
Brian: The Victoria and Albert. I ³_____ there was so much in there.
Steve: It's fascinating isn't it? And what show ⁴_____ ?
Brian: Oh, a musical about cowboys. I forget what it's called. I ⁵_____ it.
Steve: Where ⁶_____ ?
Brian: At a small hotel I know in Bayswater.
Steve: And ⁷_____ the weekend?
Brian: Yes, she did. She did some shopping too, but I ⁸_____ to look at shops.

□ you have
1 not try
2 you go
3 not know
4 you see
5 not like
6 you stay
7 Sarah enjoy
8 not want

6 Present perfect or past simple?

A Introduction

Look at this:

Now compare:

Sam and Kay have bought a new car. Sam uses the present perfect to tell us about the past and the present. They bought the car, and it's theirs <u>now</u>.	They bought the car <u>last week</u>. Kay uses the past simple to tell us about the past, a time which is finished.

We do not use the present perfect with phrases like **yesterday**, **last week**, **ten years ago**.
NOT ~~They've bought the car last week.~~

B I have done/I did

Compare:

PRESENT PERFECT	PAST SIMPLE
We use the present perfect to talk about the past and the present:	We use the past simple to talk about the past:
Jane **has packed** her case, look.	Jane **packed** her case last night.
PAST → NOW	PAST NOW
United **have won** the Cup!	United **won** the Cup in 1989.
have won → NOW	won NOW

The present perfect tells us about the present. There is a present result of a past action:
    Jane **has packed** her case. (So the case is full <u>now</u>.)
    United **have won** the Cup! (So the Cup is theirs <u>now</u>.)
    Tim **has repaired** the chair. (So the chair is all right <u>now</u>.)
But the past simple does not tell us about the present:
    Jane **packed** her case last night. (Her things may not be in the case now.)
    United **won** the Cup in 1989. (United may not have the Cup now.)
    Tim **repaired** the chair. (It may be broken again now.)
We often give a piece of news in the present perfect and use the past simple for the details:
    I've found my wallet. ~ Oh, good. Where **did** you **find** it?
    Someone **has left** this door open. ~ I expect Phil **did** when he **went** out.
    Your parcel **has arrived**. The postman **brought** it this morning.

We often use **just**, **already** and **yet** with the present perfect:	But Americans sometimes use the past simple:
I've just remembered something.	*I just remembered* something.
The bus **has already left**.	The bus **already left**.
Has Tom **replied** to your letter **yet**?	**Did** Tom **reply** to your letter **yet**?
For these adverbs see Unit 90.	For more examples see p 288.

6 Present perfect or past simple?

C I've been/I was

Compare:

PRESENT PERFECT	PAST SIMPLE
We use the present perfect for a state which has gone on up to the present: *We've lived here for ten years.* (And we **still** live here.)	We use the past simple for a state in the past, in a period which is finished: *We lived there for ten years.* (We don't live there now.)
have lived → NOW	lived　　　　NOW

Here are some more examples:

I've had this briefcase for ages. (And I've **still** got it now.) *Emma has loved Bali since she first saw it.* (And she **still** loves it now.)	*I had a briefcase once. I don't know if I've still got it. Emma loved Bali when she first saw it.*

D Have you ever . . .?/Did you ever . . .?

Compare:

PRESENT PERFECT	PAST SIMPLE
We use the present perfect for actions in a period of time up to the present: *This young producer has made four films so far.*	We use the past simple for actions in the past, a period which is finished: *The producer made lots of films in his long career.*
has made → NOW	made　　　　NOW
He's made films means that it is possible he will make more films.	**He made films** means that his career in films is over. He won't make any more.

Here are some more examples:

We like climbing. We've climbed this mountain many times. *Have you ever been to America?* ~ *Yes, I've been there twice.* *I've played volleyball before.*	*My grandparents liked climbing. They climbed this mountain many times.* *Did Churchill ever go to America?* ~ *No, I don't think so.* *I played volleyball at college.*

E today, this week etc.

We use **today** and phrases with **this** for a period up to the present:

PRESENT PERFECT	PAST SIMPLE
It hasn't rained today. *Have you seen this week's magazine?*	*It rained yesterday.* *Did you see last week's magazine?*

But note these examples:

I haven't seen Jody today. (It's still day time.) *Has the post come this morning?* (It is still morning.)	*I didn't see Jody at school today.* (The school day is over.) *Did the post come this morning?* (It is later in the day.)

6 Exercises

6.1 I have done/I did (A, B)

Put in the correct verb form.

- have done / did
  I *'ve done* all the housework. The house is clean.
- have bought / bought
  A young couple *bought* the house. But they didn't live there long.

1. have arrived / arrived
   Our visitors _____. They're sitting in the garden.
2. has repaired / repaired
   Susan _____ the television, but then it broke down again.
3. have lost / lost
   I _____ my purse. I can't find it anywhere.
4. has started / started
   The match _____. They're playing now.
5. has run / ran
   Joanne _____ away from home. But she came back two days later.
6. has earned / earned
   James _____ some money last week. But I'm afraid he's already spent it all.
7. have planted / planted
   We _____ a tree in the garden. Unfortunately it's died.
8. have gone / went
   Prices _____ up. Things are more expensive this week.
9. has turned / turned
   Someone _____ on the hi-fi. I can hear it.
10. have phoned / phoned
    I _____ the office at eleven. Helen isn't there today, they said.
11. have made / made
    I _____ a cake. Would you like a piece?
12. has broken / broke
    The runner Amos Temila _____ the world record for the mile in Frankfurt. Then two days later in Helsinki, Lee Williams ran the mile in an even faster time.

6.2 I've been/I was (C)

Complete the letter. Put in the present perfect or past simple of the verbs on the right.

I □ *was* angry and sad to hear that someone plans to knock down the White Horse Inn in Brickfield. This pub □ *has been* the centre of village life for centuries. It ¹_____ at our crossroads for about 500 years. It ²_____ famous in the old days, and Shakespeare once ³_____ there, they say. I ⁴_____ in Brickfield all my life, and I know all about it. We ⁵_____ for some time of the danger to our pub. There ⁶_____ some talk a year or two ago about knocking it down. But all the villagers are against the plan. We will stop it, you'll see.	□ be □ be 1 stand 2 be 3 stay 4 live 5 know 6 be

6.3 The son has done .../The father did ... (D)

Reginald was a rich and successful businessman, but now he's an old man and doesn't work any more. His son Hugo is a very rich and very successful businessman. Put in the verbs. Use the present perfect or past simple.

▫ Most business people make mistakes. Reginald _made_ mistakes, but his son _has_ never _made_ a mistake.

1. Business people travel a lot. Hugo _____ all over the world. His father _____ on business too, but not so much.
2. Good business people make money. Hugo _____ £50 million now. His father _____ £10 million.
3. Business people can win prizes. Reginald _____ the Exporter of the Year prize twice. His son _____ it four times already.
4. A lot of business people don't take risks. Old Reginald _____ risks because he was afraid to. But his son _____ quite a few risks so far in his career.

6.4 today, this week etc. (E)

Put in **this**, **last**, **today** or **yesterday**.

▫ _Last_ month prices went up, but _this_ month they have fallen a little.

1. It's been dry so far _____ week, but _____ week was very wet.
2. I went shopping earlier _____ and spent all the money I earned _____.
3. We didn't have many tomatoes _____ year. We've grown a lot more _____ summer.
4. I don't feel so tired now. We got up quite late _____ morning. I felt really tired _____ morning when we got up so early.

6.5 Present perfect or past simple? (A–E)

Put in the verbs.

Craig: ▫ _Have you heard_ the news about Cathy?	▫ you hear
Nicola: No, what ¹_____?	1 happen
Craig: She ²_____ an accident. She was running for a bus when she ³_____ down and ⁴_____ her leg.	2 have 3 fall 4 break
Nicola: Oh, how awful! When ⁵_____?	5 this happen
Craig: Yesterday afternoon. Sarah ⁶_____ me about it last night.	6 tell
Nicola: Last night! You ⁷_____ last night, and you ⁸_____ me!	7 know 8 not tell
Craig: Well, I ⁹_____ you last night. And I ¹⁰_____ you today, until now.	9 not see 10 not see
Nicola: I hope she's all right. She ¹¹_____ lots of accidents, you know. She ¹²_____ the same thing about two years ago.	11 have 12 do

7 Past continuous or simple?

A The past continuous

Look at this question and answer:
> Alice: *I rang yesterday, but you weren't in.* **Were** you **playing** *tennis?*
> Dave: *No, I* **was helping** *Bob. We* **were working** *on his car. I* **wasn't playing** *yesterday.*

The past continuous is the past tense of **be** + the ing-form:

I/he/she/it **was working**	you/we/they **were working**
I/he/she/it **wasn't working**	you/we/they **weren't working**
was he/she/it **working?**	**were** you/we/they **working?**

We use the past continuous to say that we were in the middle of an action.

B Continuous or simple?

Look at this paragraph:
> *It was a lovely day, and the sun* **was shining**. *I* **was walking** *across the field when I* **saw** *a plane. It* **was flying** *very low. It* **was making** *a strange noise, and I* **knew** *there was a problem. It* **came** *down in the next field, and I* **heard** *a crash. I* **ran** *to the village and* **phoned** *for help.*

Compare:

PAST CONTINUOUS	PAST SIMPLE
We use the past continuous to say that we were in the middle of an action:	We use the past simple for a complete action in the past:
I **was walking** *across the field.*	*I* **walked** *across the field.*
(I was in the field.)	*(I crossed it completely.)*
The plane **was flying** *very low.*	*The plane* **crashed** *in a field.*

We often use the past continuous to describe the background and the past simple for the actions in a story:
> *The sun* **was shining**. . . . *I* **ran** *to the village.*
> *The crowds* **were waiting**. . . . *The Princess* **arrived**.

Verbs of thinking and feeling and state verbs are usually simple, not continuous. (For more details see Unit 3.)
> *I* **thought** *everything was OK.*   *We* **liked** *the film.*
> *I* **knew** *there was a problem.*   *Mr Young once* **owned** *the field.*

We often use the past continuous and simple together when a shorter action interrupted a longer one (came in the middle of it):
> *I* **fell** *asleep while I* **was watching** *television.*
> *We* **were sitting** *in the garden when it suddenly* **started** *to rain.*
> *The phone* **rang** *while Gary* **was making** *lunch.*

Longer action: ... Gary was making lunch ...

Shorter action: The phone rang

We use two past simple verbs for one action after another:
> *When I* **heard** *the crash, I* **ran** *to the village.* (= I heard it and then I ran.)

7 Exercises

7.1 The past continuous (A)

Complete the conversation. Put in a past continuous form of the verb on the right.

Jeremy: I'm afraid I've broken this dish.
Sue: Oh no! What ¹_____ ?
Jeremy: I ²_____ it into the dining-room. I bumped into Emma. She ³_____ out just as I ⁴_____ in.
Emma: It was your fault. You ⁵_____ . You ⁶_____ where you ⁷_____ .

1 you do
2 take
3 come
4 go
5 dream
6 not look
7 go

7.2 Past continuous or simple? (B)

Put in the past continuous or past simple.

Kim: I hear the lights □ _went_ out last night.
Charles: Yes, I □ _was watching_ television at the time. The programme ¹_____ interesting, too. But the electricity ²_____ on again after about ten minutes. I ³_____ very much of it.
Angela: Sarah ⁴_____ down the stairs when the lights went out. She almost ⁵_____ over.
Jessica: Tom and I ⁶_____ table tennis at the time.
Peter: I ⁷_____ at my computer. When it ⁸_____ , I ⁹_____ work and ¹⁰_____ to bed.

□ go
□ watch
1 get
2 come
3 not miss
4 come
5 fall
6 play
7 work
8 happen
9 stop   10 go

7.3 Past continuous or simple? (B)

Find the second part of each sentence. Put each verb in brackets into the past continuous or past simple.

□ I (dream)
□ When Mary (see) the question,
1 The train (wait)
2 Ella (have) a puncture
3 When I (try) the pudding,
4 When Karen (lift) the chair,
5 When the gates (open),
6 I (read) a library book

she (feel) a sudden pain in her back.
when she (drive) on the motorway.
when I (find) a £10 note between two pages.
the crowd (walk) in.
she (know) the answer.
when the alarm clock (ring).
I (like) it.
when we (arrive) at the station.

□ _I was dreaming when the alarm clock rang._
□ _When Mary saw the question, she knew the answer._

1 _____
2 _____
3 _____
4 _____
5 _____
6 _____

8 Present perfect continuous

A Form

The present perfect continuous is the present tense of **have** + **been** + the ing-form:
We've been waiting ages.
It has been raining all day.
How long have you been learning English?
Our horses haven't been winning many races.

I/you/we/they **have been waiting**	OR	I**'ve been waiting**
he/she/it **has been waiting**	OR	he**'s been waiting**
I/you/we/they **haven't been waiting**		**have** I/you/we/they **been waiting?**
he/she/it **hasn't been waiting**		**has** he/she/it **been waiting?**

B Use

We use the present perfect continuous for an action over a period of time up to now:
We've been lying in the sun all afternoon.
I've been waiting here for twenty minutes.
That burglar alarm has been ringing since eight o'clock this morning.

We must use the perfect when we are talking about a period 'up to now':
NOT *I wait here twenty minutes* or *I'm waiting here twenty minutes.*

We can talk about repeated actions up to now:
Melissa has been playing the piano since she was four.
Fred has been going to evening classes this year.

The action can end just before the present:
Brian has been painting the house all afternoon, and now he's having a rest.
I've been swimming. That's why my hair is wet.

We often use **for**, **since**, **recently/lately** and **how long**:
Mrs Wilkins has been staying at the hotel for three weeks.
You've been writing that letter since ten o'clock.
I haven't been feeling very well recently.
How long have you been waiting?
For details about **for** and **since** see Unit 97.

8 Exercises

8.1 Form (A)

Put in the verbs. Use the present perfect continuous.

Maria: Sorry I'm late.
Kay: It's okay. I ☐ _haven't been waiting_ long. What ¹_____? ☐ not wait
1 you do
Maria: I've been with Mrs King. She ²_____ me with my English. 2 help
Kay: Your English is very good. You don't need lessons. How long ³_____ it? 3 you study
Maria: Eight years now. But my accent wasn't so good before I came to England. I ⁴_____ on it. I think it ⁵_____ better lately. 4 work
5 get
Kay: Your accent is fine, Maria.

8.2 Use of the present perfect continuous (B)

Add a sentence with the present perfect continuous. Use the words in brackets.

☐ Mr Davis has back-ache. _He's been digging the garden._ (dig – the garden)
1 Joe has no money left. _____ (shop)
2 The girls are tired. _____ (work – hard)
3 The boys have got a suntan. _____ (sunbathe)
4 Emma's shoes are dirty. _____ (walk – in the field)
5 Jane and Neil look annoyed. _____ (argue)
6 The ground is wet. _____ (rain)
7 Tim has some washing up to do. _____ (bake – cakes)

8.3 Use of the present perfect continuous (B)

Write a sentence with the present perfect continuous and **for** to describe each situation. Use these verbs: **camp, play, read, swim, talk, travel, work**.

☐ The video began two hours ago, and it hasn't finished yet.
  It's been playing for two hours.

1 James went into the water ten minutes ago. He doesn't want to come out yet.

2 Alice rang Peter half an hour ago, and they're still on the phone.

3 Robert picked up a book an hour ago. He hasn't put it down yet.

4 Ed and Jennifer started their journey around the world three months ago. They've gone about halfway now.

5 Sue got to the office early this morning. Ten hours later she's still there.

6 The Dobsons left on holiday four weeks ago and they're not back yet. They took their tent.

9   I have been doing or I have done?

A   Present perfect continuous (have been doing) or simple (have done)?

Compare:

have been doing	**have done**
We use the present perfect continuous for an action over a period (Unit 8): *We've been touring Scotland. A strong wind has been blowing all day.*	We use the present perfect simple for a complete action (Unit 4): *We've finished our tour of Scotland. The wind has blown our fence over.*

The choice of form depends on whether we see the action as continuing over a period or as complete. Compare:

OVER A PERIOD (**have been doing**)   COMPLETE (**have done**)

*Tim **has been repairing** his bike. He's got oil on his hands.*
*Jane is out of breath. She**'s been running**.*

*I**'ve been writing** an essay. I'm tired now.*

We normally use the continuous form with a phrase saying <u>how long</u>:
*Mandy **has been picking** apples **all afternoon**.*
*I**'ve been writing** letters **since this morning**.*

*Tim **has repaired** his bike. It goes all right now.*
*Jane hopes she isn't late. She**'s run** all the way.*

*I**'ve written** an essay. I can hand it in now.*

We use the simple form with a phrase saying <u>how many</u>:
*Mandy **has picked hundreds** of apples.*

*I**'ve written ten** letters.*

B   Actions and states

We cannot normally use the continuous form for a state (see Unit 3):
*I**'ve known** the secret for a long time.* NOT ~~I've been knowing...~~
*The Browns **have had** that car for at least ten years.*
*We've never **been** very happy here.*

Live and **work** (= have a job) can be continuous or not, with little difference in meaning:
We've been living here since 1988. OR *We've lived here since 1988.*
*Tom **has been working** at the bank for three years now.* OR *Tom **has worked** at the bank for three years now.*

9 Exercises

9.1 I have been doing or I have done? (A)

Put the verb forms in these conversations.

A: I feel really tired.
B: It's because you □ *'ve been doing* too much. □ do
A: Well, at least I □ *'ve finished* that report now, and I can have a rest. □ finish

A: Someone ¹_____ the ladder outside, look. 1 leave
B: I expect that's Brian. He ²_____ windows. I don't think he's finished yet. 2 clean

A: You've got grass on your shoes.
B: I ³_____ the lawn. 3 mow
A: Yes, I ⁴_____ it. It looks a lot better. 4 see
   You ⁵_____ it nice and short. 5 cut

9.2 I have been doing or I have done? (A)

Put in the verb forms. Use the present perfect continuous or simple.

□ (build) The Thorpes *have been building* a house for some time.
  They *'ve built* more than half of it now.

1 (run) Those young men _____ nearly two miles.
  They _____ for ten minutes.
2 (do) Since tea time Elaine _____ sums in her exercise book.
  She _____ fifty.
3 (drink) You _____ tea all day.
  You _____ at least ten cups.
4 (deliver) Simon _____ about two hundred newspapers.
  He _____ them since early this morning.
5 (play) Bob and his friends _____ golf since lunch time. They _____ ten holes.

9.3 I have been doing or I have done? (A, B)

Complete the dialogue. Put in the verbs in the present perfect continuous or simple.

Linda: What are you doing, Jeff?
Jeff: I ¹_____ out this cupboard most of the afternoon. There's a lot of old stuff in here. 1 clear
   I ²_____ this, look. 2 find
Linda: You ³_____ that book for the last five minutes. I ⁴_____ you. 3 read
                                                                                  4 watch
Jeff: It's my old diary. I ⁵_____ it since I was ten. It ⁶_____ in here for years. 5 not see
                                                                                                6 be
Linda: And is that old tennis racket yours?
Jeff: No, it must be yours. I ⁷_____ a tennis racket. 7 never have

29

10 Past perfect

Look at this paragraph from a story:
> When Alex left for the office that morning, he wasn't feeling very awake. He **had been** tired the evening before, and he **hadn't slept** very well. He **had** only **travelled** about a mile when he realized he**'d forgotten** his wallet. **Had** he **left** it in the office the day before, or **had** he **left** it at home?

A Form

The past perfect is **had** + a past participle:
> He **had travelled** about a mile. OR He**'d travelled** . . .
> He **had not slept** very well the night before. OR He **hadn't slept** . . .
> Where **had** Alex **left** his wallet?

For irregular participles (e.g. **slept**, **left**) see p 292.

B Present perfect and past perfect

We use the past perfect for an action before a past time. Compare these examples:

PRESENT PERFECT (before now)	PAST PERFECT (before then)
My wallet isn't here. I**'ve left** it behind.	My wallet wasn't there. I**'d left** it behind.
The match is over. The Lions **have won**.	The match was over. The Lions **had won**.
I have won → NOW	I had won → PAST NOW

Here are some more examples of the past perfect:
> It was six o'clock. All the shops **had closed**.
> We got home at midnight. It **had been** a wonderful day.
> By 1960 most of Britain's old colonies **had become** independent.

C Past simple and past perfect

To talk about one action in the past, we use the past simple:
> I **posted** the letter yesterday. NOT ~~I had posted the letter yesterday.~~

When one action comes straight after another, we use the past simple for both:
> When Jack **saw** the bomb, he **shouted** a warning.

To say that one thing finished and then something else happened, we use either **when . . . had done** or **after . . . did/had done**:
> **When** Carol **had taken** the photos, she developed the film.
> **After** Carol **had taken** (OR **After** Carol **took**) the photos, she developed the film.

Note the different meanings:
> When we arrived, the others all **left**. (We arrived and then they left.)
> When we arrived, the others **had** all left. (They left before we arrived.)

We sometimes use the past perfect with **before** or **until**:
> The ball hit the back of the net **before** the goalkeeper **had moved**.
> The chairman didn't speak **until** he **had heard** all the arguments.

10 Exercises

10.1 Present perfect and past perfect (B)

Put in the verbs in the present perfect (**have done**) or past perfect (**had done**).
- ☐ It isn't raining now. It _has stopped_ . — ☐ stop
- ☐ We had no car at that time. We _had sold_ our old one. — ☐ sell
1. The square looked awful. People _____ litter everywhere. — 1 leave
2. You can have that newspaper. I _____ with it. — 2 finish
3. There's no more cheese. We _____ it all. — 3 eat
4. There was no sign of a taxi although I _____ one half an hour before. — 4 order
5. This bill isn't right. They _____ a mistake. — 5 make
6. I spoke to Melanie at lunch time. Someone _____ her the news earlier. — 6 tell
7. I was really tired last night. I _____ a hard day. — 7 have
8. Do you want to see this programme? It _____ . — 8 start
9. It'll get warmer in here. I _____ the heating on. — 9 turn
10. At last the committee were ready to announce their decision. They _____ up their minds. — 10 make

10.2 Past simple and past perfect (C)

Say what happened first.
- ☐ Ten people had eaten chicken. They all fell ill. — _First they ate chicken._
1. Two men delivered the sofa. I had already paid for it. — First _____
2. When the headmaster came in, everyone stood up. — First _____
3. We didn't stop until we'd finished the work.
4. The light came on when I pressed the switch.

10.3 Past simple and past perfect (C)

Write the two sentences as one. Use **when** and the past perfect in either the first or the second part of the sentence.
- ☐ I gave the book to a friend. I read it.
  I gave the book to a friend when I'd read it.
- ☐ The pupils did the experiment. They wrote a report on it.
  When the pupils had done the experiment, they wrote a report on it.
1. Joe saved enough money. He bought a motor-bike.

2. Max put all the dishes away. He dried them.

3. Jane signed the letter. She typed it on her word processor.

4. We completed the forms. We handed them in.

5. I looked both ways. I pulled out into the road.

6. The golfers went into the club house. They played the last hole.

11 Past perfect continuous

Read this paragraph:
> Mr Dennis Fowler died last Friday evening in Highfield Hospital at the age of 58. Mr Fowler suffered a heart attack at his home three weeks ago after he **had been cooking** a meal for some guests. According to friends, he **had been working** very hard at his mobile telephone business, which **had been losing** money.

A Form

The past perfect continuous is **had been** + the ing-form:
> He **had been working** very hard. OR He**'d been working** very hard.
> We **had not been waiting** long. OR We **hadn't been waiting** long.
> Was the grass wet? **Had** it **been raining**?

B Use

We use the past perfect continuous for an action over a period up to a past time:
> The business **had been losing** money.
> I went to the dentist on Thursday. My tooth **had been aching** since Monday.
> I found the calculator yesterday. **I'd been looking** for it for some time.
> There were some dirty pans in the kitchen. Someone **had been cooking** a meal.

Compare the <u>present</u> perfect continuous (**has been doing**) and the <u>past</u> perfect continuous (**had been doing**):
> Bill's eyes are red. He **has been crying**.
> Bill's eyes were red. He **had been crying**.

C The past perfect continuous and other past tenses

Compare the past perfect continuous and simple (**had done**). We use the continuous for an action over a period and the simple for a complete action:

OVER A PERIOD (**had been doing**)	COMPLETE (**had done**)
I'd been washing the car. My hands were wet.	**I'd washed** the car. It looked nice and clean.
Jane **had been reading** most of the afternoon.	Jane **had read** five chapters by tea time.

We cannot normally use the continuous for a state (see Unit 3):
> George **had seemed** unwell for some time before he died.
> NOT ~~George had been seeming unwell.~~

Now compare the past continuous (**was doing**) and the past perfect continuous (**had been doing**):
> When I phoned Janet, she **was having** a piano lesson.
> (I phoned in the middle of the lesson.)
> When I phoned Janet, she**'d been having** a piano lesson.
> (I phoned after the lesson.)

11 Exercises

11.1 Form (A)

Put in the past perfect continuous of the verbs.

A: I had a terrible back-ache last week.
B: Oh, dear. What □ _had you been doing_? □ you do
A: I ¹_____ the garden. It was on Sunday 1 dig
afternoon. I ²_____ it long when I felt a pain in 2 not do
my back. It was still aching the next day. When I finally got to see the
doctor, I ³_____ over an hour. He was late. He 3 wait
⁴_____ with an emergency. But he was able to 4 deal
help me. It's much better now.

11.2 Use (B)

Add a sentence with the past perfect continuous to explain how the accidents happened. Use these words:

□ **play – with matches**   1 **clean – a window**   2 **walk – on the ice**   3 **hitch-hike**
4 **play – on the railway line**   5 **walk – in her sleep**   6 **use – a faulty electric drill**

□ Some children started a house fire. _They'd been playing with matches._
1 A man fell off a ladder. _____
2 A girl drowned in the lake. _____
3 A young woman was hit by a car. _____
4 Two boys were killed by a train. _____
5 A woman fell down the stairs in the middle of the night. _____
_____
6 A man died of an electric shock. _____

11.3 had done, had been doing or was doing? (C)

Put in the correct form of the verbs.

□ Steve could hear shouts from the flat next door. His neighbours _were_ □ argue
arguing.
1 Lucy went into the living-room. It was empty but the television was still
warm. Someone _____ it. 1 watch
2 I _____ tennis, so I had a shower. I was annoyed 2 play;
because I _____ a single game. not win
3 The walkers finally arrived at their destination. They
_____ all day, and they needed a rest. They 3 walk;
_____ thirty miles. walk
4 When I saw Ben last week he said he _____ 4 stop;
smoking. But when I saw him two days later, he
_____ a cigarette. He took the cigarette from his smoke
mouth and looked rather ashamed.
5 Harry found a note from Graham in Celia's coat. That's how Harry found
out they _____ an affair. In fact they 5 have;
_____ each other for months. Graham's wife see;
_____ about it all the time. know

33

12 Review of present and past tenses

Look at these verb forms. They tell us something about the present.
>Louise **is playing** tennis.
>She **plays** tennis, badminton and hockey.
>She **likes** sport.

A I am doing or I do?

Compare:

PRESENT CONTINUOUS (Unit 2)
We use the present continuous for something happening now, for when we are in the middle of something:
>I **am writing** a letter.
>It**'s snowing**, look.
>We**'re getting** lunch now.
>Sarah **is listening** to the news.

We use the present continuous for a temporary feeling (one that lasts for only a short period):
>I **am enjoying** this holiday.

We use the present continuous for a temporary situation or routine:
>I'm here for a week. I **am staying** at the Waldorf Hotel.
>Mandy **is going** to work by bus while her car is off the road.

PRESENT SIMPLE (Unit 2)
We use the present simple for repeated actions, for things that happen again and again:
>I **write** home every week.
>It **snows** here most winters.
>We usually **get** lunch for about one.
>She **listens** to the news every morning.

We normally use the present simple for thoughts and feelings and for states and permanent facts:
>I **believe** in ghosts.
>I **like** camping.
>The company **owns** three factories.
>Four plus two **makes** six.

We use the present simple for a permanent situation or routine:
>I always **stay** at the Waldorf Hotel when I come here.
>She usually **drives** to work.

Now look at these verb forms:

```
DYSON'S Sports shop
Brighton
                    Date 16 MAY
1 tennis racket         £75.69
cheque                  £75.69
            total       £75.69
THANK YOU FOR YOUR CUSTOM
```

Louise **has bought** a new tennis racket.
She **bought** it last Saturday.
She **has been using** it since Saturday.
She **was going** past Dyson's sports shop when she saw the racket in the window.
She **had** already **decided** to buy a new racket.
She **had been looking** for one for a few weeks.

12 Review of present and past tenses

B I have done or I did?

Compare:

PRESENT PERFECT (Unit 6)	PAST SIMPLE (Unit 6)
The present perfect tells us about the past and the present: I **have cleaned** the floor. It's clean now. They **have locked** the door. No one can get in there.	The past simple tells us about the past: I **cleaned** the floor yesterday. They **locked** the door at ten o'clock last night.
We use the present perfect for a state which has gone on up to the present: I **have had** this bike for ten years. I'**ve known** Gary for a long time. He's a good friend of mine.	We use the past simple for a state in the past: I **had** a bike once, but I sold it. I **knew** Gary at college.
We use the present perfect for actions in a period up to the present: I **have seen** this film several times. **Have** you **played** this game before?	We use the past simple for actions in the past: I **saw** this film several times in 1990. We **played** this game a lot when we were on holiday.

C I was doing or I did?

Compare:

PAST CONTINUOUS (Unit 7)	PAST SIMPLE (Unit 7)
We use the past continuous to say that we were in the middle of something: I **was reading** the paper at half past ten. We **were looking** for the coffee bar when we met Kirsty.	We use the past simple for a complete action in the past or for a past state: I **left** the house at half past ten. Kirsty **knew** the way.

D I have been doing

PRESENT PERFECT CONTINUOUS (Unit 8)
We use the present perfect continuous for an action over a period of time up to now:
  I **have been waiting** here for ages.
  I'm tired. I'**ve been working**.

E I had been doing or I had done?

Compare:

PAST PERFECT CONTINUOUS (Unit 11)	PAST PERFECT (Unit 10)
We use the past perfect continuous for an action over a period up to a past time: I **had been waiting** there for ages when they finally arrived. I was tired. I'**d been working**.	We use the past perfect for something before a past time: I **had seen** the film before, so I didn't want to see it again. I **had had** the bike for ten years, so I sold it.

12 Exercises

12.1 Present and past (A, B)

Complete the sentences. Use the words on the right. The verbs can be present continuous (**is doing**), present simple (**does**), or present perfect (**has done**).

☐ We bought this picture many years ago. _We've had it_ for ages.   ☐ we – have – it

1 Colin's car phone is very useful. _____ all the time.   1 he – use – it
2 Joanna doesn't know where her watch is. _____   2 she – lose – it
3 We're in the middle of decorating our kitchen. Meals are a problem. _____ from a take-away restaurant this week.   3 we – get – them
4 Robert is on a skiing holiday. _____ very much, he said on the phone.   4 he – enjoy – it
5 This colour is absolutely awful. _____   5 I – hate – it
6 I hope these figures are correct. _____ several times already.   6 I – check – them
7 Ed and Kay like Scrabble. _____ at the moment.   7 they – play – it
8 These flowers are dying. _____ for ages.   8 you – not water – them

12.2 Present and past (C–D)

Complete the conversations. Put in a pronoun and the correct form of the verb. Use the past continuous (**was doing**), the past simple (**did**), or the present perfect continuous (**have been doing**).

☐ I rang at one, but you weren't in your office. ~ No, _I was having_ lunch.   ☐ have

1 You look tired. ~ Well, _____ all day.   1 work
2 Is Helen still here? ~ No, _____ about half an hour ago.   2 leave
3 I haven't finished this letter yet. ~ It must be a long letter. _____ it since lunch time.   3 write
4 Someone's living in that house now. ~ Yes, a young couple. _____ in last month.   4 move
5 Did Kirsty drive you home? ~ Yes, _____ and gave me a lift while _____ for a bus outside the cinema.   5 stop, wait

12.3 Present and past (A–E)

Complete the conversation. Choose the correct form.

Hugo: Hello, Simon. [1]_____ you for ages.   1 I don't see/I haven't seen
Simon: Hello, Hugo. How are you?
Hugo: Fine, thanks. [2]_____ a new job as a car salesman. [3]_____ on Monday.   2 I just started/I've just started
    3 I started/I had started
Simon: How many cars [4]_____?   4 did you sell/have you sold

36

12 Review of present and past tenses

Hugo: Well, none yet. Up to now
⁵_____ about the
job. ⁶_____ I'm
going to like it.

Simon: ⁷_____ a sports car
when you were at college, ⁸_____.

Hugo: Yes, and I've still got it.
⁹_____ it for years.
¹⁰_____ sports cars.

5 I learn/I've been learning
6 I think/I'm thinking

7 You had/You were having
8 I remember/I'm remembering

9 I had/I've had
10 I love/I'm loving

12.4 Present and past (A–E)

Complete the news report. Put each verb into the correct form.

An eight-year-old boy ⁰ *has disappeared* . Mark Davidson
¹_____ yesterday from the park near his home in
Copley Road, Dulverstone. The Davidsons ²_____
five minutes' walk away from the park.
Mark ³_____ to the park at four o'clock and
⁴_____ football with his friends. After they
⁵_____ for about an hour, they
⁶_____ down for a rest. Mark
⁷_____ the park at quarter past five. He
⁸_____ alone. A man who
⁹_____ his dog ¹⁰_____
him go out through the gate. No one ¹¹_____
Mark since then. Police ¹²_____ local residents,
and so far they ¹³_____ to about two hundred
people. They ¹⁴_____ to question a middle-
aged man in a green sweater who ¹⁵_____ on
the grass near the park exit at five o'clock. At the moment police and
other helpers ¹⁶_____ nearby fields and woods
in the hope of finding the missing boy.

0 disappear
1 not return
2 live
3 go
4 play
5 play
6 sit
7 leave
8 be
9 walk   10 see
11 see
12 question
13 speak
14 want
15 lie

16 search

12.5 Present and past (A–E)

Complete the radio news report. Put in the correct form of the verbs.

'Hello. I ¹_____ to you from Oxford, where the finals
of the World Quiz Championships will begin tomorrow. The favourite is
Claude Jennings from Cornwall, the man who ²_____
everything. Twelve months ago no one ³_____ of
Claude Jennings, although he ⁴_____ part in quiz
competitions for years. Now suddenly he is a big star. So far this year he
⁵_____ every single question correctly. And he is
popular too. When he ⁶_____ here two days ago,
hundreds of fans ⁷_____ to welcome him at the station.
Since his arrival Claude ⁸_____ encyclopedias in his
hotel bedroom. He is clearly the man to watch. And now back to the Radio
Ten News Desk.'

1 speak
2 know
3 hear
4 take
5 answer
6 arrive
7 wait
8 read

13 be going to and will

A Be going to in the present

Look at these examples:
> *I'm going to watch* this next programme.
> *We're going to meet* at the station.
> When *are* you *going to pay* this bill?
> *Is* it *going to rain*?
> I hope she *isn't going to fall*.

| I **am going to** watch |
| you/we/they **are going to** watch |
| he/she/it **is going to** watch |

We use **be going to** for the future. *I'm going to watch a programme* means that I intend now to watch a programme in the future. For more details see Unit 14.

We can use **be going to** with the verb **go**: *I'm going to go out later*. But the present continuous is more usual: *I'm going out later*. (See Unit 15.)

B Was/were going to

We can use **be going to** in the past tense:
> *I was going to tidy* the flat, but I didn't have time.
> Tim *wasn't going to spend* any more money, but he saw a pair of trousers he just had to buy.
> The girls left early. They *were going to catch* the eight o'clock train.

I was going to tidy the flat means that I intended <u>in the past</u> to tidy the flat. Often the action does not really happen. (In fact I did not tidy the flat. I didn't have time.)

Look at this example with **just as**:
> The woman walked away *just as* I was going to speak to her. (**just as** = at the moment when)

C Will

The form is **will** (OR **'ll**):
> The West *will have* rain tomorrow.   *I will be* at home this evening.
> You*'ll be* late if you don't hurry.   The world *will end* in the year 2050.
> We*'ll know* soon.   I'm sure you*'ll enjoy* the show.

The negative is **will not** or **won't**:
> The cost *will not be* more than £50.   *I won't stay* long.

We use **will** for the future, for what we think will happen. For more details see Unit 14.

D Shall

We can use **shall** for the future, but only in the first person:
> *I will be* (OR *I shall be*) on holiday in August.
> *We will be* (OR *We shall be*) pleased to help you.
> But NOT ~~Jemima shall be on holiday in August.~~

For **shall** in offers and suggestions (e.g. **Shall** *I do it for you?*) see Unit 33.
For **will, would, shall** and **should** see Unit 36.
For **will/shall** in the USA see p 288.

13 Exercises

13.1 be going to (A)

Add a sentence. Use the verbs in brackets.
- □ (wash) Martin's sweater is dirty. _He's going to wash it._
- 1 (read) Mike has just bought a magazine. _____
- 2 (fry) I've decided to eat these eggs. _____
- 3 (sell) Mary doesn't need the sofa. _____
- 4 (correct) My work has several mistakes in it. _____
- 5 (accept) Someone has offered Carol a job. _____

13.2 be going to (A)

Put in the verbs. Use **be going to**.

Julia: Oh, you've got the lawn-mower. Good. It's time you cut the grass.
Paul: I □ _'m not going to cut_ it now. I ¹_____ the mower round to Steve's house. He ²_____ it for a couple of days. His mower has broken down.
Julia: ³_____ his lawn today?
Paul: I don't know. I expect so.
Julia: I just hope it ⁴_____.

□ not cut
1 take
2 borrow
3 he mow
4 not rain

13.3 was/were going to (B)

Complete the sentences. Use **was/were going to** and these verbs: **drive, get, go, pick, see**.
- □ The train left just as Harold _was going to get_ on it.
- 1 The shop closed just as I _____ in it.
- 2 The phone stopped ringing just as I _____ it up.
- 3 We went to the cinema, where we _____ a film about the Mafia, but it was so popular we couldn't get in.
- 4 Bob had trouble parking. A car took the last place in the car park just when he _____ into it.

13.4 will and won't (C)

Use the notes to write predictions about the world fifty years from now.
- □ there – be – twice as many people   _There will be twice as many people._
- 1 the world – have – one government   The world will _____
- 2 there – not be – any wars   _____
- 3 computers – decide – our future   _____
- 4 everyone – have – a personal robot   _____
- 5 there – not be – any oil left   _____
- 6 people – travel – to other planets   _____

14 be going to or will?

Look at this conversation:
- Mrs Wells: *How old are you now, Jackie?*
- Jackie: *I'll be eighteen next Friday.*
- Mrs Wells: *Oh, really? Are you going to have a party?*
- Jackie: *I'm going to have a meal in a restaurant with a few friends.*
- Mrs Wells: *That'll be nice.*

A Intentions and decisions

Compare:

be going to	**will**
We use **be going to** for an intention (what we've decided):	We use **will** for an instant decision (deciding at the moment of speaking):
We're going to have a meal.	*I know. We'll have a party.* ~ *Yes, good idea.*
Neil is going to buy a new sweater.	*It's cold. I'll shut the window.*
I'm going to visit my uncle tomorrow.	(NOT *It's cold. I shut the window.*)
	We also use **will** in offers and promises:
	I'll post that letter for you.

Remember that we use **be going to** (and not **will**) for an intention:
  Max and Sarah are planning something very exciting. They're going to sail round the world.
In this context NOT ... *They'll sail round the world.*

B Predictions

Compare:

be going to	**will**
We use **be going to** for a prediction based on the present situation (what we can see is going to happen):	We use **will** for a prediction (what we think will happen):
There isn't a cloud in the sky. It's going to be a lovely day.	*I'll be eighteen next Friday.*
The jockey can't stay on the horse. He's going to fall, look!	*One day people will travel to Mars.*
	The festival will last for ten days.

So we can use either form for a prediction:
- *We're going to win the match.*
- (*We're playing really well.*)
- *We'll win the match.*
- (*We've got the best team.*)

We often use **be going to** for an intention and **will** for the details and comments:
  I'm going to have a meal with a few friends. There'll be about ten of us. ~ *Oh, that'll be nice.*

We often use **will** with **I'm sure**, **I think**, **I expect** and **probably**:
- *I'm sure it'll be all right.*
- *I think we'll get there on time.*
- *I expect we'll lose the match.*
- *I'll probably have a meal.*

14 Exercises

14.1 be going to or will? (A)

Complete the replies. Use **be going to** or **will** with the verbs.

▢ Oh, you've got a ticket for the play. ~ Yes, I *'m going to see* it on Friday.   ▢ see
▢ The phone's ringing. ~ OK, I *'ll answer* it.   ▢ answer
1 Did you buy this book? ~ No, Nancy did. She _____ it on holiday.   1 read
2 Tea or coffee? ~ I _____ coffee, please.   2 have
3 I'm going to miss this film on TV because I'll be out tonight. ~ Well, I _____ it on the video, then.   3 record
4 I'm just going to the newsagent's for a paper. ~ What newspaper _____?   4 you buy
5 Can you meet me at seven? ~ I might be a bit late. ~ That's all right. I _____ for you.   5 wait

14.2 be going to or will? (A, B)

Complete the conversation. Decide which is best for the context, **be going to** or **will**.

Anita: What about your plans, Carlo? ▢ *Are you going to return* home after the exams?   ▢ you return
Carlo: I expect ▢ *I'll go* back home at some time in the future, but first I ¹_____ six months in the USA.   ▢ go   1 spend
Anita: Oh, that ²_____ interesting.   2 be
Carlo: I've fixed up a job. I ³_____ for a chemical company in California. I'm looking forward to it. I'm sure it ⁴_____ good experience.   3 work   4 be
Anita: I don't know what I ⁵_____. At the moment I'm trying to revise for the exams. But I don't know enough. I ⁶_____.   5 do   6 fail
Carlo: I'm sure you ⁷_____.   7 not fail

14.3 be going to or will? (A, B)

Complete the news report. Decide which is best for the context, **be going to** or **will**. Sometimes either is possible.

We have learnt this week that Brimley Town Council has plans for Westside Park. The Council ▢ *is going to sell* the land to a builder, A. Forbes and Son.   ▢ sell
'The plans are all ready. We ¹_____ fifty houses,' said Mr Forbes. 'In two years everything ²_____ finished. I'm sure people ³_____ the houses. Some of them ⁴_____ for young families.' But people living near the park are angry. 'This is a terrible idea. We're against it. We ⁵_____ a protest march on Saturday,' said Mrs Alice Marsh. 'I expect everyone in Brimley ⁶_____ there. We want to make our intentions clear. We ⁷_____ this plan.'   1 build   2 be   3 like   4 be   5 have   6 be   7 stop

15 Present tenses for the future

A Present continuous for arrangements

Look at this question and answer:
Melvyn: **Are** you **doing** anything this evening?
Bill: Yes, **I'm going** to the ice hockey match. The Tigers **are playing** the Kings. I bought my ticket yesterday.

APOLLO ICE STADIUM
THE TIGERS v THE KINGS
Wed 15th Feb 7.30 pm
ROW B SEAT 36

We use the present continuous for what someone has arranged to do. Here Bill has arranged to go to the match. (He has bought a ticket.)
I'm meeting Ann at six o'clock.   Phil **is coming** round later on.
They're playing ice hockey tonight.   Judy **is going** to Malta next week.

The present continuous and **be going to** have similar meanings:
We're having a party soon. (We have made the arrangements.)
We're going to have a party soon. (We have decided to have one.)

B Present simple for a timetable

Polly: What time **does** your train **leave** tomorrow?
Mike: Ten twenty-five. And it **arrives** in Gloucester at eleven ten.

City-direct				
Swindon	dp.	10.25	11.15	12.25
Kemble	ar.	10.39	11.29	12.39
Stroud	ar.	10.59	11.49	12.59
Gloucester	ar.	11.10	12.00	13.10

We can use the present simple for the future when it is part of a timetable:
The train **leaves** at ten twenty-five tomorrow morning.
The match **starts** at seven thirty.
Next Friday **is** the thirteenth.

But we do not use the present simple for intentions and decisions:
NOT ~~I buy my ticket tomorrow~~ or ~~I give you a lift this evening.~~

C Present simple after **when**, **before** etc.

We use the present simple for the future after **when, as, while, before, after, as soon as** and **until**:
We'll have coffee **when** the visitors **get** here.
I must get to the bank **before** it **closes**.
As soon as you **hear** any news, will you let me know?

Both actions are in the future. But we do not use **will** after **when, as** etc.
NOT We'll have coffee ~~when the vistors will get here~~.

The same thing happens after **if, who/which** and **that**:
If you **see** Elaine, can you give her a message?
The people **who arrive** early will get the best seats.
I'll make sure **(that)** everything **is** ready.

15 Exercises

15.1 The present continuous (A and Unit 1A)

Say if the verb refers to the present or the future.

Tim: What <u>are</u> you <u>reading</u>?   *present*
Fiona: Oh, it's a book about China. I ¹'<u>m going</u> there next month.   1 _____
Barry and I ²<u>are having</u> a holiday there.   2 _____
Tim: That sounds exciting.   3 _____
Fiona: Yes, I ³'<u>m</u> really <u>looking</u> forward to it. We ⁴'<u>re doing</u> a   4 _____
tour of the country. So I ⁵'<u>m finding</u> out as much as I can   5 _____
about it.

15.2 Present continuous for arrangements (A)

For each situation write a sentence with the present continuous. Use the verbs in brackets.

▷ Louise has accepted an invitation to Dave's party next week. (go)
 She's going to Dave's party next week.

1 Elaine has agreed to be in the office on Saturday. (work)

2 Karen has just bought her plane ticket to Acapulco. (fly)

3 Tim and Mike have booked a badminton court for tomorrow afternoon. (play)

4 All the arrangements have been made for Princess Diana to spend a day at the New World Fun Park on June 10th. (visit)

15.3 Present simple for a timetable (B)

This is today's programme for a group on a package tour of England. Describe their day. Use these verbs: **arrive, do, have, leave, take**.

▷ 9.30 am Bus to Stratford   *At half past nine they take a bus to Stratford.*
1 12.30 pm Arrival in Stratford _____
2 1.00 pm Lunch _____
3 2.00 pm Tour of the town _____
4 5.30 pm Departure _____

15.4 Present simple after **when**, **before** etc. (C)

Put in the verbs. Use **will** or the present simple.

A: What about my money?
B: I ▷ *'ll send* the cheque to you as soon as I ▷ *have* it.   ▷ send ▷ have
A: Why can't you write me a cheque now?
B: The manager writes the cheques. He's away until Tuesday.
I can't do anything until he ¹_____ back. When   1 get
he ²_____ in on Tuesday morning,   2 come
I ³_____ him about it. I ⁴_____ sure   3 remind   4 make
that he ⁵_____ you want the money immediately.   5 know
If I ⁶_____ the cheque first class,   6 post
you ⁷_____ it on Wednesday.   7 receive

43

16   will be doing and will have done

Look at this conversation:
> Don: *I need to know all the arrangements. Can you phone me tomorrow?*
> Judy: *Yes, I'll phone you tomorrow afternoon at about three.*
> Don: *Oh, I'll be out then. **I'll be playing** golf. But **I'll have finished** by about five.*
> Judy: *Well, **I'll be passing** your house at half past five. It's on my way home. I'll call in and see you.*

A   will be doing for continuous actions

We use **will be** + ing-form for an action over a period of future time. It means that we will be in the middle of an action:
> *I'll be out. **I'll be playing** golf.*
> *When the men leave the building, the police **will be waiting** for them.*
> *This time next week we**'ll be driving** through France.*

Compare the past continuous (see Unit 7):
> *This time last week we **were driving** through France.*

Compare these sentences:
> *The band **will play** when the President enters.*
> (The President will enter and then the band will play.)
> *The band **will be playing** when the President enters.*
> (The band will start playing before the President enters.)

B   will be doing for routine actions

We also use **will be** + ing-form for an action which is the result of a routine:
> *I'**ll be passing** your house this afternoon. It's on my way home from work.*
> *Barbara **will be cleaning** the flat tomorrow. She always does it on Sundays.*

Compare the present continuous and **will be doing**:
> Arrangement: *I'm seeing Nigel tomorrow. We've arranged to meet.* (See Unit 15.)
> Routine: *I'll be seeing Nigel tomorrow. We work in the same department.*

We can use **will be doing** to ask if someone's plans fit in with what we would like them to do:
> ***Will** you **be going** anywhere near a chemist's this morning?* ~ *Yes, why?* ~ *Could you get me some aspirin, please?*
> *How long **will** you **be using** this computer?* ~ *You can have it in a minute.*

C   will have done

We use **will have** + a past participle for something before a future time, something that we will finish before a time in the future:
> *We'll **have finished** our game of tennis by six o'clock.*
> (The game will be at an end before six o'clock.)
> *This book isn't very long. I'll **have read** it by lunch time.*
> *The Watsons **will have lived** here ten years next April.*

16 Exercises

16.1 will be doing (A)

A gang of criminals have a plan to steal millions of pounds from a London bank and leave the country. They're talking about what they will be doing a week from now, after the robbery.

☐ we – live – in luxury   _We'll be living in luxury._
1 we – relax – at our villa   _____
2 I – sit – by the pool   _____
3 the sun – shine   _____
4 we – enjoy – ourselves   _____
5 the police – look for us   _____
6 but – we – laugh – at them   _____

16.2 will be doing (B)

You want to ask a friend to do something for you or to let you do something. Find out if it is convenient for your friend. Use the verbs in brackets.

☐ You want to have a look at your friend's magazine tonight. (read)
   Will you be reading your magazine tonight?
1 You want your friend to send a note to Emma for you soon. (write to)
   Will you be _____
2 You want your friend to take your library book back today. (go to)
   _____
3 You want to use your friend's calculator this afternoon. (use)
   _____
4 You want your friend to give a photo to Henry tomorrow. (see)
   _____
5 You want your friend to video the late-night film. (watch)
   _____
6 You want your friend to give a message to her sister. (phone)
   _____

16.3 will have done (C)

Oswald is at art school. He wants to be a successful artist. He's reading about the famous Richard Plummer.

> Richard Plummer was a great artist. He won lots of prizes before he was twenty. By the age of twenty-five he had had his own exhibition. He had been the subject of a TV programme before he was thirty. By the age of thirty-five he had become world-famous. He made millions of pounds from his pictures before he was forty.

What does Oswald think?
☐ I hope _I'll have won lots of prizes_ _____ when I'm twenty.
1 I hope _____ my own exhibition by the age of twenty-five.
2 I hope _____ before I'm thirty.
3 I hope _____ by the age of thirty-five.
4 I hope _____

17 Review of the future

I'm leaving school in July. From September I'll be studying engineering at the polytechnic. The term starts on September 10th. I'll be free for seven weeks before then. I'm going to get a holiday job.

There are a number of different ways of expressing the future. The form of the verb depends on whether the speaker is talking about what he/she intends (*I'm going to get a job*), or talking about a timetable (*The term starts on September 10th*), and so on. Sometimes more than one form is possible, e.g. *I'm leaving* school OR *I'll be leaving* school.

A I'm going to or I will? (Unit 14)

We use **be going to** for an intention:
I'm going to get a job, I've decided.
We're going to have a picnic.

We also use **be going to** for a prediction based on the present:
Look at the time. We're going to be late.

We use **will** for an instant decision:
I feel really ill. ~ *I'll call the doctor then.*
We'll give you a lift.

We also use **will** for a prediction about the future:
I'll be free at five o'clock.
You'll enjoy the course, I'm sure.

We can often use either **be going to** or **will** for a prediction:
We're going to need some help. OR *We'll need some help.*

B I'm doing or I do? (Unit 15)

We use the present continuous for an arrangement:
I'm playing basketball tonight. I'm in the team.

We use the present simple for a timetable:
We leave tomorrow morning at half past seven.

We also use it after **when**, **before** etc:
I'll tell you when I see you.

C I'll be doing and I'll have done (Unit 16)

We use **will be doing** for an action over a period of future time:
At this time tomorrow I'll be driving up the motorway.

We use **will have done** for something that we will finish in the future:
I'll have finished my homework by eight o'clock.

We also use **will be doing** for the result of a routine:
I'll be visiting my parents tomorrow. I visit them every Sunday.

D be about to and be to

We use **be about to** for the very near future:
The plane is at the end of the runway. It is about to take off.
Hurry up. The programme is about to start.

We use **be to** for an official arrangement:
The Queen is to visit Portugal in November.
The Student Games are to take place in Melbourne next year.

17 Exercises

17.1 The future (A–C)

Choose the correct verb form from the phrases on the right.
1. How's your flat? ~ Well, the rent is very expensive. _____ to a new place. I decided last week.
2. I can cycle home. ~ Have you got lights? _____ dark, don't forget.
3. I'd like a photo of Adrian and me. ~ Well, _____ one with your camera then.
4. Have you booked a holiday? ~ Yes, _____ to Spain.
5. Look at that car! _____
6. Can I borrow your bike on Monday, please? ~ Oh, I'm afraid _____ it. I always cycle to work.

1. I'll move/I'm going to move
2. It'll be/It'll have been
3. I'll take/I'm going to take
4. we go/we're going
5. It'll crash!/It's going to crash!
6. I'll be using/I'll have used

17.2 The future (A–D)

What do these people say? Pay special attention to the underlined words.
- Maria is <u>predicting</u> a win for Italy in their next match.
  Maria: *Italy will win their next match.*
1. Bob <u>intends</u> to get up early tomorrow.
   Bob: I _____
2. Steve's train <u>timetable</u> says 'Arrival 10.30'.
   Steve: The train _____
3. Louise has <u>arranged</u> to see her bank manager tomorrow.
   Louise: _____
4. Dan will leave in the <u>very near future</u>.
   Dan: _____
5. Sarah's next visit to her aunt is on Sunday, the day she <u>usually</u> visits her.
   Sarah: _____

17.3 The future (A–D)

Complete the conversation. Look at the context and choose the best form of the verb to express the future. Sometimes more than one answer is correct.

A: Hello. Where are you going?
B: To my evening class. I'm learning Swedish. And I ¹_____ it for real this time next week. I ²_____ to Sweden for three weeks. I ³_____ on Friday evening. I ⁴_____ friends there.
A: Oh, that ⁵_____ nice.
B: Oh, it's nearly half past. My lesson ⁶_____ in a minute.
A: Well, have a good time. I ⁷_____ you next month.
B: Thanks. I ⁸_____ you all about it when I ⁹_____ back.

1. speak
2. go
3. leave
4. visit
5. be
6. start
7. see
8. tell
9. get

18 have and have got

A The use of have (got)

We use **have** and **have got** for possession and related meanings.
  Peter **has** a cassette recorder.   Linda **has got** fair hair.
  You **have** a good memory.   **I've got** an idea.
  We **had** several jobs to do.   **Haven't** you **got** any friends?
In these examples **have (got)** expresses a state, not an action. For the action verb **have** see Unit 19.

B have and have got

have	have got
Present simple	Present simple
I/you/we/they **have**	I/you/we/they **have got** OR **I've got**
he/she/it **has**	he/she/it **has got** OR he**'s got**
Past simple	Past simple
everyone **had**	everyone **had got** OR they**'d got**

In many contexts either **have** or **have got** is possible. But **got** is more informal, more everyday.

We use **got** more in the present and not so often in the past tense:
  I **had** the letter in my hand a moment ago. (I **had got** . . . is less usual.)

We do not use **got** with the forms **have had/has had**, **to have** or **having**:
  I've had this jacket for years. NOT *I've had got this jacket.*
  We're allowed **to have** pets. NOT *We're allowed to have got pets.*
  It's a nuisance not **having** a watch. NOT *a nuisance not having got a watch*
And we do not use **got** in short answers:
  Has Helen got a car? ~ Yes, she **has**. NOT *Yes, she has got.*

We can use the short forms **'ve** (= have) and **'s** (= has) before **got**:
  I've got two sisters.
  Simon**'s got** a new motor-bike.

C Negatives and questions

These are the most usual ways of forming negatives and questions in the present:

have	have got
I **don't have** a ticket.	I **haven't got** a ticket.
Sadie **doesn't have** any money.	Sadie **hasn't got** any money.
Do you **have** a ticket? ~ Yes, I **do**.	**Have** you **got** a ticket? ~ Yes, I **have**.
Does Sadie **have** any money? ~ No, she **doesn't**.	**Has** Sadie **got** any money? ~ No, she **hasn't**.

Americans normally use the forms with **do/does**. See p 289.

In the past we normally use **did**:
  I **didn't have** my passport.
  Did you **have** your passport?

18 Exercises

18.1 The use of **be** and **have** (A)

Put in **are**, **is**, **have** or **has**.

We □ _have_ a new girl in our class. Her name □ _is_ Melissa. She ¹_____ very nice. She ²_____ tall and ³_____ long dark hair. She ⁴_____ a very popular girl. She ⁵_____ hundreds of friends. She ⁶_____ lots of clothes and she ⁷_____ very smart. Her parents ⁸_____ quite rich, I believe. They must ⁹_____ lots of money. Melissa ¹⁰_____ very lively and ¹¹_____ lots of energy, much more than I ¹²_____.

18.2 **have** and **have got** (B)

Put in a present or past form. You can use either **have** or **have got**.

□ Luke is very good at tennis. He _has got_ a lot of ability.
1. The boys aren't usually very busy. They _____ lots of spare time.
2. I missed the train. I couldn't run very fast. I _____ a big suitcase.
3. We don't need to wash up. We _____ an automatic dishwasher.
4. I felt cold yesterday evening, even though I _____ a pullover on.
5. Rosemary loves music. She _____ over two hundred compact discs.
6. I can't do any work at all. I _____ a bad back.

18.3 Positive and negative forms of **have (got)** (C)

Put in a positive or negative form. You can use either **have** or **have got**.

□ The family are homeless. They _haven't got_ anywhere to live.
1. Sorry, I can't help you today. I _____ a busy day ahead of me.
2. More people came than we expected, but luckily we _____ just enough chairs.
3. The Taylors always keep their house so tidy. They _____ any children, of course.
4. I walked home yesterday. I couldn't get a bus because I _____ any money.
5. Paul _____ something wrong with his leg. He can't walk very well.
6. Linda leaves her car out in the street because she _____ a garage.

18.4 Negatives and questions (C)

Complete the dialogue. Put in the negative or question form of **have** or **have got**.

A: □ _Have_ you _got_ your bike here?
B: Yes.
A: ¹_____ it _____ lights?
B: Yes, why?
A: Can I borrow it to get home? Mine ²_____ any lights. It ³_____ any when I bought it. I meant to get some last week, but I ⁴_____ time.
B: OK, but it's raining, look. ⁵_____ you _____ something to wear?
A: Yes, I've got a coat.

19 The action verb **have**

A The meanings of **have**

We use **have** or **have got** to talk about a state, something staying the same (see Unit 18):
*Tessa **has** a new camera.*   *I'**ve got** a bit of a problem.*

But **have** can also be an action verb:
*Tessa **has** lunch around one.* (= eats)
*We **have** coffee at breakfast.* (= drink)
*We **had** a wonderful weekend in the mountains.* (= We spent a wonderful weekend ...)
*The children **had** a game of cards.*
*We must **have** a talk some time.* (**have** a talk = talk; see C)

B The action verb **have**

The action verb is **have**, not **have got**:
NOT *Tessa has got lunch around one.*
We do not use a short form of **have** when it is an action verb:
NOT *She's lunch around one* or *We'd a wonderful holiday.*

In negatives and questions in simple tenses, we use a form of **do**:
*We **didn't have** a very good time.*   *We **don't have** parties very often.*
*What time **does** she **have** lunch?*   *How often **do** you **have** a holiday?*

The action verb **have** can be continuous:
*Tessa **is having** lunch now.*
*We'**re having** a marvellous time.*
*The students **were having** a conversation in English.*

C **have a talk** = **talk** etc.

Compare these two sentences, which have the same meaning:
*We must **talk**.* (verb)
*We must **have a talk**.* (**have** + **a** + noun)

The pattern **have a talk** is quite common in English. Here are some more examples:
*Shall we **have a walk/a run/a ride/a swim**?*
*I usually **have a rest/a sleep** in the afternoon.*
*I ought to **have a wash/a bath**.*
*The two men were **having a talk/a chat/an argument/a fight**.*
*Can you **have a look** at this camera? There's something wrong with it.*

There are similar expressions with a few other verbs. Here are some examples:

> **go for a walk/a run/a jog/a ride/a swim**
> **make a complaint/a request/a suggestion**
> **pay someone a visit**
> **give a laugh/a smile**
> **make/take a decision**

19 Exercises

19.1 The meanings of have (A)

What does **have** mean in these sentences? Rewrite the sentences using a form of these verbs:
drink, eat, play, receive, smoke, spend.

☐ I never have breakfast.
  I never eat breakfast.

1. We've had three games of Scrabble.
   _____

2. My father has a glass of beer every evening.
   _____

3. We've just had three weeks in Yugoslavia.
   _____

4. I've already had a sandwich.
   _____

5. James had lots of presents on his birthday.
   _____

6. The manager was having a cigarette in his office.
   _____

19.2 The action verb have (B)

Complete the conversation. Use a form of the action verb **have**.

Claire: Are you enjoying yourselves?
Philip: Yes, thanks. We ☐ *'re having* a great time.
Claire: It's a long time since our last party. We ¹_____ parties very often.
Jemima: This is a super party, Claire. Everyone ²_____ fun.
Claire: And how was Normandy? ³_____ you _____ a good holiday?
Jemima: Yes, we ⁴_____ a lovely time thanks. You must ⁵_____ a look at our photos some time.
Philip: But we ⁶_____ very good weather, unfortunately.

19.3 have a talk = talk etc. (C)

Put in phrases like **have a ride, had a sleep, make a complaint** etc.

☐ Did you go out? ~ Yes, I *had a walk* round the village.
1. It's hot today, isn't it? ~ Yes, I think I'll _____ in the pool.
2. Why are Daniel and Joanna looking so annoyed? ~ Oh, they've _____ about something. They're always arguing.
3. What did Lucy say when she heard the news? ~ Nothing. She just _____. I think she was pleased.
4. Is the water hot? ~ Yes, there's plenty of hot water if you want to _____.
5. I'm sorry. Were you asleep? ~ No, I was just lying down. I was _____.
6. How is your aunt? ~ She's still in hospital. I'm going to _____ her _____ tomorrow.
7. There's something wrong with the car. It's making a funny noise. ~ I'll take it to the garage and ask them to _____ at it.

20 Short forms (e.g. 's, 've)

A The use of short forms

Look at this conversation:
- Alan: Hello, Barry. How are you? I heard you **haven't** been well.
- Barry: Yes, **I've** been ill, but **I'm** much better now, thanks.
- Alan: Oh, **that's** good.

A short form like **I'm** or **that's** stands for the full form **I am** or **that is**. We leave out one or more letters and we write an apostrophe (') instead. We use short forms in conversational English and in informal writing such as a letter to a friend.

We cannot use the short form when the word is stressed, e.g. in a short answer:
Have you seen a doctor? ~ *Yes, I 'have.* NOT *Yes, I've.*
But we can use **n't** at the end, e.g. *No, I haven't*.

B The most common short forms

Some verbs can have short forms when they come after a pronoun:

VERB	SHORT FORM
am	I'm
are	you're, we're, they're
is/has	he's, she's, it's
have	I've, you've, we've, they've
had/would	I'd, you'd, he'd, she'd, it'd, we'd, they'd
will	I'll, you'll, he'll, she'll, it'll, we'll, they'll

A short form can also come after a noun:
Susan's lost her pen.   Do you think the **bus'll** be full?
(Susan **has** ...)   (... the bus **will** ...)

Some verbs can also have short forms after a question word or after **here**, **there** or **that**:
who's, what's, where's, when's, how's; who'd; who'll, what'll
here's, there's, that's; there'll, that'll; there'd, that'd

There is a negative short form **n't**, which can come after some verbs:
aren't, isn't, wasn't, weren't; haven't, hasn't, hadn't; don't [dəʊnt]**, doesn't, didn't;**
won't (= will not)**, shan't** (= shall not)**, can't** [kɑ:nt]**, couldn't, mustn't** ['mʌsnt]**, needn't,**
mightn't, shouldn't, wouldn't, daren't

C Some special points about short forms

's can be **is** or **has**, and **'d** can be **had** or **would**:
She's short and she's got fair hair. (She **is** short ... she **has** got ...)
If I'd known, I'd have told you. (If I **had** known, I **would** have ...)

Sometimes we can shorten either **not** or the verb:
It is not funny. → *It **isn't** funny.* OR *It's not funny.*
You will not believe it. → *You **won't** believe it.* OR *You'll not believe it.*
But we cannot use **n't** after **I**:
I am not sure. → *I'm not sure.* NOT *I amn't...*

20 Exercises

20.1 Short forms (A)

Write the sentences in a more informal style, with short forms instead of full forms.

	Business letter	Letter to a friend
☐	You are right.	You're right.
1	That is the problem.	
2	I have seen the article.	
3	I am sorry.	
4	We have not decided.	

20.2 Short forms (B)

Two students of English are having a conversation. But it sounds strange because they aren't using short forms. Make their conversation more natural.

A: I am ready.   ☐ I'm ready.
B: Where is your ticket?   1 _____
A: I do not know. I have not got it.   2 _____
Oh, it is here.   3 _____
B: It is ten past. We will be late.   4 _____
A: Do not worry. We need not hurry.   5 _____
A: I would like to be on time.   6 _____
B: We are early. We have got time.   7 _____
We will not be late.   8 _____

20.3 Short forms (B)

What do these sentences mean? Write the full forms.

☐ I'm quite sure.   *I am quite sure.*
1 We're ready.
2 The letter hasn't come.
3 What'll you do?
4 You've made a mistake.
5 I didn't know.
6 That book's mine.
7 Here's your ticket.
8 They won't win.

20.4 The short forms 's and 'd (C)

Write the sentences with full forms. Use **is**, **has**, **had** or **would**.

☐ What's your name?   *What is your name?*
1 I'd like a coffee.
2 There's been an accident.
3 That's correct.
4 I'd seen the film before.
5 Who's got the key?
6 We'd have stopped if we'd seen you.

21 Negative statements

A The use of the negative

Read this information about two bridges in London. Note the negative forms.

There have been several bridges called London Bridge across the Thames. The present London Bridge **is not** very old, and it **does not** look very special. The last one was sold to the USA and is now in Arizona. The old London Bridge in the song 'London Bridge is Falling down' **doesn't** exist any more. You **must not** confuse London Bridge with Tower Bridge, the next bridge down the river. Tower Bridge is the one with two tall towers, but it **isn't** called Tower Bridge because of these towers. It gets its name from the nearby Tower of London. The Tower of London **isn't** just a tower – it is really a castle.

B Negative verb forms

In a negative statement **not** or **n't** comes after the auxiliary verb. The auxiliary verb is a form of **be** or **have** or a modal verb, e.g. **can**, **must**, **should**.

The girls **are not** dancing.   The cooker **isn't** working properly.
Terry **hasn't** got a car.   I **haven't** seen Kate for ages.
You **can't** turn right here.   I **mustn't** stay long.

We write **n't** without a space in front of it, e.g. **isn't**, **haven't**.

Not or **n't** also comes after the main verb **be**:

The photos **are not** ready yet.   It **isn't** very warm.

If there are two or more auxiliary verbs, we put **not/n't** after the first one:

This plate **hasn't** been washed.   You **shouldn't** have bothered.

In the present simple and past simple, we use a form of **do**:

I **don't** work on Saturdays. NOT ~~I work not on Saturdays.~~
This soup **doesn't** taste very nice.
We **didn't** enjoy the holiday very much.

The verb after **not/n't** does not end in **s** or **ed**:

NOT ~~It doesn't tastes very nice.~~ or ~~We didn't enjoyed the holiday.~~

Look at this table:

	POSITIVE	NEGATIVE (FULL FORM)	NEGATIVE (SHORT FORM)
be	are	are not	aren't
have	have seen	have not seen	haven't seen
Modal	must stay	must not stay	mustn't stay
Present simple	work	do not work	don't work
	tastes	does not taste	doesn't taste
Past simple	enjoyed	did not enjoy	didn't enjoy

C no or not?

We can use **no** before a noun. The verb is positive:

No music is allowed (OR Music is not allowed) after eleven o'clock.
There are **no** shops (OR There aren't any shops) in the village.

We do not use **no** with a verb: NOT ~~Music is no allowed~~ or ~~The shops are no open.~~

21 Exercises

21.1 The use of the negative (A)

Read the information in A. Then put in a positive or a negative verb.

☐ London Bridge _isn't_ the same as Tower Bridge.   ☐ is/isn't
1 The Americans _____ Tower Bridge.   1 bought/didn't buy
2 The present London Bridge _____ very beautiful.   2 is/isn't
3 You _____ Tower Bridge near the Tower.   3 will find/won't find
4 Tower Bridge _____ towers.   4 has got/hasn't got
5 Tower Bridge _____ its name from its two towers.   5 gets/doesn't get
6 'The Tower of London' _____ a good name.   6 is/isn't

21.2 Negative verb forms (B)

Put in **isn't**, **aren't**, **wasn't**, **hasn't** (×2), **haven't**, **don't** (×2), **doesn't** (×2) or **didn't**.

Bert is a strange man. He ☐ _hasn't_ got a job, so I ¹_____ know where he gets his money from. He bought his small house years ago, and he ²_____ pay much for it. It ³_____ very expensive when he bought it. I ⁴_____ think he's rich. His clothes certainly ⁵_____ new. He lives alone, and he ⁶_____ got any friends. He ⁷_____ in good health but he ⁸_____ go to the doctor. He ⁹_____ like doctors, he says. I usually see Bert most days, although I ¹⁰_____ seen him this week. He always seems happy enough.

21.3 Negative verb forms (B)

Trevor and Rex are brothers, but they have very different personalities. Change the sentences into the positive or negative.

☐ Trevor hasn't got a lot of friends. But Rex _has got a lot of friends._
☐ Trevor worries about the future. But Rex _doesn't worry about the future._
1 Trevor is a nervous person. But Rex _____
2 Trevor wants a quiet life. But Rex _____
3 Trevor doesn't take risks. But Rex _____
4 Trevor was a very clever child. But Rex _____
5 Trevor passed all his exams. But Rex _____
6 Trevor can relax. But Rex _____
7 Trevor isn't a good talker. But Rex _____
8 Trevor has read a lot of books. But Rex _____

21.4 no or not? (C)

Complete this paragraph from a travel article. Put in **no** or **not**.

Metropolis is ¹_____ an attractive town. There are ²_____ parks or gardens in the city centre. I saw ³_____ interesting buildings, only factories, offices and blocks of flats. The hotels are ⁴_____ very good. ⁵_____ tourists visit Metropolis, and I certainly do ⁶_____ want to go there again.

22 Questions

A The use of questions

Look at this conversation:
> Tony: **Are you ready?**
> Kate: *Yes, just about.* **What time does the film start?**
> Tony: *Quarter to eight, I think.*
> Kate: **Have you seen my bag?**
> Tony: *Yes, it's on the chair.*
> Kate: *Right.* **Shall we go then?**

A question asks for information, e.g. if someone is ready or not, or the time when a film starts. But questions sometimes have other uses, especially questions with modal verbs (e.g. **shall**, **could**). Here are some examples:

Making a suggestion:	**Shall** *we go then?* ~ *All right.*
Requesting:	**Could** *you pass the sugar, please?*
Offering:	**Can** *I carry something for you?* ~ *No, it's OK, thanks.*
Inviting:	**Would** *you like to come to a party?* ~ *Yes, I'd love to. When is it?*
Asking permission:	**May** *I use your phone?* ~ *Yes, of course.*

B The form of questions

There are two kinds of question. Compare:

YES/NO QUESTION	WH-QUESTION
A yes/no question can have the answer **yes** or **no**:	A wh-question begins with a question word, e.g. **what**, **where**:
Are you ready? ~ **Yes**, *just about.*	**What** *have you done?* ~ *Broken a glass.*
Have you got a pen? ~ **No**, *sorry.*	**Where** *do you work?* ~ *At a supermarket.*
Is it raining? ~ *I don't think so.*	**When** *did you arrive?* ~ *Just now.*

In a question, an auxiliary verb comes before the subject. An auxiliary verb is a form of **be** or **have** or a modal verb (e.g. **can**, **should**). For example:

STATEMENT	QUESTION		
		Auxiliary	Subject	
*It **is** raining.*		*Is*	*it*	*raining?*
***Paula was** dancing.*	*What*	*was*	*Paula*	*doing?*
***Bob has** got a car.*		*Has*	*Bob*	*got a car?*
***The boys have** gone out.*	*Where*	*have*	*the boys*	*gone?*
***Andrew can** type.*		*Can*	*Andrew*	*type?*
***I should** travel by train.*	*How*	*should*	*I*	*travel?*

The main verb **be** also comes before the subject in a question:
> ***Is it*** *windy out there?*   ***Are you*** *ready?*

If there is more than one auxiliary, only the first one comes before the subject:
> *What **has Paula** been doing?*
> ***Can the letter** have got lost in the post?*

22 Questions

In the present simple and past simple, we use a form of **do**. For example:

STATEMENT	QUESTION			
		Auxiliary	Subject	
*The shops **stay*** *open late.*		*Do*	*the shops*	*stay open late?*
*The coach **leaves*** *tonight.*	*When*	*does*	*the coach*	*leave?*
*You **liked*** *the film.*		*Did*	*you*	*like the film?*
*Joanna **bought*** *something.*	*What*	*did*	*Joanna*	*buy?*

A question cannot begin with an ordinary verb like **stay**, **leave**, **like** or **buy**.
    NOT *When leaves the coach?* or *Liked you the film?*

The verb after the subject does not end in **s** or **ed**.
    NOT *When does the coach leaves?* or *Did you liked the film?*

Note: The question form is different when the question word is the subject (e.g. *Who liked the film?*). For details see Unit 23.

C Question words and phrases

All question words begin with **wh**, except **how**:
    Who *are you meeting?* ~ *A friend.*
    What *did you say?* ~ *Nothing.*
    Which *of these do you prefer?* ~ *The blue one, I think.*
    Whose *coat is this?* ~ *Mine.*
    Where *are you from?* ~ *Italy.*
    When *are the visitors arriving?* ~ *This evening.*
    Why *did you walk out?* ~ *Because I felt ill.*
    How *can we find out?* ~ *We can ask someone.*
For more details about **who**, **what** and **which**, see Unit 24.

There are also question phrases with **what** and **how**:
    What time *are the visitors arriving?* ~ *Half past eight.*
    What colour *is your toothbrush?* ~ *Yellow.*
    What kind *of/***What sort** *of club is it?* ~ *A night club.*
    How old *is your sister?* ~ *She's twenty.*
    How often *do you go out?* ~ *About once a week.*
    How far *is the beach?* ~ *Only five minutes' walk.*
    How long *will the meeting last?* ~ *An hour or so, I expect.*
    How many *televisions have you got?* ~ *Three.*
    How much *money did you spend?* ~ *Over fifty pounds.*

D Prepositions in questions

In formal English, a preposition can sometimes come before a question word:
    On *what will the winner spend his money?*
But usually the preposition comes in the same place as in a statement:
    What will the winner spend his money **on**?   *Who are you waiting* **for**?
    Where do those students come **from**?   *What was your brother talking* **about** *just now?*

22 Exercises

22.1 The use of questions (A)

Write down the use of each question: asking for information, making a suggestion, requesting, offering, inviting, or asking permission.

☐ Would you post this letter for me? — *requesting*
☐ Can we get a 35 bus from this stop? — *asking for information*
1. Shall I help you with that? _____
2. Shall we stop for a rest? _____
3. Can I come in? _____
4. Can you wait a moment, please? _____
5. Will you stay and have some tea with us? _____
6. Will your friends be in London next weekend? _____
7. May I sit down? _____
8. Could you help me with this? _____

22.2 The form of questions (B)

Jessica has just had an interview for a job. Look at the interviewer's notes and write down what his questions were.

☐ (<u>No</u>, she hasn't done this kind of work before.)
  Have you done this kind of work before?
☐ (She went to <u>Croft Park</u> School.)
  Which *school did you go to?*
1. (She left school <u>three years ago</u>.)
   When _____
2. (Her best subject was <u>music</u>.)
   What _____
3. (<u>Yes</u>, she passed her maths exam.)

4. (Her hobbies are <u>music and computers</u>.)
   What _____
5. (She lives in <u>Middleton</u>.)

6. (<u>Yes</u>, she has got a car.)

7. (<u>Yes</u>, she would like to work evenings.)

22.3 The form of questions (B)

Wayne Livingstone is a young actor in the TV programme 'Round the Corner'. Put in the reporter's questions.

☐ Reporter: *Do you enjoy acting?*
  Wayne: Yes, I enjoy acting very much.
☐ Reporter: *What are your plans* for the future?
  Wayne: I don't know. I haven't got any plans.
1. Reporter: How long _____
  Wayne: I don't know how long the programme will continue.

58

2 Reporter: _____
  Wayne: I'm not going to tell you. How much money I earn is my business.
3 Reporter: _____
  Wayne: I started acting when I was twelve.
4 Reporter: _____
  Wayne: Yes, my parents are proud of me.
5 Reporter: _____
  Wayne: Yes, I've got a girl-friend.
6 Reporter: _____
  Wayne: Karen. Her name is Karen.
7 Reporter: _____
  Wayne: She lives in Fulham.
8 Reporter: _____
  Wayne: I've known her about a year.
9 Reporter: _____
  Wayne: I don't know if we're going to get married.
10 Reporter: _____
  Wayne: What a question! No, I've never taken drugs.

22.4 Question words and phrases (C)

Complete the questions. Put in these words and phrases: **who, what, whose, where, when, what time, what colour, what kind, how often, how far, how long, how many**.

☐ _Where_ is Melbourne? ~ In Australia.
☐ _What colour_ is the Greek flag? ~ Blue and white.
1 _____ was the first President of the USA? ~ George Washington.
2 _____ did the Second World War end? ~ In 1945.
3 _____ inches are there in a foot? ~ Twelve.
4 _____ do banks open in England? ~ Half past nine.
5 _____ is a foal? ~ A young horse.
6 _____ is it from San Francisco to Los Angeles? ~ About 400 miles.
7 _____ home is 10 Downing Street? ~ The Prime Minister's.
8 _____ are the Olympic Games held? ~ Every four years.
9 _____ of food is Cheddar? ~ Cheese.
10 _____ is a game of rugby? ~ 80 minutes.

22.5 Prepositions in questions (D)

Reply with a question. Put the preposition at the end.
☐ I'm afraid. ~ _What are you afraid of?_ (of)
☐ Your friends are pleased. ~ _What are they pleased about?_ (about)
1 I often worry. ~ What do _____ (about)
2 People are fed up. ~ What are _____ (with)
3 I feel ashamed. ~ _____ (of)
4 I'm going to complain. ~ _____ (about)
5 Polly's sister is famous. ~ _____ (for)
6 I'm concentrating. ~ _____ (on)

23 Subject/object questions

A who and what as subject and object

Look at these examples:

Who is interviewing Jane?    *Who is Jane interviewing?*

Now compare:

Who and **what** can be the subject of a question. The word order is the same as in a statement. Compare **someone** and **something** as subject:	**Who** and **what** can also be the object. The word order is different from a statement. An auxiliary (e.g. **did**, **will**) comes before the subject:
SUBJECT	OBJECT
Who rang you? ↑ (**Someone** rang you.)	*Who did you ring?* ↑_____ (You rang **someone**.)
Who is helping you? ↑ (**Someone** is helping you.)	*Who are you helping?* ↑_____ (You are helping **someone**.)
What will happen next? ↑ (**Something** will happen next.)	*What will they do next?* ↑_____ (They will do **something** next.)

Compare **who** and **what** as subject of the sentence and object of a preposition (e.g. **to**):

SUBJECT	OBJECT
Who was talking to you? (**Someone** was talking to you.) *What wine goes with fish?* (**Some wine** goes with fish.)	*Who were you talking to?* (You were talking to **someone**.) *What did Emma ask for?* (Emma asked for **something**.)

B which and whose as subject and object

A phrase with **which** or **whose** can also be either subject or object:

SUBJECT	OBJECT
Which computer can draw pictures? (**One of the computers** can draw pictures.) *Whose dog is barking over there?* (**Someone's dog** is barking over there.)	*Which computer can the pupils use?* (The pupils can use **one of the computers**.) *Whose dog is Darren looking after?* (Darren is looking after **someone's dog**.)

23 Exercises

23.1 who and what as subject and object (A)

Read about the situations and answer each question in a single phrase.

Sam was building a wall. Eric came and laid some bricks for him. Graham watched them for a while.
- Who helped Sam? _Eric_
- Who did Sam help? _No one_

Ed wants to marry Lola, but she's crazy about Carl. He isn't interested in women.
1. Who is Ed in love with? _____
2. Who is in love with Carl? _____

Elaine met Louise at the airport. The plane was very late. On the way out they saw Tom standing at a bus stop.
3. Who met Louise? _____
4. What was Tom waiting for? _____

Jason and Craig were having a boxing match. Craig knocked Jason out. Someone threw a chair at the referee and hit him on the head.
5. What hit the referee? _____
6. Who did Craig hit? _____

23.2 who and what as subject and object (A)

Ask questions with **who** or **what**.
- Something has happened. ~ Oh? _What has happened?_
- I've invited someone to tea. ~ Oh? _Who have you invited?_
1. Somebody is having a party. ~ Oh? _____
2. I was laughing at something. ~ Oh? _____
3. I've learnt something. ~ Oh? _____
4. We should do something. ~ Oh? _____
5. Someone is looking for you. ~ Oh? _____
6. I'm looking for someone. ~ Oh? _____
7. Jill is planning something. ~ Oh? _____
8. Somebody has moved in next door. ~ Oh? _____
9. Something is worrying me. ~ Oh? _____
10. I want to meet someone. ~ Oh? _____

23.3 which and whose as subject and object (B)

You don't quite hear what someone says. Complete the questions.
- The children's rabbit is missing. ~ Whose rabbit _is missing_?
- I made that table, you know. ~ Sorry, which table _did you make_?
1. We can use these tennis rackets here. ~ Sorry, which rackets _____?
2. That painting has won first prize. ~ Sorry, which one of them _____?
3. I like the blue suit best. ~ Which one _____?
4. I've borrowed Simon's car. ~ Pardon? Whose car _____?
5. Andrew's uncle has died. ~ Whose uncle _____?

24 who, what or which?

A what or which?

We can use **what** or **which** before a noun:
What sport do you play?
What books do you need for your course?
Which way do we go here?
Which questions did you answer in the exam?

We use **what** when there is a wide choice of answers. We ask *What sport?* because there are lots of different sports. We use **which** when there is a limited number of possible answers. We ask *Which way?* because there are only two or three ways to go.

> *What **sport**?* (Tennis or golf or football or hockey or . . .?)
> *Which **way**?* (Right or left?)

After **which** we sometimes say the possible answers:
*Which café did you go to, **Snoopy's, the Coffee Pot or the Tea Gardens**?*
*Which phone shall I use, **the one upstairs or the one downstairs**?*

In some contexts, **what** and **which** are both possible:
What day (OR Which day) is your evening class?
What train (OR Which train) will you catch?
What platform (OR Which platform) does it go from?
What part (OR Which part) of Italy are you from?

B Patterns with who, what and which

We can use these words without a noun:
Who knows the answer?
What do you think?
Which is quicker, bus or train?

We can use **what** and **which** before a noun, but not **who**:
Which pupil knows the answer? NOT ~~Who pupil knows the answer?~~

We can use **which** with **one** or **ones** or with **of**:
*You can have a photo. **Which one** would you like?*
*You can have some photos. **Which ones** would you like?*
Which of these photos would you like?

We cannot use **who** or **what** before **of**. We can say *Which of the pupils?* but NOT ~~Who of the pupils?~~

Who always means a person. **What** usually means a thing; it can mean a person only when it is before a noun. **Which** can mean a person or a thing.
Who did you see? (person)
What did you see? (thing)
What doctor/What film did you see? (person or thing)
Which (doctor/film) did you see? (person or thing)

24 Exercises

24.1 what or which? (A)

Rewrite the questions with **what** or **which**. Use **what** if the list of answers is incomplete. Use **which** if it is complete.

☐ (Is this wine 1965 or 1982 or 1979 or 1990 or . . .?)
  What year is this wine?
☐ (Did you go to the Little Theatre or the Theatre Royal?)
  Which theatre did you go to?
1 (Did you take the morning flight or the afternoon one?)

2 (Did you stay at the Wessex Hotel or the Bristol?)

3 (Do you go to Blake School, or Sydenham School, or Haygrove School, or . . .?)

4 (Is yours the red car or the black one?)

5 (Do you buy the Times newspaper, or the Telegraph, or the Mirror, or . . .?)

6 (Are you learning English, or Spanish, or Arabic, or Japanese, or . . .?)

24.2 what or which? (A)

Isabel is moving into a new flat in London. Jerry has come to see the flat and help her move in. Complete his questions. Put in **what** or **which**.

1 _____ number is this house? ~ Forty-two.
2 _____ floor is the flat on? ~ The first floor.
3 Oh, it's a nice flat. _____ room will be your living-room? ~ This one here, I thought.
4 _____ colour are you going to paint it? ~ Oh, I don't know yet.
5 _____ time is your furniture arriving. ~ Three o'clock, they said.
6 _____ way is the nearest tube station, right or left? ~ It's left at the end of the street.
7 _____ station is nearest, Earls Court or West Brompton? ~ Earls Court, I think.

24.3 who, what or which? (B)

Two detectives are investigating the murder of Lord Weybridge at his country house. Put in **who**, **what** or **which**.

A: [1]_____ of the guests in this house is the murderer, do you think? [2]_____ one put the cyanide in Lord Weybridge's coffee?
B: I don't know yet. Someone did it. But [3]_____ had the opportunity? [4]_____ of the guests had the chance to do it?
A: [5]_____ happened after dinner last night? That's what we've got to find out.
B: There must be a reason for the murder. [6]_____ reason could the murderer have?
A: Love or money, one or the other. [7]_____ of them is it, I wonder?
B: [8]_____ did Lord Weybridge leave his money to? That's the question.

25 Short answers (e.g. **Yes, it is**.)

A Answering **yes** or **no**

Look at the answers to these questions:
Did you say something? ~ ***No***.
Did you get the tickets? ~ ***No, I didn't***.
Did you open my letter? ~ ***No, I didn't open your letter***.

We can sometimes answer with a simple **yes** or **no**, but in many contexts this can sound not full enough and not very polite. A short answer (e.g. **No, I didn't**) is more usual. We do not normally use a full sentence, but we can do if we want to add emphasis to the answer (e.g. **No, I didn't open your letter**).

We can add a sentence to the answer:
Did you get the tickets? ~ *No, I didn't.* ***There wasn't time, unfortunately***.

B Short answers

A positive short answer has the pattern **yes** + pronoun + auxiliary (e.g. **Yes, I am**). A pronoun is **I, you, he, she** etc. or **there**. The auxiliary is the verb at the beginning of a question (e.g. **is, have**).
Are *you working tomorrow?* ~ ***Yes, I am***, *unfortunately*.

Have *you got a stamp?* ~ ***Yes, I have***. ***Will*** *I need my passport?* ~ ***Yes, you will***.

We can also use the main verb **be** in a short answer:
Is *it time to go?* ~ ***Yes, it is***, *I'm afraid*.
In the present simple and past simple we use a form of **do**:
Do *you play tennis?* ~ ***Yes, I do***. *I love it.* NOT *Yes, I play*.
And ***does*** *your brother go to college too?* ~ ***Yes, he does***.
Did *the letter come?* ~ ***Yes, it did***.

A negative short answer has the pattern **no** + pronoun + auxiliary + **n't**. The auxiliary + **n't** is one word (e.g. **isn't, don't**).
Is *this phone working now?* ~ ***No, it isn't***.
Has *your sister left school?* ~ ***No, she hasn't***.
Can *we turn right here?* ~ ***No, we can't***.
Will *there be a disco?* ~ ***No, there won't***, *unfortunately*.
Do *you like chocolate?* ~ ***No, I don't***. *I never eat chocolate*.
Does *this train stop at Derby?* ~ ***No, it doesn't***.
Did *they cut the grass in the park?* ~ ***No, they didn't***.

C Answering requests, suggestions, offers and invitations

To answer a request etc. we normally use a phrase like **Yes, of course** or **Yes, please**, not just a short answer.

Request: ***Could*** *you help me move these chairs, please?* ~ ***Yes, of course***. OR ***I'm afraid I'm rather busy just now***.
Suggestions: ***Shall*** *we have a coffee?* ~ ***Yes, OK***. OR ***Well, I've got to go***.
Offer: ***Shall*** *I carry this bag for you?* ~ ***Yes, please***. *That's very kind of you.* OR ***It's all right, thanks***. *I can manage*.
Invitation: ***Would*** *you like to come to the barbecue?* ~ ***Yes, please***. *I'd love to.* OR ***I'd love to but I'll be away***. *Thanks all the same*.

25 Exercises

25.1 Short answers (B)

These conversations take place at a party. Complete the short answers.
- Have you got a drink? ~ Yes, _I have._
- Are you French? ~ No, _I'm not._
1. Can you speak Italian? ~ Yes, _____
2. Is it raining outside? ~ Yes, _____
3. Did that girl come with you? ~ No, _____
4. Are those people friends of yours? ~ No, _____
5. Do you know Phil Compton? ~ Yes, _____
6. Is your brother here? ~ No, _____
7. Have you seen Debbie? ~ No, _____
8. Will you be in town next month? ~ No, _____
9. Did you come by car? ~ Yes, _____

25.2 Short answers (B)

Look at the conversation and put in short answers.
- Psychiatrist: Do you ever feel angry?
  Patient: _Yes, I do._ I feel angry about lots of things.
1. Psychiatrist: Has life been unfair to you?
   Patient: _____ I've been very unlucky.
2. Psychiatrist: Do other people like you?
   Patient: _____ I've got no friends at all.
3. Psychiatrist: Are you married?
   Patient: _____ I've been married for five years.
4. Psychiatrist: And do you and your wife still live together?
   Patient: _____ We live in a flat.
5. Psychiatrist: Does your wife understand you?
   Patient: _____ She doesn't understand me at all.
6. Psychiatrist: I see. Were you happy as a child?
   Patient: _____ I was very unhappy.
7. Psychiatrist: Did your parents love you?
   Patient: _____ But their love didn't make me happy.
8. Psychiatrist: Will you be happy in the future?
   Patient: _____ I'm quite sure I never will be.
9. Psychiatrist: Can you explain why you think that?
   Patient: _____ But I know it's true.

25.3 Answering requests etc. (C)

Complete the answers. Put in **of course**, **OK** or **please**.
1. Shall I help make the sandwiches? ~ Yes, _____.
2. Would you lend me 20p? ~ Yes, _____.
3. Would you like to look round our garden? ~ Yes, _____.
4. Shall we go for a walk? ~ Yes, _____.
5. Can I have a glass of water, please? ~ Yes, _____.
6. Can I give you a lift? ~ Yes, _____.

26 Question tags (e.g. It's nice, **isn't it?**)

A The use of question tags

Look at this conversation:
>Ted: *It's nice today,* **isn't it?**
>Julia: *Yes, we're having a lovely summer,* **aren't we?** *You've been on holiday,* **haven't you?**
>Ted: *No, not yet. We're going to Greece next month. You haven't been away this summer,* **have you?**
>Julia: *No, but we're going to France in the autumn.*

A question tag is a short question (e.g. **isn't it?**) added on to a statement. When a tag is spoken, the voice can go down or up:
>*It's nice today,* ↘ *isn't it?*   *You've been on holiday,* ↗ *haven't you?*

A <u>falling</u> intonation (↘) means that the speaker is sure (or almost sure) that the statement is true. Ted knows that it is a nice day. The tag is not really a question. Ted is inviting Julia to continue the conversation. A <u>rising</u> intonation (↗) means that the speaker is less sure. Julia thinks that Ted has been on holiday, but she isn't sure. The tag is a more like a real question.

For tags in American English see p 289.

B The form of question tags

The two main sentence patterns are these:

POSITIVE STATEMENT + NEGATIVE TAG	NEGATIVE STATEMENT + POSITIVE TAG
It **is** raining, **isn't** it?	It **isn't** raining, **is** it?

A negative tag is an auxiliary verb + **n't** + pronoun. A positive tag is an auxiliary verb + pronoun. The pronoun (**you**, **he** etc.) refers to the subject of the sentence (e.g. **you**, **Steve**).

You've played before, **haven't you?**	*Steve hasn't got a car,* **has he?**
The children can swim, **can't they?**	*I shouldn't laugh,* **should I?**
It'll be dark soon, **won't it?**	*You aren't going to watch this awful*
Sarah was winning, **wasn't she?**	*programme,* **are you?**

We can also use the main verb **be**:
| *There's a mistake,* **isn't there?** | *The answer isn't right,* **is it?** |

In the present simple and past simple we use a form of **do**:
You live near here, **don't you?**	*We don't have to pay,* **do we?**
This coat looks nice, **doesn't it?**	*The shower doesn't work,* **does it?**
I turned left, **didn't I?**	*Your horse didn't win,* **did it?**

There is no one tag that we can use all the time. NOT *The answer is wrong, no?*

C Question tags with requests and suggestions

After an order or request with an imperative, we can use **can you?** or **could you?**:
>***Wait** here a moment,* **can you?**   ***Put** it in writing,* **could you?**

We can also use **You couldn't . . .** and **You haven't . . .** for a request:
>*You couldn't help me,* **could you?**   *You haven't got a pound,* **have you?**

After **Don't . . .**, the tag is **will you?**: ***Don't** make any noise,* **will you?**
After **Let's** we use **shall we?**: ***Let's** sit in the garden,* **shall we?**

26 Exercises

26.1 The use of question tags (A)

Three of these sentences must have a falling intonation(↘). They keep the conversation going, but they are not true questions. Write the three sentences.

You work here, don't you?
It was a super show, wasn't it?
It feels much colder, doesn't it?
These sweaters are lovely, aren't they?
We've got time for a coffee, haven't we?
The bus goes at ten past, doesn't it?

1 _____   3 _____
2 _____

26.2 Question tags (B)

You are at a barbecue. Add tags to help start a friendly conversation.
- These sausages are delicious, _aren't they?_
- You haven't lived here long, _have you?_

1 It's a big garden, _____
2 There aren't many people here yet, _____
3 You're Celia's friend, _____
4 You came together, _____
5 These burgers look good, _____
6 We can sit on the grass, _____
7 We've been lucky with the weather, _____
8 The forecast wasn't very good, _____

26.3 Question tags (B)

Complete the conversation. Put in the question tags.

Joanna: You don't really want to marry me, _do you?_
Dominic: Of course I do. But I need time.
Joanna: You love me, ¹_____
Dominic: You know I love you. I've told you enough times, ²_____
Joanna: You're quite happy, ³_____ The situation doesn't bother you, ⁴_____
Dominic: Why are we arguing? There's nothing to argue about, ⁵_____
Joanna: You can't ever see things from my point of view, ⁶_____

26.4 Question tags with requests and suggestions (C)

Complete the conversation. Put in the question tags.

Mary: Let's go out somewhere tonight, ¹_____
Jeff: All right. Where?
Mary: You haven't got a local paper, ²_____ Pass it over here, ³_____ Thanks. Well, there's a disco at the Grand Hotel.
Jeff: Fine, but I haven't got any money. You couldn't lend me five pounds, ⁴_____
Mary: OK, I'll pay then. I'll meet you outside at eight o'clock. Don't be late, ⁵_____

27 The patterns So/Neither do I and I hope so/not

A so and neither

After a statement we can use this pattern: **so/neither** + auxiliary + subject. We use **so** after a positive statement and **neither** after a negative one. The auxiliary verb is a form of **be** or **have** or a modal verb (e.g. **can**, **must**).

I'm going. ~ **So am I**. (= And I'm going. OR I'm going too.)

*The washing-machine has broken down, and **so has the dishwasher**.*

We've got a problem. ~ **So have we**, *unfortunately.*
Kevin can't drive. ~ **Neither can Scott**. (= And Scott can't drive. OR Scott can't drive either.)

The subject comes at the end. NOT *I'm going.* ~ ~~So I am.~~

We can also use the main verb **be** in this pattern:
The manager isn't at the meeting. **Neither is the secretary**.

In the present simple and past simple we use a form of **do**:
I hate parties. ~ **So do I**.
Our dog doesn't like loud noises. ~ **Neither does ours**.
Arsenal won. ~ **So did Manchester United**.
*Sadie didn't get the answer right, and **neither did I**.*

We can use **nor** instead of **neither**. **Nor** is rather more formal.
David isn't here tonight. **Neither/Nor is Sarah**.
*The sweater didn't fit, and **neither/nor did the trousers**.*

B I think so, I hope not etc.

Look at these examples with **so**:
Do you think you'll pass the exam? ~ *Well, I hope **so***. (= I hope I'll pass the exam.)
*I don't know if that shop sells bread, but I think **so***.
Are you going to the concert next week? ~ *Yes, I expect **so***.

In these examples we cannot leave out **so**. NOT ~~Well, I hope~~ or ~~Well, I hope it.~~

We can use **so** after **think**, **expect**, **imagine**, **believe**, **suppose**, **guess**, **hope** and **be afraid**. But we cannot use it after **know** or **be sure**:
There's been an accident. ~ *Yes, **I know***. NOT ~~I know so.~~
Are you sure you're doing the right thing? ~ *Yes, **I'm sure***. NOT ~~I'm sure so.~~

There are two negative patterns:

NEGATIVE + **so**	POSITIVE + **not**
Is it raining? ~ ***I don't think so***.	*Is it raining?* ~ ***I hope not***.

We can use **suppose** and **believe** in either pattern:
Will there be no seats left? ~ ***I don't suppose so***. OR ***I suppose not***.

Think, **expect** and **imagine** usually form the negative with **so**:
Is it going to rain? ~ ***I don't think so***.

But with **guess**, **hope** and **be afraid** we form the negative with **not**:
Are we in time for the evening meal? ~ ***I'm afraid not***, *sir*.

27 Exercises

27.1 so and neither (A)

Felix has just met Vicky at a party. They are finding out that they have a lot in common. Put in the sentences with **so** and **neither**.

Felix: I haven't been to a party for ages.
- Vicky: _Neither have I._ I hate crowded rooms.
- Felix: _So do I._ I'm not a party-goer, really.
1. Vicky: _____ I can't make conversation.
2. Felix: _____ I'm a quiet sort of person.
3. Vicky: _____ I live alone in a bedsitter.
4. Felix: _____ I haven't got many friends.
5. Vicky: _____ And I would really like a good friend.
6. Felix: Oh, _____

27.2 so and neither (A)

Look at the table and complete the sentences.

	Mike	Lorna	Paul	Marie
Swimming	✓	✓		
Tennis		✓	✓	
Cycling	✓			✓
Chess			✓	✓

- Mike can swim, and _so can Lorna._
- Marie isn't keen on tennis, and _neither is Mike._
1. Paul doesn't like swimming, and _____
2. Marie has got a bike, and _____
3. Mike can't play chess, and _____
4. Lorna isn't keen on cycling, and _____
5. Paul plays tennis, and _____
6. Marie is a chess player, and _____

27.3 I think so, I hope not etc. (B)

Complete these short conversations. Put in sentences with **so** or **not**.

- A: Does the library open on Saturdays?
  B: Yes, _I think so._ But I'm not absolutely certain.   □ think
- A: You can't go out for an evening meal wearing shorts.
  B: _I guess not._ I'd better put some trousers on.   □ guess
1. A: Will there be lots of people at the concert tonight?
   B: _____ There aren't usually very many.   1 expect
2. A: Are you going to apply for the job?
   B: _____ It's the only one available.   2 suppose
3. A: Do you think it's going to rain?
   B: _____ I've just hung out the washing.   3 hope
4. A: Will the match take place in this weather?
   B: _____ In fact, I'm sure it won't.   4 think
5. A: Are my photos ready, please?
   B: _____ We've had a problem with the machine.   5 afraid

28 can, could and be able to

A can

We use **can** to say that someone has the ability or opportunity to do something:
*Sarah is very musical. She **can** play three instruments.*
***Can** you do this sum in your head?*
*It's nice today. We **can** sit in the garden.*

The negative of **can** is **cannot** ['kænɒt]. It has a short form **can't** [kɑ:nt].
*I **can't** come and see you tomorrow morning. I'll be at work.*

B be able to

In the present tense **be able to** is a little more formal and less usual than **can**:
*Karen knows all about computers. She **can** write (OR **is able to** write) programs.*

But in some patterns we always use **be able to**, not **can**:
To-infinitive: *It's nice **to be able to** go to the opera.*   (NOT ~~to can go~~)
Present perfect: *It's been a quiet day. **I've been able to** get some work done.*

We use **can** or **will be able to** (but NOT ~~will can~~) for the future:
*If I pass my exams, I **can** go (OR **I'll be able to** go) to university next year.*
*I'm afraid I **can't** come (OR **I won't be able to** come) to the dance on Friday.*

But we normally use **can** (not **will be able to**) to suggest a possible future action:
*Let's have lunch together. We **can** go to that new restaurant.*

C could or was/were able to?

For ability or opportunity in the past, we use **could** or **was/were able to**:
*Sarah **could** play (OR **was able to** play) the piano when she was five.*
*In those days we didn't have a car, so we **couldn't** travel (OR **weren't able to** travel) very easily.*

To say that the ability or opportunity resulted in a particular action, we use **was/were able to** but not **could**:
*Paul felt much better on Saturday, and so he **was able to** play in the match.*
*Luckily I had my camera with me, so I **was able to** take some photos.*
*The pool was open today, so the children **were able to** have a swim.*
*The driver **was able to** stop (OR **managed to** stop) just before he hit the wall.*

But in negatives and questions we can use either **could** or **was/were able to** because we are not saying that the action really happened:
*Paul was ill. He **couldn't** play (OR **wasn't able to** play) in the match.*
***Could** you take (OR **Were** you **able to** take) photos in the cathedral?*

We normally use **could** (not **was/were able to**) with verbs of seeing, hearing, etc. and verbs of thinking:
*We **could see** the village in the distance.*
*As soon as Harriet opened the door, she **could smell** gas.*
*I **couldn't understand** what was happening.*

28 Exercises

28.1 can and can't (A)

Complete these sentences about old people. Use **can** or **can't** and these verbs:
hear, look, read, see, walk.

☐ I'm afraid Mr Groves is deaf. _He can't hear_ what you say.
1 Mrs Lawrence has to wear glasses. _____ very well.
2 Mr Goddard likes books with large print. _____ them more easily.
3 Mr Hogg uses a wheelchair. _____ very far.
4 Mrs Bernstein is quite happy living alone. _____ after herself.

28.2 be able to (B)

Put in **be able to**, **to be able to** or **been able to**.

Sharon: Hello, Jackie. I'm sorry I haven't ¹_____ come and see you before. How are you?
Jackie: Getting better, thanks. It'll be nice ²_____ go back to college next week. The trouble is, I've missed so much I won't ³_____ understand what we're doing in maths. I haven't ⁴_____ do any studying.
Sharon: Oh, you're good at maths. You'll ⁵_____ catch up.

28.3 could or was/were able to? (C)

Put in **could** or **was/were able to** with the verbs. Use the negative if necessary.

'There was a fire at Oxford Circus Underground Station last night. It was awful. I was really afraid. I was walking along a corridor, and suddenly I ☐ _could see_ smoke. It was everywhere.
I ¹_____ people screaming and shouting. I turned round, and luckily I ²_____ away from the smoke.
There was a loudspeaker announcement, but I ³_____ what it was saying. But fortunately I ⁴_____ the way out of the station. No one was hurt, I found out later. The ticket collectors ⁵_____ all the passengers to safety.'

☐ see
1 hear
2 get
3 understand
4 find
5 help

28.4 could or was/were able to? (C)

Put in **could** or **was/were able to**. Use a negative if necessary. Sometimes two different answers are possible.

☐ It was dark. We _couldn't_ see a thing.
1 The concert was sold out. I'm afraid I _____ get tickets.
2 The fence fell down in the storm. Luckily I _____ repair it myself.
3 Someone in our street was having a party last night. You _____ hear the music half a mile away.
4 I learnt to swim very early in life. I _____ swim when I was three.
5 The residents heard warnings about the flood, and they _____ move their belongings upstairs in time.

71

29 can, may, could and be allowed to

A Asking permission

We use **can**, **could** or **may** to ask for permission:
Can I use your pen? ~ *Yes, of course.*
Could we borrow your ladder, please? ~ *Well, I'm using it at the moment.*
May I see the letter? ~ *Certainly.*

Could is often more polite than **can**. **May** is rather formal.

B Giving and refusing permission

We use **can** or **may** to give permission (but not **could**). **May** is formal and not often used in speech.
*You **can** wait in my office if you like.*
Could I borrow your calculator? ~ *Of course you **can**.*
*You **may** telephone from here.* (a written notice)

To refuse permission we use the negative forms:
*I'm sorry, but you **can't** picnic here.*
*Members **may not** bring more than two visitors into the club.*

We can also use **must not**:
*Bicycles may not (OR **must not**) be left here.*

C Talking about permission

We sometimes talk about rules made by someone else. To do this we use **can**, **could** and **be allowed to**.

We use **can** to talk about the present or the future, and we use **could** for the past:
Present: *Each passenger **can** take one bag onto the plane.*
Future: *I **can't** have another day off work tomorrow.*
Past: *Years ago you **could** park your car anywhere.*

We can also use **be allowed to**:
Present: *Passengers **are allowed to** take one bag onto the plane.*
Future: *Will I **be allowed to** record the interview on tape?*
Past: *We **weren't allowed to** feed the animals at the zoo yesterday.*

For a general permission in the past we use either **could** or **was/were allowed to**:
*I **could** always stay (OR I **was** always **allowed to** stay) up late as a child.*

But we cannot use **could** when we mean that an action really happened at a time in the past:
*I **was allowed to** leave work early yesterday.*
NOT *I could leave work early yesterday.*

Compare questions with **may** and **be allowed to**:
***May** I take a photo of you?*
(Asking for permission: 'Will you allow it?')
***Are** we **allowed to** take photos?*
(Asking about permission: 'What is the rule?')

29 Exercises

29.1 Asking permission (A)

How would you ask permission in these situations. Use **Can I . . . ?** / **Could I . . . ?** / **May I . . . ?** and these verbs: **borrow, join, look at, sit down, use.**

☐ You are at a friend's flat. You want to make a phone call.
   Can I use your phone?

1 You need a ruler. The student sitting next to you has got one.
   _____

2 You are in the manager's office. You want to discuss something with him, but you don't want to stand the whole time.
   _____

3 You have gone into a café. Three people who you know fairly well are sitting at a table. You go over to the table.
   _____

4 You had to go to a lecture but you were ill. Your friend went to the lecture and took notes. Next day you are well again, and you see your friend.
   _____

29.2 Giving and refusing permission (B)

Say what the signs mean. Use **can** and **can't** and these verbs:
go, have, leave, park, play, smoke, turn.

☐ *You can't go this way.*
☐ *You can park.*
1 _____
2 _____
3 _____
4 _____
5 _____

29.3 be allowed to (C)

Put in the correct form of (**not**) **be allowed to**.

A: Our flat is OK, but the landlady is a real dictator. We aren't ¹_____ do anything. It was my birthday last month, and I ²_____ have a party.

B: Oh, we ³_____ have parties at our place, luckily. We're hoping to have an all-night party soon, but I don't know if we ⁴_____ do that.

29.4 May I . . . ? or Am I allowed to . . . ? (C)

Put in **May I** or **Am I allowed to**.

☐ *May I* use your typewriter?
☐ *Am I allowed to* smoke in a cinema?
1 _____ cross the road here?
2 _____ ask you a question?
3 _____ go in this park?
4 _____ take money out of England?
5 _____ read your paper?

30 Saying something is possible or certain

A may, might and could

Look at this conversation:
> Angela: *Are you going to the disco, Kate?*
> Kate: *I'm not sure. I **may** go.*
> Laura: *It **might** be difficult to get a ticket. It **could** be sold out.*

May and **might** express the idea that something is very possible. We can use them for the present or the future:
> *I **may/might** go to the disco tomorrow.* (= Perhaps I will go there tomorrow.)
> *There **may/might** be some tickets left.* (= Perhaps there are some left.)
> *The train **may/might** be late.*   *It **may/might** rain.*

We can also use **could** to say that something is possible:
> *I **could** go to the disco tomorrow.*   *There **could** be some tickets left.*
> *You **could** win £100,000!*   *It **could** be good fun.*

But NOT ~~There can be some tickets left.~~

For the use of **could** to talk about the past see Unit 28.
For **can** and **could** in suggestions (e.g. *We **can/could** go tomorrow*) see Unit 33C.

B may, might and could in the negative

The forms are: **may not**   **might not** OR **mightn't**   **could not** OR **couldn't**

Compare:

| **May not** and **might not** express the idea that something negative is possible:
*I'm running in the marathon, but I **may/might not** finish it.*
(It is possible that I will not finish it.)
*I **may/might not** have time to go.*
*There **may/might not** be any tickets left.* | **Couldn't** expresses the idea that something is impossible:
*You're not fit. You **couldn't** run a marathon.*
(It would be impossible for you to run it.)
*I'm afraid of heights. I **couldn't** climb onto a roof.* |

C must and can't

Look at this conversation:
> Alice: *Have you done this puzzle?*
> Paul: *Yes, and I've got the same answer as you. It **must** be correct.*
> Alice: *Well, the answer in the book is different. So we **can't** be right.*

Must and **can't** are opposites:
> *The story **must** be a joke. It **can't** be true.*

We use **must** when we see something as necessarily true, as logically true:
> *Dave isn't answering the phone. He **must** be out.*
> *I had my keys a moment ago. They **must** be here somewhere.*

We use **can't** when we see something as logically impossible:
> *I need a rest.* ~ *But we haven't been working long. You **can't** be tired yet.*
> *Life **can't** be easy when you're permanently in a wheelchair.*

30 Exercises

30.1 may and might (A, B)

Put in a pronoun (e.g. **it**, **she**) and **may** (**not**)/**might** (**not**) + verb. Use the verbs in brackets.

▷ There are lots of clouds. _It may rain_ you know. (rain)
▷ Don't give your grandmother these sweets. _She might not like_ them. (like)
1 I'm thinking of learning Italian. _____ to evening classes. (go)
2 I wonder why Jeff is late. ~ Well, there's a lot of traffic. _____ in a hold-up. (be)
3 It's a long way to go in a day. We think _____ the journey somewhere. (break)
4 The car has been standing outside in the cold all week. _____ first time. (start)
5 Emma is pleased that she's got an interview for a job. _____ the job, of course. (get)
6 The caravan is a bit small for all of us. _____ it and buy a bigger one. (sell)
7 Don't you think that box is a bit too heavy for you? _____ it. (drop)

30.2 mightn't or couldn't? (A, B)

Put in **mightn't** or **couldn't**.

▷ I _mightn't_ have time to come out tonight. I've got one or two little jobs to do.
▷ I _couldn't_ be a taxi driver. I can't drive.
1 We're going to need lots of plates. We _____ have enough, you know.
2 Bruce _____ be in the office tomorrow. He thinks he's getting a cold.
3 We _____ have a dog, living in a small flat like this.
4 How do you manage to work with all this noise going on? I _____ study in these conditions.
5 There _____ be a drama festival this year. We don't know if anyone will be willing to organize it.
6 Ring me on Saturday. Don't ring me tomorrow because I _____ be in. I'm not sure what I'm doing.

30.3 must, can't and might (A, C)

Complete the conversation. Put in **must**, **can't** or **might**.

A: I'm going to do a parachute jump next week.
B: You're going to jump out of an aeroplane! But you're seventy-three years old! You ¹_____ be serious. You ²_____ be mad.
A: It really ³_____ be wonderful looking down on everything. I've always wanted to try it.
B: But anything could happen. You ⁴_____ be injured, or even killed. I wouldn't take the risk.
A: Well, your life ⁵_____ be much fun if you never take risks. You ought to try it too. You never know – you ⁶_____ enjoy it.
B: Enjoy it! You ⁷_____ be joking.

31 must and have to

A Present, past and future

In the present we use **must** and **have to** to say that something is necessary:
  You **must** be careful.   We **must** win this game.
  I **have to** work on Saturday mornings.   Tim **has to** do some washing.
We use **must** and **have to** to talk about the present or the near future.

But for the past and in other patterns we use a form of **have to**:
  Josie **had to** go to work yesterday. NOT ~~She must go to work yesterday.~~
  We'**ll have to** do better next time.
  Sue **has had to** sell her car.
  I don't want **to have to** wait ages.

We use **do** to form negatives and questions with **have to**:
  I **don't have to** work on Sundays.
  Did you **have to** pay for your second cup of coffee? ~ No, I **didn't**.
For the meaning of **don't have to** see Unit 32.

B must or have to?

Compare:

We use **must** when the necessity is inside the speaker and **have to** when the necessity is outside the speaker, when it comes from the situation:

You **must** finish this today.	I **have to** finish this today.
(I'm telling you.)	(The boss says so.)
You **must** be quiet.	You **have to** be quiet.
(I'm telling you.)	(That's the rule.)

I/we **must** ... can also express a wish. Compare:

  I **must** buy a paper. I want to see the racing results.
  We **must** invite Marjorie. She's wonderful company.

  I **have to** buy a paper. My boss asked me to buy one for him.
  We **have to** invite the Bells. They invited us last time.

C have got to

Have got to means the same as **have to**, but **have got to** is informal. We use it mainly in the present:
  I **have to** make (OR I'**ve got to** make) my sandwiches.
  My father **has to** take (OR **has got to** take) these pills.
  Do we **have to** apply (OR **Have** we **got to** apply) for a visa?

31 Exercises

31.1 have to (A)

Put in the correct form of **have to**.

☐ Vera has a bad leg. She _has to_ go to hospital. ~ How long will she _have to_ stay in there? ~ She doesn't know.

1 I parked my car outside a shop, and while I was in the shop, the police took the car away. I've got it back now. But I _____ pay a lot of money. ~ How much _____ you _____ pay? ~ Over £100.
2 That door doesn't close properly. You _____ really slam it every time. ~ You'll _____ fix it, won't you?
3 You're always taking exams. _____ you really _____ take so many? ~ Yes, and I'll _____ take a lot more if I want a good job.
4 We're in a new house now. We've _____ move. The old house was too small. ~ Did it take a long time to find a house? ~ No, we found one very quickly. We _____ look very hard.
5 My brother is a milkman. He starts work at half past four. ~ What time _____ he _____ get up? ~ Half past three. He _____ be quiet because everyone else is asleep.

31.2 must or have to? (B)

Write a sentence with **must, have to** or **has to**.

☐ The sign says: 'Passengers must show their tickets.'
So _passengers have to show their tickets._
☐ Tracy has to be home by eleven.
Her parents said: _'You must be home by eleven.'_
1 Jeremy has to get to work on time.
His boss told him: _____
2 The police said: 'You must keep your dog under control, Mr Forbes.'
So Mr Forbes _____
3 The pupils have to listen carefully.
The teacher says: _____
4 The new sign says: 'Visitors must report to the security officer.'
So now _____

31.3 must or have to? (B)

Put in **must, have to** or **has to**. Choose which is best in the context.

☐ I _have to_ go to the airport. I'm meeting someone.
1 You _____ lock the door when you go out. I don't want burglars in here!
2 Rex _____ go to the bank. He hasn't any money.
3 I _____ stay late at the office tomorrow. We're very busy at the moment.
4 You really _____ make less noise. I'm trying to concentrate.
5 Louise really _____ hurry up. I don't want to be late.
6 I think you _____ pay to park here. I'll just have a look at that notice over there.
7 I _____ put the heating on. I feel really cold.

32 mustn't or needn't/don't have to?

A mustn't or needn't?

We use **must** to say that something is necessary:
>You **must** be careful with these glasses.   I **must** remember my key.

Now compare **mustn't** and **needn't**:

We use **mustn't** to stop or forbid someone from doing something: You **mustn't** drop these glasses. They'll break. I **mustn't** forget my keys or I won't get in. You **mustn't** wear your best clothes. You'll get them dirty.	We use **needn't** when it is not necessary to do something: You **needn't** bring sandwiches. We can stop at a café. We **needn't** get up early, but we can if you want. You **needn't** wear your best clothes. You can wear what you like.

B don't have to and don't need to

We can use **don't have to** and **don't need to** when it is not necessary to do something. The meaning is the same as **needn't**.
>You **don't have to** bring (OR **don't need to** bring) sandwiches. We can stop at a café.
>Sylvia **doesn't have to** finish (OR **doesn't need to** finish) her essay today. She's got until Friday to hand it in.

For American usage see p 289.

In the past we use **didn't**:
>All the food was free. We **didn't have to** pay (OR **didn't need to** pay) for it.

C didn't need to or needn't have?

Compare:

We use **didn't need to** to say that we knew it was not necessary to do something: Laura **didn't need to** hurry. She had plenty of time. She drove slowly along the motorway. We **didn't need to** go to the supermarket because we had plenty of food. I **didn't need to** take a coat. It was a lovely day.	We use **needn't have** + a past participle (e.g. **gone**) for something we did which we now know was not necessary: Laura **needn't have** hurried. After driving at top speed she arrived half an hour early. We **needn't have** gone to the supermarket. I had forgotten about the chicken we already had in the fridge. You **needn't have** brought a coat. Look what a lovely day it is. ~ I know. But it was cloudy when I left home.

Didn't need to usually shows that the action did not happen. But sometimes the action happened, even though it was not necessary:
>Laura **didn't need to** hurry, but she drove at top speed. She likes driving fast.

32 Exercises

32.1 must, mustn't or needn't? (A)

Put in **must**, **mustn't** or **needn't**.

☐ Mother: You _needn't_ take an umbrella. It isn't going to rain.
   Son: Well, I don't know. It might do.
   Mother: Well, look after it, please. You _mustn't_ lose it.
1 Mervyn: Come on. We _____ hurry. We _____ be late.
   Isabel: It's only ten past. We _____ hurry. We've lots of time.
2 Pupil: Jason and I are just going for a walk.
   Teacher: No, you _____ go off on your own. I want you all together.
   We _____ keep together.
3 Sandra: I'll put these glasses in the dishwasher.
   Natalie: No, you _____ put them in there. They might break. In fact,
   we _____ wash them at all. We didn't use them.
4 Secretary: I _____ forget to type this letter.
   Boss: It _____ go in the post today because it's urgent. But the report isn't so
   important. You _____ type the report today.

32.2 don't have to (B)

Two old people are comparing life today and life in the past. Complete the sentences using **don't have to, doesn't have to** or **didn't have to**.

☐ There wasn't any television then. We had to make our own fun. These days people _don't have to make their own fun_.
1 There's so much traffic now. You have to wait ages to cross the road. In those days you _____
2 When I was young, I had to work long hours. But children today _____
3 My brother had to work in a factory when he was twelve. But today a twelve-year-old child _____
4 There's so much crime today. People have to lock their doors now. In the old days we _____
5 In those days we had to wash our clothes by hand. Nowadays people _____

32.3 didn't need to or needn't have? (C)

Write each verb with **didn't need to** or **needn't have**.

☐ The previous owners had recently decorated the flat, so we _didn't need to decorate_ it ourselves.   ☐ decorate
1 We've done the journey much more quickly than I expected. We _____ so early.   1 leave
2 A friend had already given me a free ticket to the exhibition, so I _____ to go in.   2 pay
3 Luckily, the cheque arrived before the bill, so we _____ money.   3 borrow
4 Service was included in the bill, so you _____ the waiter. It was a waste of money.   4 tip

79

33 Requests, offers and suggestions: Would you...? Shall I...? etc.

A Requests

We can use **can** or **could** to ask someone to do something:
  Can *everyone be quiet for a minute, please?*
  Could *you lend me ten pounds until tomorrow?* ~ *I haven't got ten pounds.*
  I wonder if you **could** *explain something to me.*
Could is often more polite than **can**.

We can also use **mind** (+ ing-form) and **would like** (+ to-infinitive). They are both polite.
  Do you **mind** (OR *Would you* **mind**) *waiting a moment?* ~ *No, I'll wait.*
  Would *you* **like** *to lay the table for me?* ~ *Yes, of course.*
We do not use **Do you like**...? when we make a request.
  NOT *Do you like to lay the table for me?*

We can also use **Can I/we**...? and **Could I/we**...? when we ask someone to give us something:
  Can we *have our room key, please?* ~ *Certainly, sir.*
  Could I *see your ticket?*

B Offers

We can use **I'll/we'll** or **I/we can** to offer to do something:
  I'll *carry* (OR *I can carry*) *your bag.* ~ *Oh, thanks.*
  We'll *give* (OR *We can give*) *you a lift if you like.* ~ *Oh, thank you.*

We can also use **Shall I/we**...? or **Can I/we**...?:
  Shall I *get* (OR *Can I get*) *a taxi for you?* ~ *Yes, please.*
  Shall we *pay* (OR *Can we pay*) *you the money now?* ~ *Oh, there's no hurry.*

To offer food or drink, we can use **would like**:
  Would *you* **like** *one of these chocolates?* ~ *Yes, please. Thank you.*
  Would *anyone* **like** *more coffee?* ~ *No, thanks.*

We also use **would like** (+ to-infinitive) or **will** to invite someone:
  Would *you* **like** *to have lunch with us?* ~ *Yes, I'd love to. Thank you.*
  Will *you come and see us again?* ~ *I'd like to very much.*

C Suggestions

We can use **Shall we**...? or **can/could** to make a suggestion:
  It's a lovely day. **Shall we** *go for a walk?* ~ *Yes, OK.*
  We **can/could** *watch this comedy on TV tonight.* ~ *Well, I've seen it before.*

To ask for a suggestion, we use **shall** or **can**:
  What **shall/can** *I get Debbie for her birthday?*

33 Exercises

33.1 Requests (A)

In each situation, make a request using the word in brackets.
- ☐ It is cold in the restaurant. Ask the waiter to shut the window. (could)
  Could you shut the window, please?

1 You are buying a coat and want a receipt. Ask the assistant for one. (can)

2 You need someone to help you. Ask a friend. (can)

3 You are carrying a tray. Ask someone to open the door for you. (would mind)

4 You are on the phone. You want to speak to the manager. (could)

33.2 Offers (B)

Use **Shall I ... for you?** and these verbs: **buy, carry, open, post, repair.**
- ☐ I haven't got enough money for this magazine. ~ *Shall I buy it for you?*
1 This chair is falling to pieces. ~
2 I can't get the top off this bottle. ~
3 These groceries are heavy. ~
4 I've finished the letter. ~

33.3 Requests, offers and suggestions (A–C)

Put in **could, shall** or **would**.

Gavin: This is a nice place. ¹_____ we have our picnic here?
Louise: Yes, all right. ²_____ you all sit round here, please?
Gavin: Oh, I've forgotten the sausages. They're in the car.
Vicky: ³_____ I get them?
Gavin: Oh, thanks Vicky.
Darren: We ⁴_____ sit by those trees. It looks nicer over there.
Louise: No, it's fine here.
Mark: ⁵_____ you mind passing the sandwiches along, please? Thanks.
⁶_____ you like a sandwich, Louise?
Louise: Oh, thank you.
Vicky: Here are the sausages. ⁷_____ anyone like one?

33.4 Requests, offers and suggestions (A–C)

What do you say? (Sometimes more than one answer is correct.)
- ☐ A friend has called at your flat. Invite him to come in.
  Would you like to come in?
1 A woman you know is afraid to walk home alone. Offer to walk home with her.

2 You want to know the time. Ask someone in the street to tell you.

3 You are walking in town with a friend. Suggest having a cup of coffee.

34 should, ought to, had better and be supposed to

Look at what these people are saying:

We ought to go soon.

I'd better ring for a taxi.

You're supposed to put the money in first.

A should and ought to

We use **should** and **ought to** to say what is the best thing or the right thing to do:
   You're not very well. Perhaps you **should** see (OR you **ought to** see) a doctor.
   We **should** write (OR We **ought to** write) a letter of thanks.
   People **shouldn't** tell (OR **oughtn't to** tell) lies.
   I'm in a difficult situation. What **should** I do? (OR What **ought** I **to** do?)

B had better

We use **had better** (OR **'d better**) to say what is the best thing to do in a situation:
   It's cold. You **had better** wear a coat.
   The neighbours are complaining. We**'d better** turn the music down.
   My wife is waiting for me. I **had better not** be late.
Had better is stronger than **should** or **ought to**. The speaker expects that the action will really happen.

C be supposed to

We use **be supposed to** for what we expect to happen because it is the normal way of doing things or because someone has ordered it or arranged it:
   The guests **are supposed to** buy flowers for the hostess.
   You**'re not supposed to** walk on the grass.
   How **am I supposed to** cook this? ~ Well, look at the instructions.
   You **were supposed to** be here at ten thirty, you know.

34 Exercises

34.1 should and ought to (A)

Put in **should, shouldn't, ought** or **oughtn't**. (Look for the word **to**.)

A: I ☐ _ought_ to do some work, but I'll just have a cigarette first.
B: Don't you know cigarettes are bad for you? You ¹_____ smoke.
A: I know. I ²_____ to give it up. I ³_____ smoke, but I can't help it. I try to forget about what it's doing to me.
B: There's an article about smoking in this magazine. You ⁴_____ read it. You really ⁵_____ to stop, you know. You ⁶_____ to put your health at risk.

34.2 had better (B)

Add a sentence with **'d better**. Use these verbs: **answer, find, mend, pay, return, wash**.

☐ Carol's bike has got a puncture. _She'd better mend it._
1. Ben's sweaters are all dirty. He _____
2. Your phone is ringing. You _____
3. I've had these bills for weeks. _____
4. Laura thinks she's lost her passport. _____
5. The neighbours have had my cassette player for ages. _____

34.3 be supposed to (C)

Complete the sentences using **be (not) supposed to** and these verbs: **leave, report, stand, take, watch**.

☐ You shouldn't bring your bike inside the building. You_'re supposed to leave_ it outside.
1. I've got these pills. I _____ two before a meal.
2. The film is not for children. Under sixteens _____ it.
3. Foreigners staying in that country _____ to the police every week.
4. In England people waiting for a bus _____ in a queue.

34.4 should/ought to, had better and be supposed to (A–C)

Complete the conversation. Use **should, ought to, had better** or **be supposed to** and the verbs on the right. Usually more than one answer is correct.

A: What time ☐ _are we supposed to be_ at the reception?   ☐ we be
B: The invitation says seven o'clock.
A: Well, it's ten to seven now. We ¹_____ .   1 hurry
   We ²_____ late.   2 not be
B: Oh, it won't matter if we're a bit late.
A: Well, I think it would be rude. We ³_____   3 arrive
   on time if we can.
B: You worry too much. You ⁴_____   4 not take
   everything so seriously. It doesn't mean exactly seven o'clock. We
   ⁵_____ there exactly on time.   5 not get

83

35 It may/could/must have been etc.

We can use a modal verb (e.g. **may, could**) with the perfect (e.g. **have done**):
Sue: *Where's Alec, I wonder? We **ought to have started** fifteen minutes ago.*
Phil: *He **may have lost** his way. It isn't very easy to find this place.*
Sam: *We **should have come** here together.*
Sue: *He **could have forgotten** all about it, I suppose.*
Kay: *He **can't have forgotten**, I reminded him only this morning.*
Phil: *Well, something **must have delayed** him.*

A may have and might have

We use **may/might have** to say that very possibly something happened in the past:
*He **may have lost** his way.* (= Perhaps he has lost his way.)
*You **might have left** your keys at work.* (= Perhaps you left them at work.)

We can also use the negative to say that possibly something did not happen:
*Tom **mightn't have heard** the news.* (= Perhaps he didn't hear the news.)
*I **may not have put** everything away in the right place.*

B could have

We use **could have** to say that possibly something happened in the past:
*Someone **could have taken** the keys from your bag.*
(= It is possible that someone took the keys from your bag.)

We also use **could have** for an opportunity that we didn't take or a possible result that didn't really happen:
*We **could have gone** out somewhere, but we were too tired.*
*You were very lucky. There **could have been** a terrible accident.*

We use **couldn't have** to say that it is impossible that something happened:
*Phil **couldn't have taken** a bus yesterday. There aren't any buses on Sundays.*
(= It is impossible that he took a bus yesterday.)

C must have and can't have

We use **must have** for things in the past that we see as logically true. We use **can't have** for things we see as logically impossible:
*My watch says only ten past. It **must have stopped**.*
*You've spent five minutes on the job. You **can't have done** it properly.*

D should have and ought to have

We use **should have** and **ought to have** when something was the best thing to do, but we didn't do it:
*We didn't play very well. We **should have played** better.*
*I got lost. ~ Sorry, I **ought to have drawn** you a map.*

For **needn't have** see Unit 32C, and for **would have** with if-clauses see Unit 115D.

35 Exercises

35.1 might have and could have (A, B)

Agree with what people say. Use **might have, mightn't have, could have** or **couldn't have**. Sometimes more than one answer is correct.

☐ Perhaps the missing girl has run away from home.
   Yes, she might have run away from home.
☐ The computer didn't make a mistake. That's impossible.
   No, the computer couldn't have made a mistake.
1 It's possible that Louise didn't receive our message.
   No, she _____
2 I suppose it's possible the thief had a key.
   Yes, he _____
3 You didn't press the wrong button. That's impossible.
   No, I _____
4 Perhaps Phil has missed the train.
   _____
5 It's possible that the driver didn't see the warning sign.
   _____

35.2 must have and can't have (C)

Put in **must have** or **can't have** and the past participle of the verb on the right.

Mike:	I can't wind the film on in this camera.	
Robert:	You ☐ *must have finished* the film, then.	☐ finish
Mike:	I ¹_____ a whole film. I've only taken four photos.	1 use
Robert:	Well, you ²_____ the film in correctly, then. You ³_____ it wrong. You'll have to take it out.	2 put 3 do

35.3 should (have) and ought to (have) (D and Unit 34)

Write a sentence with **should/ought to** or **should have/ought to have**.
☐ Jeremy didn't lock his door when he went out. *He should have locked it.*
☐ Mr Little smokes at meal times. *He oughtn't to smoke at meal times.*
1 The picnickers left litter everywhere. _____
2 Sue didn't look before crossing the road. _____
3 Alan never says hello to people. _____
4 Mary was late for her job interview. _____

35.4 It may/could/must have been etc. (A–D)

Put in **might have, shouldn't have, must have** and **can't have** with the past participle of the verbs.

A: There's a parcel outside. The postman ☐ *must have left* it.		☐ leave
B: Well, he ¹_____ it outside. Someone ²_____ it. Why didn't he ring the bell?		1 leave 2 take
A: He always rings. You ³_____ out when he came.		3 be
B: I haven't been out. So he ⁴_____ the bell.		4 ring

85

36 Review of **will**, **would**, **shall** and **should**

A   **will** and **would** for predictions

We use **will** for a prediction (see Unit 14B):
*Alison has walked a long way. She'**ll** sleep well tonight.*
We're going to Cornwall for the weekend. ~ *Oh, that'**ll** be nice.*

We use **would** for a past prediction or a prediction about a possible situation:
Past: *Alison had walked a long way. She **would** sleep well that night.*
Possible: *How about going to Cornwall next weekend?* ~ *That **would** be nice.*

Would like is less direct than **want**. It is a more polite way of asking for something that you want, or inviting someone to do something:
*I'**d like** some hot water, please.*
***Would** you **like** to visit the museum?*

We can use **shall** instead of **will** and **should** instead of **would** – but only after **I** and **we** – not after other persons:
*I **will/shall** be twenty-five in June.* NOT *David shall be twenty-five . . .*
*We **would/should** like to meet your family.* NOT *My friend should like . . .*

B   Other meanings of **will** and **would**

We can use **will** for a decision or an offer:
Decision: *Tea or coffee?* ~ *I'**ll** have coffee, please.*
Offer: *I'**ll** wait for you if you like.*

We use **will** and **would** in the negative for a refusal:
*The strikers **won't** go back to work until they get a wage increase.*
*The key goes in the lock, but it **won't** turn.*
*The key went in the lock, but it **wouldn't** turn.*

I won't . . . expresses a strong refusal:
*I **won't** listen to any more of this nonsense.*

C   **shall** and **should**

We use **Shall I** . . .? for offers and **Shall we** . . .? for suggestions:
Offer: ***Shall I** wait for you?* ~ *Oh, thank you.* (Unit 33B)
Suggestion: ***Shall we** go to the park?* ~ *Good idea.* (Unit 33C)

We use **should** to say what is the right thing or the best thing to do (Unit 34A):
*People **should** exercise regularly.*
*You **shouldn't** spend all your wages as soon as you get them.*

We use either **shall** or **should** to ask for advice:
*I'm in terrible trouble. What **shall/should** I do?*
*What **shall** we have for lunch?*

36 Exercises

36.1 will and would for predictions (A)

Put in 'll, won't, would or wouldn't.

A: Have you heard? A ten-year-old boy was knocked down by a car outside the school this afternoon.
B: Oh no! I always said this □ _would_ happen sooner or later.
A: He's badly injured, but he ¹_____ live, they say. But he ²_____ be out of hospital for a few weeks.
B: Why can't they build a footbridge over the road there? Then everyone ³_____ be able to cross safely. There ⁴_____ be any danger.
A: I ⁵_____ like to cross the road there, myself. I always avoid it.
B: They ⁶_____ have to do something about it now.

36.2 Other meanings of will and would (B)

Put in **will, won't** or **wouldn't** with these verbs: eat, give, go, help, let, open, stand.

□ Anne has got very thin. She's on a diet. She _won't eat_ very much.
1 Julie and I _____ you get everything ready. We're quite willing to lend a hand.
2 I couldn't get away from work early enough yesterday, I'm afraid. My boss _____ me go.
3 Andrew and I _____ you a lift. We're going your way.
4 Tim has quarrelled with Melanie. He doesn't want to see her. He _____ to the party if she's invited.
5 I tried to use the washing machine yesterday, but the door _____.
6 This lamp is always falling over. It _____ up properly.

36.3 will, would, shall and should (A–C)

Write the sentences.
□ Offer to make the tea.
  Shall I make the tea?
1 Suggest going for a walk.

2 Refuse to take any risks.

3 Invite someone to stay at your flat.

4 Offer to park someone's car.

5 Say politely that you want a shower.

6 Tell someone it's best they don't decide in a hurry.

7 Predict the end of the world in the year 2500.

37 Passive verb forms

A The passive with be

A passive verb form is a form of **be** + a passive participle (e.g. **transported**).
    The steel **is transported** on trains.   The house **has been sold**.
    The pupils **are taught** in the main building.   Several people **were injured**.

Some participles are irregular, e.g. **taught**. For irregular verbs see p 292.

Here is a summary of verb tenses:

	ACTIVE	PASSIVE
Present simple	They **wash** the car.	The car **is washed**.
Present continuous	They **are washing** the car.	The car **is being washed**.
Present perfect	They **have washed** the car.	The car **has been washed**.
Past simple	They **washed** the car.	The car **was washed**.
Past continuous	They **were washing** the car.	The car **was being washed**.
Past perfect	They **had washed** the car.	The car **had been washed**.

We form negatives and questions in the same way as in active sentences:
    It **is not transported** by road.   The house **hasn't been sold**.
    How **is** it **transported**?   **Has** the house **been sold**?

B The future and modal verbs in the passive

After **will, be going to, can, must, have to, should, ought to** etc. we use **be** + a passive participle:
    The house **will be sold**.   Seats **cannot be reserved**.
    The steel **has to be transported**.   The news **could be announced** soon.
    How **can** more jobs **be created**?   This rubbish **should be thrown** away.

	ACTIVE	PASSIVE
Future	They **will wash** the car.	The car **will be washed**.
	They **are going to wash** the car.	The car **is going to be washed**.
Modal verb	They **should wash** the car.	The car **should be washed**.
	They **ought to wash** the car.	The car **ought to be washed**.

C The passive with get

We sometimes use **get** in the passive rather than **be**:
    Lots of postmen **get bitten** by dogs.   I'm always **getting chosen** for the unpleasant jobs.
    How **did** the painting **get damaged**?
    Charles hadn't lived in Surrey long when he **got moved** to another area.

We use **get** mainly in informal English. We use **get** to emphasize action or change. We often use it for something happening by accident, unexpectedly or in an unplanned way. NOT ~~The picture got painted several years ago.~~

We also use **get** in idiomatic expressions, e.g. **get washed** (= wash oneself), **get dressed/changed, get engaged/married/divorced, get started** (= start).

37 Exercises

37.1 Passive verb tenses (A)

Complete the paragraph. Put in a passive verb in the correct tense.

Barford Hall

The building at the top of the High Street is Barford Hall.
It □ _was built_ in 1827 and today it ¹_____ as
the finest Georgian building in the county.
A number of changes ²_____ since it was built,
but the front of the building ³_____ .
Today the Hall ⁴_____ by Bardale Council, and for
the last ten years it ⁵_____ as a home for Barford Arts
Centre. At the moment a small art gallery ⁶_____
behind the Hall.

□ build
1 regard
2 make
3 not change
4 own
5 use
6 build

37.2 The future and modal verbs in the passive (B)

A press conference is being held. Put in the correct form of the verbs.

□ Reporter: Can this new drug prolong human life?
   Professor: Yes, we believe that human life _can be prolonged_ by the drug.
1 Reporter: Are you going to do any more tests on the drug?
   Professor: Yes, further tests _____ .
2 Reporter: What _____ the drug _____ ?
   Professor: It will be called Bio-Meg.
3 Reporter: Can people use the drug now?
   Professor: No, the drug _____ yet.
4 Reporter: Who will produce the drug?
   Professor: It _____ by the Bentrix drug company.
5 Reporter: Do you think they should sell it to anyone who wants it?
   Professor: Yes, I think it _____ freely.
6 Reporter: And what quantity could Bentrix produce?
   Professor: We believe the drug _____ in large quantities.

37.3 The passive with **get** (C)

Look at these newspaper headlines and tell your friend what's in the news. Use the passive with **get** in the present perfect (e.g. **has got**) or the present continuous (e.g. **are getting**).

□ POST OFFICE LOSES IMPORTANT DOCUMENT
   You: _An important document has got lost._
□ THIEVES STEALING MORE BICYCLES, SAY POLICE
   You: _More bicycles are getting stolen._
1 HEAVY LORRIES DAMAGING MOTORWAYS
   You: The motorways _____
2 VANDALS KNOCK WALL DOWN
   You: A wall _____
3 STORM BLOWS OFF ROOF
   You: A roof _____
4 COMPANIES PAYING INDUSTRIAL WORKERS HIGHER WAGES
   You: Industrial workers _____

38 Active or passive?

A What is the sentence about?

Compare these examples:

> **Alexander Graham Bell**
> British inventor who went to live in Canada and then the USA. Bell invented the telephone.

> **Telephone**
> Apparatus with which people can talk to each other over long distances. The telephone was invented by A.G. Bell.

Now compare these two sentences from the examples:
> **Bell** invented the telephone. | **The telephone** was invented by Bell.

The two sentences have the same meaning, but they are about different things. The subject of one sentence is **Bell**, and the subject of the other is **the telephone**. The subject is the starting-point of the sentence, the person or thing we are talking about. In both of these sentences the subject is old information, something already mentioned.

The new information comes at the end of the sentence. We say **Bell invented the telephone** because we are talking about **Bell**, and the new information is that he invented **the telephone**.

When the subject is the person or thing doing the action (the agent), then we use an active verb (**invented**). When the subject is not the agent, then the verb is passive (**was invented**). Compare:

> ACTIVE (about **Bell**):
> **Bell** invented the telephone.
> ↑
> Subject & agent

> PASSIVE (about **the telephone**):
> **The telephone** was invented by **Bell**.
> ↑   ↑
> Subject   Agent

The subject of the passive sentence is the same as the object of the active sentence (**the telephone**). It is not the agent. It is the thing that the action is directed at.

B Passive sentences with and without *by*

In a passive sentence, when we want to say who or what did the action, we use **by**:
> *We were stopped **by the police**.*
> *The building will be opened **by the Queen**.*
> *The decision must be taken **by the full committee**.*
> *The paper was all blown away **by the wind**.*

We can give other details about the action. For example, when we want to say when or where something happens, we can use **in, to** or **at**:
> *The telephone was invented **in 1876**.*
> *The visitors will be driven **to the airport**.*
> *The concerts are held **at the university**.*
> *The swimming-pool was built **last year**.*

In a passive sentence we mention the agent, the person or thing doing the action, only if it is important. We do not mention the agent when:

1. the agent does not add any new information:
   The money was stolen.
   The men were arrested last night.
   We do not need to say that the money was stolen **by a thief** or that the men were arrested **by the police**.

2. the agent is not important:
   The streets are cleaned every day.
   Oil has been discovered in Bavaria.
   Who discovered the oil is less important than the fact that it is there.

3. it is difficult to say who the agent is:
   This kind of jacket is considered very smart.
   A number of attempts have been made to find the Loch Ness monster.

C Empty subjects (**you, they, people** etc.)

We can use an 'empty subject' such as **you, one, they, people** or **someone**. We can sometimes use them instead of the passive, especially in conversation. Compare:

ACTIVE	PASSIVE
You/One should check the details.	The details should be checked.
They're increasing the rents.	The rents are being increased.
People use this footpath every day.	This footpath is used every day.
Someone took my purse.	My purse was taken.

D When do we use the passive?

We use the passive both in speech and writing, but it is more common in writing. We see it especially in textbooks and reports. We use it to describe activities in industry, science and technology, and also for official rules:

*Bananas **are exported** to the USA.*
*The liquid **is heated** to boiling point.*
*Payment **can be made** at any post office.*
*These gates **will be locked** at 9.00 pm.*

In these kinds of context, the person doing the action is often not important, or it is difficult to say who it is.

The passive is often used in news reports:
*A number of political prisoners **have been released**.*
*Talks **will be held** in London next week.*

38 Exercises

38.1 Active or passive verb? (A)

Put the missing verb forms into this news report.

Millions of pounds worth of damage ☐ *has been caused* by a storm which ¹_____ across the north of England last night. The River Ribble ²_____ its banks after heavy rain. People ³_____ from the floods by firemen, who ⁴_____ numerous calls for help. Wind speeds ⁵_____ ninety miles an hour in some places. Roads ⁶_____ by fallen trees and electricity lines ⁷_____ down, leaving thousands of homes without electricity. 'Everything possible ⁸_____ to get the situation back to normal,' a spokesman ⁹_____ .

☐ has caused/has been caused
1 passed/was passed
2 burst/was burst
3 rescued/were rescued
4 received/were received
5 reached/were reached
6 blocked/were blocked
7 brought/were brought
8 is doing/is being done
9 said/was said

38.2 Active or passive sentence? (A, B)

Use the notes to write sentences about American history. Put the important underlined information at the end of the sentence.

☐ Britain – rule – the American colonies
   The American colonies were ruled by Britain.
☐ the colonies – win – their independence – 1783
   The colonies won their independence in 1783.
1 Washington – become – President – 1789
   Washington _____
2 buy – Louisiana – from France
   Louisiana _____
3 discover – gold – California
   _____
4 the North – win – the Civil War
   _____
5 black people – want – equal rights
   _____
6 shoot – Kennedy – 1963
   _____

38.3 Active or passive sentence? (A–C)

You are telling a friend some news. Use the notes and write each sentence in the present perfect, active (**has done**) or passive (**has been done**).

☐ (someone – repair – phone box)
   You know the phone box at the end of the road? *It has been repaired.*
☐ (Trevor – leave – his wife)
   Have you heard about Trevor? *He has left his wife.*
1 (someone – steal – Kate's new car)
   You know about Kate's new car? It _____

38 Active or passive?

2 (Parkers – buy – a video camera)
You know the Parkers? They _____
3 (an ambulance – take – Mr Deacon – hospital)
Poor old Mr Deacon. He _____
4 (owner – sell – house)
You know the house on the corner? It _____
5 (picture – win – the competition)
You remember that picture Mark painted? _____
6 (company – sack – Caroline)
I feel sorry for Caroline. _____
7 (something – run over – cat)
Bad news about the cat next door. _____

38.4 Passive sentences with and without **by** (A–C)

Read this information about what happened to the Watsons.

> Someone broke into the Watsons' house at the weekend. The burglar took some jewellery. But he didn't do any damage. A young policewoman interviewed Mrs Watson. The police found some fingerprints, and the police computer identified the burglar. The police have arrested a man and are questioning him.

Complete the passive sentences in this conversation. Use a phrase with **by** only if it adds information.

Mrs Watson: Our house ▷ *was broken into at the weekend.*
Mrs Owen: Oh no!
Mrs Watson: Some jewellery ¹_____. But no damage ²_____.
Mrs Owen: Did the police come and see you?
Mrs Watson: Yes, of course. I ³_____.
Mrs Owen: Do they know who the burglar was?
Mrs Watson: Oh, yes. Some ⁴_____, and the ⁵_____.
A man ⁶_____.
Mrs Owen: Oh, good. Well, I hope you get your jewellery back.

38.5 Active or passive sentence? (A–D)

Write the paragraph from the notes on the right. Some sentences are active and some are passive. Use a phrase with **by** only if it adds information.

The First Motor Car

The first _____

But Marcus _____

Commercial _____

Benz _____

1 an Austrian called Siegfried Marcus – make – first motor car
2 but – Marcus – not produce – cars – for sale
3 a German called Carl Benz – start – commercial production
4 people – now – see – Benz – as – the father of – the motor car

39 Special passive patterns

A I was given . . .

In an active sentence, a verb of giving can have two different patterns after it. They both have the same meaning.
>The Queen gave **a medal to the pilot**.
>The Queen gave **the pilot a medal**.

For more details see Unit 68.

Either **a medal** or **the pilot** can be the subject of a passive sentence:
>**A medal** was given to the pilot.
>**The pilot** was given a medal.

The first of these two sentences is about **a medal**, and it tells us who received it. The second is about **the pilot**, and it tells us what he received.

It is quite normal in English for the person receiving something to be the subject in a passive sentence. Here are some more examples:
>**A government minister** was sent a letter bomb.
>**The workers** are paid £200 a week.

Verbs in this pattern are: **give, send, pay, lend, hand, sell, promise, show, offer, teach, owe, award, grant, allow, leave** (in a will) and **feed**.

B It is said (that) . . .

We can use a special pattern with verbs of reporting when we do not need to know who is doing the reporting. Compare:

ACTIVE	it + PASSIVE verb + clause
People say the bridge is unsafe.	It is said the bridge is unsafe.

We often see this pattern with **it** in news reports:
>**It was reported** that the President had suffered a heart attack.
>**It is thought** that the company is planning a new advertising campaign.
>**It has been agreed** that changes to the scheme are necessary.

Verbs in this pattern are: **say, report, mention, announce, think, believe, understand, agree, decide, know, find, expect, hope, regret, fear, intend, arrange**.

C He is said to . . .

We can also use a pattern with an infinitive. Compare:

ACTIVE	subject + PASSIVE verb + to-infinitive
People say the bridge is unsafe.	The bridge **is said to be** unsafe.

We also see this pattern in news reports:
>The President **was reported to have suffered** a heart attack.
>The company **is thought to be planning** a new advertising campaign.
>The home team **had been expected to win** easily.

In this pattern we can use: **say, report, think, believe, understand, know, find, expect** and **intend**.

39 Exercises

39.1 I was given ... (A)

A large company is explaining how well it looks after its employees. Rewrite the sentences as in the examples. The underlined information is important, so put it at the end of the sentence.

☐ Useful work skills are taught to our staff.
   Our staff are taught useful work skills.

1 Company shares are offered to most employees.
   _____

2 Six weeks' holiday is allowed to all employees.
   _____

☐ People with initiative are given opportunities.
   Opportunities are given to people with initiative.

3 People moving house are given help.
   _____

4 Women who leave to have children are paid a sum of money.
   _____

39.2 It is said ... (B)

Report these rumours. Instead of the active (e.g. **People say** ...), use the passive (e.g. **It is said** ...).

☐ The actress Tania Revesky has refused a part in the film *Volcano*.
   People say this.

   It is said that the actress Tania Revesky has refused a part in the film 'Volcano'.

1 The newsreader Ann Slater is furious at losing her job.
   Her friends have reported this.

   It has _____
   that the newsreader Ann Slater is furious at losing her job.

2 The Prime Minister and his wife are getting divorced.
   Lots of people believe this.

   It _____
   _____
   _____

3 The footballer Gary Johnson earns £1 million a year.
   Journalists have said this.

   _____
   _____
   _____

39.3 He is said to ... (C)

You are a journalist. Report the rumours in Exercise 39.2, like this.

☐ *The actress Tania Revesky is said to have refused a part in the film 'Volcano'.*
1 The newsreader Ann Slater _____ to be furious at losing her job.
2 The Prime Minister and his wife _____ getting divorced.
3 _____

40 have/get something done

A Professional services

Compare:

Sadie decorated the room.
(She did the work herself.)

*Sadie **had** the room **decorated**.*
(A decorator did the work.)

We use **have** in a passive pattern which means to arrange for someone to do something for you as a professional service. Look at these examples:

	have	**something**	**done**
We	had	the sofa	delivered.
Our neighbours	have had	a new garage	built.
You ought to	have	that video	repaired.
I might	have	this jacket	cleaned.

B have and get

We can also use **get something done** with the same meaning. Compare:
   We must **have** another key **made**. OR We must **get** another key **made**.
   The company **had** a market survey **done**. OR The company **got** a market survey **done**.
Get is more informal than **have**.

C have and get as ordinary verbs

Both **have** and **get** are ordinary verbs and can have auxiliaries (e.g. **did** you have, **is** getting):
   Where **did** you **have** (OR **did** you **get**) your hair cut?
   Leon **is having** (OR **is getting**) his photos developed.

D have something happen

We can use **have** in this pattern with the meaning 'experience something', often something unpleasant:
   We **had** our passports **stolen**.   The car has **had** its aerial **pulled** off.

40 Exercises

40.1 Professional services (A)

Write sentences with the pattern **have something done**.
☐ Susan is at the optician's. He's going to test her eyes.
   Susan is going to have her eyes tested.
1 Peter went to the dentist. She filled his tooth.
   Peter had _____
2 The actress went to the photographer's studio. He took her photo.
   The actress _____
3 Adrian is talking to the mechanic who has serviced his car.
   _____
4 Our window cleaner comes once a month.
   _____
5 The Watsons' dishwasher has broken down. The engineer is repairing it.
   _____

40.2 get something done (B)

Write the sentences from Exercise 40.1, but use **get**.
☐ _Susan is going to get her eyes tested._
1 _____
2 _____
3 _____
4 _____
5 _____

40.3 have and get as ordinary verbs (C)

Complete the conversation. Use **have something done** with each verb.

A: Oh, what's happening in here?
B: We're ☐ _having_ this room _decorated_. We got tired of the old wallpaper, so we're ¹_____ the walls _____. And when we've ²_____ that _____, we're going to ³_____ a new carpet _____.
A: When did you ⁴_____ these shelves _____? Are they new?
B: Oh no. Those have been there a long time.

☐ decorate
1 re-paper
2 do
3 lay
4 fit

40.4 have something happen (D)

Say what happened to people.
☐ The tourists' luggage was searched in customs.
   The tourists had their luggage searched in customs.
1 Angela's car was stolen from outside her house.
   Angela _____
2 The family's electricity was cut off.

3 Old people's pensions have been increased by five per cent.
   _____

97

41 to be done and being done

A Active and passive forms

Some verbs take a to-infinitive (e.g. **want to do, expect to do, hope to do, agree to do, ought to do, have to do**). Some take an ing-form (e.g. **enjoy doing, keep doing**). For more details see Unit 42. After a preposition we use an ing-form, not an infinitive (e.g. **insist on doing, tired of doing**).

The to-infinitive or ing-form can be active or passive. Compare:

ACTIVE
*I want **to meet** the visitors at the airport.*
*I insist on **meeting** all your friends.*
(I meet people.)

PASSIVE
*I want **to be met** at the airport.*
*I insist on **being met** at the airport.*
(Someone meets me.)

Look at this table of forms:

	ACTIVE	PASSIVE
to-infinitive	to do	to be done
ing-form	doing	being done

Here are some more examples with active and passive forms:
*The minister **agreed to answer** questions. He **agreed to be interviewed** on television.*
*Judy **tried to blame** Max for the accident. He didn't **expect to be blamed**.*
*I **want to play** volleyball. I **hope to be chosen** for the team.*
*I don't **enjoy being laughed** at.*
*Famous people get **tired of being recognized** everywhere they go.*
*I can't **remember being told** about this arrangement.*

B Active forms with a passive meaning

The active form after **need** has a passive meaning:
*The bicycle **needs oiling**. (= The bicycle needs **to be oiled**.)*
*The windows **need cleaning**. (= The windows need **to be cleaned**.)*
We cannot use the passive ing-form here. NOT ~~The bicycle needs being oiled.~~

We sometimes use an active infinitive to refer to jobs to **be** done:
*I've got some letters **to write** today.*
*We've got this bill **to pay**.*
We must use the active (**to write**) here because the subject of the sentence (**I**) is the person who has to do the job. But if the subject is <u>not</u> the person doing the job, then we use the passive infinitive:
*These letters are **to be written** today.*
*The bill is **to be paid** without delay.*

After the subject **there** we can use either an active or a passive infinitive:
*There are some letters **to write** (OR **to be written**) today.*
*There's a bill **to pay** (OR **to be paid**).*

41 Exercises

41.1 **to be done** and **being done** (A)

An immigrant has arrived in Britain. This is what he is saying.

'I am asking the government to allow me into Britain. I am worried about them refusing me entry. I am afraid of your officials sending me away. I don't want you to misunderstand me. I hope someone in Britain will offer me a job. I don't mind them paying me low wages. I am willing for my employer to re-train me. I would like Britain to give me a chance.'

Report what the man says. Use the passive to-infinitive or ing-form.

☐ *He is asking to be allowed into Britain.*
☐ *He is worried about being refused entry.*
1 He is afraid of _____
2 _____
3 _____
4 _____
5 _____
6 _____

41.2 Active and passive forms (A)

Some workers are protesting about not being paid enough. Put in a to-infinitive or ing-form. Some forms are active and some are passive.

☐ We want _to be paid_ better wages.   ☐ pay
1 We don't enjoy _____ as cheap labour.   1 use
2 We're tired of _____ for low wages.   2 work
3 We expect _____ like human beings.   3 treat
4 We won't agree _____ what the bosses want.   4 do
5 We hope _____ to discussions with the company.   5 invite
6 We insist on _____ .   6 hear

41.3 Active forms with a passive meaning (A, B)

Put in an active or passive to-infinitive or an ing-form.

Rory: Are you going to be busy this evening?
Claire: Well, I've got a few things ☐ _to do_ . This room ought   ☐ do
    1_____ up a bit. And we've got some   1 clean
    clothes 2_____ to the launderette.   2 take
Rory: Yes, my trousers need 3_____ . I'll put   3 wash
    them in the bag.
Claire: Those trousers have 4_____ , don't they?   4 dry-clean
Rory: Oh yes, of course.
Claire: I've got too much 5_____ . I'll take it in   5 carry
    the car.
Rory: Well, if this mess in here needs 6_____ up,   6 clear
    I can do that when you've gone.

42 Verb + to-infinitive or verb + ing-form?

Some verbs take a to-infinitive and some take an ing-form. Compare:

> Sarah **decided to go** out.
> NOT ~~Sarah decided going out.~~
> **Decide** takes a to-infinitive.

> Sarah **suggested going** out.
> NOT ~~Sarah suggested to go out.~~
> **Suggest** takes an ing-form.

Here are some more examples:

+ TO-INFINITIVE
> The committee **agreed to pay** half the cost.
> I **refuse to wait** here in the cold.
> We're **training to run** a marathon.
> The man had **chosen not to buy** a ticket.

+ ING-FORM
> The committee **recommended paying** half the cost.
> I **can't face waiting** here in the cold.
> We're **practising running** uphill.
> The man **admitted not buying** a ticket.

+ TO INFINITIVE	+ ING-FORM
agree, guarantee, undertake	admit, confess, deny
ask, demand, beg	appreciate
attempt, seek	avoid, save, escape, resist
can't afford	can't face
can't wait, long	can't help
choose, decide	delay, postpone, put off
claim, pretend	dislike, detest, can't stand
expect	enjoy, fancy
fail, omit, neglect, hesitate	finish, quit, give up
happen, turn out, prove	imagine, consider
hope, aim	involve
learn, train	justify, excuse
manage	keep, keep on, carry on
offer, promise, swear	mention
plan, arrange, prepare	miss
refuse	practise
seem, appear	resent, mind
tend	risk
threaten	suggest
wish, want	tolerate

Some verbs take either a to-infinitive or an ing-form, e.g. **start, continue, intend, like** and **hate**. See Unit 43.

> Andrew **started to unpack** (OR **started unpacking**) his suitcase.

Some verbs take an object and a to-infinitive. See Unit 44.

> We **persuaded Sharon to come** with us.

Some verbs take a preposition + ing-form. See Unit 48.

> I've **thought of changing** my job.

42 Exercises

42.1 Verb + to-infinitive or ing-form?

Put in the verbs. Use a to-infinitive or ing-form.

Elaine: Are we going to have a holiday this year?
Gary: I thought we'd decided □ _to spend_ our holidays on a Spanish beach somewhere.
Paula: Oh, good. I enjoy □ _lying_ on the beach. I might manage ¹_____ a suntan.
Elaine: But I dislike ²_____ in one place all the time. I refuse ³_____ on the beach all day.
Martin: I don't mind ⁴_____ around in the car.
Elaine: You promised ⁵_____ to Scandinavia with me. We could take the car.
Gary: I'm not going to drive. I do too much driving. I can't face ⁶_____ all holiday.
Martin: I wasn't planning ⁷_____ abroad. I can't afford ⁸_____ too much money.

□ spend
□ lie
1 get
2 stay
3 sit
4 tour
5 go
6 drive
7 go
8 spend

42.2 Verb + to-infinitive or ing-form?

Put in the verbs. Use the to-infinitive or ing-form.

A: Where's your new hi-fi?
B: Oh, it went wrong. It kept □ _making_ a funny noise. I took it back to the shop.
A: Did you get your money back?
B: Well, first they offered ¹_____ it, so I asked ²_____ the manager. In the end she agreed ³_____ me back the money.
A: And are you going to get another one?
B: I don't know. I want ⁴_____ about it. I can't help ⁵_____ if I really need a hi-fi after all. And I can't afford ⁶_____ a very good one.

□ make
1 repair
2 see
3 give
4 think
5 wonder
6 buy

42.3 Verb + to-infinitive or ing-form?

Complete the sentences. Use a to-infinitive or ing-form.
  □ My sister went to college, and I hope _to go_ there too.
  1 Will you apply for university? ~ Well, I'm considering _____.
  2 Where would you like to work? In an office? ~ No, I don't fancy _____ indoors.
  3 When are you starting your job? ~ Next month. I'm really looking forward to it. I can't wait _____.
  4 I can operate the machine on my own now. It took a few days to learn _____ it properly.
  5 How much will you earn? ~ I don't know. I want _____ more than I do now.
  6 I shouldn't miss this opportunity of getting another qualification. If I don't take it now, I risk _____ my chance of promotion.

101

43 start, like etc. + to-infinitive/ing-form

A start, intend etc.

Look at these examples:
> *People **started to leave** (OR **started leaving**) the theatre before the end of the play.*
> *Do you **intend to make** (OR **intend making**) a complaint?*
> *I didn't **bother to do** (OR **bother doing**) the washing-up after breakfast.*

These verbs can take either a to-infinitive or an ing-form with no difference in meaning: **start, begin, continue; intend, propose; bother**.

But we do not usually have two ing-forms together:
> *It was **starting to get** dark.* NOT *It was starting getting dark.*

B like, love, prefer and hate

After **like, love, prefer** and **hate** we can use either a to-infinitive or an ing-form with no difference in meaning:
> *Wendy **likes to take** (OR **likes taking**) photos.*
> *I **love to watch** (OR **love watching**) the sun rise.*
> *We always **prefer to travel** (OR **prefer travelling**) by train.*
> *I **hate to stand** up (OR **hate standing** up) while I'm eating.*

But compare these two different meanings of the verb **like**:

Like takes an infinitive when it means that something is a good idea rather than a pleasure:	But when **like** means 'enjoy', the ing-form is more usual:
*I **like to check** my work carefully before I hand it in.*	*Christopher **likes skiing**.*

After **would like, would love, would prefer** and **would hate**, we use a to-infinitive but not usually an ing-form:
> *I'**d like to meet** your brother.*
> *Tom **would love to have** his own flat.*
> *We'**d prefer to make** our own decision.*
> *I'**d hate to live** in a big city.*

Compare **would like** (= want) and **like** (= enjoy):

*I'**d like to lie** on the beach today. It's too hot to do anything else.*	*I **like lying** on the beach. I always spend my holidays sunbathing.*

102

43 start, like etc. + to-infinitive/ing-form

C remember, regret, try etc.

With some verbs, the choice of a to-infinitive or an ing-form depends on the meaning. Compare:

TO-INFINITIVE	ING-FORM
remember/forget	
I must **remember to post** this letter today. It's important.	I can't **remember posting** the letter. Perhaps it's still in my coat pocket.
The clothes are still dirty because I **forgot to switch** on the machine.	I'll never **forget flying** over the Grand Canyon. It was wonderful.
We use **remember/forget** + to-infinitive for necessary actions.	We use **remember/forget** + ing-form for memories of the past.
remember to do = to first remember and then do the action	**remember doing** = to first do the action and then remember it later
regret	
I **regret to say** I don't have much sympathy with you.	I **regret spending** all that money. I've got none left now.
regret to say = to say we are sorry when expressing something unpleasant or giving bad news	**regret doing** = to feel sorry about something
try	
I'm **trying to find** Josie's phone number.	Why don't you **try ringing** Enquiries? They might have the number.
People **tried to put** out the fire.	First they **tried stamping** on the flames, but that didn't work.
try to do = to attempt an action, do your best	**try doing** = to do something which might solve the problem
stop	
An old man walking along the road **stopped to talk** to us.	There's too much noise. Can you all **stop talking** please?
stop to do = to stop so that you can do something	**stop doing** = to end an action, finish doing something
mean	
I **meant to drop** the glass. It wasn't an accident.	I'm applying for a visa. It **means filling** in this form.
mean to do = to intend an action, do it deliberately	**mean doing** = to make another action necessary
go on	
The teacher introduced herself and **went on to explain** about the course.	The teacher told everyone to be quiet, but they just **went on talking**.
go on to do = to do something different, do the next thing	**go on doing** = to continue doing
need	
Sarah **needs to get** up early tomorrow. She's going to London.	The grass **needs cutting**. It's got very long.
needs to do = has to do (Sarah **has to** get up early.)	**needs doing** = needs to be done (The grass needs **to be cut**.) (See Unit 41B.)

43 Exercises

43.1 start, intend etc. (A)

Complete the news report. Put in the to-infinitive or the ing-form of these verbs: **drive, go, lock, look, make**. (Sometimes more than one answer is possible.)

Taxi stolen

28-year-old Steve Paisley has lost his taxi. It was stolen on Friday afternoon. 'I just went into the newsagent's for a moment,' said Steve. 'I didn't bother ¹_____ the car.' Steve started ²_____ his own taxi only six months ago. 'I was just beginning ³_____ a profit,' he said. 'I intend ⁴_____ on with my work as soon as I get the taxi back.' The police are continuing ⁵_____ for the stolen car.

43.2 like, love, prefer and hate (B)

Complete the sentences using the words in brackets. Decide if the verb after **love, prefer** etc. is a to-infinitive or an ing-form.

☐ I've always wanted to visit San Francisco. (I'd love)
  I'd love to visit it some time.
1 Tom enjoys swimming very much, especially in the sea. (He loves)
  _____ in the sea.
2 I'm glad I don't work such long hours as Susan. (I wouldn't like)
  _____ eighty hours a week.
3 I think I'll go and see this new film. (I'd like)
  _____ it.
4 Can't I come? I don't want to wait around here. (I'd prefer)
  _____ with you if you don't mind.
5 It would be marvellous to fly in a balloon. (I'd love)
  _____ in one some day.
6 Queueing is my least favourite activity. (I hate)
  _____ .
7 Brian's hobby is walking. (He likes)
  _____ in the country.
8 Ordering clothes from a catalogue isn't a good idea because you can't try them on. (I like)
  _____ them on in the shop first.

43.3 remember and forget (C)

Put in the to-infinitive or ing-form of the verbs.

Sophie: Did you remember ☐ _to pick_ up those photos today?   ☐ pick
Daniel: What photos?
Sophie: Oh, no. I can remember ¹_____ it to you only this   1 mention
        morning.
Daniel: I can't remember ²_____ to pick up some photos.   2 agree
Sophie: Well, don't forget ³_____ in at the shop for them   3 call
        tomorrow.
Daniel: OK.

43 *start*, *like* etc. + to-infinitive/ing-form

Sophie:	Your memory is getting worse. Yesterday afternoon you went out and forgot ⁴_____ the door.	4 lock
Daniel:	I'm sure I didn't forget ⁵_____ it. I can clearly remember ⁶_____ for my keys. They were in my pocket.	5 lock 6 look
Sophie:	You ought to write notes to yourself to remind you.	
Daniel:	I would never remember ⁷_____ them!	7 read

43.4 remember, regret, try etc. (C)

Write each pair of sentences as one. Use a to-infinitive or ing-form.

☐ Polly didn't do her homework. She forgot.
  Polly forgot to do her homework.

☐ The boys had been playing cards for hours. But they went on with the game.
  The boys went on playing cards.

1 The driver wanted to buy some cigarettes. So he stopped.
  The driver _____

2 Laura didn't think she could move the piano. She didn't even try.
  Laura _____

3 I once met Mrs Thatcher. I'll always remember it.
  I'll _____

4 What about painting the shelves? They need it.
  The shelves _____

5 Graham was rude to Louise. But he didn't mean it.
  _____

6 Kevin missed his chance of a prize. He regrets that.
  _____

43.5 like, love, regret, try etc. (B,C)

Complete the story. Put in the to-infinitive or ing-form of the verb.

'Last year I finally stopped ☐ *smoking* . I'd been trying ¹_____ up for ages. I needed ²_____ because it was costing me a lot of money. And of course if I went on ³_____, I would be putting my health at risk. Well, I wasn't having much success until one day a friend said, 'Why don't you try ⁴_____ sweets instead of smoking? That might break the habit.' And it worked! I don't smoke now, which is fine. But there's one problem. I like ⁵_____ to the dentist for a check-up now and again. Last time he said, 'I regret ⁶_____ you this, but your teeth don't look very healthy.' He went on ⁷_____ that three of my teeth needed ⁸_____ out! This was all because of the sweets. 'Eating sweets means ⁹_____ a lot of damage to your teeth,' he said. I don't regret ¹⁰_____ up smoking of course. I'd hate ¹¹_____ addicted to tobacco again. But I'd love ¹²_____ healthy lungs <u>and</u> healthy teeth.'

☐ smoke	
1 give	
2 stop	
3 smoke	
4 eat	
5 go	
6 tell	
7 say	
8 pull	
9 do	
10 give	
11 become	
12 have	

44 Verb + object + to-infinitive

A Introduction

Some verbs can take an object and a to-infinitive:

	VERB	OBJECT	TO-INFINITIVE
Kate	**reminded**	**us**	**to bring** our passports.
The police wouldn't	**allow**	**the protestors**	**to march** along the High Street.

With some verbs (e.g. **remind, allow**) we must use an object before the to-infinitive. But we can use others (e.g. **expect**) without an object. Compare:

VERB + TO-INFINITIVE	VERB + OBJECT + TO-INFINITIVE
I **expected to win**.	I **expected Tracy to win**.
(= I expected that I would win.)	(= I expected that Tracy would win.)

B The verbs **tell, order, command; ask, beg; remind;** and **warn**

The boss **told us to hurry** up.   Dave couldn't **persuade Sharon to dance**.
I **asked the waiter to fetch** the manager.

Ask and **beg** can be without an object, e.g. I **asked to see** the manager.

C The verbs **cause; force, drive; teach; invite; intend, mean;** and **expect**

The hot weather has **caused ice-cream sales to increase**.
Simon's mother is **teaching him to play** the piano.

After **help** can we leave out **to**, e.g. We **helped Karen (to) look** for her purse.

We can use **help, intend** and **mean** with or without an object:
I **meant my words to sound** friendly.   I **meant to sound** friendly.

D The verbs **want, (would) like, (would) love, (would) prefer** and **(would) hate**

Tom **wants everyone to go**.   I don't **want you to get** the wrong idea.
I'd **like you to listen** carefully.   We'd **hate the house to be** left empty.

We cannot normally use a that-clause. NOT ~~Tom wants that everyone goes.~~

We can also use these verbs without an object, e.g. Tom **wants to be** alone.

E The verbs **allow, permit; advise, recommend** and **encourage**

These verbs also come in the pattern of verb + ing-form. Compare:

+ ING-FORM	+ OBJECT + TO-INFINITIVE
They **allow fishing** here.	They **allow people to fish** here.
I'd **advise taking** out some insurance.	I'd **advise you to take** out some insurance.
I wouldn't **recommend walking** home alone at night.	I wouldn't **recommend you to walk** home alone at night.

We do not use **suggest** in the pattern with an object + to-infinitive:
I **suggested** to Eric **(that)** he should buy a new car.   NOT ~~I suggested Eric to buy a new car.~~

44 Exercises

44.1 tell, ask etc. (B)

Report what was said. Use the verbs in brackets.
- Police to motorists: 'Take special care.'
  (warn) _The police warned motorists to take special care._
1. Pupils to teacher: 'Could you explain, please?'
   (ask) The pupils _____
2. Doctor to patient: 'You should stay in bed.'
   (tell) _____
3. Kay to Joe: 'Don't forget to pay the bill.'
   (remind) _____
4. Police to gunman: 'Come out with your hands up.'
   (order) _____

44.2 cause, help etc. (C)

Write the two sentences as one.
- The lorry skidded. The icy road caused it.
  The icy road _caused the lorry to skid._
1. Kelly can speak Italian. Her mother taught her.
   Kelly's mother _____
2. The team lost. We'd all expected it.
   We'd all _____
3. The hostages lay down. The kidnappers forced them.
   The kidnappers _____
4. Bob's smile wasn't friendly. But he meant it to be.
   Bob _____

44.3 want and would like (D)

Complete the sentences using **would like** or **not want**.
- Neil won't wear a tie. His girl-friend is annoyed.
  She would like _him to wear one._
1. Sarah is going to hitch-hike. But her parents don't like the idea.
   They don't want _____
2. The girls want to stay out late. But their father is against it.
   He _____
3. Lucy refuses to take the exam. Her mother thinks it would be a good idea.
   _____

44.4 allow, advise etc. (E)

Complete the paragraph. Use the to-infinitive or the ing-form.

We wouldn't recommend ¹_____ into London in the rush hour. If you need to go there, we'd advise you ²_____ by train. We'd recommend ³_____ a special saver ticket, which is less expensive. But British Rail don't allow you ⁴_____ it before ten o'clock. This is to encourage people ⁵_____ a later train.

1. drive
2. travel
3. buy
4. use
5. take

45 Infinitive with and without **to**

A The to-infinitive

We use a to-infinitive (e.g. **to do**):

1 after **it** + **be** + adjective
   *It's nice **to see** you again.*
   ***It** would be wonderful **to travel** round the world.*

2 after a noun
   *I must take a **book to read**.* (= a book that I **can** read)
   *We've got a few **things to do**.* (= jobs that we **must** do)

3 in phrases like **going to buy** and **about to start**. Also: **have to, able to, allowed to, ought to** and **used to**
   *We're **going to buy** a caravan.*   *The race is **about to start**.*
   *We **aren't allowed to take** photos here.*   *You **have to fill** in a form.*

4 After some verbs, e.g. **hope, manage, decide, offer** (see Unit 42)
   *I **hope to see** you soon.*   *Did you **manage to find** the way?*
   *We **decided to leave** early.*   *Jane **offered to pay** for the meal.*

5 after some verbs with an object, e.g. **invite, want, persuade** (see Unit 44)
   *They've **invited the Prime Minister to open** the new building.*
   *I **want you to do** something for me.*

6 after a question word (see Unit 46)
   *We don't know **where to leave** our coats.*
   *This book tells you **how to train** race horses.*

7 to express purpose (see Unit 119)
   *Adrian went out **to get** a paper.*   *I need the money **to pay** the phone bill.*

B The infinitive without **to**

We use the infinitive without **to** (e.g. **do**):

1 after **must, needn't, can, could, will, would, shall, should, may** and **might**
   *You **must give** your work in on time.*   *We'**ll be** away a couple of days.*
   *We **could go** to a night club.*   *Things **might get** better.*

2 after **had better** ('**d better**) and **would rather** ('**d rather**)
   *It's cold. You'**d better wear** a coat.*   *We'**d rather play** golf than tennis.*

3 after **make** + object and **let** + object
   *That programme was funny. It really **made me laugh**.*
   *The boss gave us the afternoon off. He **let everyone go** home early.*

4 after **see/hear/feel** etc. + object (see Unit 53)
   *They **saw the street lights come** on.*   *We all **felt the house shake**.*

45 Exercises

45.1 The to-infinitive (A)

Join each pair of sentences using a to-infinitive.
- I might win a prize. That would be nice.
  It would be nice to win a prize.
1. I don't eat chocolate. I'm not allowed.
   I'm not allowed _____
2. Zoe is coming to lunch. I persuaded her.
   I _____
3. We're having a holiday. We've decided.
   _____
4. We might miss our train. That would be silly.
   It _____
5. What can I eat? I must have something.
   _____
6. I'd like to go somewhere. But I don't know where.
   _____
7. Susan is buying some stamps. She's gone to the post office.
   _____

45.2 The infinitive without to (B)

Put in these verbs: **crash, cry, explode, go, know, see, snow, wash**.

- My hands are dirty. I really must *wash* them.
1. My back is hurting again. I think I'd better _____ a doctor.
2. When I've got the information, I'll let you _____.
3. People miles away heard the bomb _____.
4. It was a terribly sad story. It made me _____.
5. It's very cold. It might _____.
6. I would rather _____ to the ballet than to the opera.
7. We saw the accident. We saw the car _____ into the wall.

45.3 Infinitive with and without to (A, B)

Put in the infinitive of the verbs. Decide whether or not you need **to**.

A: Are you sure you'll □ *be* all right on your own?
B: Yes, of course. I can manage □ *to look* after myself.
   I'm pleased Kate invited you ¹_____.
A: We're going ²_____ some fun, I just know it.
B: It's a long journey. Let me ³_____ you a magazine ⁴_____.
A: Not when I'm travelling. You know it makes me ⁵_____ sick, even in a train. I'd rather just ⁶_____ out of the window.
B: OK. Well, you'd better ⁷_____ in. I think it's about ⁸_____. Oh, did I remind you ⁹_____ at Birmingham?
A: Yes, you did. I won't ¹⁰_____.

- be
- look
1. stay
2. have
3. buy
4. read
5. feel
6. look
7. get
8. leave
9. change
10. forget

109

46 Question word + to-infinitive

A The pattern **know what to do**

After some verbs we can use a question word or phrase (e.g. **what, how much**) and a to-infinitive:

*It was a real problem. I didn't **know what to do**.*
*We were **wondering where to put** our coats.*
*Have you **decided when to have** your party?*
*We were **discussing how much to pay** the waiter.*

This pattern expresses a question about what the best action is:
what to do = *what I **should** do*
where to put *our coats* = *where we **should** put our coats*

These are some of the verbs that can come before the question word: **know; learn, find out, discover; understand, remember, forget; think, consider, discuss; decide; explain; ask, wonder, want to know**.

B Other patterns with **what to do**

We can also use **sure, clear, obvious, have an idea** and **make up your mind** before the question word:

*I wasn't **sure who to ask** for help.*
*Gary had no **idea how to operate** the machine.*

We can use the verbs **ask, tell, show, teach** and **advise** with an object (e.g. **the tourists**) and a question word:

*The guide didn't **tell the tourists when to be** back at the coach.*
*Our teacher **showed us how to change** a wheel.*

A preposition (e.g. **of**) can come before the question word:

*There's the problem **of how to transport** everyone to the airport.*
*Can you give me some advice **on where to apply**?*
*You need to be informed **about what to do** in an emergency.*

C **why, what, whose, which** and **whether**

We cannot use **why** in this pattern with the to-infinitive:

*No one could explain **why we needed to wait**.*
NOT *No one could explain why to wait.*

After **what, which, whose, how many** and **how much** we can use a noun:

*Graham and Sue were discussing **what colour to paint** the walls.*
*I wonder **whose story to believe**.*
*It's difficult to know **how much luggage to take**.*

We can use **whether** (but not **if**):

*We'll have to decide **whether to go** ahead with the project (or not).*
NOT *... decide if to go ahead ...*
*Tom wasn't sure **whether to sign** the form (or not).*
*I was wondering **whether to order** some tea.*

46 Exercises

46.1 The pattern **know what to do** (A)

Write the two sentences as one.
- How do you open the window? Felix didn't know.
  Felix didn't know how to open the window.
1. 'Who shall I invite to the party?' Natasha wondered.
   Natasha _____
2. 'What shall I play next?' the pianist asked.
   The pianist _____
3. Who should he choose for the team? The trainer hadn't decided.

4. How do you fill in the form? Ralph didn't understand.

5. What should they expect in the exam? The students wanted to know.

46.2 Question word + to-infinitive (B)

Look at the questions and then complete the paragraph about a man coming out of prison.
- How should Don start a new life?
1. What should he expect?
2. Where should he go for help?
3. How can he find somewhere to live?
4. What should he do?

Don will have problems when he leaves prison. He needs advice on □ *how to start* a new life. After a long time in prison he isn't sure ¹_____ in the outside world. And he has no idea ²_____ for help. There's the problem of ³_____ somewhere to live. But he won't be completely alone. A social worker will advise him ⁴_____.

46.3 Question word + to-infinitive (A–C)

Answer the questions using a question word + to-infinitive.
- Are you going to buy that sweater?
  You: I'm not sure *whether to buy it.*
- How many seats do you think we ought to book?
  You: I don't know *how many to book.*
1. What number should we ring?
   You: I don't know _____
2. Do you want to do the history course?
   You: I'm wondering _____
3. How much money should we give?
   You: I have no idea _____
4. Do you intend to join the sports club?
   You: I can't decide _____
5. Which path should we take?
   You: It's difficult to know _____
6. Have you solved the puzzle, then?
   You: I can't think _____

47 for with the to-infinitive

A Verb/Adjective + for

Look at these examples:

Verb + **for** + object + to-infinitive
  I'm **waiting for someone to serve** me.
  We **arranged for someone to look** after the house.
  Fiona was **longing for her parcel to arrive**.

Adjective + **for** + object + to-infinitive
  It's **difficult for untrained people to find** work.
  The bridge is not **safe for cars to use**.
  Their help was **essential for the plan to work**.
  The crowd were **impatient for the match to begin**.
  It's **dangerous for children to play** near the railway line.
  The organizers were **anxious for the event to be** a success.

[Illustration: Two women talking; speech bubble: "We're waiting for the plumber to come."]

B for expressing purpose

We can use the to-infinitive with **for** to express purpose:
  We brought some toys **for the children to play** with.
  (= We brought some toys **so that** the children could play with them.)
  At the station there were trolleys **for passengers to put** their luggage on.
  For the diet to work properly, you have to follow it very strictly.

C too and enough

We can use the pattern with **for** after **too** and **enough**:
  The road is **too busy for the children to be** able to cross safely.
  The table was **too** small **for all of us to sit** round.
  The table was big **enough for all of us to sit** round.
  The guide didn't speak clearly **enough for everyone to understand** her.

D for or of?

We can use **of** after these adjectives describing people's behaviour: **good, nice, kind, helpful; mean, generous; brave; honest; clever, sensible; silly, stupid, foolish, careless; wrong; polite, rude**.
  It's **kind of your parents to give** me a lift. (= Your parents are kind ...)
  It was **clever of you to work** out the answer. (= You were clever ...)

Compare **good of** and **good for** in these two sentences:

It was good **of** you to go jogging with me. (= It was a kind action by you.)	It was good **for** you to go jogging with me. (= It was a good, healthy experience for you.)

47 Exercises

47.1 Verb/Adjective + **for** (A)

Write the two sentences as one.
- ☐ Everyone must play their part. It's important.
  It's important for everyone to play their part.
1. Children shouldn't play with matches. It's dangerous.
   It's dangerous _____
2. The taxi is coming at eight o'clock. Phil has arranged it.
   Phil has _____
3. The party should begin soon. Tina is impatient.
   Tina _____
4. People should know the truth. It's important.
   _____

47.2 **for** expressing purpose (B)

Match the sentence pairs and rewrite them with **for** and the to-infinitive.

There's a visitors' book.	You can listen to it.
There's a pool.	You can picnic at them.
There are tables.	Tourists can buy souvenirs in them.
There's music.	Guests can write their names in it.
There are gift shops.	Guests can swim in it.

- ☐ *There's a visitors' book for guests to write their names in.*
1. _____
2. _____
3. _____
4. _____

47.3 **too** and **enough** (C)

Add a sentence with **too** or **enough** and: big, difficult, heavy, high, loud, warm.

- ☐ The boys couldn't lift the piano. *It was too heavy for them to lift.*
- ☐ Melanie can't read the sign. *It isn't big enough for her to read.*
1. Mary can't reach the top shelf. _____
2. We can't understand the poem. _____
3. Not everyone could hear the music. _____
4. Mark couldn't swim in the sea. _____

47.4 **for** or **of**? (A, D)

Put in **for** or **of**.
Sally: It was good ^{1}_____ Simon to help us clear away after the party.
Pat: Yes, it was kind ^{2}_____ him.
Sally: It was honest ^{3}_____ him to admit breaking that glass. But it wasn't really necessary ^{4}_____ him to pay for it.
Pat: He seemed very anxious ^{5}_____ us to accept the money.

48 Verb/Adjective + preposition + ing-form

A Introduction

Some verbs and adjectives can have a preposition after them:
*I **apologized for** my mistake.*   *Melanie is very **keen on** horses.*

Sometimes we can use an ing-form after the preposition:
*I apologized **for making** a mistake.*   *Melanie is very keen **on riding**.*

We can use **not** before the ing-form:
*I apologized **for not answering** the letter.*

B Verb + preposition + ing-form: **I don't approve of smoking**.

*I don't **approve of smoking**. I think it's a disgusting habit.*
*I **believe in discussing** things openly.*
*I don't **feel like cooking** tonight.*
*Unfortunately Ian **insisted on telling** us all about his medical problems.*
*People **objected to having** to wait so long.*
*You ought to book in advance. You can't **rely on finding** a hotel room.*
*I'm **thinking of going** to France in the summer.*
*I've **succeeded in getting** hold of the telephone number.*

We can use **about** after **speak, talk, think, ask, wonder, dream** and **complain**:
*They're **talking about building** a new swimming-pool.*
*The tourists **complained about not getting** any sleep.*

C Verb + object + preposition + ing-form: **No one blames you for thinking that**.

*He **accused his political enemies of inventing** stories about him.*
*I don't **blame you for thinking** about your own safety.*
*May I **congratulate you on reaching** such a high standard?*
*Higher prices will **discourage customers from buying**.*
*The firemen **prevented** (OR **stopped**) **the fire from spreading**.*
*The club has **punished its players for fighting** during a match.*
***Thank you for being** so helpful the other day.*

D Adjective + preposition + ing-form: **I'm bored with waiting here**.

*People were **annoyed at not being** able to see properly.*
*I'm **bored with waiting** here doing nothing.*
*Is this car **capable of getting** us all the way to Aberdeen?*
*Debbie is really **excited about going** to New York.*
*I'm **fed up with living** in this awful place.*
*Ted is **fond of fishing**.*
*Andrew is very **good at telling** jokes.*
*The man was found **guilty of stealing** from his employer.*
*Some of us are **interested in starting** a discussion group.*
*Sophie is very **keen on going** to art college.*
*I'm **pleased about getting** into university.*
*I'm **tired of studying**. I need a rest.*

48 Exercises

48.1 The pattern with a verb: **believe in doing** (A,B)

Put in the verbs with these prepositions: **for, in, like, of, on**.

Rachel: What's happened to your cassette-player?
Kirsty: Oh, James broke it. He knocked it off the table. He tried to repair it,
but unfortunately he hasn't succeeded ☐ _in getting_ it to work.   ☐ get
Rachel: Oh, dear.
Kirsty: He not only apologized ¹_____ it, but he insisted   1 break
² _____ me a new one. There's no need, because   2 buy
I'd been thinking ³_____ a new one anyway.   3 get
This one wasn't very good. But I didn't feel
⁴_____ about it.   4 argue

48.2 The pattern with a verb or a verb + object (B,C)

Combine each pair of sentences into one. Use a preposition and an ing-form.
☐ The police prevented the crime. It didn't take place.
The police prevented _the crime from taking place_.
1 We congratulated Ann. She passed her driving test.
We congratulated Ann _____
2 The doctors succeeded. They saved the woman's life.
The doctors _____
3 The customer complained. He didn't get his money back.
The customer _____
4 Everyone blamed the van driver. He didn't stop at the crossroads.
Everyone _____
5 Vegetarians don't approve. They think you shouldn't eat meat.

6 The complicated rules will discourage people. They won't play this game.

7 The workers have accused the management. They say the management is doing nothing about the problem.

8 The courts should punish drivers. They break the speed limit.

48.3 Verb/Adjective + preposition + ing-form (A–D)

Complete these sentences from a letter. Put in a preposition and ing-form.
Dear Jessica,
Thank you ☐ _for telling_ us all your news. You must be very pleased   ☐ tell
¹_____ the job you wanted. Personally, I wouldn't   1 get
be very keen ²_____ sixty miles to work. And don't   2 travel
you get bored ³_____ in the country? I apologize   3 live
⁴_____ sooner. A week in bed with flu has   4 not reply
prevented me ⁵_____ anything at all. Luckily, Mark   5 do
is very good ⁶_____ after me. I'm OK now, but . . .   6 look

49 afraid to do or afraid of doing?

A afraid

Compare:

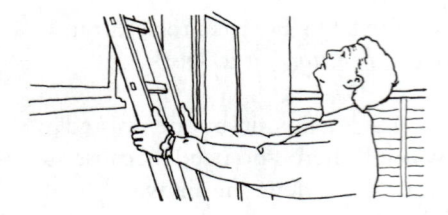

*He is **afraid to climb** the ladder.*
(= He **doesn't want to climb** the ladder because he's afraid.)

*He is **afraid of falling**.*
(= He is afraid **because he might fall**.)

Here are some more examples:

*I was **afraid to say** anything in front of all those people.*
*Henry was **afraid to wander** too far from the hotel.*

*I was **afraid of sounding** foolish.*

*He was **afraid of getting** lost.*

B anxious, ashamed and interested

Compare:

*We're **anxious to find** out the truth.*

(= We **want** to find out the truth.)

*Brian was **anxious about speaking** to a large audience.*
(= He was worried because he had to speak to a large audience.)

*I'm **ashamed to tell** you what I scored in the test.*
(= I **don't want** to tell you because I'm ashamed.)

*I'm **ashamed of getting** such a low score.*

(= I'm ashamed because I got such a low score.)

*I'd be **interested to meet** your **sister**.*
(= I **would like** to meet her.)

*My sister is **interested in photography**.*
(= It is an interest / a hobby of hers.)

C Patterns after sorry

To apologize for something in the present, we use a to-infinitive:
*I'm **sorry to tell** you this, but your score is rather low.*
*I'm **sorry to ring** you so late, but it's important.*

To apologize for something in the past we can use **about** + ing-form:
*I'm **sorry about making** all that noise last night.*
(OR *I'm **sorry I made** all that noise.*)

49 Exercises

49.1 afraid (A)

Rewrite the second sentence using **afraid to** or **afraid of**.
- ☐ There was a large dog in the garden. Stella didn't want to open the gate.
  She was afraid to open the gate.
- ☐ I arrived at the airport in good time. I thought I might get stuck in a traffic jam.
  I was afraid of getting stuck in a traffic jam.
1 I'm just checking that my wallet is safe. I might lose my money.
  I'm afraid _____
2 The young woman took a taxi. She didn't want to walk home alone.
  She _____
3 The policeman looked angry. Maria didn't want to argue with him.
  She _____
4 Nick is keeping his shirt on. He thinks he might get too sunburnt.
  _____
5 I don't know anything about electricity. I don't want to touch these wires.
  _____
6 I didn't like to say my room was cold. I thought I might offend my hostess.
  _____

49.2 anxious, ashamed and interested (B)

Put in a to-infinitive (e.g. **to show**) or a preposition + ing-form (e.g. **of showing**).

- ☐ It's an awful photo. I'm ashamed *to show* it to anyone. ☐ show
- ☐ Let's not be in too big a hurry. I'm a bit anxious *about making* the wrong decision. ☐ make
1 Carol hates aeroplanes. She's really anxious _____ to Los Angeles next week. 1 fly
2 It's my fault, I know. I'm ashamed _____ so badly. 2 behave
3 Brian is reading a book about food. He's interested _____. 3 cook
4 These discussions have gone on too long. We're anxious _____ things as quickly as possible. 4 settle
5 I didn't score many points in the quiz. I'm ashamed _____ you how few questions I got right. 5 tell

49.3 Patterns after sorry (C)

Complete the conversation using a to-infinitive or **about** + ing-form. Look at the information on the right.

Alex: I'm sorry ¹_____, but could I speak to you for a moment? 1 (I'm disturbing you.)
Roger: Yes, of course.
Alex: I'm sorry ²_____ last night. I didn't mean what I said. 2 (I was so rude.)
Roger: Oh, that's all right. I'm sorry ³_____. 3 (I lost my temper.)

50 used to do or used to doing?

A Verb + to

To can be part of a to-infinitive, or it can be a preposition. Compare:

VERB + TO-INFINITIVE	VERB + **to** + ING-FORM
I hope **to see** you soon.	I look forward **to seeing** you soon.
The man claimed **to be** a tourist.	The man admitted **to being** a spy.
We use a to-infinitive after many verbs, e.g. **hope, claim, decide, offer, expect, refuse, manage**.	We use **to** with a few verbs: **look forward to, admit to, confess to, face up to, resort to, object to**.

Compare **would prefer to do something** and **prefer one thing to another**:

I don't want to play tennis. I'd prefer **to go** for a walk.	I don't walk much. I prefer jogging **to going** for a walk.

B Adjective + to

Compare:

ADJECTIVE + TO-INFINITIVE	ADJECTIVE + **to** + ING-FORM
It would be silly **to give** up now.	We came close **to giving** up the idea.
It's wrong **to kill** animals.	I'm opposed **to killing** animals.
We use a to-infinitive after many adjectives, e.g. **silly, wrong, safe, important, exciting**.	There are a few adjectives with **to**, e.g. **close to, opposed to, used to** (see C), **accustomed to, resigned to**.

C used to

Compare:

used + TO-INFINITIVE (in the past)
 We **used to play** that game when we were younger.
 I **used to smoke**, but I gave it up.

Here **used** is a verb. **Used to** refers to something that happened regularly, or that went on for a time in the past.

We normally use **did** in negatives and questions:
 We **didn't use to have** computers.
 Did you **use to live** in London?

be used to + ING-FORM (be accustomed to)
 We're **used to getting** up early. We do it every day.
 I'm **used to living** alone.

Here **used** is an adjective. **Used to** means 'accustomed to', 'familiar with'. We can say **is used to, was used to** etc.

We use a form of **be** in negatives and questions:
 We aren't **used to cooking**.
 Are you **used to working** nights?

We can also say **get used to**:
 I'll **get used to driving** on the left.

50 Exercises

50.1 to-infinitive or to + ing-form? (A,B)

Put in the correct form (e.g. **to get** or **to getting**).
- Did you get to the concert on time? ~ Yes, I just managed _to get_ there before it started.
- Did you eat the last chocolate? ~ Sorry. I must admit _to being_ very fond of chocolate.
1. Are you enjoying yourselves? ~ No, we wish it was time to go. We're looking forward _____ home.
2. Why do we have to stand in a queue? ~ Yes, I object _____ here in the freezing cold.
3. No one has seen Boris all week. ~ No, I expected _____ him at the club last night.
4. Has anyone paid the bill? ~ Well, Tim has offered _____ it.
5. Did you write to Louise or ring her up? ~ In the end I decided _____ her up.
6. I understand Anthony doesn't want to come on the treasure hunt. ~ That's right. He simply refused _____ with us.
7. The motor-cyclist almost hit that tree, didn't he? ~ Yes, he came very close _____ it.
8. Will you be going to the club tonight? ~ No, but I hope _____ next week.

50.2 used to for the past (C)

An interviewer is talking to the oldest person in a village. Put in **used to** with the verb.

Old Woman:	I've always lived in the village, but not always in this house.	
Interviewer:	Where □ _did you use to live_ ?	□ you live
Old Woman:	When I was a girl, we lived at Apple Tree Farm. We 1_____ it there.	1 like
Interviewer:	But life was hard, wasn't it?	
Old Woman:	Oh, yes. In those days we 2_____ electricity. My father milked the cows by hand.	2 not have
Interviewer:	And 3_____ with the farm work?	3 you help
Old Woman:	Yes, I 4_____ after the hens.	4 look

50.3 I used to do or I'm used to doing? (C)

Put in **to** and the verbs in brackets.
- (want) I used _to want_ to be an astronaut when I was a child.
- (speak) I'm nervous. I'm not used _to speaking_ to a large audience.
1. (live) It took us ages to get used _____ in a block of flats.
2. (stop) Lots of trains used _____ here, but not many do now.
3. (work) Didn't your sister use _____ in this office?
4. (be) There didn't use _____ so many cars fifty years ago. The roads were much quieter.
5. (drink) I'll have an orange juice. I'm not used _____ alcohol.
6. (travel) Marcia wasn't used _____ such long distances every day. She'd never done it before.

51 Preposition or linking word + ing-form (e.g. **before leaving**)

A Preposition + ing-form

We can use an ing-form after some prepositions:

	PREPOSITION	ING-FORM
This all happened	**as a result of**	**missing** the bus.
Are you	**in favour of**	**banning** cars from the city centre?
I've got a job to do	**as well as**	**looking** after the children.
I've got a job to do	**besides**	**looking** after the children.
Why not save some money	**instead of**	**spending** it all?
Can you touch your toes	**without**	**bending** your knees?
What	**about**	**giving** us some help?
How	**about**	**giving** us some help?
Laurie went to work	**in spite of**	**not feeling** well.
Laurie went to work	**despite**	**not feeling** well.

We cannot use an infinitive after a preposition.
NOT ... ~~in spite of to feel ill.~~

We use these prepositions: **as a result of; in favour of, against; as well as, besides; without; what about, how about; in spite of, despite; for; by; on**.

We use **for** to express purpose (what we use a thing for) and **by** to express means (how someone does something):
This cloth is **for cleaning** the floor.
The thief got in **by breaking** a window.

We use **on** + ing-form to mean 'as soon as':
On hearing the news Fiona burst into tears.
(= As soon as Fiona heard the news, ...)

B Linking word + ing-form

We can use an ing-form after some linking words (e.g. **before, when**):
I read the letter through again **before sealing** the envelope.
I always have a shower **after playing** football.
You should always lock the door **when leaving** your room.
I was listening to the car radio **while sitting** in a traffic jam.
Although hoping for success, I wasn't really expecting it.
Harold has been unemployed **since losing** his job at the town hall.

This pattern with the ing-form is a little more formal than putting a subject after the linking word, e.g. ... since **he lost** his job.

We use these linking words with an ing-form: **when, while; although; before, after, since**.

51 Exercises

51.1 Preposition + ing-form (A)

Complete the sentence using the word in brackets.
- ☐ Marion: Do you want to walk? ~ Rita: Yes, let's not take a taxi.
  (instead of) Rita wants to walk _instead of taking a taxi_.
1. Lisa: Did you finish writing the report? ~ Julia: Yes, I worked all night.
   (by) Julia finished the report _____
2. Norma: When do you take your medicine? ~ Ed: The minute I wake in the morning.
   (on) Ed takes his medicine _____
3. Derek: Tom was unable to go abroad. ~ Lorna: He lost his passport, didn't he?
   (as a result of) Tom was unable to go abroad _____
4. Darren: So you worked out the answer? ~ Andy: And I didn't use a calculator.
   (without) Andy worked out the answer _____
5. Sonia: Why the rucksack? ~ Gavin: So I can carry the food.
   (for) The rucksack is _____
6. Dave: Sorry, I forgot the sugar. ~ Eric: And you had it on your list.
   (in spite of) Dave forgot the sugar _____

51.2 Linking word + ing-form (B)

Put in **before** or **after** and the ing-form of the verbs on the right.
- ☐ Replace the top on the bottle _after taking_ the medicine. ☐ take
1. Read the contract carefully _____ it. 1 sign
2. You shouldn't have a bath straight _____ a meal. 2 eat
3. Ring the airport to check that your flight is on schedule
   _____ home. 3 leave
4. Wash your hands _____ the toilet. 4 use
5. Switch off the electricity _____ a fuse. 5 change

51.3 Preposition or linking word + ing-form (A,B)

Dan Mason owns a supermarket business. Write sentences about his life. Make two sentences into one using the word in brackets.
- ☐ He saw an empty shop. He was walking around town one day. (while)
  He saw an empty shop while walking around town one day.
1. He thought carefully. He decided to buy it. (before)
   He thought carefully _____
2. He bought the shop. He had little money of his own. (despite)

3. He became successful. He gave the customers what they want. (by)

4. He fell ill. He worked too hard. (as a result of)

5. He was happy. He was running his own business. (when)

6. He has made a lot of money. He bought his first shop ten years ago. (since)

52 go shopping and do the shopping

A go shopping

We use an ing-form after **go** to talk about some leisure activities outside the home:
*Shall we **go dancing** tonight?*   *One day we **went sailing** on the lake.*
*The others have all **gone skating**.*   *Kate sometimes **goes riding**.*
*We quite often **go swimming** in the summer.*
*I like to **go shopping** if I've got some money to spend.*

Other examples are: **go walking, go hiking, go jogging, go cycling, go skiing** and **go fishing**.

B do the shopping

We use an ing-form after **do the** for some kinds of work, especially housework:
*I'd better **do the cleaning**, I suppose.*
*Have you **done the typing** yet?*
*I **do the painting** and Eric **does the wallpapering**.*
*How about **doing the washing** up?*
*I usually **do the shopping** at the supermarket on Friday evening.*

Other examples are: **do the cooking, do the hoovering** and **do the ironing**.

We can also use **this** or **that**:
*I hurt my back when I **did that digging** yesterday.*
*I've got all **this ironing** to do.*

Compare:

going shopping   doing the shopping

C do some . . . / do a lot of . . .

After **do** we can use **some, any, a lot of, much, a little, a bit of, more** and **less**:
*My parents are coming today. I'm just **doing some tidying** up.*
*We usually eat out. We don't **do much cooking**.*

We can also use **do some . . . , do a lot of . . .** etc. for leisure activities:
*We used to **do a lot of walking** when we lived in the country.*
*There wasn't really enough snow to **do any skiing**.*

But we cannot use **the** for leisure activities. NOT ~~do the skiing~~ or ~~do the cycling~~.

52 Exercises

52.1 go shopping (A)

Add a sentence with ... **sometimes go** ... or ... **sometimes goes** ...
- ☐ Max has got a fishing rod. _He sometimes goes fishing._
1. Lucy has got some skis. _____
2. The girls have got dancing shoes. _____
3. Tom has got a bike. _____
4. Carol has got a pony. _____
5. The Managing Director has got his own yacht. _____

52.2 do the shopping (B)

Two couples went on holiday together and stayed in a flat by the sea. Who did what? Write sentences from the notes.
- ☐ cooking – Diana   _Diana did the cooking._
1. shopping – Nigel   _____
2. driving – Anne   _____
3. map-reading – Mark   _____
4. cleaning – everyone _____

52.3 go or do? (A, B)

Complete the conversation. Put in a phrase with **go** or **do** in the correct form.

A: You look a bit hot.
B: I am hot. I've just been ☐ _doing the cleaning_ .   ☐ clean
A: Do you want to ¹_____ this afternoon?   1 swim
B: I won't have time. I haven't ²_____ yet.   2 wash
A: Oh, come on. It's a lovely day, too nice for housework.
B: All right. I'll ³_____ tonight.   3 wash
A: Good idea.
B: Is Sharon coming?
A: No, she's gone out. She has ⁴_____ .   4 ride
B: Well, I'll just get ready.
A: We can go tomorrow as well if the weather stays like this.
B: Oh, tomorrow I'll be ⁵_____ .   5 iron
A: Oh no!

52.4 do a lot of .../much ... (C)

Add a sentence with **do + a lot of** or **not ... much**.
- ☐ I like cooking. _I do a lot of cooking._
- ☐ Don hates walking. _He doesn't do much walking._
1. Mrs Brown loves gardening. _____
2. Gary's hobby is fishing. _____
3. We hate decorating. _____
4. Jeff doesn't like dancing. _____
5. Julia isn't very keen on ironing. _____
6. Swimming is Giles and Mandy's favourite sport. _____

53   see it happen or see it happening?

A   see it happen

After some verbs we can use an object and an infinitive without **to**:

	VERB	OBJECT	INFINITIVE
I	*saw*	*Frank*	**light** *a cigarette.*
Fiona	*heard*	*someone*	**close** *the door.*
Let's	*watch*	*the conjuror*	**do** *a trick.*
We	*felt*	*the house*	**shake**.

We can use the verbs **see, watch, notice; hear, listen to;** and **feel**.

B   see it happening

We can also use an ing-form after the object:
> *I* **saw Frank smoking** *a cigarette.*
> *Can you* **hear someone playing** *the piano?*
> *We* **noticed two boys fishing** *from the river bank.*
> *I could* **feel an insect crawling** *up my leg.*

In this pattern we can use the verbs in A. We can also use **find** and **smell**:
> *We* **found Graham and Liz lying** *on the beach.*
> *I can* **smell something cooking**.

C   see it happen or see it happening?

Look at this conversation:
> Alex: *I saw them* **knock** *the old bridge down yesterday. It only took them about half an hour.*
> Debbie: *I saw them* **knocking** *it down as I drove past, but I didn't have time to stop and watch.*

Alex saw the complete action, but Debbie saw only part of it. When Debbie passed, they were in the middle of knocking it down. Compare:

see it happen	see it happening
We saw Louise **plant** *the tree.* (Louise **planted** the tree. We saw her do the whole job.)	*We saw Louise* **planting** *the tree.* (Louise **was planting** the tree. We saw her in the middle of the job.)
The reporters watched the players **train** *in the gym.* (They watched all the training.)	*The reporters watched the players* **training** *in the gym.* (They watched some of the training, perhaps not all of it.)
We noticed a man **sit** *down and order a meal.*	*We noticed a man* **sitting** *at the table eating a meal.*

Note: When we talk about a relatively short action, it does not matter which pattern we use:
> *They heard a car* **turn** (OR **turning**) *the corner.*
> *I didn't see anyone* **leave** (OR **leaving**) *any litter.*

53 Exercises

53.1 see it happen (A)

Answer **yes** and use the verbs on the right.

- Did Jill catch the ball? ~ _Yes, I saw her catch it._ — see
1. Did Richard lock the door? ~ _____ — 1 hear
2. Did Melissa take this photo? ~ _____ — 2 watch
3. Did Phil get on the train? ~ _____ — 3 notice
4. Did the rope break? ~ _____ — 4 see

53.2 see it happening (B)

Add a sentence with **can see**, **can hear** or **can smell**, and use the ing-form of these verbs: **bark, burn, come, play, ring**.

- The postman will be here soon. _I can see him coming._
1. There's a dog outside. _____
2. The footballers are in the park. _____
3. That's the phone. _____
4. You've forgotten your toast. _____

53.3 see it happen or see it happening? (C)

People are talking about a bomb explosion. Write the two sentences as one. Use the infinitive without **to** (e.g. **happen**) or the ing-form (e.g. **happening**).

- 'A man was running away. I noticed him.' _I noticed a man running away._
- 'The bomb exploded. I heard it.' _I heard the bomb explode._
1. 'The building shook. I felt it.' _____
2. 'People were shouting. I heard them.' _____
3. 'An alarm was ringing. I could hear it.' _____
4. 'The police arrived. I saw them.' _____
5. 'I saw a woman. She was crying.' _____

53.4 see it happen or see it happening? (C)

Put in the verbs. Use the infinitive without **to** or the ing-form.

- Horrified, we watched the van _crash_ into the house. — crash
- I rang Ben just now, and we could hear two other people _talking_ on the phone. — talk
1. Emma was in town yesterday. I noticed her _____ for a bus outside the town hall. — 1 wait
2. The horse was almost at the winning post when we saw it suddenly _____. — 2 fall
3. As I walked past the window, I could see all the old people _____ television inside. — 3 watch
4. We heard Jemima _____ the whole piece from beginning to end on the piano. — 4 play
5. We stopped for a moment outside the church to watch someone _____ a picture of it. — 5 paint
6. I saw Somerset _____ Middlesex. It was a wonderful game of cricket. — 6 beat

54 Some patterns with the ing-form (e.g. I lay in bed **reading**.)

A Two actions at the same time

When someone does two actions at the same time, we can use a main verb and an ing-form:
   We had to **stand** in the queue **waiting** for the bank to open.
   (We stood in the queue **and** we waited.)
   You can't **sit watching** television all day.
   All afternoon, Stella **lay** on the sofa **thinking** about life.
We often use the ing-form after **stand, sit** and **lie**.

We can also use this pattern when one action comes in the middle of another. We use the ing-form for the longer action:
   Andy **injured** his knee **doing** gymnastics.
   (He injured his knee **while** he was doing gymnastics.)
   I **fell** asleep **listening** to the radio.

B One action after another

We can use an ing-form when there are two short actions, one immediately after the other:
   Opening the bottle, Sam poured the drinks.
   (He opened the bottle **and then** poured the drinks.)
   Turning right into Madison Avenue, the car drove north for two blocks.

We can also use the perfect (e.g. **having done**):
   Having opened the bottle, Sam poured the drinks.

When the first action is a long action, we must use the perfect:
   Having photocopied all the papers, the secretary put them back in the file.
   NOT *Photocopying all the papers*, the secretary ...
   Having repaired the car, Simon took it out for a road test.

The perfect always means the first action, so we can change the order:
   The secretary put all the papers back in the file, **having photocopied** them.
But NOT *Sam poured the drinks, opening the bottle*.

All these patterns in B are more common in written English. In spoken English we normally use sentences like these:
   The car turned right into Madison Avenue and drove north for two blocks.
   The secretary photocopied all the papers and then put them back in the file.

C The ing-form saying why

We can use the ing-form to give a reason:
   The fans queued for hours **hoping** to get tickets.
   (They queued for hours **because** they hoped to get tickets.)
   Being the youngest child, Neil was his mother's favourite.
   Not knowing the way, I had to ask for directions.

We can also use the perfect to give a reason:
   Having spent all my money, I couldn't buy anything else.
   We decided not to travel, **having heard** the weather forecast.

54 Exercises

54.1 One action in the middle of another (A)

Write sentences from the notes using an ing-form (e.g. **doing**).
☐ Antonia – burn – her fingers – light – a fire
   Antonia burnt her fingers lighting a fire.
1 Tom – break – his arm – play – rugby

2 Ella – cut – her hand – open – a tin

3 Helen – injure – her leg – climb – a mountain

4 Peter – hurt – his back – dig – this hole

54.2 One action after another (B)

Rewrite the sentences. Begin with an ing-form (e.g. **doing** or **having done**).
☐ Judy picked up the phone and dialled a number.
   Picking up the phone, Judy dialled a number.
☐ Martin did his essay, and then he handed it in.
   Having done his essay, Martin handed it in.
1 The man pulled out a gun and fired a shot.
  Pulling
2 Sharon used the whole film, and then she developed it.
  Having
3 Teresa cut the grass, and then she put the mower away.

4 Roger took out his wallet and offered a £20 note.

5 Mike solved the puzzle, and then he sent the answer to the magazine.

54.3 The ing-form saying why (C)

Match the two parts and join them using an ing-form (e.g. **doing** or **having done**).

Because she didn't see the danger,   Lorna turned on the heating.
As he had worked hard all day,   Tony took it back to the library.
Because he had studied the map,   Tina found it hard to communicate.
She felt cold, so   Nicola ran towards the cliff edge.
Because she didn't know the language,   Paul knew which way to go.
He had finished the book, so   Derek was exhausted.

☐ *Not seeing the danger, Nicola ran towards the cliff edge.*
☐ *Having worked hard all day, Derek was exhausted.*
1
2
3
4

55 Word classes: noun, adjective etc.

A What kind of word is it?

Look at this news item:

A man in Colchester returned a library book yesterday thirty-four years late. Alex Williams, a newsagent, found the book in his mother's house after she died recently. It was under some old clothes at the bottom of a cupboard. The book was a romantic novel called 'I See You Everywhere'. Alex's mother borrowed it thirty-four years ago, so Alex thought it was time to take it back. The library will decide next week if Mr Williams has to pay the fine, which is over two hundred pounds. 'I hope they won't make me pay,' he said anxiously. 'It's a lot of money, and I'm not a rich man.'

There are eight different word classes (parts of speech) in English.
1. Verb: **returned, found, died, was, see, borrowed, thought, take**
2. Noun: **man, book, years, newsagent, house, clothes, cupboard**
3. Adjective: **old, romantic, rich**
   (e.g. some **old** clothes, the clothes were **old**)
4. Adverb: **yesterday, recently, everywhere, anxiously**
5. Preposition: **in, under, at, of**
6. Determiner: **a, the, his, some**
   (Determiners come before a noun, e.g. **a** man, **his** mother.)
7. Pronoun: **she, it, I, you, which, they, me, he**
   (**she** = Alex's mother, **it** = the book, **I** = the speaker, **which** = the fine)
8. Linking word: **after, so, if**
   (A linking word joins sentences together.)

B Words in context

Some words can belong to different classes in different contexts:
   The **book** wasn't in the cupboard. (noun)
   I musn't forget to **book** a hotel room. (verb)
   He might have to **pay** some money. (verb)
   I like the job, but the **pay** isn't very good. (noun)

C Determiners and pronouns

There are different kinds of determiners and pronouns. Compare:

DETERMINERS
Articles: **a** book, **the** library
Possessive determiners: **my** ticket, **your** house, **his** mother, **her** book etc.
Demonstratives: **this** door, **that** time, **these** keys, **those** pages
Quantifiers: **a lot of** money, **most** books, **some** clothes

We use a DETERMINER before a noun:

   The book was in a cupboard.
   Look at **this** photo.
   I've got **a lot of** money.

PRONOUNS
Personal pronouns: **I, you, he, she** etc.
Possessive pronouns: **mine, yours, his, hers** etc. (I've got **mine**.)
Demonstratives: **this, that, these, those** (**This** is nice.)
Quantifiers: **a lot, most, some**
Relative pronouns: **who, which, that**

We use a PRONOUN instead of a determiner + noun:

   It was in a cupboard.
   Look at **this**.
   I've got **a lot**.

55 Exercises

55.1 What kind of word is it? (A)

Read this story and say what kind of words they are.

On Tuesday night a burglar broke into a shop in a small Sussex town and stole £600. The shop sells burglar alarms! 'It's terrible. We opened very recently, so we haven't had time to fit an alarm,' the manager said sadly.

- ☐ on — *preposition*
- ☐ night — *noun*
1. a _____
2. broke _____
3. into _____
4. small _____
5. and _____
6. the _____
7. sells _____
8. it _____
9. terrible _____
10. recently _____
11. so _____
12. we _____
13. time _____
14. an _____
15. alarm _____
16. manager _____
17. said _____
18. sadly _____

55.2 Words in context (B)

Is the underlined word a verb, a noun or an adjective?
- ☐ I'm going to the shop. — *noun*
- ☐ I don't want to shop on Saturday. — *verb*
1. The door was open. _____
2. The burglar didn't open the door. _____
3. You ought to fit an alarm. _____
4. Our best player isn't fit. _____
5. The alarm didn't ring. _____
6. The news will alarm everyone. _____

55.3 Determiners and pronouns (C)

Read the dialogues and write an example of each kind of word.

	DETERMINERS	PRONOUNS
What's the matter with that girl? ~ She's cut herself on a tin.	☐ Article: *the* ☐ Demonstrative: *that* ☐ Article: *a*	☐ Personal: *she*
Is this your bag? ~ No, I've got mine here.	1 Possessive: _____	2 Demonstrative: _____ 3 Personal: _____ 4 Possessive: _____
We'll need lots of plates. ~ There aren't many, I'm afraid.	5 Quantifier: _____	6 Personal: _____ 7 Quantifier: _____ 8 Personal: _____
What's this film about? ~ A man who loses all his money at Monte Carlo.	9 Demonstrative: _____ 10 Article: _____ 11 Quantifier: _____ 12 Possessive: _____	13 Relative: _____

56 The parts of a sentence: subject, object etc.

A Phrases

Look at this conversation:
- Sophie: *You look tired.*
- Ben: *I feel absolutely awful. This tooth is aching.*
- Sophie: *Well, I can give you an aspirin. We've got a bottle, I think.*
- Ben: *That's good.*
- Sophie: *It's somewhere upstairs. I think it's in the bathroom.*

Here are some examples of phrases from the conversation:
- Verb phrase: **look, is aching, can give**
- Noun phrase: **you, I, this tooth, an aspirin, the bathroom**
- Adjective phrase: **tired, absolutely awful**
- Adverb phrase: **somewhere upstairs**
- Prepositional phrase (preposition + noun phrase): **in the bathroom**

We use phrases to form sentences. A phrase is sometimes one word. For example, a noun phrase can be **this tooth** (two words) or **it** (one word). An adjective phrase or adverb phrase can be one word (e.g. **good**) or more (e.g. **very good**).

B Sentence patterns

The parts of a sentence are subject, verb, object, complement and adverbial. These are the main sentence patterns:

1	SUBJECT	VERB
	This tooth	is aching.

2	SUBJECT	VERB	OBJECT
	We	have got	a bottle.

3	SUBJECT	VERB	COMPLEMENT
	That	is	good.
	The pill	was	an aspirin.

4	SUBJECT	VERB	ADVERBIAL
	The aspirins	are	upstairs.
	The bottle	is	in the bathroom.

5	SUBJECT	VERB	OBJECT	OBJECT
	I	can give	you	an aspirin.

(For details about two objects see Unit 68.)

For the different parts of a sentence we use different kinds of phrases:
- Subject and object: noun phrase, e.g. **we, a bottle**
- Complement: adjective phrase (e.g. **good**) or noun phrase (e.g. **an aspirin**)
- Adverbial: adverb phrase (e.g. **upstairs**) or prepositional phrase (e.g. **in the bathroom**)

A complement (Pattern 3) comes after **be** and other linking verbs, e.g. **seem, appear, become, get, stay, look, sound, feel**. (For American English see p 289.)

C Adverbials

We can add adverbials (an adverb or prepositional phrase) to all the sentence patterns in B:
- *We have **probably** got a bottle **in the bathroom**.*
- *The aspirins are **usually** upstairs.*
- ***Of course** I can give you an aspirin.*

56 Exercises

56.1 Phrases (**A**)

Read this message on a postcard and then write each underlined phrase in the correct place.
Hi! We're having a super time. The hotel is very good. The food is OK. The weather is marvellous. We're outside by the pool at the moment. We might go on a trip into the country tomorrow. I'll see you on Saturday.

1 Verb phrases	2 Noun phrases	3 Adjective phrases	4 Adverb phrases	5 Prepositional phrases
_____	_a super time_	_____	_____	_____
_____	_____			

56.2 Sentence structure (**B**)

Look at each underlined phrase and say what part of the sentence it is: verb, subject, object, complement or adverbial.

☐ Jill had a good time. _object_
1 Everything was marvellous. _____
2 She really enjoyed it. _____
3 She liked the hotel. _____
4 Oh, I'm glad. _____
5 Her next break will be at Christmas. _____
6 That's a long time. _____

56.3 Sentence structure (**B**)

You are writing a postcard. Put the phrases in the right order.

☐ are – in this hotel – we _We are in this hotel._
1 I – must tell – the bad news – you _____
2 an awful place – is – this town _____
3 is – raining – it _____
4 very expensive – is – everything _____
5 hate – I – the food _____
6 is – on Friday – our last day _____

56.4 Adverbials (**C**)

Write down the two adverbial phrases in each sentence of this news item.

☐ Prince Charles opened a new youth centre in Stoke yesterday. _in Stoke_ / _yesterday_
1 He also spoke with several young people. _____
2 The £2 million centre was first planned in 1986. _____
3 Naturally, the local Council could not finance the project without help. _____
4 Fortunately the money was raised from sponsorship. _____

57 Count nouns (e.g. a **cup**) and mass nouns (e.g. **milk**)

A What is the difference?

Compare:

COUNT NOUNS
A count noun (e.g. **horse**) can be singular or plural. We can count horses. We can say *a horse* or *two horses*.

MASS NOUNS
A mass noun (e.g. **grass**) is neither singular nor plural. We cannot count grass. We can say **grass** but NOT ~~a grass~~ or ~~two grasses~~.

a horse   cow**s**   water   grass

Here are some examples of count nouns:
*a **horse**, **cows**, a **cup**, three **weeks**, four **days**, the **house**, an **idea**, a **problem**, a **meal**, two **newspapers***

Here are some examples of mass nouns:
water, grass, milk, bread, sugar, paper, money, music, literature, sadness.

A mass noun goes with a singular verb:
*The grass **is** nice and green.*
*This water **tastes** strange.*

Some nouns can be either count or mass. See Unit 58.

B Nouns after **the, a, some** etc.

There are some words that go with both count and mass nouns, e.g. **the**. We can say *the cow* (singular), *the cows* (plural) and *the water* (mass). We can also use **my, your** etc. with count and mass nouns (e.g. *my house, my cows* and *my money*).

This and **that** go with singular or mass nouns (e.g. *this horse, that water*). **These** and **those** go only with plural nouns (e.g. *these animals*).

A/an or **one** goes only with a singular noun. We can say *a horse* but NOT ~~a grass~~ or ~~a water~~.

Some and **any** go with plural or mass nouns (e.g. *some cows, some grass*). We can also use plural and mass nouns alone, without a word in front of them:
Cows eat grass.   *Money is always useful.*

Numbers above one go only with plural nouns (e.g. *six cows*). NOT ~~six waters~~ or ~~three musics~~.

A lot of goes with both plural and mass nouns. **Many** and **a few** go only with plural nouns (e.g. *many cows*), and **much** and **a little** only with mass nouns (e.g. *much grass*).

Adjectives can go with both count and mass nouns:
*a **white** horse   the **new** houses   some **hot** water   **brown** sugar*

57 Count nouns and mass nouns

Look at this summary:

	SINGULAR	PLURAL	MASS
Noun on its own		*fields*	*milk*
the	**the** *field*	**the** *fields*	**the** *milk*
my, your etc.	**my** *field*	**my** *fields*	**my** *milk*
this, that	**this** *field*		**this** *milk*
these, those		**these** *fields*	
a/an/one	**a** *field*		
some/any		**some** *fields*	**some** *milk*
two etc.		**four** *fields*	
a lot of		**a lot of** *fields*	**a lot of** *milk*
many, a few		**many** *fields*	
much, a little			**much** *milk*

C a glass of water, two pounds of butter etc.

We cannot use **a** or a number before a mass noun. We cannot say ~~a water~~ or ~~two butters~~. If we want to say how much water or how much butter, then we use a count noun + **of** (e.g. *a glass of water, two pounds of butter*). Here are some examples of count nouns in this pattern:

> a **cup of** coffee, a **glass of** wine, a **bottle of** milk, a **box of** matches, a **packet of** washing powder, a **tin of** soup, a **jar of** jam, a **tube of** toothpaste;
> five **metres of** cable, a **kilo of** sugar, twenty **litres of** petrol, half a **pound of** margarine;
> a **piece of** wood, a **slice of** toast, a **sheet of** paper, a **bar of** chocolate, a **loaf of** bread

We can also use this pattern with a plural noun after **of**, e.g. *a **packet of** crisps, five **pounds of** potatoes*.

D information, news etc.

Information, news and **advice** are mass nouns:
> We got **some information** from the tourist office. NOT ~~some informations~~
> I've just heard **some** great news. NOT ~~a great news~~
> Can I give you **some advice**? NOT ~~an advice~~

We can use **a piece of, a bit of, three items of**, etc. to say how much information:
> We got **two bits of information** from the tourist office.
> There's **an item of news** that might interest you.
> Can I give you **a piece of advice**?

Some other mass nouns are: **accommodation; behaviour; camping; equipment; fun; laughter; furniture; health; knowledge, education, research; leisure; luck; luggage, baggage; progress; rubbish, litter; scenery; traffic, travel, transport; weather; work, homework, housework.**
But some nouns with similar meanings are count nouns: ***a journey*** (NOT ~~a travel~~), ***a job*** (NOT ~~a work~~).

57 Exercises

57.1 What's the difference? (A)

What can you buy at the little shop on the corner? Look at the nouns and write two lists. Put the count nouns in the plural.

beer	crisp	mineral water	sweet
book	egg	newspaper	toilet paper
bread	magazine	pen	toothpaste
cigarette	milk	soap	washing powder

1 Count nouns
books,
_____
_____

2 Mass nouns
beer,
_____
_____

57.2 Nouns after **the, a, some** etc. (B)

Put in the correct form of the noun, with or without **s**.

A: You're a ☐ *student* at the ¹_____, aren't you?
B: Yes, I've been there six ²_____ now. I'm studying ³_____.
A: You've got a lot of ⁴_____.
B: Yes, I've just bought these ⁵_____. I spend too much on books, you know. Quite often I have no money left to buy ⁶_____.
A: Why don't you get a ⁷_____ at ⁸_____ and earn some ⁹_____. Not eating can't be much ¹⁰_____.
B: Well, I paint ¹¹_____ sometimes. I've sold a few to some of my ¹²_____.

☐ student
1 university
2 month
3 literature
4 book
5 paperback

6 food
7 job
8 weekend 9 money
10 fun
11 picture
12 friend

57.3 **a bottle of milk** etc. (C)

Say what the customer bought. Use a count noun + **of**.

```
    COOKING OIL      0.74
    COOKING OIL      0.74
  1 KILO FLOUR       0.69
    JAM              0.72
    MATCHES          0.39
    BREAD            0.65
    BREAD            0.65
    CHOCOLATE        0.95
  5 KILOS POTATOES   1.59
    WASHING POWDER   1.38
    MILK             0.35
    MILK             0.35
    TOOTHPASTE       0.89

  TOTAL            £10.09
```

☐ *two bottles of cooking oil*
☐ *a kilo of flour*
1 _____
2 _____
3 _____
4 _____
5 _____
6 _____
7 _____
8 _____

57.4 information, news etc. (D)

Complete the sentences. Put in **a/an** or **some**.

☐ I really ought to do _some_ housework.
1. The people who camped in the field have left _____ rubbish.
2. I've been working on my essay. I think I've made _____ progress.
3. That isn't right. Look, you've made _____ mistake.
4. I'm here for two nights, and I'm looking for _____ accommodation.
5. The room is quite empty. We need _____ furniture.
6. The second-hand shop had _____ sofa.
7. You pay extra for the taxi if you've got _____ luggage.
8. I can't fit this guitar into _____ suitcase.
9. The scientists are doing _____ interesting experiment.
10. They are doing _____ research into radioactivity.
11. You need _____ luck to win at this game.
12. I'm just about to set off on _____ long journey.

57.5 Count nouns and mass nouns (A–D)

Put in the correct form.
1. Would you like to play _____?   1 a music/some music
2. There seemed to be a lot of _____   2 traffic/traffics
   on the road.
3. I've just had _____.   3 an idea/some idea
4. I'm afraid I've got _____ to do.   4 some work/a work
5. Let me give you _____.   5 an advice/some advice
6. We've got a bit of _____ I'm afraid. 6 problem/a problem
7. Do you need _____ information?   7 an/any
8. Ian hasn't been in _____ lately.   8 good health/a good health

57.6 Count nouns and mass nouns (A–D)

Carol and Roger are talking about their holiday. Complete the sentences. Use **a/an** or **some** with these words: **day, fun, terrible journey, meal, money, lovely scenery, nice weather**.

☐ (They won £100 in a lottery.)
   'We won _some money_ in a lottery.'
1. (The sun shone most of the time.)
   'We had _____ while we were there.'
2. (One evening they went out to a restaurant with some other people.)
   'We had _____ with some people we met.'
3. (They enjoyed themselves.)
   'We had _____.'
4. (They went up into the mountains one morning and came back in the evening.)
   'We spent _____ in the mountains.'
5. (They saw a beautiful part of the country.)
   'We saw _____ when we went on a trip.'
6. (Travelling home was awful.)
   'We had _____ home.'

58   Count or mass?

A   A cake or cake?

Some nouns can be either count or mass. For example, **an onion** (count noun) is a separate, individual thing, but **onion** (mass noun) is a kind of food. Compare:

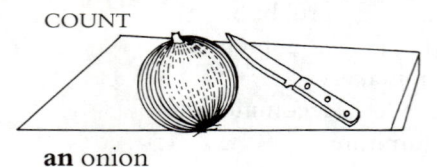

COUNT — **an** onion

MASS — onion

Here are some more examples to compare:

COUNT	MASS
Have **an apple**.	Is there **apple** in this salad?
Dave baked **a cake**.	Have **some cake**.
Someone threw **a stone**.	The house is built of **stone**.

B   A sport or sport?

Often the count noun (e.g. **a sport**) means one specific example, and the mass noun (e.g. **sport**) means something in general. Compare:

COUNT	MASS
Volleyball is **a sport**.	Do you like **sport**?
That's **a nice painting**.	Alice is good at **painting**.
We heard **a sudden noise**.	**Noise** can make you ill.
She had **an interesting life**.	**Life** is too short to do everything.

C   An ice or ice?

Some nouns can be count or mass with different meanings:

COUNT	MASS
an ice (= an ice-cream)	**ice** on the road
a paper (= a newspaper)	**some paper** to write on
a glass of orange juice	**some glass** for the window
an iron (for ironing clothes)	**iron** and steel (a metal)
The **lights** came on.	the speed of **light**
There's **a hair** in my soup.	Brush your **hair**. (NOT ~~your hairs~~)
I know this place. I've been here lots of **times** before.	I'm in a hurry. I haven't got much **time**.
The journey was **a great experience**.	He has enough **experience** for the job.
a small business (= a company)	to do **business** (= to buy and sell)

D   A coffee or a cup of coffee?

Words for drink are usually mass nouns, but they can be count nouns when we are offering or ordering drinks. We can say **a coffee** instead of **a cup of coffee**:

   Would you like **a beer**? (= a **glass of** beer)   **Two teas**, please. (= two **cups of** tea)

Some mass nouns can be count when we mean 'what kind':

   the **wines** of Italy (= different **kinds of** Italian wine)
   the use of **plastics** (= different **kinds of** plastic)

58 Exercises

58.1 A cake or cake? A sport or sport? (A,B)

Put in the correct form.

☐ I heard _an apple_ fall from the tree.
1. I think _____ is boring.
2. I find that _____ helps me to relax. I paint quite often.
3. Laura went into the vegetable garden to dig _____.
4. _____ woke me up in the night.
5. Is there _____ in this soup?
6. I had _____ with Alan last night.
7. I'll put _____ in your sandwiches.
8. If you're a pacifist, you don't believe in _____.
9. _____ isn't fair sometimes.
10. You've got _____ on your shirt.

☐ an apple/ some apple
1. sport/a sport
2. painting/a painting
3. some potato/some potatoes
4. Noise/A noise
5. cheese/a cheese
6. conversation/a conversation
7. a chicken/some chicken
8. war/a war
9. Life/A life
10. some egg/some eggs

58.2 An ice or ice? (C)

Put in these words: **business, experience, glass, ice, iron, light, paper, time**.

Use **a/an** before a count noun and **some** before a mass noun.

☐ Seeing the Grand Canyon was certainly _an experience_.
1. Neil hadn't gone to bed yet. There was _____ on in the sitting-room.
2. I must just write a few notes. I've got a pen, but could you give me _____, please?
3. After lunch we spent _____ in the National Museum.
4. It's freezing outside. I slipped on _____ and nearly fell down.
5. We aren't going to take _____ with us. I refuse to do any washing on my holiday.
6. I'll pour you a lemonade as soon as I can find _____.
7. Pamela works very long hours. She runs _____ of her own now.

58.3 A coffee and plastics (D)

Say whether the meaning is **cup of, glass of**, etc. or **different kinds of**.

☐ I'll have a beer.   = _a glass of beer_
☐ I'm reading about the use of metals.   = _different kinds of metal_
1. Two coffees, please.   = _____
2. It's an article about French cheeses.   = _____
3. Could you get me an orange juice?   = _____
4. Which of these medicines would be best? = _____
5. I'd better order an extra milk from the milkman. = _____

59 Agreement (e.g. **My foot hurts/My feet hurt**.)

A Subject and verb

There is agreement between a subject and a verb when the verb is **is/are, was/were, has/have** or present simple (e.g. **tastes/taste**). Compare:

SUBJECT	VERB
The **window**	**is** open.
The **road**	**was** wet.
It	**has** been raining.
The **soup**	**tastes** good.

After a singular or mass noun and after **he, she** or **it**, we use a singular verb.

SUBJECT	VERB
The **windows**	**are** open.
The **roads**	**were** wet.
They	**have** repaired the fence.
The **biscuits**	**taste** nice.

After a plural noun or **they**, we use a plural verb.

After two nouns joined by **and**, we use a plural verb:
   *The door **and** window **are** open.*

B **everyone, something** etc. and **every, all** etc.

After **everyone, something** etc. the verb is singular:
   *Everyone **was** pleased by the news.*   *Something **is** wrong.*

But compare:

We use a singular verb after a phrase with **every** or **each**:
   *Every seat **has** a number.*
   *Each door **is** a different colour.*

We use a plural verb after **all** and a plural noun:
   *All the seats **have** a number.*

C **one of, a number of** and **a lot of**

After **one of** ... the verb is singular:
   *One of the photos **is** missing.*

After **a number of** ... the verb is normally plural:
   *A number of questions **were** asked.*

After **a lot of** ... the verb agrees with the noun:
   *A lot of **wood is** burnt.*   *A lot of **trees are** cut down.*

D **any of, either of, neither of** and **none of**

When a plural noun comes after **any of, either of, neither of** and **none of**, we can use a singular or plural verb:
   Is (OR Are) any of these old maps worth keeping?
   I wonder if either of those alternatives is (OR are) a good idea.
   Neither (of these cameras) works (OR work) properly.
   None (of the plants) has (OR have) grown very much.

E An amount + singular verb

We use a singular verb after an amount of money, a distance, a weight or a length of time:
   *Twelve pounds **is** our sale price.*   *A hundred metres **isn't** far from the beach.*
   *Two hours **seems** a long time to have to wait for the next train.*
We are talking about the amount as a whole, not the individual pounds or hours.

59 Exercises

59.1 Subject and verb (A)

Complete the conversation. Put in the correct form.

A: This table □ *is* lovely, look. The wood ¹_____ beautiful.
B: Yes, these chairs ²_____ very stylish too.
A: But they ³_____ rather expensive.
B: And ⁴_____ the table got a price on it?
A: Yes, it ⁵_____ £300.
B: I'm sure prices ⁶_____ gone up. Things ⁷_____ so expensive last year.

□ is/are 1 is/are
2 looks/look
3 is/are
4 has/have
5 costs/cost
6 has/have
7 wasn't/weren't

59.2 everyone, every etc. and phrases with of (B–D)

Put in **was** or **were**.

'We really enjoyed the party. All the rooms ¹_____ crowded with people. Everyone ²_____ enjoying themselves. A lot of people ³_____ dancing. All the people there ⁴_____ very smart. One of the guests ⁵_____ quite well-known; he was the actor Melvyn Harper. Each guest ⁶_____ welcomed by the hostess in person. It's a lovely house, you know. A number of people ⁷_____ swimming in the pool in the garden. I didn't know many of the guests. None of my friends ⁸_____ there.

59.3 Agreement (A–D)

A policeman is talking about his job. Put in the correct form.

1 Every policeman _____ given special training for the job.
2 Each day _____ different from the one before.
3 A number of police officers here _____ with dogs.
4 A lot of people _____ a wrong image of police work.
5 Not all policemen _____ allowed to carry guns.
6 None of the officers here _____ allowed to have guns.
7 Crime _____ exciting or glamorous.
8 One of our jobs _____ to help prevent crime.
9 A lot of crime _____ caused by people being careless.
10 I must go. Someone _____ just reported a robbery.

1 is/are
2 is/are
3 works/work
4 has/have
5 is/are
6 is/are
7 isn't/aren't
8 is/are
9 is/are
10 has/have

59.4 An amount + singular verb (E)

Put in **is** or **are**.

□ Eighty pounds a week *is* not a good wage.
□ Ten days in the year *are* public holidays.
1 Ten miles _____ quite a long walk.
2 Ten students _____ in the group going to France.
3 Three tourists _____ waiting for the museum to open.
4 Most of our luggage is here, but three suitcases _____ missing.
5 Forty six grammes _____ the maximum weight of a golf ball.

60 Singular or plural?

A clothes etc.

Some nouns have only a plural form (with **s**) and take a plural verb:
   The **clothes were** hanging on the line. NOT *The clothe was* ...
   The **goods have** been sent to you by post. NOT *The good has* ...
   My **belongings are** all packed up in suitcases.

> Plural nouns:
> **clothes; goods, belongings; earnings** (= money you earn);
> **surroundings** (= things around you), **outskirts** (= outer part of a town);
> **customs** (when you enter a country); **troops** (= soldiers), **arms** (= weapons);
> **contents** (= what is inside something); **remains** (= what is left);
> **thanks, congratulations**

Some nouns have a singular and a plural form with a difference in meaning:

SINGULAR	PLURAL
Our price means a **saving** of £10.	My **savings** are in the bank.
The storm did a lot of **damage**.	The airline had to pay **damages** to the families of passengers who died.
I get a lot of **pain** in my back.	I took great **pains** to get the figures exactly right.

B news etc.

Some nouns have a plural form (with **s**) but take a singular verb:
   The **news was** worse than I expected. NOT *The news were* ...
   Politics is an interesting subject. NOT *Politics are* ...

> Nouns taking a singular verb:
> **news;**
> the subjects: **politics, economics, mathematics, statistics, physics;**
> the activities: **athletics, gymnastics;**
> the games: **billiards, darts, dominoes;**
> the illness: **measles**

C means etc.

Some nouns have the same singular and plural form:
   This means of transport **is** expensive.
   Both **these means** of transport **are** expensive.

> Nouns with one form:
> **means; works** (= factory/factories), **headquarters** (= main office), **crossroads;**
> **series** (e.g. a **series** of TV documentaries); **species** (= kind, type)

60 Exercises

60.1 clothes etc. (A)

Put in the nouns and add **s** if necessary.

☐ We had to take our luggage through _customs_ .   ☐ custom
1. Please accept this gift as an expression of our _____.   1 thank
2. The woman is demanding _____ for her injuries.   2 damage
3. The _____ was so bad I called the doctor.   3 pain
4. The old man carried his few _____ in a plastic bag.   4 belonging
5. The man twisted Tim's left _____ behind his back.   5 arm
6. If we pay in cash, we make a _____ of 10%.   6 saving
7. More _____ should travel by rail instead of by road.   7 good
8. The explosion caused some _____.   8 damage
9. We're going to spend all our _____ on a new car.   9 saving
10. The company always takes _____ to protect its image.   10 pain

60.2 clothes, news etc. (A,B)

Put in the correct verb form.

☐ The television news _is_ at ten o'clock.   ☐ is/are
☐ These clothes _are_ the latest fashion.   ☐ is/are
1. Maths _____ my favourite subject.   1 is/are
2. The troops _____ involved in a training exercise.   2 was/were
3. The contents of the case _____ disappeared.   3 has/have
4. Darts _____ often played in pubs.   4 is/are
5. The athletics we watched _____ quite exciting.   5 was/were
6. The remains of the meal _____ thrown in the bin.   6 was/were
7. Carol's earnings _____ as much as she would like.   7 isn't/aren't
8. Physics _____ to interest Janet.   8 seems/seem

60.3 clothes, news, means etc. (A–C)

Put in the correct form of the nouns and verbs.
Dear Maureen,

☐ _Thanks_ for your letter. We're living in the   ☐ thank/s
1_____ of the 2_____ about three   1 outskirt/s   2 town/s
3_____ from the 4_____. Our new house is   3 mile/s   4 centre/s
quite nice, but the surroundings 5_____ very   5 isn't/aren't
pleasant. We're on a busy 6_____, near a paint   6 crossroad/s
7_____ and a steel 8_____. I'm   7 factory/ies   8 work/s
back at 9_____ doing the course I told you   9 university/ies
about. Statistics 10_____ an easy subject, I find, but   10 is/are
11_____ is very difficult! The other students   11 economic/s
are all very nice. Mike works at the company
12_____ now. There's a good sports and social   12 headquarter/s
club. Lots of people do 13_____. We play   13 athletic/s
14_____ at weekends, and sometimes Mike   14 tennis/es
has a game of 15_____. Come and see us soon.   15 billiard/s
Love, Kate.

61 Pair nouns (e.g. **trousers**) and group nouns (e.g. **team**)

A Pair nouns

We use a pair noun for some things made of two parts which are the same. Pair nouns are: **jeans, trousers, shorts, pants, tights; pyjamas; glasses, binoculars; scissors**.

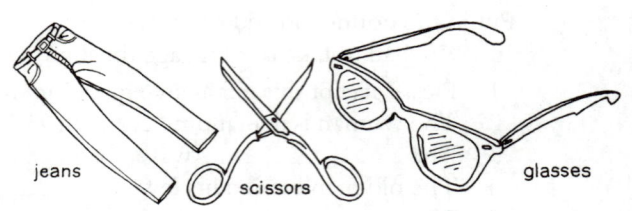

A pair noun is plural and takes a plural verb:
*My **jeans need** washing.* NOT *My jean* ...
***These tights were** quite cheap.* NOT *This tight* ...
*We've got **some scissors** somewhere.* NOT ... *a scissor* ...

We cannot use **a/an** or a number with a pair noun. But we can use **pair of**:
*I bought **a pair of** jeans.* NOT *a jean*
*I bought **four pairs of** tights.* NOT *four tights*

B Group nouns

A group noun refers to a group of people. It can take a singular or a plural verb:
*The **team was** playing well.* OR *The **team were** playing well.*
The choice depends on whether we see the group as a whole or as a number of individuals. (But for American English see p 289.) Compare:

We always use the singular when we mean a whole group:	We normally use the plural for the feelings and thoughts of the people in the group:
*The **family is** a very old and famous one.*	*The **family are** delighted with their presents.*
*The **orchestra consists** of eighty-six musicians.*	*The **orchestra don't** know what to play.*

We use **it** and **its** with the singular and **they** and **their** with the plural:
*The **committee has** made **its** decision.*
*The **class** will miss **their** lessons because **they are** all going on a trip.*

Some common group nouns are: **group; crowd; team, club; public, population, community; government, council, committee; army, enemy; company, firm; union, management; staff, crew** (of a ship); **family; class, school, college, university; orchestra, choir; audience; press** (= newspapers); **majority, minority**. Also **the BBC, the United Nations, Harrod's** etc. and **England** (= the England team).

C **police, people** and **cattle**

These nouns have a plural meaning and take a plural verb:
*The **police have** warned motorists to take extra care.*
***People don't** agree with the idea.*
*The **cattle are** going to be sold with the farm.*

61 Exercises

61.1 Pair nouns (A)

Complete the conversation. Put in the correct form of the verb.

Keith: These trousers ¹_____ a bit tight. And I think the blue ones ²_____ better with the jacket.
Jill: That jacket ³_____ too long.
Keith: Well, the jeans ⁴_____ all right. Perhaps I'll buy the jeans instead.
Jill: Yes, the jeans ⁵_____ good on you. I like the style. They really ⁶_____ you.

1 feels/feel
2 goes/go
3 is/are
4 fits/fit
5 looks/look
6 suits/suit

61.2 Pair nouns (A)

Put in the correct words.

▢ I'm long-sighted, I wear _glasses_ to read.
1 You can't wear _____ to a job interview.
2 There must be two _____ in the wash.
3 I need a _____ to spread the butter.
4 I need _____ to cut this article out.
5 I found a _____ in the drawer.
6 I'm going to buy _____.

▢ a glass/glasses
1 a jean/jeans
2 shorts/pairs of shorts
3 knife/pair of knives
4 a scissor/some scissors
5 tights/pair of tights
6 a pyjama/some pyjamas

61.3 Group nouns (B)

Put in the correct form of the verb.

The ICB Company ¹_____ just announced that it made a big loss last year. The management ²_____ well aware that they have made mistakes. The press ³_____ all printing stories about ICB's problems. The ICB Board ⁴_____ that they have some difficult decisions to take. The staff ⁵_____ worried about their jobs and ⁶_____ a meeting with management. The engineers' union ⁷_____ promised to do its best to help ICB workers.

1 have/has
2 is/are
3 is/are
4 knows/know
5 is/are
6 wants/want
7 has/have

61.4 Group nouns (B,C)

Put in a group noun and **is** or **are**. Use these nouns:
audience, choir, club, crew, crowd, police, population.

▢ The _crowd are_ really enjoying the game.
1 This sports _____ the most popular one in this area.
2 The _____ hoping to take part in a national singing contest.
3 The _____ very tired after a long sea voyage.
4 The country's _____ increasing rapidly, mainly because of immigration.
5 The _____ one of the biggest we have ever had for one of our concerts.
6 The _____ looking into the robberies.

62 a/an or the?

Look at this newspaper story:
> *A farmer*, Mr Richard Culver, has found **a cup** worth £5000. He found **the cup** two weeks ago when he was driving **a tractor** across **a field** on his farm. It is **a gold cup** at least 3500 years old, experts say. Now **the government** is going to pay Mr Culver £5000, and **the cup** will go to **a museum**. 'It's **the best news** I've had for **a long time**,' said Mr Culver. 'This is **a great day** for me and my wife. We're going to spend part of **the money** on **a holiday**.'

A a/an and the in context

When the story first mentions a thing, the noun has **a** or **an**:
> *A farmer has found **a cup**.*

This phrase is new information. We do not know <u>which</u> cup.

When the same thing is mentioned again, the noun has **the**:
> *He found **the cup** two weeks ago.*

This phrase is old information. Now we know <u>which</u> cup – the one we are talking about.

We use **the** when it is clear from the context <u>which</u> one we mean. Compare:

a/an	the
Would you like to see **a show**? (We don't say which show.)	Would you like to see **the show**? (= the show we are talking about)
The boy was knocked down by **a car**. (We don't say which car.)	Whose is **the car parked outside**? (**Parked outside** tells us <u>which</u> car.)

In some contexts there is only one, and so we use **the**:
> **The sun** was going down.   **The government** is unpopular.

Also: **the sky, the earth, the sea, the coast, the weather**

Now compare these examples:

a/an	the
In the office **a phone** was ringing. (This office has lots of phones.)	I was in bed when **the phone** rang. (My house has one phone.)
Has Tim's house got **a garden**? (We do not know if there is one.)	Tim was at home in **the garden**. (He has one garden.)
We're buying **a new door**.	There was a knock at **the door**.
The train stopped at **a station**. (We don't know which station.)	Turn left here for **the station**. (= the station in this town)
We took **a taxi**.	We went in **the car**. (= our/your car)
Is there **a doctor** in the audience?	I'm going to **the doctor**. (= my doctor)
We could hear **a noise**.	We could hear **the noise** of a party.
I wrote the number on **an envelope**.	I wrote it on **the back** of an envelope.
A/an goes only with a singular noun. We use **some** with a plural or a mass noun: He found **a coin** in a field. He found **some coins** in a field. He found **some money** in a field. We use **some** (like **a/an**) when we do not know <u>which</u>.	**The** goes with both singular and plural nouns and with mass nouns: He took **the coin** to the local museum. He took **the coins** to a local museum. He took **the money** to the police station. We use **the** when we know <u>which</u>.

62 a/an or the?

B Indefinite and definite phrases

A/an and **someone/something** are indefinite (we don't say which one). **The** and **he/she/it** are definite (we know which one).

A farmer (OR *Someone*) found a cup in a field. ***The** farmer* (OR ***He***) took the cup to a museum.
Phil wrote ***a** note* (OR ***something***) on a piece of paper. ***The** note* (OR ***It***) was a message about the disco.

C a/an to describe or classify

A phrase which describes something has **a/an**:
*It was **a gold cup**.*   *This is **a lovely flower**.*
*This is **a nicer colour**.*   *It's been **a bad day**.*

We also use **a/an** to say what something is, to classify it:
*The play was **a comedy**.*   *Kent is **a county** in south-east England.*

We use **a/an** to say what someone's job is:
*Mr Culver is **a farmer**.* NOT *... is farmer.*   *She's **an engineer**.* NOT *She's engineer.*

But we use **the** with superlatives:
*It's **the best news** I've had for a long time.*   *You're **the fastest runner** here, aren't you?*

D a or an?

The form of **a/an** and **the** depends on the next sound:

a [ə] / **the** [ðə] + consonant sound				**an** [ən] / **the** [ðɪ] + vowel sound			
a cup	[k]	*the* [ðə] cup		*an* aspirin	[æ]	*the* [ðɪ] aspirin	
a picnic	[p]	*the* [ðə] picnic		*an* exam	[e]	*the* [ðɪ] exam	
a shop	[ʃ]	etc.		*an* Indian	[ɪ]	etc.	
a maths exam	[m]			*an* old photo	[əʊ]		
a record	[r]			*an* umbrella	[ʌ]		

It is the sound of the next word that matters, not the spelling:

a one-way street	[w]		*an* open door	[əʊ]
a uniform	[j]		*an* uncle	[ʌ]
a holiday	[h]		*an* hour	[aʊ]
a U shape	[j]		*an* MP	[e]

E a/an or one?

A/an and **one** both refer to one thing. Using **one** emphasizes the number.
*The farmer found **a cup** (not a bowl).*
*The farmer found **one cup** (not two).*

We use **one** (not **a/an**) when we mean one of a larger number:
***One coin** was gold, but the others were silver.*   ***One of the fields** had cows in it.*

62 Exercises

62.1 a/an and the in context (A)

Put in **a** or **the**.

☐ Look outside. _The_ sky is getting very dark. ~ I hope there isn't going to be _a_ storm.

1. Is there _____ table I can put these parcels on? ~ Oh, just put them on _____ floor, can you?
2. Would you like _____ tomato? There's one in _____ fridge. ~ Oh, yes please. I'll make myself _____ cheese and tomato sandwich.
3. Can you post these letters for me? ~ I'll take them to _____ main post office. I have to go into _____ town centre in any case.
4. I have to get _____ visa. Do you know where _____ passport office is? Someone told me it's in this building. ~ Yes, it's on _____ fifth floor. _____ lift is along the corridor. ~ Oh, thank you.
5. Why haven't we got _____ swimming-pool in this area? I like _____ swim now and again. ~ Yes, I think _____ Council should build one, shouldn't they?
6. I've got _____ pain in my stomach. I've had it all day. ~ Perhaps you ought to go and see _____ doctor. He'll be at the Health Centre until six.
7. It's my lucky day. I've found _____ ten-pound note on the pavement. ~ Well, you really ought to take it down to _____ police station.

62.2 Indefinite and definite phrases (B)

Replace the underlined words. Put in **a, an** or **the** with these nouns:
article, bomb, criminal, game, pedestrian, pizza, teacher, waitress.

☐ We had <u>something</u> for lunch.   _We had a pizza for lunch._
☐ <u>She</u> dropped the plates.   _The waitress dropped the plates._

1. We played <u>it</u> on holiday.   _____
2. <u>Someone</u> stepped into the road. _____
3. I read <u>something</u> in the paper. _____
4. <u>It</u> exploded at midnight.   _____
5. The pupils didn't like <u>him</u>.   _____
6. The police arrested <u>someone</u>.   _____

62.3 a/an or the? (A,C)

Complete this true story. Put in **a, an** or **the**.

¹_____ man walked into ²_____ bank in America and handed ³_____ note to one of the cashiers, ⁴_____ young woman. ⁵_____ woman read ⁶_____ note, which told her to give ⁷_____ man some money. Afraid that he might have ⁸_____ gun, she followed ⁹_____ instruction. ¹⁰_____ man then walked out of ¹¹_____ building, leaving ¹²_____ note behind. However, it was not ¹³_____ successful crime. ¹⁴_____ man had no time to spend ¹⁵_____ money because he was arrested ¹⁶_____ same day. He had made ¹⁷_____ stupid mistake. He had written ¹⁸_____ note on ¹⁹_____ back of ²⁰_____ envelope. On ²¹_____ other side of ²²_____ envelope was ²³_____ man's name and address. This information was quite enough for the police to get their man.

62.4 a/an or the? (A,C)

Put in **a, an** or **the**.

☐ How was your trip to _the_ coast? ~ Wonderful. _The_ sun shone all day. We had _a_ great time.

1. Is this _____ film that you videoed yesterday? ~ That's right. ~ What's it about? ~ Oh, it's _____ Western.
2. Would you like _____ cigarette? ~ I don't smoke, thanks. ~ It's _____ bad habit.
3. Does your brother work? Has he got _____ job? ~ Yes, he's _____ soldier. He's in _____ army. It's _____ great life, he says.
4. Do you go to Dr Palmer? ~ Yes, he's _____ best doctor I've ever had. ~ He's very nice. You couldn't meet _____ nicer man.
5. You were _____ long time at _____ supermarket. ~ Yes, I was. I was in _____ enormous queue.
6. There isn't a playing-field in _____ village. Do you think it would be _____ good idea for us to have one? ~ Yes, if we can get _____ money to buy some land.
7. Why were you so late? ~ Well, I took _____ taxi from _____ airport to _____ hotel where I was staying and _____ driver got completely lost. _____ man was _____ real idiot.

62.5 a or an? (D)

Put in the abbreviations.

☐ A Personal Assistant — _a PA_
☐ A Member of Parliament — _an MP_
1. A Disc Jockey — _____
2. A Very Important Person — _____
3. An Intelligence Quotient — _____
4. A Public Relations Officer — _____
5. A State Registered Nurse — _____
6. An Unidentified Flying Object — _____
7. An Annual General Meeting — _____
8. A Local Education Authority — _____

62.6 a/an or one? (E)

Put in **a** or **one**.

1. I was thirsty. I was looking for _____ shop where I could buy something to drink.
2. It was Sunday. _____ shop was open, but all the others were closed.
3. _____ of these photos is of you. Would you like it?
4. Would you like me to take _____ photo of the two of you? ~ Oh, thank you. That would be very kind.
5. The old woman fell downstairs. Unfortunately she broke _____ leg and was taken to hospital.
6. The climber broke _____ leg, not both his legs as we thought at first.

63 General statements

A Singular nouns

We can make general statements with **a/an** or **the** and a singular noun:
  A tiger can be dangerous.   *The tiger* is a dangerous animal.
Here *a tiger* and *the tiger* mean all tigers, tigers in general. We usually use **the** in scientific, formal and academic contexts. **A/an** with a singular noun is more informal.

Here are some more examples:
  A dishwasher can be very useful.   *The fly* is a common insect.
  A butcher is someone who sells meat.   Who invented *the camera*?

B cars or the cars? money or the money?

We can also use a plural noun (e.g. **cars**) or a mass noun (e.g. **money**) with a general meaning. Compare the nouns on their own and with **the**:

A plural noun on its own has a general meaning:	With **the**, a plural noun has a specific meaning:
GENERAL	SPECIFIC
Cars are expensive to buy.	*The cars* were both damaged in the accident.
Tigers are dangerous animals.	We saw *the tigers* at Bristol Zoo.
I like *birds*. I often go bird-watching.	I put some bread out for *the birds*. (= the birds in our garden)
Computers save time.	At work *the computers* often fail.
A mass noun on its own also has a general meaning:	A mass noun with **the** also has a specific meaning:
GENERAL	SPECIFIC
You always need *money*.	I paid *the money* into my bank account.
Glass is made from sand.	Dave swept up *the broken glass*.
Do you like *cricket*?	He was listening to *the cricket* on the radio.
Curry is an Indian food.	*The curry* was delicious, thank you.
I am studying *maths, physics* and *music*.	They had *the music* on very loud.

A phrase or clause after the noun often makes it specific:

GENERAL	SPECIFIC
Oil is the life-blood of industry.	*The oil in the garage* is motor oil.
Oranges have Vitamin C.	*The oranges I got yesterday* were nice.

Notice that before an adjective + noun with a general meaning we do not use **the**. But we use **the** before a noun + **of** phrase with the same meaning. Compare:
  adjective + noun: *I'm reading a book on **Irish history**.*
  noun + **of** phrase: *I'm reading a book on **the history of Ireland**.*

C Special uses of the

We can also use **the** with musical instruments, means of transport, and with **country(side), seaside, cinema, theatre** and **radio**.
  Tina can play *the piano*   I usually go to work on *the bus*.
  I love *the countryside* in autumn.   Do you ever go to *the theatre*?
  We listen to *the radio* a lot. (But: *We watch **television**.*)

63 Exercises

63.1 General statements with **the** (A)

Write sentences from the notes, using **the**.

☐ Rutherford – split – atom   *Rutherford split the atom.*
1. A Dutchman – invent – submarine
2. Galileo – invent – telescope
3. A Frenchman – develop – IQ test
4. Thomson – discover – electron
5. A Scotsman – invent – bicycle

63.2 General statements with **a/an** (A)

Match each word with the right explanation and write sentences with **a/an**.

carrot	line of people
violin	fruit
queue	vegetable
apple	answer to a problem
pistol	musical instrument
solution	kind of gun

☐ *A carrot is a vegetable.*
1.
2.
3.
4.
5.

63.3 **cars** or **the cars**? **money** or **the money**? (B)

Complete the conversations. Put in the plural and mass nouns on the right. Decide if you need **the**.

☐ Did you see _the football_ on television last night? ~ No, I hate _football_. I was watching _the news_ on the other channel.   ☐ football, football, news

1. Is Hamley's the shop that sells things for _____? ~ Yes, it sells _____ and _____.   1 children, toys, games

2. You're always reading books about _____. ~ Yes, I'm interested in _____ of this country. ~ I was glad to give up _____. I prefer _____.   2 history, history, history, geography

3. _____ is a problem everywhere these days. ~ Yes, _____ is responsible for _____ of our air and water.   3 pollution, industry, pollution

63.4 Special uses of **the** (C)

Put in the words. Decide if you need **the**.

1. (radio)   I heard the news on _____ .
2. (television)   The children watch _____ most of the time.
3. (basketball)   We play _____ at college.
4. (guitar)   Can you play _____ ?
5. (country)   Would you rather live in a town or in _____ ?

64 go to school, stay in bed etc.

A school or the school?

Compare:

WITHOUT **the**	WITH **the**
With some nouns we do not use **the** when we talk about the normal purpose of a building or other place:	We use **the** when we mean a specific building or thing:
School is over at four o'clock. (**School** = school activities)	*The school is near the park.*
*The injured man is in **hospital**.* (He is there as a patient.)	*There are 200 beds in **the hospital**.*
*The gang are in **prison** now.* (They are there as prisoners.)	*The visitors are in **the prison** now.*
*Sarah is going to **church**.* (She is going to a service.)	*We went to **the church**, but we couldn't get in because it was locked.*
*I felt ill, so I stayed in **bed**.* (I was sleeping or resting.)	***The bed** was very expensive.*

B Notes on individual nouns

	WITHOUT **the**	WITH **the**
school	*in/at school* (as a pupil) *go to school* (as a pupil)	
class	*do work in class*	
university	*at university* (as a student) *go to university* (as a student)	in the USA always: *at/to the university*
college	*at/to college* (as a student) *go to college* (as a student)	
prison	*in prison* (as a prisoner) *go to prison* (as a prisoner)	
jail	*in/to jail* (as a prisoner) *go to jail* (as a prisoner)	
hospital	*in hospital* (as a patient) *go to hospital* (as a patient)	in the USA always: *in the hospital* But: *at the hospital* (as a visitor)
church	*in/at church* (at a service) *go to church* (to a service)	
market	*take animals to market*	But: *at/in the market*; *put a house on the market* (= offer it for sale)
town	*in town*; *go to town*; *leave town* (your home town)	But: *in the town centre*
home	*at home*; *go/come home*	But: *in/to the house*
work	*go to work*; *leave work*; *at work*	But: *the office*; *the factory*
bed	*in bed*; *go to bed*	But: *sit on the bed*; *make the bed*
sea	*at sea* (= sailing); *go to sea* (as a sailor)	But: *on the sea*; *by the sea*; *at the seaside*

We do not leave out **the** before other nouns for buildings and places e.g. **the station**, **the shop**, **the cinema**, **the library**, **the pub**, **the city**, **the village**.

64 Exercises

64.1 school or the school? (A)

Put in the words. Decide if you need **the**.
- □ (school)   The children go to _school_ every morning.
- □ (school)   The parents are going to _the school_ to a meeting.
- 1 (hospital)   My sister is a nurse at _____ .
- 2 (hospital)   My father isn't very well. He's in _____ .
- 3 (prison)   The murderer went to _____ .
- 4 (prison)   The prisoner's wife drove to _____ .
- 5 (church)   Brian goes to _____ on Sundays.
- 6 (church)   The tourists went to _____ to look round it.
- 7 (bed)   Tim walked over to _____ and sat down on it.
- 8 (bed)   Tim was tired, so he went to _____ early.

64.2 go to school, stay in bed etc. (A, B)

Complete the sentences. Use **in**, **at** or **to** and these words:
bed, church, home, hospital, library, market, prison, seaside, town, work.
Decide if you need **the**.
- □ We haven't got any food. I'd better go _to town_ and do some shopping.
- □ These apples were cheap. I bought them _in the market_ .
- 1 The weather is too bad to go out. I'm staying _____ today.
- 2 I had an early night last night. I was _____ at ten.
- 3 Kate has just had a baby. We're going _____ to visit her.
- 4 Mr and Mrs Lee are religious. They go _____ every Sunday.
- 5 We like lying on the beach. We always spend our holidays _____ .
- 6 I don't like my job. I just go _____ to earn a living.
- 7 I'm taking these books back _____ .
- 8 The men who robbed the bank are no longer _____ . They were let out last month.

64.3 go to school, stay in bed etc. (A, B)

Complete this paragraph. Put in the words with or without **the**.

Alan Broome
Today Alan Broome is a world-famous actor. Forty years ago he was an unhappy child. He didn't do well at □ _school_ , and he never went to ¹_____ . His greatest pleasure was to go to ²_____ . The family lived in an unattractive Midland town. Their home was next to ³_____ . Alan's father was a sailor, and he spent months at ⁴_____ . He was seldom at ⁵_____ . When he was, he didn't do much. Sometimes he would spend all day in ⁶_____ . His wife had to get up at five o'clock to go to ⁷_____ . Mr Broome lost his job in ⁸_____ and then went to ⁹_____ for stealing. Read the first part of Alan Broome's life story in next week's Sunday News.

- □ school
- 1 university
- 2 cinema
- 3 railway station
- 4 sea
- 5 home
- 6 bed
- 7 work
- 8 navy
- 9 prison

65 on Thursday, for lunch, by car etc.

Compare:

WITHOUT **a/an** OR **the**	WITH **a/an** OR **the**
Phrases of time are usually without **a/an** or **the**:	But we must use **a/an** or **the** if there is an adjective before **lunch**, **Thursday** etc, or if there is a phrase or clause after it:
*I'll see you after **lunch**.* *They came on **Thursday**.*	*We had **a nice lunch**.* *They came **the Thursday** before last.* *It was **the Thursday** after we moved house.*

A Years, seasons and months

*I was born in **1966**.*   But: *in **the year** 1966*
*We play cricket in **summer**.*   Or: *in **the summer**, in **the spring*** etc.
***Winter** is a quiet time here.*   But: *It was **the winter** of 1970.*
*I start the course in **September**.*   NOT *I start in the September.*

B Special times of the year

*We go away at **Christmas**.*   But: *We had **a wonderful Christmas**.*
***Easter** is early this year.*   *I started work **the Easter** before last.*
*I'll be home for **Thanksgiving**.*

C Days of the week

*Yes, **Friday** will be convenient.*   But: *The storm was on **the Friday** of that week.*
*It's my class on **Tuesday evening**.*   *We went to Cornwall **at the weekend**.*
But NOT *at weekend*

D Parts of the day and night

*We were on the beach at **sunset**.*   But: *It was **a beautiful sunset**.*
*I can't sleep at **night**.*   *in/during **the day**/**the night**/**the morning**/**the afternoon**/**the evening**;*
*I prefer to travel by **day**/**night**.*   *I couldn't see in **the dark**.*
*They arrived before **dark**.*
*I must get to bed before **midnight**.*

E Meals

***Lunch** is at one o'clock.*   But: ***The lunch** Simon gave us was delicious.*
*They had **supper** in the garden.*   *We had **a quick breakfast**.*
*We had eggs for **breakfast**.*   ***The meal** was very nice.*
But NOT *Meal is* ... or *for meal*.   *The guests will need **an evening meal**.*

F Transport

*go **by car** / **by bus** / **by train** / **by plane*** etc.   But: *go **in the car** / **on the bus** / **on the train*** etc.

For more details about transport see Unit 99B.

65 Exercises

65.1 **a/an** or **the** with years, months, days etc. (**A–D**)

Put in the words on the right. Use **a/an** or **the** if you need to.

☐ My birthday is _the Sunday_ after next. ☐ Sunday
1. It doesn't often snow here at _____. We haven't had _____ for many years. 1 Christmas; white Christmas
2. We came here in _____ of _____. 2 summer; 1969
3. _____ is in _____. 3 Thanksgiving; November
4. The Church of England dates from _____ 1534. 4 year
5. I like driving at _____. The roads are quiet. ~ Oh, I don't like driving in _____. I'd rather travel during _____. 5 night; dark; day
6. Are you doing anything at _____? ~ I don't think so. ~ Well, come over on _____. 6 weekend; Saturday

65.2 **a/an** or **the** with meals (**E**)

Sadie is talking about the food she and her husband had on holiday. Put in the words. Use **a/an** or **the** if you need to.

'☐ _The meals_ we had weren't very good. We had ☐ meals
¹_____ in the hotel and that wasn't too bad. We 1 breakfast
usually went out for ²_____ because 2 lunch
³_____ they served in the hotel was always the 3 lunch
same. ⁴_____ we had on our first evening was 4 dinner
pretty awful, so we tried a few restaurants. On our last evening
we had ⁵_____ in a Chinese restaurant, but 5 marvellous dinner
that was an exception.'

65.3 **on Thursday**, **for lunch**, **by car** etc. (**A–F**)

Put in the words. Decide if you need to use **the**.

Sue: Hello, Paul. Are you having ☐ _lunch_ already? ☐ lunch
Paul: No, this is ¹_____. I had a late night. It was long 1 breakfast
after ²_____ when I got back. 2 midnight
Sue: You're leaving us soon, aren't you?
Paul: This is my last weekend here for a while. I'm flying home on
³_____. 3 Wednesday
Sue: Oh, you're going by ⁴_____, are you? What 4 plane
time do you leave?
Paul: Oh, in ⁵_____ some time. About ten. 5 morning
Sue: I can drive you to the airport if you like. I'm usually free on
⁶_____ morning. 6 Wednesday
Paul: Well, thanks. I was going to go on ⁷_____. 7 bus
Sue: Unless it's ⁸_____ when I have my job 8 day
interview. Let me look in my diary. No, it's OK. I can do it.
When will you be back?
Paul: After ⁹_____. I've got a job here starting in 9 Christmas
¹⁰_____. 10 January

66 quite, such and what with a/an

A quite, fairly etc.

A/an goes before words like **very** and **fairly**:
*It's **a very old** house.* *I have **a fairly long** journey to work.*

But **quite** usually goes before **a/an**:
*It's **quite an old** house.* *We had **quite a nice** meal.*

Rather can go either before or after **a/an**:
*It's **rather an old** house.* OR *It's **a rather old** house.*

We can also use these words with mass or plural nouns:
*This is **quite nice** coffee.* *They're **very old** houses.*

B so and such

We cannot use **so** or **such** after **a/an**.
  NOT *a so easy test* or *a such easy test*
We use these patterns instead. Compare:

be + **so** + adjective:	**such** + **a/an** + adjective + noun:
*The test was **so easy**.*	*It was **such an easy test**.*
*The film is **so boring**.*	*It's **such a boring film**.*
*It was **so nice** to see everyone.*	*I got **such a nice welcome**.*

We can also use **so** and **such** with a mass noun (e.g. **food**) or a plural noun (e.g. **portions**):

*The food was **so rich**.*	*We had **such rich food**.*
*The portions are **so big**.*	*They give you **such big portions**.*

Note these sentences with **long**, **far**, **many/much** and **a lot of**:

*It's **so long** since I saw you.*	*It's **such a long time** since I saw you.*
*Why are we **so far** from the beach?*	*Why are we **such a long way** from the beach?*
*There were **so many** people.*	*There were **such a lot** of people.*
*You waste **so much** time.*	*You waste **such a lot** of time.*

After a phrase with **so** or **such** we can add a clause:
*The film is **so** boring **(that)** no one wants to watch it.*
*We were **such** a long way from the beach **(that)** we had to take a bus.*
*I had **such** bad luck you wouldn't believe it.*

C what

We can use **what a/an** with a singular noun:
***What an** idea!* ***What a** good photo that is.*

We can also use **what** with mass or plural nouns:
***What** rubbish!* ***What** awful weather we're having.*
***What** lovely flowers!* ***What** lies that child tells!*

66 Exercises

66.1 quite, fairly etc. with a/an (A)

Agree with what people say. Use **a** or **an**.
- This hill is very steep. ~ _Yes, it's a very steep hill._
- The show was quite good. ~ _Yes, it was quite a good show._
1. The flight was fairly good. ~ _____
2. This train is quite fast. ~ _____
3. This coat is rather expensive. ~ _____
4. The evening was quite enjoyable. ~ _____
5. The hotel is very grand. ~ _____

66.2 so and such (B)

Put in **so** or **such**.

A: Sorry I'm □ _so_ late. There's been □ _such_ a lot to do at work. And I'm ¹_____ tired.
B: You shouldn't do ²_____ much. It can't be ³_____ important.
A: The boss gets in ⁴_____ a terrible panic about things. He makes ⁵_____ a big fuss.
B: Well, you shouldn't be ⁶_____ willing to work ⁷_____ long hours. You'll make yourself ill.

66.3 so/such with a clause (B)

Match the sentences. Join each sentence pair using **so** or **such**.

The piano was heavy.	She never has time to talk.
We'd walked a long way.	They never last long.
Karen is always busy.	We had to have a rest.
I haven't cooked for a long time.	There's no room to sit on the beach.
Neil buys cheap clothes.	We couldn't move it.
You made a noise.	I've forgotten how to.
There are a lot of tourists.	You woke everyone up.

- _The piano was so heavy we couldn't move it._
- _We'd walked such a long way we had to have a rest._
1. _____
2. _____
3. _____
4. _____
5. _____

66.4 what (C)

Put in **what** or **what a**.
1. Come into the sitting room. ~ Oh, _____ nice room!
2. Helen believes in ghosts. ~ _____ nonsense she talks.
3. Let's go for a midnight swim. ~ _____ suggestion!
4. You can see for miles. ~ Yes, _____ lovely view.
5. Smile please. Oh, _____ perfect teeth you've got.
6. This is my record collection. ~ Well, _____ lot of records.

67 Place names and **the**

Compare:

WITHOUT **the**	WITH **the**
Most place names do not have **the**, e.g. **Europe, California, Melbourne.** Sometimes a noun such as **lake** or **street** is part of a name, e.g. **Lake Victoria, Princes Street.**	Some names with a noun have **the**, e.g. *the* **North Sea**, *the* **Classic Cinema**.

Whether a name has **the** depends on two things: the kind of place it is – for example, a lake (**Lake Ontario**) or a sea (*the* **South China Sea**) – and the grammatical pattern of the name:

We do not use **the** with a possessive (**'s**): **Pete's Snack Bar**	We often use **the** in these patterns: With **of**: *the* Avenue *of the* Americas With an adjective: *the* **White** House With a plural: *the* **Bahamas**

Although we say or write *the* **North Sea** or *the* **Classic Cinema** in a sentence, **the** is usually left out when the name is on a map or a sign.

A Continents, countries, islands, states and counties

Most are without **the**: *travelling through* **Africa** *a holiday in* **Portugal** *on* **Jersey** *to* **Florida** *in* **Sussex**	Exceptions are words like **republic** and **union**, e.g. *the* **Irish Republic**, *the* **USSR**, *the* **UK**, and plural names, e.g. *the* **Netherlands**, *the* **USA**, *the* **Canary Islands**. Also: *the* **Gambia**, *the* **Yemen**, *the* **Sudan**

B Regions

Regions ending with the name of a continent or country are without **the**, e.g. **Central Asia, South Wales.**	Most other regions have **the**, e.g. *the* **West**, *the* **Middle East**, *the* **Riviera**, *the* **Baltic**, *the* **Highlands**, *the* **Midlands**. Phrases with **of** have **the**, e.g. *the* **South of France**.

C Hills and mountains

Most are without **the**: *She climbed* **(Mount) Everest.** *down* **North Hill**	An exception is *the* **Matterhorn**. Hill ranges and mountain ranges have **the**: *skiing in* *the* **Alps**

D Lakes, seas, rivers and canals

Only lakes are without **the**: *near* **Lake Michigan** *beside* **Coniston Water**	Seas, rivers and canals have **the**: *the* **Mediterranean (Sea)** *across* *the* **Atlantic (Ocean)** *on* *the* **(River) Thames** *the* **Mississippi (River)** *through* *the* **Suez Canal**

67 *Place names and* **the**

E Cities, towns, suburbs and villages

Most are without **the**:
in **Boston**
Harehills, *a suburb of* **Leeds**
from **south London**
in **central Birmingham**

Exceptions are **The Hague** and **The Bronx**.

F Roads, streets, squares and parks

Most are without **the**:
along **Morden Road**
in **Church Street**
on **Lexington Avenue**
near **Berkeley Square**
through **Central Park**

Exceptions are **the High Street** and e.g. **The Avenue**, **The Strand**, **The Mall**.

Note also **the Bristol road** (= the road to Bristol), **the A38**, **the M5 (motorway)**.

G Bridges

Most bridges are without **the**:
across **Vauxhall Bridge**
on **Brooklyn Bridge**
near **Tower Bridge**

But there are many exceptions:
the Golden Gate Bridge
the Severn Bridge (= the bridge over the River Severn)

H Stations and airports; religious, educational and official buildings; palaces, houses

Most are without **the**:
to **Waterloo (Station)**
at **Orly (Airport)**
St Mary's (Church)
at **York University**
Cardiff Museum
near **Lambeth Palace**
at **Chatsworth House**

Exceptions are names with **of** or with an adjective or noun, e.g. **open**, **railway**.
the University of York
the Palace of Westminster
the Railway Museum
the Open University
the White House

I Theatres, cinemas, hotels, galleries and centres

Possessive forms (**'s**) are without **the**:
St Martin's Theatre
Durrant's (Hotel)
(In the USA names with **center** do not have **the**, e.g. *near* **Lincoln Center**.)

But most theatres etc. have **the**:
at **the Globe (Theatre)**
the Plaza (Cinema)
outside **the Dorchester (Hotel)**
in **the Tate (Gallery)**
the Brunel shopping centre

J Shops and restaurants

Most are without **the**:
shopping at **Selfridge's**
in **Laura Ashley**
at **Sally's Coffee Shop**

Patterns without a person's name sometimes have **the**:
I got it at **the Body Shop**.
The Steak House

67 Exercises

67.1 Geographical names (A–E)

How good is your geography? Put in these names: **Andes, Anglesey, Brussels, Irish Republic, Italy, Lake Michigan, Mount McKinley, North, Pennsylvania, River Seine, United Kingdom, West Indies**. Decide if you need **the**.

- ☐ Harrisburg is the capital of _Pennsylvania_ .
- ☐ Dublin is in _the Irish Republic_ .
1. _____ is in the USA.
2. Sicily is a part of _____ .
3. _____ are a mountain range in South America.
4. _____ is England, Scotland, Wales and Northern Ireland.
5. _____ is an island off the north coast of Wales.
6. Jamaica is an island in _____ .
7. _____ flows through Paris.
8. _____ is the capital of Belgium.
9. Leeds is in _____ of England.
10. _____ is the highest mountain in the USA.

67.2 Roads and buildings etc. (D–I)

Complete these sentences from a guide to London. Put in the words on the right. Decide if you need **the**.

- ☐ The boat train leaves from _Victoria Station_ . ☐ Victoria Station
- ☐ _The National Theatre_ is south of the river. ☐ National Theatre
1. You can take a trip by boat along _____ .   1 Thames
2. The Serpentine is a lake in _____ .   2 Hyde Park
3. You can see planes taking off at _____ .   3 Heathrow Airport
4. Nelson's Column is in _____ .   4 Trafalgar Square
5. Walk a little way along _____ .   5 Westminster Bridge
6. From there you get a view of _____ .   6 Houses of Parliament
7. The Queen lives at _____ .   7 Buckingham Palace
8. Arsenal Football Club is in _____ .   8 north London
9. _____ is in _____ .   9 Savoy Hotel; Strand

67.3 Roads, buildings etc. (E–J)

Complete the conversation. Put in the words and decide if you need **the**.

A: Have you been away?
B: Yes, we've been to ¹_____ .   1 New York City
A: Oh, really? A holiday?
B: That's right. We saw ²_____ , we   2 Statue of Liberty
    walked in ³_____ . We did all the   3 Central Park
    sights. We spent a day in ⁴_____   4 Metropolitan Museum
    of Art. And we walked along ⁵_____   5 Broadway
    and around ⁶_____ department store.   6 Macy's
A: And where did you stay?
B: In a small hotel near ⁷_____ not   7 Washington Square
    far from ⁸_____ .   8 New York University

67 Place names and the

67.4 Roads, buildings etc. (F–I)

Put in the words. Decide if you need **the**.

A: Excuse me, can you tell me the way to ¹_____?

B: Yes, go along here and turn left by ²_____. The turning is just before a building called ³_____. The road is ⁴_____. Go along there, straight across ⁵_____, past ⁶_____, and you'll see it in front of you.

A: Thank you very much.

1 Millthorpe Station
2 Classic Theatre
3 Kingston House
4 Wood Lane
5 High Street
6 Norfolk Hotel

67.5 Roads, buildings etc. (F–J)

Look at the addresses and write the sentences.

Useful addresses for visitors to Seaport

Seaport Bus Station, Queen's Road
Grand Theatre, George Street
Odeon Cinema, The Boulevard
Clarendon Art Gallery, Newton Lane
King Edward College, College Road
St John's Church, South Street
Webster's department store, High Street
Bristol Hotel, Westville Way

☐ *Seaport Bus Station is in Queen's Road.*
1 The Grand Theatre _____
2 _____
3 _____
4 _____
5 _____
6 _____
7 _____

67.6 Place names and the (A–J)

These headlines are from a magazine about travel and tourism. Write each phrase in full.

☐ Walk along Princes St — *a walk along Princes Street*
☐ Holiday in USA — *a holiday in the USA*
1 Day at Blenheim Palace
2 Train journey in North Wales
3 Tour of White House
4 Beach on Riviera
5 Shopping trip to Harrod's
6 Small town in France
7 Trip across Severn Bridge
8 Walk around Lake Windermere
9 Visit to Tower Bridge
10 Journey across Rockies
11 Look around National Gallery
12 Boat trip along River Dart

68 Direct and indirect objects

Look at this conversation:
Jody: *Kate gave **me this cassette** for my birthday, but I've already got it.*
Susie: *Oh, that's a pity. You'll have to give **it to someone else** then.*
Jody: *I could send **it to my cousin** for Christmas, I suppose.*

A Patterns with **give**, **send** etc.

Some verbs can have two objects – an indirect object (the person receiving something) and a direct object (the thing that someone gives):

	INDIRECT OBJECT	DIRECT OBJECT
Kate gave	*me*	*this cassette.*
I'll send	*my cousin*	*a present.*
We bought	*all the children*	*an ice-cream.*

We can say the same thing with a different pattern:

	DIRECT OBJECT	PHRASE WITH **to** OR **for**
Kate gave	*the cassette*	*to someone else.*
I'll send	*a present*	*to my cousin.*
We bought	*ice-creams*	*for all the children.*

B **to** or **for**?

We can use the **to** pattern or an indirect object with these verbs: **give**, **lend**, **hand**, **pass**, **throw**; **send**, **post**, **bring**, **take**; **pay**, **sell**; **promise**; **show**, **offer**; **read**, **write**, **tell**, **teach**; **owe**; **leave** (in a will):
*Jill paid the money **to** the cashier.* OR *Jill paid the cashier the money.*
*We showed the photos **to** Simon.* OR *We showed Simon the photos.*
*Let me read this news item **to** you.* OR *Let me read you this news item.*

We can use the **for** pattern or an indirect object with these verbs: **buy**, **get**, **fetch**, **bring**; **find**; **leave**, **save**; **reserve**, **order**, **book**; **make**, **cook**, **build**; **pick**, **choose**:
*They found a spare ticket **for** me.* OR *They found me a spare ticket.*
*I've saved a seat **for** you.* OR *I've saved you a seat.*
*I'm making a cake **for** our guests.* OR *I'm making our guests a cake.*

C **She gave me the tape** or **She gave the tape to me**?

We put the new and important information near the end of a sentence. Look at these sentences from Jody and Susie's conversation:
*Kate gave me **this cassette** for my birthday.*   *You'll have to give it **to someone else** then.*
This cassette and **someone else** are the new information. **Me** and **it** are old information, something already known or already mentioned, so we put them first.

Now compare these sentences. The important information comes at the end:
*The duchess was rich. She gave her daughter **a million pounds**.*
*The duchess was very odd. She gave her money **to complete strangers**.*

68 Exercises

68.1 Patterns with **give**, **send** etc. (A)

Write the information in one sentence. Put the underlined part at the end of the sentence. Sometimes you need **to**.

☐ Tim lent something to Sarah. It was <u>his calculator</u>.
   Tim lent Sarah his calculator.
☐ Brian sent a message. It was to <u>his wife</u>.
   Brian sent a message to his wife.
1 I sold my bike. <u>My brother</u> bought it.
   I _____
2 The boss promised something to the workers – <u>a pay rise</u>.
   The boss _____
3 Someone passed the sugar. <u>Dave</u> wanted it.
   Someone _____
4 Sam told the joke. He told <u>all his friends</u>.
   Sam _____
5 Jeremy gave <u>some help</u>. He helped his flat-mate.
   _____
6 I wrote to my teacher. I wrote <u>a letter of apology</u>.
   _____
7 Sarah threw the ball. <u>Kirsty</u> caught it.
   _____

68.2 **to** or **for**? (B)

The boss of a big company is telling people to do things. Put in **to** or **for**.

☐ Give these papers _to_ my secretary.
☐ Make some coffee _for_ us, could you?
1 Book a seat on the plane _____ me.
2 Can you post the key _____ the hotel?
3 Don't show these plans _____ anyone.
4 Leave a message _____ my secretary.
5 Fetch the file _____ me, please.
6 Write a memo _____ all managers.

68.3 **She gave me the tape** or **She gave the tape to me**? (C)

Complete the conversation. Put in the two phrases on the right and decide which pattern to use. Put the new information at the end.

A: When I got some petrol at the garage, they gave ☐ _me this card_. You can buy things with it, it says here.   ☐ this card – me

B: Yes, when you buy petrol, they give
   1 _____ to stick on the card.   1 a little sticker – you
   When you've filled all the spaces on the card, you take
   2 _____ and hand   2 the card – the garage
   3 _____. He'll give   3 it – the cashier
   4 _____ from the catalogue.   4 something – you
   The more cards you fill, the better. Twenty cards will buy
   5 _____.   5 a sports bag – you

A: I haven't got a catalogue.
B: Well, I'll show ⁶_____ then.   6 mine – you

69 this, that, these and those

A Things near and far

Look at this:

(Speech bubbles: "This album is interesting. Look at these photos." / "That table is nice, isn't it?" / "I don't like those chairs.")

We use **this** and **these** for things near the speaker (e.g. *this album here*) and **that** and **those** for things further away (e.g. *that table there*).

This and **that** go with a singular noun (or a mass noun, e.g. *this money*), and **these** and **those** go with a plural noun.

We can leave out the noun if the meaning is clear:
   This is interesting. Look at these.
   That's nice, isn't it?

B More uses of this, that, these and those

When we are in a place or situation, we use **this** (not *that*) to refer to it:
   There's a wonderful view from this office. Just come to the window.
   This play isn't very interesting, is it? Shall we go home?

We can use **this** to introduce people:
   Carol, this is Dave. ~ Hi, Carol. ~ Hallo, Dave.
And on the phone we use **this** to say who we are and **that** when we ask who the other person is:
   Hello? This is Angela Henderson (speaking).
   Who's that please?
   (In the USA: *Who's this?*)

This/these can mean 'near in time' and **that/those** 'distant in time':
   I'm doing my exams this summer. I'm pretty busy these days.
   Do you remember that summer when we all went on holiday together? Those were the days.

We normally use **that** to refer back to an idea mentioned before:
   Moira has to babysit. That's why she can't come out with us.
   I've lost my key. ~ Well, that's a silly thing to do.

But we use **this** to refer to an idea we are just about to mention:
   I don't like to say this, but I'm not happy with the service here.

69 Exercises

69.1 Things near and far (A)

Write the sentences. Use these nouns:
clock, dog, flowers, horse, shirt, shoes, socks, telephone.

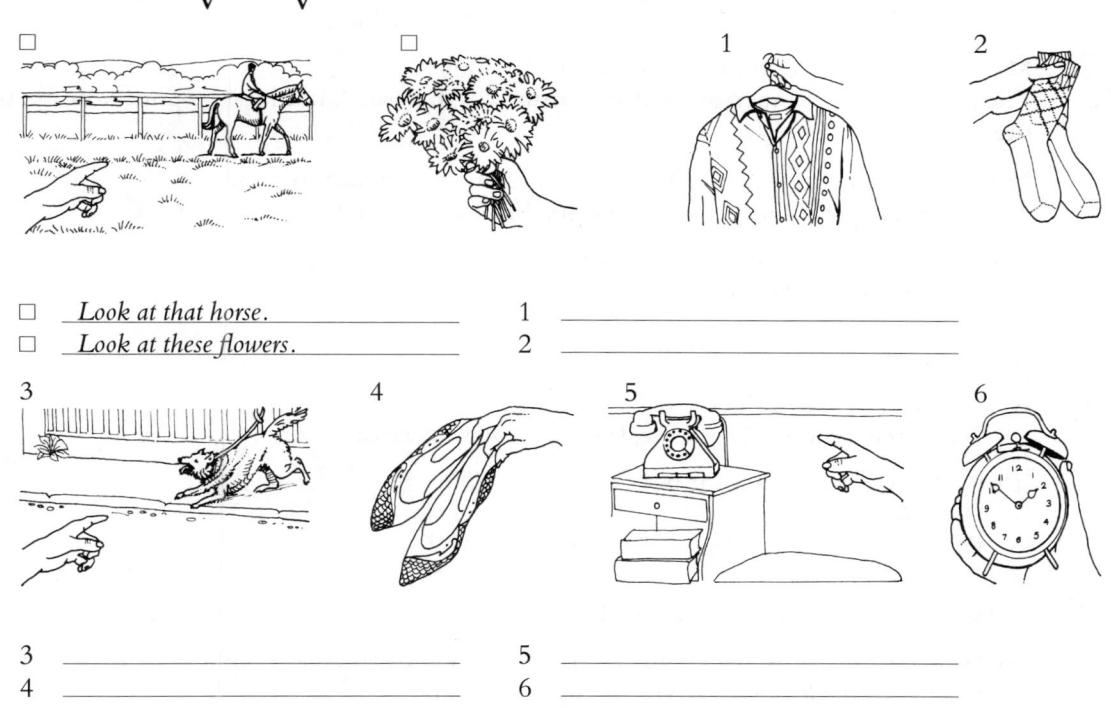

☐ *Look at that horse.*
☐ *Look at these flowers.*
1 _____
2 _____
3 _____
4 _____
5 _____
6 _____

69.2 this, that, these and those (A, B)

Complete the conversations. Put in **this**, **that**, **these** or **those**.
1 Are we going out _____ evening? ~ I can't really. I'm working late at the office today.
2 I hear you've got a new job. ~ _____'s right. I start on Monday.
3 What's the matter? ~ It's _____ boots. They don't fit properly. They're hurting my feet.
4 I'm bored. ~ So am I. Nothing ever happens in _____ town.
5 What's happened? You look terrible. ~ You won't believe _____, but I've just seen a ghost.
6 What kind of planes are _____? ~ I don't know. They're too far away to see properly.
7 The match is three weeks from today. ~ Sorry, I won't be able to play in the team. I'll be away all _____ week.
8 _____ is a great party, isn't it? ~ Yes, I'm really enjoying it.
9 Sheffield 637419. ~ Hello. _____ is Steve. Is _____ Debbie? ~ No, it's Kate. I'll go and get Debbie for you.
10 I've got _____ bump on my head where my girl-friend hit me with a frying pan. ~ Oh. Well, _____ wasn't a very nice thing to do.

70 my, your etc; mine, yours etc.

A Possessive determiners and pronouns

Look at this question and answer:
  Laura: *Shall we go in **my** car?*
  Neil: *Well, I'd rather not take **mine**. There's something wrong with it.*

My is a possessive <u>determiner</u>. It comes before a noun.
The possessive determiners are: **my** car, **your** coat, **his** name, **her** idea, **its** price, **our** house, **their** names.

Mine is a possessive <u>pronoun</u>. When Neil says **mine**, he means **my** car.
The possessive pronouns are: **mine, yours, his, hers, ours, theirs**.

These words express possession, the fact that something belongs to someone (***my car***), and similar meanings (***his name, her idea***).

B its and it's

Its is a possessive determiner:
  *The street is along here somewhere, but I've forgotten **its** name.*

It's is a short form of **it is** or **it has**:
  *I think **it's** time to go.* (= it is)
  *Yes, **it's** got a lot colder, hasn't it?* (= it has)

C Possessives with parts of the body

We normally use a possessive with parts of the body and someone's clothes:
  *Sarah shook **her** head sadly.* NOT *... shook the head ...*
  *Someone came up behind me and grabbed **my** arm.*
  *You take off **your** shoes before you enter a mosque.*

But we normally use **the** in this pattern: verb + person + prepositional phrase.

	VERB	PERSON	PHRASE
Someone	grabbed	me	by **the** arm.
The stone	hit	Peter	in **the** back.

D own

We use **own** to say that something belongs to us and to no one else:
  *I've got **my own** dictionary. I don't need to borrow one.*
  *Jemima has **her own** flat. She doesn't share any more.*

E a friend of mine

We use the pattern **a friend of mine** to mean one of a number of friends:
  *Tim is **a friend of mine**.* (= one of my friends)
  *Sadie came with **a cousin of hers**.* (= one of her cousins)
  *I borrowed **some magazines of yours**.* (= some of your magazines)

70 Exercises

70.1 Possessive determiners and pronouns (A)

Put in the missing words.
Roger: Did you and □ _your_ friends have a nice holiday?
Sam: Yes, thanks. We had the best holiday of ¹_____ lives. The only problem was at Gatwick Airport when Tony discovered he had left ²_____ passport behind.
Roger: Oh, dear. What happened?
Sam: Well, luckily he doesn't live far away. He rang ³_____ parents; and they brought the passport over in ⁴_____ Mini, just in time.
Roger: You remembered ⁵_____ , I hope.
Sam: Yes, I had ⁶_____ , but Sarah thought for a minute she'd lost ⁷_____ . Luckily it was in ⁸_____ suitcase.

70.2 its and it's (B)

Put in the correct form.
□ The town has lost _its_ only cinema.
□ The meeting won't last long. I'll see you when _it's_ over.
1 You should give the book back to _____ owner immediately.
2 The sofa was a nice colour, but I didn't like _____ shape much.
3 I want to go out, but _____ raining.
4 I'm not buying this table-cloth because _____ got a hole in it.
5 The company wants to improve _____ image.

70.3 Possessives with parts of the body (C)

Put in **my**, **your** etc. or **the**.
□ I fell down and hurt _my_ leg.
□ The ball hit Amanda on _the_ knee.
1 A wasp stung me on _____ neck.
2 Mary put both _____ arms around the child.
3 Aunt Caroline kissed Martin on _____ cheek.
4 The fans are all shouting at the top of _____ voices.
5 Don't just stand there with _____ hands in _____ pockets!

70.4 my own flat and a friend of mine (D,E)

Write a phrase with **their own**, **of hers** etc.
□ The boys have got a garden just for them. = _their own garden_
□ Susan introduced me to one of her friends. = _a friend of hers_
1 Coin-collecting is one of my hobbies. = _____
2 We've got a private swimming-pool at home. = _____
3 Phil lent me some of his tapes. = _____
4 Melanie says walking on the moon is one of her ambitions.
  = _____
5 I'd like a room which is mine and no one else's.
  = _____

71 the boy's name or the name of the boy?

A Forms

We form the possessive of a noun like this:

With a singular noun we add an apostrophe and **s**,
e.g. **boy → boy's, Jill → Jill's**.
With a plural noun ending in **s**, we add an apostrophe,
e.g. **boys → boys', tourists → tourists'**.
With a plural noun <u>not</u> ending in **s**, we add an apostrophe and **s**,
e.g. **men → men's, children → children's**.

Compare:

THE POSSESSIVE FORM		THE **of** PATTERN
Singular + **'s**:	the *boy's* name	the *name* **of the boy**
s-plural + **'**:	the *boys'* names	the *names* **of the boys**
Other plurals + **'s**:	the *men's* names	the *names* **of the men**

B Which pattern?

Sometimes we can use either pattern, e.g. **the boy's name** or **the name of the boy**. But often only one is possible.

We normally use the possessive with people and animals:

my friend's house   *Erica's* computer
Peter's brother   *the dog's* bed
the students' union   *the Parkers'* car
the policemen's uniforms   *the women's* changing room

We normally use **of** with things, and not the possessive form:

the side **of the house**   NOT *the house's side*
the end **of the street**   NOT *the street's end*
the result **of the match**   NOT *the match's result*
the day **of the meeting**   NOT *the meeting's day*

But we use **of** with people when there is a long phrase:

the house **of one of our teachers at college**
the address **of those people we met in Spain**

We can use both patterns for places, organizations and writings:

London's museums   *the museums* **of London**
the earth's atmosphere   *the atmosphere* **of the earth**
the company's future   *the future* **of the company**
the newspaper's opinions   *the opinions* **of the newspaper**

C The possessive of time

We can use the possessive in some expressions of time:

*last **week's*** concert   ***today's** TV programmes*
about ***a month's*** work   *a **year's** salary*
in ***two months'*** time   ***ten minutes*** *walk from the beach*

71 Exercises

71.1 The possessive form (A)

Put in the possessive form of the nouns on the right.

Olivia: And where was this photo taken?
Sally: Oh, that's in my □ _friend's_ garden, my friend Pat. It was at the ¹_____ party. This is Sandy, ²_____ girl-friend. And that's ³_____ sister.
Olivia: And who are these two?
Sally: That's ⁴_____ mother. She's talking to Nancy Davis, her ⁵_____ teacher. And that's the ⁶_____ dog sitting on ⁷_____ foot.
Olivia: And who's that on ⁸_____ right?
Sally: Oh, that's ⁹_____ friend Wayne.

□ friend
1 twins
2 Carl
3 Sandy
4 Debbie
5 children
6 Simpsons
7 Pat
8 Kevin
9 Steve

71.2 The possessive form or *of*? (B)

Ed Buckman writes detective stories. Here are the titles of some of his stories. Write them using a possessive form or *of*. Sometimes more than one answer is possible.

□ the mistake – the policeman   _The Policeman's Mistake_
□ the bottom – the bottle   _The Bottom of the Bottle_
1 the gun – Mr Hillman
2 the smell – blood
3 the car – the terrorist
4 the middle – the night
5 the death – someone very important
6 the chairman – the bank
7 the money – the gangsters
8 the day – the wedding
9 the handbag – the old woman
10 the computer – the teacher
11 the plan – Mrs Fletcher
12 the price – a meal

71.3 The possessive of time (C)

Put in a possessive form.

□ The prices this year are even lower.   = this _year's_ prices
□ From here it's a drive of two hours.   = two _hours'_ drive
1 I read about it in the paper yesterday.   = in _____ paper
2 That's the brochure from last year.   = last _____ brochure
3 I just thought I'd have a rest for ten minutes.   = ten _____ rest
4 It's the special offer for this month.   = this _____ special offer
5 I'll see you in a week.   = in a _____ time

72 some and any

A some or any?

Some and **any** go before a plural or mass noun, not a singular noun:
  On the table there was **a** bowl, **some** cornflakes and **some** milk.

Some has a positive meaning, but **any** means that there may be none. We normally use **some** in positive sentences and **any** in negative sentences or ones with a negative meaning:
  Positive: *We've got **some** milk in the fridge.*
             *I need **some** stamps.* ~ *There are **some** in the drawer.*
             *There were **some** nice shops in the main street.*
             *We had **some** fun when we went to Disneyland.*
  Negative: *We **haven't** got **any** milk.* (= We've got **no** milk.)
             *There **aren't any** trees in the garden.*
             *I **never** meet **any** interesting people.*
             *There's **hardly any** money left.* (= There's almost **no** money left.)

But we can use **any** in a positive sentence with **if**:
  *If you have **any** questions, I'll be pleased to answer them.*
  *Discuss **any** problems with your group leader.* (= **if** there are any problems)
  *I'll tell **any** callers that you're out.* (= **if** there are any callers)

Any is more usual in questions, and it leaves the answer open. The answer can be **yes** or **no**:
  *Have we got **any** milk?* ~ *Yes. / No. / I think so.*
  *Did you buy **any** clothes?* ~ *Yes, I did. / No, I didn't.*
  *Will there be **any** music at the party?* ~ *I don't know.*

But we can use **some** to make the question more positive, especially in offers and requests. **Some** means that we expect the answer **yes**:
  *Did you buy **some** clothes?* (I expect you bought **some** clothes.)
  *Would you like **some** coffee?* (Have **some** coffee.)
  *Could you peel **some** potatoes?* (Please peel **some** potatoes.)

We choose between **someone** and **anyone** and between **something** and **anything** in the same way as between **some** and **any**:
  ***Someone** has spilt all this water, look.*
  *Has **anyone** seen Natalie lately?*
  *Would you like **something** to eat?*
  *I couldn't think of **anything** to say.*

B Another meaning of any

We can use **any** in a positive sentence to mean 'it doesn't matter which':
  *You can buy these maps at **any** filling station. They all have them.*
  *I'm free all day. Call **any** time you like.*
  ***Any** student will be able to tell you where the college library is.*
  *It's a very simple puzzle. **Anyone** could solve it.*
  What would you like for lunch? ~ *Oh, **anything**. I don't mind.*
We say ***any** filling station* because <u>all</u> filling stations have the maps and it doesn't matter <u>which one</u> you go to. They are all equally good.

72 Exercises

72.1 some or any? (A)

Complete what the radio disc jockey is saying. Put in **some** or **any**.
'That beautiful song was 'I can't find ▫ _any_ love' by Arlene Black. Now I've had
¹_____ letters asking for a record by Express. One listener says she hasn't heard
²_____ records by Express on this programme for months. Well, I'm going to put that right straight away. And this will be our last record because there isn't ³_____ more time left. We've had ⁴_____ great records tonight, and I'll be here next week to play
⁵_____ more. Now here's ⁶_____ music from Express, with 'I never have
⁷_____ luck'. And this is Justin Cooper saying goodbye and goodnight.'

72.2 some, any, someone, anyone etc. (A)

Complete the dialogues. Put in **some**, **any**, **someone**, **anyone**, **something** or **anything**. Sometimes more than one answer is correct.
1 We haven't got _____ bread. ~ I'd better go to the supermarket and get _____, then. We need _____ tomatoes too.
2 Would you like _____ cheese and biscuits? ~ Oh, no thank you. I don't want _____ else to eat. That was delicious.
3 There's _____ at the door. ~ Oh, were you expecting _____ visitors? ~ No, I don't think so.
4 I'm looking for _____ matches, but I can't find _____. ~ There may be _____ on the shelf by the cooker.
5 There's _____ interesting on television tonight. _____ told me about it today. Now what was it? ~ I've no idea. There isn't _____ sport on.
6 Is _____ going to help you move all these tables? ~ I don't know. Would you mind giving me _____ help, please? ~ Of course. Let's get started.
7 I can't find _____ to write with. ~ There should be a pen by the phone. ~ I can't see one. _____ must have taken it.

72.3 any (B)

Complete the answers. Use **any** + noun, **anyone** or **anything**.
▫ Are these seats reserved? ~ No, you can have _any seat_ you like.
▫ There's so much to see here. What shall I take a photo of? ~ I don't know. _Anything_ you like.
1 What time shall I phone you? ~ Ring _____ .
2 What shall we do at the weekend? ~ Oh, I don't mind. _____ you like.
3 Who shall I invite to the party? ~ I don't know. Invite _____ you want.
4 Which buses go into the city centre? ~ They all do. Take _____ that comes along this road.
5 What colours are these telephones available in? ~ Oh, we do them in lots of different colours. You can have practically _____ .
6 What do people wear to go to the theatre here? ~ Well, it isn't very formal. People can wear _____ they like, more or less.
7 My father has the television on all weekend. It doesn't matter what's on. He'll watch _____ .

169

73 a lot of, many, much, a few and a little

A Plural and mass nouns

Compare:

Many and **few** go before plural nouns:	**Much** and **little** go before mass nouns:
many places, *many* programmes	*much* money, *much* trouble
a few people, *a few* buildings	*a little* sunshine, *a little* food

A lot of and **lots of** go before both plural and mass nouns:
    a lot of students, *lots of* games   *a lot of* sugar, *lots of* fun

We can use these words without a noun, but note that we say **a lot** without **of**:
    *I take photos but not as **many** as I used to. At one time I took **a lot**.*

B a lot of, many and much

These words express a large quantity, e.g. *A million pounds is **a lot of** money*. As a general rule, we use **a lot of** and **lots of** in positive statements and **many** and **much** in negatives and questions:
Positive: *We get **a lot of** storms here.*   *We get **a lot of** rain here.*
Negative: *We don't get **many** storms here.*   *We don't get **much** rain here.*
Questions: *Do you get **many** storms here?*   *Do you get **much** rain here?*
             *How **many** newspapers did you buy?*   *How **much** salt do you put in?*

Many and **much** in positive statements are more formal than **a lot of** and less usual in conversation:
    ***Many** students have financial problems.*   ***Much** progress has been made in recent weeks.*

A lot of in a negative or question is informal:
    *We haven't got **a lot of** time to spare.*
    *Were there **a lot of** people at the dance?*

We always use **many** or **much** (not **a lot of**) after **too**, **so**, **as**, **very** and **how**:
    *There are **too many** cars on the road.*   *There was **so much** noise I couldn't hear myself speak.*

A lot of and **lots of** mean a large quantity, but **plenty of** means 'more than enough', 'more than we need':
    *I was expecting more people to come, so there's **plenty of** food.*
    *You can pick some apples from our tree. We've got **plenty**.*

C few and little with and without a

a few	**few**
With **a**, the meaning is positive:	Without **a**, the meaning is negative:
a few = some, a small number	**few** = not many
a little = some, a small amount	**little** = not much
*A **few** customers have come into the shop. It has been fairly busy.*	***Few** customers have come into the shop. It has been quiet.*
*Mike has made **a little** progress and so is feeling quite pleased.*	*Mike has made **little** progress and so is not feeling very pleased.*

In informal speech **not many / not much** is more common than **few / little**:
    ***Not many** customers have come in.*   *Mike **hasn't** made **much** progress.*

73 Exercises

73.1 a lot of, many and much (B)

Put in **a lot of**, **many** or **much**. More than one answer may be correct.

A: There are □ _a lot of_ athletes taking part in these Student Olympics, aren't there? And there's been ¹_____ interest.
B: Our runners haven't won ²_____ medals, have they?
A: Well, not as ³_____ medals as last time. But there are still ⁴_____ events to come.
B: Unfortunately I haven't got ⁵_____ time for watching sport at the moment. I'm rather busy.
A: Well, I'm hoping to get a ticket for the weekend. But there aren't ⁶_____ seats left, I hear.
B: I heard the cheapest ticket is £25. That's too ⁷_____ in my opinion.

73.2 lots of or plenty of? (B)

Put in **lots of** or **plenty of** and a noun. Use the best word for the context.

□ There are only twenty people coming to the meeting, and there are thirty-four chairs in here. ~ Oh, so we've got _plenty of chairs_.
1 I'm buying three batteries at £2 each, and I've got a £10 note. ~ You've got _____, then.
2 One of our neighbours has got two cats and the other has got about five. ~ There are _____ in this street, aren't there?
3 I ordered three litres of milk for just the two of us. We'll have _____ for today.
4 I had my camera with me all holiday. I took _____, as usual.

73.3 a few, few, a little and little (C)

Put in **a few**, **few**, **a little** or **little**.

□ Could I have _a little_ cream, please? Thank you.
□ Very _few_ people were flying because of terrorist activities.
1 The postman doesn't often come here. We receive _____ letters.
2 The snow was getting quite deep. I had _____ hope of getting home that night.
3 I'm having _____ trouble fixing this shelf. ~ Oh, dear. Can I help?
4 I shall be away for _____ days from tomorrow.
5 Tony is a keen golfer, but unfortunately he has _____ ability.
6 I could speak _____ words of Swedish, but I wasn't very fluent.

73.4 many, few, much and little (B,C)

Put in **many**, **few**, **much** or **little**.

The capital town of this island is very small and does not have □ _many_ important buildings. The islanders do not have ¹_____ money, and they have ²_____ contact with the outside world. There is not ³_____ chance of the place attracting tourists. The roads aren't very good. There are lots of bicycles but not ⁴_____ cars. There are ⁵_____ shops, and there is ⁶_____ cultural life.

74 all, most, some, every, each, both and none

Look at this conversation:
- Emma: *There are two letters, and **both** of them are for you.*
- Natalie: *Oh, thanks.*
- Emma: *You get **all** the letters. I never get **any**.*
- Natalie: *I don't get a letter **every** day. Anyway, what's so good about getting letters?*
- Emma: *Well, **most** people like to get one sometimes, don't they?*
- Natalie: *I don't really want **either** of these. They're **both** bills.*

A Meanings

All, **every**, **each** and **both** mean a whole quantity:
- *You get **all** the letters.*
- *I leave the house at eight **every** morning.*

Most and **some** mean part of a quantity:
- ***Most** people like to get a letter.* (= more than half)
- *I'm going to sell **some** of my books.* (= a part but not all)

No, **none** and **neither** are negative:
- *There are **no** letters for you, I'm afraid.*
- *I can't get in. **None** of these keys will fit.*

B all, most and some

We can use **all**, **most** and **some** before a plural noun or a mass noun:
- ***All** plants need water.*   ***All** grass is green, isn't it?*
- ***Most** drivers break the speed limit.*   ***Some** food makes me ill.*

These phrases have a general meaning. ***All** plants* means 'plants in general', 'all plants in the world'. *Most drivers* means 'most drivers in the world / in this country'.

When we mean something specific, we use **all of the**, **most of the** etc. *All of the plants* means, for example, 'all of the plants in the garden'.
- *Are you digging up **all (of) the plants**? ~ No, not **all of them**.*
- ***Most of the customers** who come in our shop are local people.*
- *I've spent **most of my money** already.*
- ***Some of the magazines** in the waiting-room were fifteen years old.*
- ***Some of that food** from the party was all right, but I threw **some of it** out.*

We can leave out **of** after **all** (e.g. *all the plants*) but not before a pronoun (e.g. *all of them*).

We can also use **all** in these patterns:
- *The plants are **all** dying. I'm going to dig **them all** up.*

We can use **most** and **some** on their own:
- *We found some old pictures. **Most** were damaged, but **some** were all right.*

We can use **all** with a clause to mean 'everything' or 'the only thing':
- *Tell me **all** (that) you know.*
- ***All** (that) we did was sit around and listen to records.*

In these sentences *(that) you know* and *(that) we did* are clauses.

C every and each

We use **every** and **each** before a singular noun to talk about a whole group:
> The police questioned *every/each* person in the building.
> *Every/Each* room has a number.

In many contexts either word is possible, but there is a difference:

Every person means 'all the people', 'everyone'.
    Every guest watched the Prince come into the room.
    I go for a walk *every day*.
Every means three or more, usually a large number.
	Each person means all the people seen as individuals, one by one.
	    Each guest (in turn) shook hands with the Prince.
	    Each day seemed to pass very slowly.
	Each is more usual with smaller groups and can mean only two.

We can use **each** (but not **every**) on its own or with **of**:
> There are six flats. *Each* has its own entrance. NOT *Every has ...*
> *Each of* the flats has its own entrance. NOT *Every of ...*

Notice the difference between **every** and **all** before **day**, **morning**, **week** etc:
> I travel *every day*. (Monday, Tuesday, Wednesday ...)
> I was travelling *all day*. (from morning till evening)

D whole

We use **whole** after **the**, **a**, **my** etc. and before a singular noun:
> The baby cried *the whole time* (OR all the time).
> We'll need *a whole loaf* for the sandwiches.

E both, either and neither

We use **both**, **either** and **neither** for two things. We use **both** in these patterns:
> ***Both letters*** are bills OR ***Both the letters*** are bills OR ***Both of the letters*** are bills.
> The letters were ***both*** bills. I've paid ***both of them*** (OR ***them both***) already.

We use **either** and **neither** in these patterns:
> I haven't met *either twin* OR *either of the twins* OR *either of them*.
> *Neither shoe* fits. OR *Neither of the shoes* fit. OR *Neither of them* fit.

We can use **both**, **either** and **neither** on their own:
> The store has two lifts and ***both*** are out of order (OR ***neither*** is working).
> Which of the two rooms would you prefer? ~ *Either*. I don't mind.

F no and none

We use **no** with a noun:
> We had **no time** to lose.   There are **no services** on the motorway.

We use **none** without a noun or with **of**:
> I wanted some cake, but there was **none** left. NOT *... there was no left.*
> **None of the hotels** have any vacancies.

74 Exercises

74.1 Meanings (A)

Put in **all**, **some** or **none**.
1. Not all these books are second-hand; _____ of them are new.
2. There aren't any biscuits left; we've eaten _____ the ones I bought.
3. The food in the freezer is completely spoilt; _____ of it is any good now.
4. You won't get into the concert; _____ the tickets have been sold.
5. Some of our relatives live near us, but _____ live a long way away.

74.2 all, most, some and none (A, B)

Six people took part in a quiz. They were asked twenty questions. Complete the sentences using **all of them**, **most of them**, **some of them** and **none of them**.
- ☐ Adam answered all twenty correctly. _He got all of them right._
- ☐ Emma answered fifteen correctly. _She got most of them right._
1. Marilyn answered eight correctly. _____
2. Steve answered fourteen correctly. _____
3. Kate answered them all correctly. _____
4. Richard couldn't answer a single one. _____

74.3 all and most (B)

Put in **all**, **all the**, **most** or **most of the**.
- ☐ You can't make milk in a factory. _All_ milk comes from animals.
- ☐ On Sundays I do a few odd jobs, but I spend _most of the_ time reading.
1. In general, people aren't interested in politics. _____ people are just bored by it.
2. When the electricity failed, _____ lights in our house went out.
3. Eat as much fruit as you can. _____ fruit is good for you.
4. _____ money for the new swimming-pool will come from the government, but the city has to pay a quarter of the cost.
5. Cars are a nuisance. _____ cars pollute the air, don't they? ~ Well, except electric ones. They don't cause pollution.

74.4 every and each (C)

Put in **every** or **each**. (Sometimes both are possible.)

A: Four of us share this flat. ☐ _Each_ of us has his own bedroom, and ¹_____ person pays a quarter of the rent. The rent is due on the first of ²_____ month.
B: Do you have parties here?
A: Oh yes, all the time. We have one ³_____ week, more or less.
B: Isn't that rather expensive?
A: Well, we ask ⁴_____ guest to bring something to drink. Actually we're not having a party this week. Just now we're spending ⁵_____ spare moment working for our exams.

74 all, most, some etc.

74.5 every and all (C)

Put in **every** or **all** and the word on the right.

☐ Diana is a religious person. She goes to church _every Sunday_ .   ☐ Sunday
1 I haven't been out today because it's been raining _____ .   1 day
2 The postman comes at about eight o'clock _____ .   2 morning
3 It's eleven o'clock. Are you going to lie in bed _____ ?   3 morning
4 I was busy last weekend. I spent _____ wallpapering the sitting-room.   4 Saturday
5 Why are you in such a hurry _____ I see you?   5 time

74.6 both, either and neither (E)

Read this paragraph about two villages and then write sentences about them.
   Cosswell and Woolford are two small villages. Cosswell has a school, a pub and a filling-station, but it hasn't got a sports field. Woolford hasn't got a school, or a sports field either, and it hasn't got a filling-station. But it has a very nice pub.

Use **both of them, one of them, either of them** or **neither of them**.
1 _____ are small.
2 _____ has a filling-station.
3 _____ have a pub.
4 _____ has a school.
5 _____ has a sports field.
6 You can't do sport in _____ .

74.7 all, most, every etc. (A–F)

People are talking about ill health. Put in the correct word.
1 I've taken _____ of the pills, but there are quite a few left.   1 all/some
2 I've had three operations. Luckily _____ of them has been successful.   2 every/each
3 I've got _____ appetite.   3 no/none
4 Now _____ my ears ache very badly.   4 all/both
5 I've had hardly any sleep. I was awake _____ of the night.   5 some/most
6 I've spent the _____ week in bed.   6 all/whole
7 I wake up tired and depressed _____ morning.   7 all/every
8 But _____ of these medicines has done me very much good.   8 no/none

74.8 all, both, none etc. (A–F)

Put in **all, every, none, both, either** and **neither**.

75 Personal pronouns (e.g. **I**, **you**)

A The meaning of the pronouns

Jessica: *Hello, Phil. Have **you** seen Sarah?*
Phil: *I don't think so. No, I haven't seen **her** today.*
Jessica: ***She** said she would meet **me** here. **We**'re going to play badminton.*
Phil: ***She** has probably forgotten all about **it**.*
Jessica: *Louise and her sister said **they** might come too. Perhaps **they**'ve gone without **me**.*

I/me means the speaker, and **you** means the person spoken to.
We/us means the speaker and someone else. Here, **we** = Jessica and Sarah.
He/him means a male person, and **she/her** a female person. Here, **she** = Sarah.
It means a thing, an action or an idea. Here, **it** = the game.
They/them is the plural of **he**, **she** and **it** and means people or things.

We can also use **they/them** for a person when we don't know if the person is male or female:
*If anyone calls, ask **them** to leave a message.*

B Subject and object forms

	1st PERSON	2nd PERSON	3rd PERSON		
Singular					
Subject	**I**	**you**	**he**	**she**	**it**
Object	**me**	**you**	**him**	**her**	**it**
Plural					
Subject	**we**	**you**	**they**		
Object	**us**	**you**	**them**		

We use the subject form (**I** etc.) when the pronoun is the subject and has a verb:
***I** don't think so.*   *****She**'s supposed to be meeting me here.*
We use the object form (**me** etc.) when the pronoun is the object of a verb or preposition:
*I haven't **seen her**.*   *Perhaps they've gone without **me**.*
The pronoun on its own or after **be** usually has the object form:
*Who spilt this paint on the floor? ~ **Me**.* OR *Sorry, it was **me**.* BUT ***I** did.*

C **you**, **one** and **they**

There is no single pronoun for 'people in general'. We use **you** or **one** to mean 'any person' or 'people in general', including the speaker:
***You** shouldn't believe what **you** read in the newspapers.*
OR ***One** shouldn't believe what **one** reads in the newspapers.*
***You** don't (OR **One** doesn't) like to have an argument in public.*

You is rather informal and conversational. **One** is more formal and rather upper-class. For American usage see p 290.

We use **they** to mean 'other people in general', or people in authority:
***They** say too much sugar is bad for you.*   ***They**'re going to build a new swimming-pool here.*
They is also informal and conversational. A passive sentence with a similar meaning sounds more formal:
*A new swimming-pool **is going to be built** here.* (see Unit 38C)

75 Exercises

75.1 The meaning of the pronouns (A)

Read Nicola and Helen's conversation. Then say what the pronouns mean.

Nicola: Have □ **you** been in that new shop?
Helen: No, not yet.
Nicola: Oh, □ **it**'s good. There are some nice clothes in there. There was a lovely dress in the window, and ¹ **it** wasn't expensive.
Helen: Sarah bought some jeans there. ² **She** said ³ **they** were quite cheap.
Nicola: ⁴ **You** ought to go there.
Helen: ⁵ **We**'d better not go now or we'll be late. ⁶ **I** told Sue and Neil we'd meet ⁷ **them** at half past five.
Nicola: Oh, Gary said ⁸ **he**'s coming too.

□ you = _Helen_
□ it = _the shop_
1 it = _____
2 she = _____
3 they = _____
4 you = _____
5 we = _____
6 I = _____
7 them = _____
8 he = _____

75.2 Subject and object forms (B)

Put in the pronouns.

Paul: Is Lisa coming to your party?
Simon: Well, I've invited □ _her_, but ¹_____ isn't sure if ²_____ can come or not. Her parents are visiting relatives, and ³_____ might have to go with ⁴_____. But I've got her tapes. She's lent ⁵_____ to ⁶_____.
Paul: And is Peter coming?
Simon: Yes, ⁷_____ can come. And his brother. ⁸_____'ll both be there.
Paul: Do ⁹_____ mean Colin? Oh, I don't like ¹⁰_____ very much.
Simon: But Paul, ¹¹_____ don't have to talk to ¹²_____.

75.3 Subject and object forms (B)

Put in the pronouns.

□ There's no need to shout. I can hear _you_.
1 You and I work well together. _____'re a good team.
2 We've got a bit of a problem. Can _____ help _____, please?
3 This is a good photo, isn't _____? Dave is in _____ somewhere. Yes, that's _____, look. _____'s next to Sophie.
4 Who did this crossword? ~ _____. I did _____ this morning.
5 Is this Carol's bag? ~ No, _____ hasn't got one. It doesn't belong to _____.
6 _____'m looking for my shoes. Have you seen _____? ~ Yes, _____'re here.

75.4 you and they (C)

Put in **you** or **they**.

A: I'm not going to drive in this weather. It's too icy.
B: □ _You_ don't want to take any risks. ¹_____ can't be too careful, really.
A: I've just heard the forecast. ²_____ say there's going to be more snow. ³_____'re better off indoors in weather like this.
B: I think ⁴_____ ought to clear the snow off the roads a bit quicker.

76 there and it

A there + be

Look at these examples of **there is** and **there are**:
> *I really ought to phone home.* ~ *Well, **there's** a phone box by the town hall.*
> *Could I make myself an omelette?* ~ *Yes, **there are** some eggs in the fridge.*

To say that something exists or is happening, we use **there + be**. We usually pronounce **there** [ðə], like **the**. **Be** agrees with the following noun phrase:
> *There **is** a phone box.* BUT *There **are** some eggs.*

Here are some more examples:
> ***There's** a bus at ten to five.*
> ***Is there** a toilet in the building?*
> ***There'll be** some food for you.*
> ***Were there** any bargains in the sale?*

We also use **there** with words like **a lot of**, **many**, **much**, **several**, **more**, **enough** and with numbers:
> ***There's too much noise** in here.*
> *Will **there be enough chairs**?*
> ***There** have been **six burglaries** in our street this year.*
> ***There** were **several problems** to discuss.*
> ***There** are **thirty days** in April.*

B Uses of it

We use **it** for a thing, an action or a situation:
> *The machine broke down and we couldn't repair **it**.*
> *Skiing is an expensive hobby, isn't **it**?*
> *You have to fill in all these stupid forms. **It's** ridiculous.*

We use **it** to mean 'the unknown person':
> *Did someone ring?* ~ ***It** was Melissa. She just called to say she's home.*

We use **it** for time, the weather and distance:
> ***It's** half past five already.*
> ***It** was much warmer yesterday.*
> ***It's** over a hundred miles from London to Birmingham.*
> ***It's** Sunday tomorrow.*
> *Isn't **it** a lovely day?*

We also use **it** in this pattern, with a to-infinitive or a that-clause:
> ***It** was nice **to meet your friends**.*
> ***It** would be a good idea **to book in advance**.*
> ***It's** important **to switch off the electricity**.*
> ***It's** a pity **(that) you can't come with us**.*

This is much more usual than, for example: ***To meet your friends** was nice.*

C there or it?

Look at this:
> ***There** was **a picture** on the wall. **It** was an abstract painting.*

We often use **there** when we mention something for the first time (e.g. *a picture*). We use **it** when we talk about the details. ***It*** means ***the picture***. Here are some more examples:
> ***There's a** girl at the door.* ~ *Oh, **it's** Sharon.*
> ***There** was **a** dog in the field. **It** was a big black one.*

76 Exercises

76.1 there + be (A)

Put in **there** and a form of **be** (e.g. **is**, **are**, **was**, **have been** or **will be**).

☐ _Are there_ any restaurants here that open on a Sunday? ~ _There's_ a café in the High Street, but I don't know if it opens on a Sunday.

1 _____ a train at twelve twenty, isn't there? We can catch that one. ~ Yes, _____ time to finish our discussion on the train.
2 What's happened? Why _____ so many police here? ~ _____ a hold-up at the bank.
3 Do you think _____ a bus strike next week? ~ I hope not, or _____ much chance of getting to college.
4 I keep hearing fire-engines. _____ a fire somewhere? ~ It looks like it. _____ two fire engines going past at the moment.
5 _____ a party last night. ~ Yes, I couldn't get to sleep. _____ a lot of noise. ~ _____ lots of people there.

76.2 Uses of it (B)

Rewrite the sentences in brackets using **it**.

☐ We sometimes go surfing in Cornwall. (Surfing is really good fun.)
  It's really good fun.

1 I bought a shirt in the market. (The shirt was really cheap.)

2 Someone wanted to see you. (The caller was a friend of yours from college.)

3 Our telephone is out of order. (The situation is a real nuisance.)

4 I've taken my pullover off. (The weather is getting quite hot.)

5 What about some lunch? (The time is one o'clock.)

6 Don't lose your credit card. (To keep it somewhere safe is important.)

76.3 there or it? (A–C)

Put in **there** or **it**.

1 Is _____ the fifteenth today? ~ No, the sixteenth.
2 Someone is injured. _____'s been an accident.
3 Take a taxi. _____'s a long way to the station.
4 _____ isn't any truth at all in that newspaper article. _____ just isn't true what they said.
5 _____ was a motor bike outside the Johnsons'. _____ was a very new and expensive-looking machine.
6 _____ was wet and _____ was a cold east wind. _____ was after midnight and _____ were few people on the streets.
7 Will _____ be any problem with my ticket? ~ Well, _____ would be a good idea to ring the airline and check.

77 Reflexive and emphatic pronouns

A Form

We form reflexive and emphatic pronouns with **self** or **selves**:

	1st PERSON	2nd PERSON	3rd PERSON
Singular	myself	yourself	himself herself itself
Plural	ourselves	yourselves	themselves

Compare **yourself** and **yourselves**:
*Have you hurt your**self**, Andrew?*   *Have you **two** hurt your**selves**?*

B Reflexive pronouns

We use a reflexive pronoun when it refers to the subject:
*I can make **myself** a sandwich.*
*Be careful with that knife or **you**'ll cut **yourself**.*
*In the end **the gunman** shot **himself**.*
***Sarah** had to force **herself** to eat.*
***We** can let **ourselves** into the flat with this key.*
***The children** watched **themselves** on video.*

We cannot use **me**, **you**, **him** etc. to refer to the subject:
*When the policeman came in, **the gunman** shot **him**. (= ... shot the policeman)*

We can also use **myself** etc. after a preposition (e.g. **after**, **for**):
*The children are old enough to look after **themselves**.*
*Alison is making a name for **herself** as a promising young athlete.*

But we use **me**, **you**, **him** etc. after a preposition of place (e.g. **with**, **behind**) when it is clear that we are referring to the subject:
*Neil didn't have any money with **him**.*   *In the mirror I could see a lorry just behind **me**.*
*Jemima thought she recognized the woman standing next to **her**.*

C Idioms with reflexive pronouns

There are some idiomatic expressions with a reflexive pronoun:
*We really **enjoyed ourselves**. (= had a good time)*
*I hope the children **behave themselves**. (= behave well)*
*Just **help yourself** to sandwiches, won't you? (= take food, drink etc.)*
*We're delighted you're staying at our house. Please **make yourself at home**.*
*I don't want to stay here **by myself**. (= on my own, alone)*

Some verbs that do not take a reflexive pronoun are: **afford**; **approach**; **complain**; **feel** + adjective; **hurry (up)**; **meet**; **rest, relax**; **stand up, get up, sit down, lie down**; **wake up**; **wonder, remember, concentrate, worry**.
*We'd better **hurry** or we'll be late.* NOT *We'd better hurry ourselves ...*
*Shall we **meet** outside the cinema?* NOT *Shall we meet ourselves ...*
*I **feel** uncomfortable in this jacket.* NOT *I feel myself uncomfortable ...*
*Just try to **relax**.*

77 Reflexive and emphatic pronouns

We do not normally use a reflexive pronoun with **wash**, **shave**, **(un)dress** and **change** (your clothes):

*Alex **washed** and **changed** before going out again.* NOT *Alex washed himself ...*

We often use **get** with these verbs:

*Alex **got washed** in the bathroom.*   *Alex **got changed**.*

D Emphatic pronouns

An emphatic pronoun has the same form as a reflexive, but the meaning is different. Look at these examples:

***The manager himself** welcomed us to the hotel.*
(= The manager welcomed us, not someone else less important.)
***The house itself** is small, but the garden is enormous.*
(= The house is small, not the garden.)

When we say these sentences, we stress **self**.

The pronoun can also mean 'without help'. In this meaning it usually comes at the end of the sentence:

*I'm building the wall **myself**.* (No one is helping me.)
*Sharon designs all these clothes **herself**.* (No one helps her.)

E each other

Look at this example with **each other**:

*Terry and Jeff help **each other** at work.*

This means that Terry helps Jeff, and Jeff helps Terry. Here are some more examples:

*Judy and Stella are certainly not friends. In fact they hate **each other**.*
*I'm still in touch with Nicky. We write to **each other**.*

One another has the same meaning:

*Terry and Jeff help **one another** at work.*

We can also use the possessive form **each other's**:

*Max and Celia wrote down **each other's** phone number.*
(= Max wrote down Celia's number, and Celia wrote down Max's number.)

Compare **themselves** and **each other**:

*They're laughing at **themselves**.*   *They're laughing at **each other**.*

181

77 Exercises

77.1 Reflexive pronouns (A, B)

Put in the reflexive pronouns (e.g. **myself** or **itself**).
☐ I'm going to Germany soon, so I'm trying to teach _myself_ German.
1. The man fell off the ladder and injured _____ .
2. You all played very well. You can be proud of _____ .
3. The team were unlucky to lose. They're feeling sorry for _____ .
4. The light in the stairway switches _____ off after a couple of minutes.
5. Wendy takes lots of photos, but she hasn't got many of _____ .
6. The accident wasn't your fault. You shouldn't blame _____ .
7. You don't need to pay my entrance fee. I can pay for _____ .
8. There wasn't much to do in the evenings, so we had to amuse _____ .

77.2 Reflexive pronouns (A, B)

Put in a reflexive pronoun after these words: **bought, get, hurt, let, locked, make**.
☐ You shouldn't study all night, you know. You'll _make yourself_ ill.
1. Are you OK? ~ No! I hit my head. I really _____ .
2. My brother is trying to _____ fit for the big race next month.
3. Where's the key? ~ It's in the house. We've _____ out.
4. I didn't know you ate chocolates. ~ Well, I felt like a treat, so I _____ some.
5. Nicola has got her own key. She'll _____ in.

77.3 Pronouns after a preposition (B)

Put in the correct pronoun, e.g. **me** or **myself**.
☐ We looked up and saw a man standing in front of _us_ .
☐ Charlotte is very self-confident. She has a high opinion of _herself_ .
1. We're very busy. We can't even allow _____ a holiday.
2. It's a pity you didn't bring your camera with _____ .
3. Peter talked to the woman sitting next to _____ .
4. I think Dave is rather selfish. He only really cares about _____ .
5. My mother likes to have all her family near _____ .
6. To be successful you must believe in _____ .

77.4 Idioms with reflexive pronouns (C)

Put in the verb on the right with or without a reflexive pronoun.

Carl:	Did you come here together?	
Emma:	Yes, we all ☐ _met_ at my house first.	☐ met
Carl:	Well, ☐ _help yourselves_ to some food, all of you. Come on Julian,	☐ help
	1 _____ at home.	1 make
Julian:	I 2 _____ a bit hot in this coat.	2 feel
Carl:	Oh, dear. Sorry. I'll take your coat.	
Louise:	Calm down, Carl. Don't 3 _____ . Just	3 worry
	4 _____ and then we can all	4 relax
	5 _____ .	5 enjoy

77 Reflexive and emphatic pronouns

77.5 Emphatic pronouns (D)

Put in an emphatic pronoun, e.g. **myself, yourself**.
1. The Queen _____ pays no income tax.
2. The song _____ was no good, but the title of the song became a popular phrase.
3. Of course I know about the rumour. You told me _____ .
4. The group was welcomed by the headmaster _____ .
5. The pilots _____ are nervous of flying because of terrorist threats.

77.6 Emphatic pronouns (D)

Add a sentence with an emphatic pronoun, e.g. **myself**. Use these verbs:
bake, clean, decorate, grow, paint, service, type.
- ☐ I don't take the car to the garage. _I service it myself._
- ☐ Laura didn't buy those pictures. _She painted them herself._
1. Bob doesn't pay to have his windows cleaned. _____
2. My bread doesn't come from a shop. _____
3. The Websters eat lots of fresh vegetables. _____
4. We finished the living-room yesterday. _____
5. Brian doesn't dictate his letters to a secretary. _____

77.7 each other (E)

Max and Penny are in love. Write sentences about them using **each other**.
- ☐ Penny often writes to Max, and Max often writes to Penny.
  They often write to each other.
1. Max really understands Penny, and Penny really understands Max.
   They really understand _____
2. Penny is always thinking about Max, and Max is always thinking about Penny.
   They're always _____
3. Max has got photos of Penny, and Penny has got photos of Max.
   _____
4. Penny enjoys Max's company, and Max enjoys Penny's company.
   _____
5. Max is crazy about Penny, and Penny is crazy about Max.
   _____

77.8 Reflexive pronoun or each other? (E)

Put in **ourselves, themselves** or **each other**.
- ☐ We could all do more to keep healthy. We don't look after _ourselves_ .
- ☐ The hostess introduced the two guests to _each other_ .
1. The two boxers did their best to knock _____ out.
2. We talk to _____ in French because it's the only language we both know.
3. People who talk to _____ may get strange looks from other people.
4. We'd better set off early to give _____ plenty of time to get there.
5. The guards who shot a gunman claimed they were defending _____ .
6. Luckily we managed to get two seats next to _____ .

78 Review of pronouns and possessives

Look at what Helen is writing to Debbie. Notice the use of the pronouns (e.g. **you**) and the possessives (e.g. **her**).

> Dear Debbie,
> How are you? Lisa and I are having a marvellous holiday. We're really enjoying ourselves. We brought three tubes of suntan cream with us and we've used them all up already. Lisa is a bit annoyed because her suntan isn't as good as mine. Our accommodation is very...

	SUBJECT PRONOUN	OBJECT PRONOUN	POSSESSIVE DETERMINER	POSSESSIVE PRONOUN	REFLEXIVE/EMPHATIC PRONOUN
Singular	I	me	my	mine	myself
	you	you	your	yours	yourself
	he	him	his	his	himself
	she	her	her	hers	herself
	it	it	its		itself
Plural	we	us	our	ours	ourselves
	you	you	your	yours	yourselves
	they	them	their	theirs	themselves

For personal pronouns see Unit 75.
For possessives see Unit 70.
For reflexive/emphatic pronouns see Unit 77.

78 Exercises

78.1 Pronouns and possessives

Complete the dialogues. Use **mine** etc. and **my** etc.
- A: Is that bag Kate's?
  B: I think _it's hers._   Yes, _it's got her name on it._
1. A: Is that briefcase yours?
   B: I think _____   Yes, _____
2. A: Is that violin Steve's?
   B: I think _____   Yes, _____
3. A: Are those tapes Joanne's?
   B: I think _____   Yes, _____
4. A: Is that book mine?
   B: I think _____   Yes, _____

78.2 Pronouns and possessives

Write sentences from the notes, as in the example.
- Alan – birthday — enjoy — parents – given – a sports car
  It's Alan's birthday today. He's enjoying himself. And his parents have given him a sports car.
1. Sue – birthday — enjoy — boyfriend – given – a leather jacket
   It's _____

2. I – birthday — enjoy — brother – given – a personal stereo
   _____

3. the twins – birthday — enjoy — parents – given – some cassettes
   _____

4. we – birthday — enjoy — friends – bought – a cake
   Karen and I were born on the same day. It's _____

78.3 Pronouns and possessives

Put in the missing words. Use **I**, **it**, **him**, **her**, **mine**, **herself** etc.

Jane: Helen's lost □ _her_ purse. There was fifty pounds in it.
Olivia: Oh, dear. [1]_____ hope [2]_____ gets [3]_____ back.
Jane: [4]_____ must have dropped [5]_____ somewhere.
         [6]_____'s rather annoyed with [7]_____ .
Tessa: That was a bit careless, wasn't [8]_____? I've never lost [9]_____ purse.
Marie: I lost [10]_____ once, but [11]_____ got [12]_____ back. A man found [13]_____ and gave [14]_____ back to [15]_____ .
Olivia: [16]_____ were lucky. That was very honest of [17]_____ .
Hannah: If I found a purse, [18]_____ would keep the money for [19]_____ .
Tessa: Most people would, wouldn't [20]_____ ?

79 The pronoun **one/ones**

A Introduction

Look at this conversation:
> Trevor: *I've brought that bottle of mineral water you wanted.*
> Rita: *Oh no, you've got a big **one**. I said a small **one**.*
> Trevor: *They didn't have any small **ones** at Priceways.*
> Rita: *That supermarket never has what I want. Why didn't you go to the **one** in the High Street?*

Here *a big **one*** means 'a big bottle', *small **ones*** means 'small bottles', and *the **one** in the High Street* means 'the supermarket in the High Street'. We use **one** for a singular noun and **ones** for a plural noun. We use **one** and **ones** to avoid repeating a noun when it is clear from the context what we mean.

We cannot use **one** or **ones** with a mass noun (e.g. **water**):
> *There was no hot water. I had to wash in **cold**.*

B Patterns with **one/ones**

We can put in or leave out **one/ones** after **this**, **that**, **these** and **those**; after **each** or **another**; after **which**; or after a superlative.
> *What about **this (one)** here? Or **that (one)** over there?*
> *I tried three phones. **Each (one)** was out of order.*
> *We have all these colours. **Which (one)** would you like?*
> *The first test is the **easiest (one)**.*

We cannot normally leave out **one/ones** after an adjective, **the** or **every**:
> *The train took ages. It was the **slow one**.* NOT *It was the slow.*
> *The play wasn't as good as **the one** we saw last week.*
> *Our house is **the one** on the left.*
> *I tried all the phones. **Every one** was out of order.*
> *I need a box of tissues. A small **one**, please.*
> *I threw away the old curtains and bought some new **ones**.*

C **a small one** and **one**

We can say ***a small one, a red one*** etc. but NOT *a one*. When there is no adjective, we say **one**, like this:
> *I've been looking for a coat, but I haven't found **one**.* (= a coat)
> *We took a taxi. There was **one** waiting.* (= a taxi)

One and **some/any** are indefinite (like **a**). **It** and **they/them** refer to something definite (like **the**):

> *I haven't got a visa, but I'll need **one**.* (***one*** = **a** visa)
> *I haven't got any stamps, but I'll need **some**.* (***some*** = **some** stamps)
> *I've got my visa. They sent **it** last week.* (***it*** = **the** visa)
> *I've got the stamps. I bought **them** yesterday.* (***them*** = **the** stamps)

79 Exercises

79.1 one and ones (A)

Add a phrase with the word in brackets and **one** or **ones**.

- (red)   I need a pen, _a red one_ .
1. (big)   Pass me the dictionary, please, _____.
2. (white)   Why have we got blue envelopes? Haven't we got any _____?
3. (second-hand) Dave's bought a fridge, _____.
4. (cheap)   I lost my watch, but it was only _____.
5. (large)   Get some eggs, _____, please.

79.2 one and ones (A,B)

Look at the pictures and answer the questions. Use these expressions:
the one on the right/on the left/in the middle   the big/small one

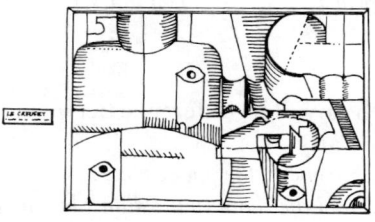

1. Which picture is a landscape?
2. Which is abstract?
3. Which one is a portrait?
4. Which is oldest, the big one or the small one?

79.3 one and ones (A–C)

Rewrite the sentences in brackets to fit the context. Use **one** or **ones**.

- (Each chair is handmade.) The chairs are nice. _Each one is handmade._
1. (I haven't got a ticket.) I need a ticket, but I haven't _____
2. (I've hired a dinner-jacket.) I need a dinner jacket, so I've _____
3. (Have you seen this photo?) These photos are good. Have _____?
4. (The cheapest camera is £100.) These cameras are OK, but the _____
5. (I made every model.) The models are all my own work. I _____

79.4 one, some, it and them (C)

Put in **one**, **some**, **it** or **them**.

- I don't know if I'll need any money. I should take _some_ , I suppose.
1. If you need a map, I can lend you _____.
2. I'm afraid the glass broke. I dropped _____ on the floor.
3. I'm having a biscuit. Would you like _____ too?
4. I had the matches a minute ago, and now I can't find _____.
5. I haven't got any tapes, but Alice has got _____.

80 everyone, something etc.

A Introduction

With **every**, **some** and **no** we can form words ending in **one**, **body**, **thing** and **where**. Look at this table:

everyone/everybody (= all the people)	**everything** (= all the things)	**everywhere** (= (in) all the places)
someone/somebody (= a person)	**something** (= a thing)	**somewhere** (= (in) a place)
no one/nobody (= no person)	**nothing** (= no things)	**nowhere** (= (in) no places)

Everyone enjoyed the show. It was a great success.
*The police searched the house but found **nothing**.*
*Let's find **somewhere** to eat.*   ***Nobody** came into the shop all afternoon.*

Words ending in **thing** can also refer to actions or ideas:
***Something** awful has happened.*   *You must tell me **everything**.*

B some and any

We can also form words with **any**. The difference between **someone** and **anyone** etc. is like the difference between **some** and **any**:

Positive: *There's **some**one in the phone box.*
Negative: *I looked round the shops, but I didn't buy **any**thing.*
Question: *Has **any**one seen today's newspaper?*
Offer/request: *Could you do **some**thing for me, please?*

We can also use **anyone**, **anywhere** etc. in a positive sentence. **Anyone** means 'it doesn't matter who', **anywhere** means 'it doesn't matter where'.
*Where shall we go? ~ **Any**where. I don't mind.*
For more details see Unit 72.

C Singular and plural

We use a singular verb after **everyone**, **something**, **anything** etc:
***Everywhere was** very crowded.*   ***Nobody wants** to go out in this weather.*

But after words ending in **one** and **body** we normally use **they/them/their** even though the verb is singular:
*Everyone is having **their** lunch.*   *Someone couldn't come because **they** were ill.*
We can use **he/she**, **his/her** etc. after **someone/somebody** when we know the person's sex:
*Someone left **her** (OR **their**) handbag behind.*

D Other patterns

We can use an adjective (e.g. **interesting**) or **else** after **everyone** etc:
*Is there **anything interesting** in that magazine?* NOT ~~... interesting anything ...~~
*We always play cards. Let's play **something else**.* (= a different game)
*Brian wore a suit, but **everyone else** had jeans on.* (= all the other people)

Words ending in **one** and **body** have a possessive form (with **'s**):
***Someone's** cat is on our roof.*   *There's **somebody's** coat here.*

80 Exercises

80.1 everyone, something etc. (A)

Complete the dialogues. Put in the correct words.
- _Someone_ rang while you were out. ~ Oh, who? ~ He didn't give his name. He wants to discuss _something_ with you.
1. I'd like to go away _____ on holiday. ~ On your own? ~ No, I hope I can find _____ to come with me.
2. Has Judy got a job yet? ~ No, she's looked _____, but she can't get one. And she hates sitting around doing _____.
3. I found _____ in the street. ~ What? ~ A five-pound note.
4. The luggage is all in the minibus. I've managed to get _____ inside. ~ Well, we can't go yet because _____ is missing. Carl isn't here yet.
5. We all know that the man is a thief. ~ Yes, _____ knows, but _____ dares to say so publicly.

80.2 some and any (B)

Put in **someone**, **anyone**, **something**, **anything**, **somewhere** or **anywhere**.
- A: Have you seen my calculator? I can't find it _anywhere_.
- B: No, I haven't. Perhaps ¹_____'s borrowed it.
- A: I haven't given ²_____ permission to borrow it. It must be ³_____ in this room.
- B: Things are in such a mess. It could be ⁴_____.
- A: I know. I can never find ⁵_____ when I want it.
- B: We'll have to do ⁶_____ about this mess. We'd better tidy it up.

80.3 Singular and plural (C)

Put in the correct form.
1. We had to wait. Someone had lost _____ ticket.   1 its/their
2. One of the policemen had injured _____ arm.   2 his/their
3. No one _____ going to the dentist, do _____?   3 likes/like; he/they
4. One guest had brought something wrapped in brown paper. She put _____ on the table.   4 it/them
5. Everyone _____ to leave _____ bags outside.   5 have/has; his/their

80.4 Other patterns (D)

Rewrite the phrases in brackets using **everyone**, **someone**, **something**, **nothing** and **somewhere**.
- (a nice thing) I'd like to buy myself _something nice_ to wear.
- (another place) It's not very nice here. Let's go _somewhere else_.
- (the results of everyone) _Everyone's results_ were very good.
1. (a famous person) I once met _____.
2. (a car belonging to someone) _____ is blocking the entrance.
3. (no exciting things) _____ ever happens in this place.
4. (a different thing) This programme is boring. Let's watch _____.
5. (the opinions of everyone) _____ will be considered.
6. (all the other people) Kate isn't coming, but _____ is coming.

81 Adjectives and word order

A What is an adjective?

An adjective is a word like **big**, **new**, **warm**, **quiet**, **expensive**, **beautiful**:
    a **big** town   the **new** house   a **warm** day   a **quiet** life

An adjective describes something (it tells us what something is like). In the phrase *a big town*, the adjective **big** describes the town.

B Word order

There are two main places where we can use an adjective. Compare:

BEFORE A NOUN	AFTER A LINKING VERB
You've got a **nice garden**.	Your garden **is nice**.
It was a **dark night**.	It was **getting dark**.

The most common linking verbs are: **be**, **seem**, **appear**, **become**, **get**, **stay**, **look**, **feel**, **taste** and **smell**.

To make an adjective stronger or weaker, we can use an adverb (e.g. **really**) before it:
    You've got a **really nice** garden.   It was getting **quite dark**.

C Adjectives used in one position only

We can use most adjectives in both positions – before a noun or after a linking verb. But a few adjectives can only go in one position but not in the other.

These adjectives can only go <u>before</u> a noun:
    main, **chief**, **principal** (= main); **only**; **inner**, **outer**, **upper**, **indoor**, **outdoor**;
    former (= earlier); **elder**, **eldest** (= older, oldest)

Here are some examples:
    This is the **main** road.   The **only** problem is that I haven't got any money.
    Chess is an **indoor** game.   The **former** champion now trains young players.

We use these adjectives only <u>after</u> a linking verb:
    asleep, **awake**, **alive**, **afraid**, **ashamed**, **alone**, **alike** (= similar);
    pleased, **glad**, **content** (= happy); **well**, **fine** (= in good health), **ill**, **unwell**

Here are some examples:
    Don't make any noise. The baby is **asleep**.
    Kate has got two brothers who are very **alike**.
    I'm **pleased** to see you.   Your friend looked **ill**, I thought.

D Nouns used as adjectives

We can also use a noun (e.g. **television**) as an adjective. We can put it before a noun (e.g. **programme**).
    a **television** programme   the **garage** door   a **night** club   **apple** trees

E The order of adjectives

When two or more adjectives come before a noun, we have to decide in what order to put them. This depends on the meaning of the adjectives. Look at the table:

	how good?	how big?	how old?	what shape?	what colour?	where from?	made of?	what kind? what for?	
a		small			green				insect
						Japanese		industrial	companies
a	wonderful		new					washing	powder
	awful						plastic		souvenirs
the			long	narrow					passage
a	nice						wooden	picture	frame

In general, the adjective closest to the noun has the closest link in meaning with the noun and expresses the most permanent quality. For example, in the phrase *a nice wooden picture frame*, the word **picture** is closely linked to **frame**. The word **nice** is not closely linked and is a matter of opinion.

F Adjectives used as nouns

There are some adjectives which we can use as nouns to talk about groups of people in society (e.g. **the hungry** or **the blind**):

*What can we do to feed **the hungry**?*   *There are special schools for **the blind**.*
***The rich** can afford to pay taxes.*   ***The disabled** need more help from the government.*
***The young** are usually keen to travel.*

The hungry means 'hungry people', **the blind** means 'blind people' etc.

Here are some adjectives which we can use as nouns:

> Social/Economic: **the rich, the poor, the strong, the weak, the (under)privileged, the disadvantaged, the unemployed, the homeless, the hungry**
>
> Physical/Health: **the blind, the deaf, the sick, the disabled, the handicapped, the living, the dead**
>
> Age: **the young, the middle-aged, the elderly, the old**

The hungry means 'hungry people in general'. When we mean a specific group of people, we say, for example, **the hungry people**:

***The disabled people** who we saw at the concert all came from a local hospital.*
NOT ~~The disabled who we saw . . .~~
*None of **the young people** in this village can afford to buy their own homes.*

When we talk about one person, we say, for example, **the hungry man**:

***The disabled man** sat by the door.*
*I know **the young woman** in reception. She lives in our street.*

81 Exercises

81.1 Adjectives (A,B)

Put a circle around all the adjectives in this description of a hotel.
This (comfortable) hotel with its pleasant gardens is ideal for people wanting a quiet holiday, but it is only a short distance from the highly popular attractions of the area. There are lovely views from your room. The atmosphere is very friendly, and the service is always helpful. A holiday here is very good value for money. You can take your meals at the hotel or feel free to try some of the excellent local restaurants.

81.2 Adjectives used in one position only (C,D)

Write song titles from these notes. Sometimes the adjective comes before the noun, and sometimes you need to form a sentence with **is** or **are**.

☐ your sister – elder   *Your elder sister*
☐ this boy – alone   *This boy is alone.*
1 the girl – only   _____
2 the world – asleep   _____
3 my ambition – chief   _____
4 these streets – city   _____
5 my heart – content   _____
6 the night – alive   _____
7 secrets – inner   _____
8 the life – outdoor   _____

81.3 The order of adjectives (D,E)

For each advertisement write a sentence with all the adjectives.
☐ This game is new. It's for the family. And it's exciting.
   It's an exciting new family game.
1 This computer is for business. It's Japanese. And it's powerful.
   It's a _____
2 This fire is electric. It's excellent. And it's small.

3 It's a chocolate bar. It's new. And it's a big bar.

4 This comedy is American. It's for television. And it's terrific.

5 These doors are aluminium. They're for your garage. And they're stylish.
   They're _____
6 These shoes are modern. They're for running. And they're super.

7 This model is blue. It's plastic. And it's attractive.

8 This phone is for your car. It's German. And it's high-quality.

81 Adjectives and word order

81.4 The order of adjectives (D, E)

Write a list of things to be sold at an auction.

- basin – sugar, antique, silver — *an antique silver sugar basin*
1. vase – glass, 19th century, lovely — a _____
2. mirror – circular, wall, attractive — _____
3. desk – modern, office — _____
4. chairs – kitchen, red, metal, four — _____
5. boat – model, splendid, old — _____
6. stamps – postage, valuable, Australian, several — _____
7. table – large, dining, mahogany — _____
8. rug – woollen, brown — _____

81.5 The position and order of adjectives (B–E)

Choose the correct sentence.

- Go to the post office along here.
  That's the main post office.
- That post office is main.
  or That's the main post office.

1. Don't wake the dog. _____
1. It's asleep.
   or It's an asleep dog.
2. What's this number? _____
2. Is it telephone?
   or Is it a telephone number?
3. I've found this bag. _____
3. It's an old shopping bag.
   or It's a shopping old bag.
4. This fish isn't dead, you know. _____
4. It's alive.
   or It's an alive fish.
5. I haven't got any money. _____
5. That problem is only.
   or That's the only problem.

81.6 Adjectives used as nouns (F)

Complete these sentences from a newspaper using the adjectives. Put in e.g. **the hungry** or **the hungry people**.

- The rich nations can afford to feed *the hungry* . □ hungry
- *The homeless people* we told you about last week have now found a flat to rent. □ homeless

1. _____ need to be looked after, so money must be spent on hospitals. 1 sick
2. Some of _____ at the local youth club are running in a marathon next week. 2 young
3. Life must be hard for _____ in our society today. 3 unemployed
4. What is the government going to do to help _____ ? 4 poor
5. There was a fire at a nursing home in Charles Street, but none of _____ who live there were hurt. 5 old
6. _____ usually have great difficulty in getting a job. 6 homeless
7. There is a special programme for _____ on television this evening. 7 deaf

82 exciting or excited?

Compare the two adjectives:

*an **exciting** game*

excited people

Both teams are playing very well. The game is **exciting**.

They are watching to see who will win. They are **excited**.

Compare:

An adjective ending in **ing** describes what something is like, what effect it has on us. For example, a game can be **exciting**, **interesting**, **boring** or **disappointing**.

An adjective ending in **ed** describes how we feel. For example, we can feel **excited**, **interested**, **bored** or **disappointed**.

Here are some more examples:

ing ADJECTIVE

This programme about astronomy is **interesting**.

I didn't enjoy the party. It was **boring**.

It was **disappointing** not to get the job.
The game went on all afternoon. It was **tiring**.

Jeremy told us an **amusing** story.
The long delay was **annoying**.

The result was **surprising**.
The talk was rather **confusing**, I thought.

Lying in a hot bath is **relaxing**.
The exhibition was **fascinating**. I could have spent all day looking at it.

ed ADJECTIVE

I'm **interested** in astronomy.

I went to the party, but I felt **bored** the whole time.

I was **disappointed** not to get the job.
After playing all afternoon they were **tired**.

We were **amused** by Jeremy's story.
The passengers were **annoyed** about the long delay.

I was **surprised** at the result.
Most people were **confused** after listening to the talk.

I feel **relaxed** when I lie in a hot bath.
I was **fascinated** by the exhibition.

82 Exercises

82.1 exciting or excited?

Put in the correct adjective.

- When we heard we'd won a trip to Florida, you can imagine how _excited_ we were. — exciting/excited
1. Tony often goes bird-watching. He's _____ in birds. — interesting/interested
2. I play chess regularly. I think it's a _____ game. — fascinating/fascinated
3. I've really got no idea what I'm supposed to do next. I'm _____. — confusing/confused
4. I was sure the car was going to crash. I was absolutely _____. — terrifying/terrified
5. I don't like this town at all. It's a rather _____ place. — depressing/depressed

82.2 exciting or excited?

Complete the conversation.

A: That was an □ _exciting_ film, wasn't it? — excit...
B: Oh, do you think so? I'm ¹_____ you liked it. I thought it was rather ²_____. — 1 surpris... / 2 disappoint...
A: Well, I was ³_____ once or twice. I didn't understand the whole story. It was ⁴_____ in places. But the end was good. — 3 puzzl... / 4 confus...
B: I was ⁵_____ most of the time. I didn't find it a very ⁶_____ film. — 5 bor... / 6 interest...

82.3 exciting or excited?

Complete the conversation about a holiday.

- I was surprised at how good the weather was. ~ Yes, the amount of sunshine we had was _surprising_.
- I was tired after we climbed the mountain. ~ Yes, I think everyone felt _tired_.
1. The older people had a nice relaxing time. ~ Yes, lying on the beach is certainly nice and _____.
2. It was annoying losing that suitcase. ~ Yes, you must be really _____ about it.
3. That film we saw was amusing. ~ Laura was certainly _____. She couldn't stop laughing.
4. The museum was interesting, I thought. ~ Yes, we had an _____ time there. There was lots to see.
5. I was fascinated by those old photos of the town. ~ Yes, I thought they were _____ too.
6. The wind-surfing was a thrilling experience for the children. ~ Yes, they were certainly _____ to have a go.
7. I think I'll go to bed. I'm exhausted. Looking after young children is an _____ job.

83 Adjective + preposition

After some adjectives we can use a preposition (e.g. **on**, **of**):
My father is very **keen on** golf.　　The town is **famous for** its architecture.
The hole was **full of** water.　　I'll be **late for** my evening class.

For an ing-form after the preposition (e.g. *He's* **keen on playing** *today*), see Unit 48.

A Adjectives expressing feelings

Here are some common adjective + preposition combinations which are to do with feelings:
**ashamed of; disappointed with/about; eager for; excited about;
interested in, keen on, fond of;
nervous of, afraid of, worried about;
pleased with/about, happy with/about, satisfied with;
proud of; surprised at/by, shocked at/by, amazed at/by;
tired of, bored with, fed up with**

Study these pairs:

I'm **sorry about** the mistake.	I feel **sorry for** Kate.
We were **angry at/about** the delay.	I was **angry with** Matthew.
We were **annoyed at/about** the delay.	We were **annoyed with** Jessica.
Tim is **anxious about** the exam.	People are **anxious for** news.
(= Tim is worried about the exam.)	(= People are waiting for news.)

B Adjectives meaning 'good' or 'bad'

To talk about a person's ability, we use **good at**, **bad at** etc:
good at tennis　　**brilliant at** crosswords　　**bad at** games　　**hopeless at** running

To talk about whether something makes you healthy or ill, we use **good for** and **bad for**:
Oranges are **good for** you.　　Smoking is **bad for** you.

To talk about how we behave towards another person, we use **good to**, **nice to**, **kind to**, **polite to** and **rude to**:
My friends have been **good to** me.　　You were very **rude to** the waitress.

C Other adjectives

Here are some more expressions with other adjectives:

It's **full of** rubbish.	We're **safe from** attack.
She's **famous for** her singing.	You're **late for** school.
This is the **same as** (OR **similar to**) last time.	This way is **different from** our usual route.
They're **ready for** (OR **prepared for**) action.	He isn't **fit for** work.
We're **used to** (OR **accustomed to**) the noise.	I'm **capable of** looking after myself.
He's **aware of** the facts.	This is **typical of** this area.
They're **involved in** a project.	I'm **responsible for** running the business.

83 Exercises

83.1 Adjectives expressing feelings (A)

Say what these people's feelings are.
- The Harpers are starting their holiday. (excited)
  They're excited about their holiday.
1. Jessica doesn't like the dark. (afraid)
   She's _____
2. Jason was watching a video, but he's going to switch it off. (bored)
   He's _____
3. Sarah is reading a magazine about computers. (interested)
   She's _____
4. Terry has just heard some news that he didn't expect. (surprised)
   He's _____
5. The team have won a victory. (proud)
   They're _____
6. Mrs Foyle's children are being silly. (annoyed)
   She's _____
7. The staff think their pay increase is all right. (satisfied)
   They're _____

83.2 Adjectives meaning 'good' or 'bad' (B)

Complete the conversation. Put in **at**, **for** or **to**.
Alice: You were very rude ¹_____ James when you said he needs to lose weight.
Trevor: Well, it's true. Exercise would be good ²_____ him.
Alice: Yes, but we aren't all as good ³_____ athletics as you are.
Trevor: Anyone can do a bit of jogging. You don't have to be brilliant ⁴_____ it. And eating so much must be bad ⁵_____ you.
Alice: Well, you could have been more polite.
Trevor: Sorry. I'm not very good ⁶_____ saying the right thing. I'll try to be nice ⁷_____ him next time I see him.

83.3 Some other adjectives (C)

Complete these paragraphs from a letter. Use these adjectives and put a preposition after each one: **aware, different, famous, full, late, ready, responsible, similar, used**.

Everything was strange here at first because this new job is ☐ *different from* any I've had before. But I've got ☐ *used to* it now, and I'm enjoying it. I'm mainly ¹_____ controlling the costs of the project. The work is quite hard, and I feel ²_____ a holiday. The company expect people to do overtime, which I wasn't ³_____ before I arrived. They hadn't told me at the interview.

I've got a nice flat which is very ⁴_____ the one I had in London. The only difference is that my flat here is ⁵_____ horrible old furniture. I live right by the harbour. I get woken very early by the noise of the boats, so I'm never ⁶_____ work. This area is ⁷_____ its sea food, and there are several good fish restaurants.

84 Adjective + to-infinitive

A The pattern **It is safe to use the ladder**

We can often use a to-infinitive after an adjective (e.g. **safe**, **easy**):
*It's **safe to use** the ladder.*
*It's **easy to criticize**.*
*It's **nice to have** lots of friends.*
*It's **difficult to keep** awake all night.*
*It is **important to read** the instructions.*
*It was very **silly to make** such a fuss.*
*I'm **delighted to see** you.*
*It's really **fascinating to see** how these baskets are made.*

B The pattern **The ladder is safe to use**

Look at these two sentences. They both have the same meaning.
It is safe to use the ladder. OR *The ladder is safe to use.*
The ladder comes after the infinitive in the first sentence. In the second sentence **the ladder** is the subject of the whole sentence. There is no pronoun (e.g. **it**) after **to use**:
NOT *The ladder is safe to use it.*

Here are some more examples:
*Your writing is **difficult to read**.*
*A small car would be **cheap to run**.*
*The race was **exciting to watch**.*

We can use this pattern with **safe, dangerous**; **cheap, expensive**; **easy, difficult, convenient**; and with adjectives meaning 'good' or 'bad', e.g. **wonderful, marvellous, exciting, nice; awful, terrible**.

C **for** and **of**

After some adjectives we can use **for** + object + to-infinitive:
*It isn't **safe for children to play** on ladders.*
*It's **important for everyone to keep** quiet.*
*The car is **ready for you to drive** away.*

We use the pattern with **for** after these adjectives: **safe, dangerous; cheap, expensive; easy, difficult; important, vital, essential, necessary; ready; willing, happy, eager, anxious, impatient; usual, normal; useful, advisable; possible, convenient; impossible; interesting; wonderful, marvellous, exciting, nice; awful, terrible**.

After an adjective describing someone's behaviour (e.g. **nice, silly**), we use a pattern with **of**:
*It was **nice of Sarah to invite** us.* (= Sarah was nice ...)
*It was **silly of me to forget** my ticket.* (= I was silly ...)

We can use the pattern with **of** after these adjectives: **good, nice, kind, helpful; mean, generous; brave; honest; clever, intelligent; sensible, reasonable; silly, stupid, foolish, careless; wrong; polite, rude**.

For more examples with **for** and **of** in this pattern, see Unit 47.

84 Exercises

84.1 The pattern **It is safe to use the ladder** (**A**)

Write the sentences with a to-infinitive after the adjective.

☐ Buy a Compex computer. It isn't expensive.
It isn't _expensive to buy a Compex computer._

1 When you use the computer, you'll see that it's very easy.
It's very easy _____
2 Understanding the handbook isn't very difficult.
It isn't _____
3 Working with the computer is fascinating.
It's _____
4 Operating the keyboard is easy.
It's _____
5 You must buy the best. That's important.
It's _____
6 When you own a Compex computer, you'll be delighted.
You'll _____

84.2 The pattern **The ladder is safe to use** (**B**)

Rewrite the first four sentences from Exercise 84.1 like this.

☐ A Compex computer _isn't expensive to buy._
1 The computer _____
2 The _____
3 _____
4 _____

84.3 **for** and **of** (**C**)

A Japanese company called Sanko is going to open a factory in Middleton, England. Write sentences from the notes using **for** or **of**.

☐ marvellous – the town – have – some new jobs
It will be _marvellous for the town to have some new jobs._
☐ clever – the Mayor – bring – Sanko – to Middleton
It was _clever of the Mayor to bring Sanko to Middleton._
1 difficult – the town – attract – new industry
It has been _____
2 very generous – the Council – give – the land – to Sanko
It was _____
3 impossible – Sanko – refuse – the offer
It was _____
4 wrong – the Middleton News – criticize – the new plan
It was _____
5 interesting – local workers – follow – Japanese methods
It will be _____
6 the company – eager – production – begin – soon
_____

85 Adjective or adverb?

A Introduction

Compare adjectives and adverbs:

An adjective (e.g. **quiet**) describes a noun (e.g. **voice**):	An adverb (e.g. **quietly**) describes a verb (e.g. **spoke**):
The man had a **quiet** voice.	He **spoke quietly**. NOT *He spoke quiet.*
Katrina wears **expensive** clothes.	She **dresses expensively**.
The runners made a **slow** start.	They **started slowly**.
We have **regular** meetings.	We **meet regularly**.
	Most adverbs end in **ly**.

An adverb (e.g. **really**, **very**) can also relate to an adjective (e.g. **hot**), or to an adverb (e.g. **carefully**):

   It was **really hot** in the sun.   They counted the money **very carefully**.

An adverb (e.g. **suddenly**, **clearly**) can also relate to a whole sentence:

   Suddenly we heard a shout.   **Clearly** there's been a mistake.

B looked nice and looked carefully

An adjective can come after **be**:

   Everyone **was happy**.   The flat **is small**.

Here **small** tells us about the noun **flat**, not about the verb. **Be** is a linking verb – it links the noun and the adjective.

Linking verbs are **be**, **seem**, **appear**, **become**, **get**, **stay**, **look**, **feel**, **taste** and **smell**. Look at these two examples:

   Everyone **seemed happy**.   The situation has **become serious**.

We use adjectives after linking verbs (e.g. **seemed happy**) and adverbs after action verbs (e.g. **played happily**). An action verb describes something happening (e.g. **play**, **start**, **open**, **put**).

Some verbs can be either linking verbs or action verbs. Compare:

LINKING VERB + ADJECTIVE	ACTION VERB + ADVERB
Mervyn **looked sad**.	He **looked carefully** at the signature.
The medicine **tasted awful**.	She **tasted** the drink **nervously**.
The man **appeared** (to be) **drunk**.	The ghost **appeared suddenly**.

C The ly ending

We form many adverbs from an adjective + **ly**. For example: **safely**, **politely**, **normally**, **softly**. But there are some special spelling rules:

1. **y** → **ily** after a consonant, e.g. luck**y** → luck**ily**
   Also: **happily, easily, heavily, angrily** etc.
2. We do not leave out **e**, e.g. nic**e** → nic**ely**
   Exceptions are **true** → **truly**, **whole** → **wholly**
3. **le** → **ly**, e.g. possi**ble** → possi**bly**
   Also: **probably, sensibly, comfortably, terribly, reasonably** etc.
4. **ic** → **ically**, e.g. dramat**ic** → dramat**ically**
   Also: **automatically, scientifically** etc. (Exception: **publicly**)

D ly adjectives

A few adjectives end in **ly**, e.g. **friendly, lively, lovely, silly, ugly, lonely, likely**.
  The professor was very **friendly**.   It was a **lively** party.

We cannot add **ly** to these words. (We canNOT say ~~friendlily~~.) And we cannot use them as adverbs. (NOT ~~He greeted us friendly.~~) But we can say **in a friendly way/manner**:
  He greeted us **in a friendly way**.

E some hard work and work hard

Compare:

ADJECTIVE	ADVERB
We did some **hard** work.	We worked **hard**.
I came on the **fast** train.	It went quite **fast**.

These words are both adjectives and adverbs: **hard, fast, high, low, deep, early, late, long, near, straight, right, wrong**.

In informal English, the adjectives **cheap, slow, quick** and **loud** can be adverbs:

ADJECTIVE	ADVERB
They sell **cheap** suits.	They sell things **cheap**/cheaply.
Back already! That was **quick**.	Come as **quick**/quickly as you can.

F hard, hardly etc.

There are some pairs of adverbs with different meanings (e.g. **hard** and **hardly**).
  I tried **hard** but I didn't succeed.
  I've got **hardly** any money left. (**hardly any** = very little, almost none)
  Luckily I found a phone box quite **near**.
  I **nearly** fell asleep in the lecture. (**nearly** = almost)
  The coach arrived **late**.
  I've been very busy (just) **lately**. (**lately** = in the last few days/weeks)
  The plane flew **high** above the clouds.
  The material is **highly** radioactive. (**highly** = very)
  We got into the concert **free**. (**free** = without paying)
  The animals are allowed to wander **freely**. (**freely** = uncontrolled)

G good and well

Good is an adjective and **well** is its adverb:

ADJECTIVE	ADVERB
Phil is a **good** dancer.	He dances **well**.
The show was very **good**.	They all performed **well**.

The opposites are **bad** and **badly**:

I made a **bad** mistake.	I did **badly** in the test.

Well can also be an adjective meaning 'in good health'. The opposite is **ill**.
  My mother was very **ill**, but she's quite **well** again now.
  How are you? ~ Very **well**, thank you.

85 Exercises

85.1 Adverbs (A)

Complete each sentence with an adverb. Form the adverbs by adding **ly** to these adjectives:
bright, careful, fluent, immediate, perfect, polite, punctual, safe, secret, serious, slow.

☐ One engine wasn't working, but the pilot still managed to land _safely_.
1 The journey took ages. We travelled really _____.
2 I didn't want to break the glasses. I packed them all _____ in paper.
3 There's no need to be rude. It doesn't cost anything to behave _____.
4 We weren't late. We arrived _____.
5 The matter is urgent. We ought to do something _____.
6 It was a beautiful day. The sun shone _____ from a clear blue sky.
7 No one else knew about the meeting. The two leaders met _____.
8 I was only joking. Why do you take everything so _____?
9 The dancer didn't make a mistake. She performed the dance _____.
10 Heidi's English is very correct. And she speaks so _____ too.

85.2 Adjective or adverb? (A, B)

Put in the correct form.

☐ This weather is _awful_. ~ Yes, it's raining quite _heavily_ now.   ☐ awful/awfully
                                                                        heavy/heavily

1 Did Paul pass his exam? ~ Yes, he passed _____. He's   1 easy/easily
   _____, isn't he?   clever/cleverly
2 You don't look very _____. ~ I can't find my wallet.   2 happy/happily
   I'm _____ I brought it with me.   sure/surely
3 How do you like Sadie? ~ She seems very _____. We   3 nice/nicely
   had a _____ chat.   nice/nicely
4 Are you all right? ~ My stomach feels a bit _____. I   4 funny/funnily
   think I'm going to be _____.   sick/sickly
5 You haven't washed these plates _____. They're still   5 proper/properly
   _____. ~ Oh, sorry. I was in a hurry. I did them rather   dirty/dirtily
   _____.   quick/quickly
6 Can you remember what happened? ~ I can't remember   6 clear/clearly
   _____. It all happened so _____.   sudden/suddenly

85.3 The ly ending (C)

Put in the adverb form. Be careful with the spelling.

☐ I felt terrible. My tooth ached _terribly_.
1 Something had made your friend angry. He shouted _____ at the waiter.
2 Wayne is happy to play computer games. He'll sit _____ in front of the
   computer for hours.
3 It's automatic. The machine switches itself off _____.
4 There's been no public debate. We haven't debated the matter _____.
5 Everyone is enthusiastic about the idea. They all discussed it _____.
6 Let's be reasonable. Can't we discuss the matter _____?
7 The building has to be secure. Did you lock all the doors _____?
8 Just use simple words. Express your meaning _____.

85 Adjective or adverb?

85.4 hard, hardly etc. (D–F)

Decide if you need **ly** with these words: **free, friend, hard, high, late, love, low, near**.

▢ The view from here is _lovely_, isn't it?
1 Employees of the airline can travel _____ on some flights.
2 The receptionist gave me a _____ smile.
3 I had very little time to spare. I _____ missed the bus.
4 The plane flew _____ over the trees.
5 I can't ask Gary to lend me money. I _____ know him.
6 We all laughed. The story was _____ amusing.
7 Does the store stay open _____ ? ~ Yes, till midnight.

85.5 good and well (G)

Put in **good, well** (×2), **bad, badly** and **ill**.
A: How did the team get on?
B: We lost. I'm afraid we didn't play very ¹_____ . Roger made a ²_____ mistake. It wasn't a very ³_____ day for us. We played really ⁴_____ .
A: I heard Dave couldn't play because he isn't very ⁵_____ at the moment.
B: Yes, I'm afraid he's been ⁶_____ for several days. He's still in bed.

85.6 Adjective or adverb? (A–G)

Give the information about each underlined word.

	Adjective or adverb?	It describes . . .
▢ This puzzle is <u>difficult</u> .	_adjective_	_puzzle_
▢ The crowd cheered <u>excitedly</u> .	_adverb_	_cheered_
1 The man had <u>fair</u> hair.	_____	_____
2 Pamela was getting <u>tired</u> .	_____	_____
3 The manager looked <u>nervous</u> .	_____	_____
4 The detective looked <u>closely</u> at it.	_____	_____
5 Sometimes I feel <u>lonely</u> .	_____	_____
6 Our visitors didn't stay <u>long</u> .	_____	_____
7 Alex plays the guitar very <u>well</u> .	_____	_____
8 There was an <u>extremely</u> loud explosion.	_____	_____

85.7 Adjective or adverb? (A–G)

Put in the correct form.

I had a ▢ _strange_ dream last night. I was in a garden. It was getting ¹_____ and it was ²_____ cold. My head was aching ³_____ . I was walking out of the garden when ⁴_____ I saw a girl sitting on a seat. She seemed very ⁵_____ . She looked up and smiled ⁶_____ at me. I felt ⁷_____ for some reason. I wanted to be ⁸_____ so I tried ⁹_____ to think of something to say. But I couldn't. I just stood there ¹⁰_____ .

▢ strange/strangely
1 dark/darkly
2 terrible/terribly
3 bad/badly
4 sudden/suddenly
5 unhappy/unhappily
6 sad/sadly   7 anxious/anxiously   8 friend/friendly   9 hard/hardly
10 foolish/foolishly

86 Comparative and superlative forms

A The comparison of adjectives

*The cassette is **cheaper** than the record. It's the **cheapest**.*
*The record is **more expensive** than the cassette, but the disc is the **most expensive**.*

A short adjective (e.g. **cheap**) and a long adjective (e.g. **expensive**) form their comparative and superlative in different ways:

	COMPARATIVE	SUPERLATIVE
Short word, e.g. **cheap**	cheaper	(the) cheapest
Long word, e.g. **expensive**	more expensive	(the) most expensive

B Short and long adjectives

One-syllable adjectives (e.g. **small, nice**) have **er/est**:
   *This screwdriver is **smaller**.*   *I need a **bigger** brush.*
   *You wore the **nicest** hat.*   *This room is the **warmest**.*
But we use **more/most** before words ending in **ed** (e.g. **pleased** → **more pleased**).

Three-syllable adjectives (e.g. **ex·cit·ing**) and longer ones have **more/most**:
   *The film was **more exciting** than the book.*   *This dress is **more elegant**.*
   *We did the **most interesting** project.*   *This machine is the **most reliable**.*

Some two-syllable adjectives (e.g. **hap·py**) have **er/est**, but others (e.g. **use·ful**) have **more/most**. Look at this table:

TWO-SYLLABLE ADJECTIVES

1. With **er/est** (e.g. **happy** → **happier**):
   Words ending in a consonant + **y**, e.g. **happy, lucky, lovely, pretty, heavy, dirty, tidy, easy, silly, funny**

2. With **er/est** OR **more/most** (e.g. **narrow** → **narrower/more narrow**):
   narrow, common, pleasant, quiet, polite, clever, simple, gentle, cruel, tired, stupid

3. With **more/most** (e.g. **useful** → **more useful**):
   Words ending in **ful** or **less**, e.g. **useful, helpful, careful, hopeless**
   Words ending in **ing** or **ed**, e.g. **boring, willing, annoyed, surprised**
   Many others, e.g. **correct, exact, certain, normal, frequent, recent, famous, modern, afraid, eager, foolish**

86 Comparative and superlative forms

C Spelling

There are some special spelling rules for the **er** and **est** endings:

> 1 **e** → **er/est**, e.g. nic**e** → nic**er**/nic**est**, larg**e** → larg**er**/larg**est**
>   Also: **safe**, **fine**, **brave** etc.
> 2 **y** → **ier/iest** after a consonant, e.g. happ**y** → happ**ier**/happ**iest**
>   Also: **lucky**, **lovely**, **pretty** etc.
> 3 Words ending in a single vowel letter + single consonant letter,
>   e.g. ho**t** → ho**tt**er/ho**tt**est, bi**g** → bi**gg**er/bi**gg**est
>   Also: **wet**, **sad**, **thin** etc. (but not **w** or **y**, e.g. ne**w** → ne**w**er)

D The comparison of adverbs

Some adverbs have the same form as an adjective, e.g. **fast**, **hard**, **high**, **near**, **long**, **late**, **early**. They form the comparative and superlative in **er/est**:
> *Can't you run **faster** than that?*   *Adrian went to bed the **latest**.*

Many adverbs are an adjective + **ly**, e.g. **nicely**, **slowly**, **carefully**, **easily**. They form the comparative and superlative with **more/most**:
> *The horse jumped the second fence **more easily** than the first.*
> *Tom was the most successful player. He planned his tactics the **most carefully**.*

In informal English we use **cheaper/cheapest**, **slower/slowest**, **quicker/quickest** and **louder/loudest** rather than **more cheaply**, **the most slowly** etc:
> *Donna reacted the **quickest**.*   *You should drive **slower** in fog.*

E Irregular forms

Good/well, **bad/badly** and **far** have irregular forms:

ADJECTIVE/ADVERB	COMPARATIVE	SUPERLATIVE
good/well	**better**	**best**
bad/badly	**worse**	**worst**
far	**farther/further**	**farthest/furthest**

> *You've got the **best** handwriting.*   *How much **further** are we going?*

We can use **elder/eldest** for people in the same family:
> *My **elder** (OR **older**) sister got married last year.*

F Comparing quantities

We use **more**, **most** and their opposites **less** and **least** to compare quantities:
> *I haven't got many tapes. You've got **more** than I have.*
> *United have won the **most** games.*
> *I'm very busy these days. I have **less** spare time than I used to.*

86 Exercises

86.1 The comparison of adjectives (**A,B**)

Complete the advertisements with the comparative form of the adjective.
- Use Clean-It and you'll get your floors _cleaner_ .
- Elegant Wallpapers simply look _more elegant_ .
1. Intelligent Books will make you _____ .
2. Wear a pair of Fast Shoes and you'll be a _____ runner.
3. Helpful Cookbooks are a _____ guide to cooking.
4. Fresh Food supermarkets have got _____ food.
5. Wear a Smart-Look suit and you'll be a _____ person.
6. Restful Beds give you a _____ night.
7. Pleasant Hotels for a _____ stay.

86.2 The comparison of adjectives (**A,B**)

Put in the superlative form of the adjectives in brackets.
- (fast)   The _fastest_ time for the 100 metres is just under 10 seconds.
- (valuable)   Is the Mona Lisa the _most valuable_ painting in the world?
1. (long)   The Pan-American Highway is the _____ road in the world.
2. (successful)   The Beatles were the _____ pop group ever.
3. (crowded)   Japan has the _____ railways in the world.
4. (old)   KLM is the _____ national airline.
5. (tall) . The Chrysler Building was once the _____ in the world.
6. (useful)   Is English the _____ language to learn?
7. (famous)   Harrod's is one of the _____ stores in the world.
8. (rich)   The Queen must be the _____ woman in England.

86.3 The comparison of adjectives (**A–C**)

Put in the comparative or superlative form of the adjectives on the right.

There are lots of hotels in the pretty town of Blexham. You get a □ _wider_ choice than in most places. The Crown is the □ _most famous_ because Charles Dickens once stayed there. It's also one of the ¹_____ . The Metropole is a ²_____ and a ³_____ hotel. It's also ⁴_____ than the Crown. The Metropole is the ⁵_____ hotel in town, and so it's ⁶_____ with business people than with tourists. Personally I can't think of anything ⁷_____ than a big modern hotel. My own favourite is the Down Court Hotel, which is ⁸_____ and ⁹_____ than the Metropole. The staff at Down Court are ¹⁰_____ than at the other hotels. Down Court is also in a ¹¹_____ place than the others. The Metropole is the ¹²_____ hotel in town because it's on the main road. The Bristol has a good restaurant. But you need to book a table because it's the ¹³_____ place in Blexham.

□ wide
□ famous
1 old
2 big   3 modern
4 comfortable
5 expensive
6 popular
7 boring

8 small
9 pleasant
10 helpful
11 nice
12 noisy

13 busy

86 Comparative and superlative forms

86.4 The comparison of adverbs (D)

Put in the comparative form of these adverbs:
carefully, easily, frequently, high, late, long, loud, smartly.

☐ I was too nervous to go _higher_ than halfway up the tower.
☐ I could have found the place _more easily_ if I had had a map.
1 Do you have to wear those old jeans? You could dress _____ .
2 You needn't go yet. You can stay a bit _____ .
3 To get to London by nine, we can't leave _____ than seven. It takes two hours.
4 There are lots of break-ins. They happen _____ nowadays than before.
5 Do it again _____ and you won't make so many mistakes.
6 We can't hear. Could you speak a bit _____ ?

86.5 Irregular forms (E)

Put in **further, furthest, better, best, worse** and **worst**.

A: I'm not used to country walks. How much ¹_____ is it?
B: Not far. And it gets better. We've done the ²_____ part. Look! The path goes down the hill from here. I hope you're feeling ³_____ now.
A: I feel dreadful actually, ⁴_____ than before.
B: Oh, dear. Do you want to have a rest?
A: No, the ⁵_____ thing would be to get there first. I'm not fit, you know. This is the ⁶_____ I've walked for a long time.

86.6 Comparative and superlative forms (A–E)

Put in the comparative or superlative form of the words on the right.

A: I'm going to the Lake District next week. We're going ☐ _earlier_ than usual.   ☐ early
B: I'd love a holiday in June, but it's ¹_____ for the children to go in the school holidays.   1 convenient
A: I know. But May and June are the ²_____ and ³_____ months. Sometimes we go in September which is the ⁴_____ time of the year with the leaves on the trees changing colour.   2 dry
3 nice
4 beautiful
B: Maybe it would be ⁵_____ to go in winter than in summer. It would certainly be ⁶_____ . It might be ⁷_____ than August. I can't think of a ⁸_____ time to go than August.   5 sensible
6 cheap
7 good
8 bad

86.7 Comparing quantities (G)

Put in **more, most, less** and **least**.

A: Our new car is smaller, so it uses ¹_____ petrol. They tested some small cars, and this one costs the ²_____ to run of all the cars in the test. It's very economical.
B: Can you get three people in the back?
A: Not very easily. We had ³_____ room in our old car. ⁴_____ cars take five people, but not this one.

207

87 Comparative and superlative patterns

A The comparative

We can use a comparative adjective before a noun:
*I've got a **younger brother**.*   *Let's play a **more interesting game**.*
We can also use it after a linking verb (e.g. **be**, **seem**, **become**, **look**):
*Your brother **looks younger**.*   *This game **is more interesting**.*
We often use a phrase with **than** after a comparative:
*He looks **younger than** you.*   *It's **more interesting than** card games.*

B The superlative

We normally use **the** before a superlative:
***The quickest** way is along this path.*   *Question 2 is **the most difficult**.*

We can use **in** or **of** after a superlative. We use **in** with places.
*Who is the **oldest** person **in the world**?*
*The Randolph is the **most expensive** hotel **in Oxford**.*
*The last question is the **most difficult of all**.*
*August is the **wettest** month **of the year**.*

We often use a clause after a superlative:
*That was the **most exciting** match **(that) I've ever seen**.*
*Dave is the **nicest** person **you could meet**.*

C as and so

We use **as ... as** in a positive sentence to say that things are equal:
*The tree is **as tall as** the house.*
NOT *The tree is so tall as the house.*

But in a negative sentence we can use **as ... as** or **so ... as**:
*It isn't **as cold as** yesterday.* OR *It isn't **so cold as** yesterday.*
(= Yesterday was colder.)

Here are some more examples:
*The chair is **as expensive as** the table.*
*Your boy-friend is **as old as** my father, you know.*
*We can't do crosswords **as quickly** (OR **so quickly**) **as** you do.*
*I don't earn **as much** (OR **so much**) money **as** I'd like.*

D than me / than I am

Compare:

than me	**than I am**
After **than** or **as**, a personal pronoun on its own has the object form (e.g. **me**):	But if the pronoun has a verb after it, then we use the subject form (e.g. **I**):
*You're taller than **me**.*	*You're taller than **I am**.*
*Her husband isn't as clever as **her**.*	*Her husband isn't as clever as **she is**.*
*They've got more money than **us**.*	*They've got more money than **we have**.*

87 Exercises

87.1 The comparative (**A**)

Write sentences with a comparative and **than**. Use these adjectives:
expensive, fast, intelligent, long, old, strong, tall.

- ☐ The film is 2½ hours, but the video tape is only 2 hours.
  The film is longer than the video tape.
- ☐ The water colour is £85, and the oil painting is £100.
  The oil painting is more expensive than the water colour.
1. The church was built in 1878 and the library in 1925.
2. Tim is 1.6 metres tall, but Wendy is 1.7 metres.
3. The Presto can do 130 mph on the race-track, but the Montero can do 140 mph.
4. Sadie is clever. She's got an IQ of 140. Lorraine has an IQ of 105.
5. Simon can lift 90 kilos, but Carl can lift 120 kilos.

87.2 The superlative (**B**)

Write sentences from the notes. Use the superlative form of the adjective.
- ☐ Ann – kind person – I know   _Ann is the kindest person I know._
1. Friday – busy day – the week   _____ of the week.
2. the Bristol – nice hotel – the town
3. this camera – expensive – you can buy
4. the latest show – successful – all
5. it – boring song – I've ever heard

87.3 as ... as (**C**)

Write sentences from the notes. Use **isn't as ... as**.
- ☐ a car – a motor bike – expensive   _A motor-bike isn't as expensive as a car._
1. Japan – China – big
2. metal – plastic – strong
3. an armchair – a stool – comfortable
4. a pop song – a symphony – long
5. the sun – the moon – hot

87.4 than me/than I am (**D**)

Put in the correct pronoun. Choose from the words on the right.

Sam: Why is Nick in the basketball team and not me? Aren't I
as good as ¹_____? Is he a better player than ²_____ am?

Jeff: I don't know. I can't understand why I'm in the team. You and
Nick are both better than ³_____.

Sam: Gary's in the team too, but I've scored a lot more baskets than
⁴_____ has.

1 he/him
2 I/me
3 I/me
4 he/him

88 much faster, faster and faster etc.

A much faster

We can put a word or phrase (e.g. **far**, **a bit**) before a comparative to say <u>how much</u> cheaper, <u>how much</u> more comfortable etc. something is. Look at these examples:

*A plastic picture frame is **far cheaper** than a wooden one.*
*This chair is **a bit more comfortable**.*
*Business has been **rather better** this year.*
*I got up **a little later** than usual.*
*Your garden is **slightly bigger** than ours.*
*You need to spend **a lot more** time practising.*
*A computer will do the job **much more efficiently**.*

Before a comparative we can use **much**, **a lot**, **far**; **rather**; **slightly**, **a bit**, **a little**; **no**, **any**.

No has a negative meaning:
*Your second shot at goal was **no nearer** than your first.*

We can use **any** in negatives and questions:
*Your second shot at goal wasn't **any nearer** than your first.*
*Are you sleeping **any better** since you've been taking the pills?*

B faster and faster

We use expressions like **faster and faster** and **more and more expensive** to say that something is increasing all the time:

*The caravan was rolling **faster and faster** down the hill.*
*As the plane approached, the noise got **louder and louder**.*
*The queue was getting **longer and longer**.*
*Prices go up and up. Everything seems to be getting **more and more expensive** all the time.*
*The crowd are becoming **more and more excited**.*
*The country is rapidly losing its skilled workers as **more and more** people want to emigrate.*

The form depends on whether the comparative is with **er** (e.g. **louder**) or with **more** (e.g. **more expensive**). See Unit 86.

C the faster the better

We use this pattern to say that a change in one thing goes with a change in another. Look at these examples:

*There's no time to lose. **The faster** you drive, **the better**.*
***The closer** we got to the waterfall, **the louder** the noise was.*
***The higher** the price, **the more reliable** the product.*
***The more** the customer complained, **the ruder** and **more unpleasant** the manager became.*
*The **sooner** we leave, the **sooner** we'll get there.*
*Shall we try to get cheap tickets? ~ **The cheaper the better**!*

88 Exercises

88.1 much faster (A)

Complete each sentence from the notes.
- ☐ I feel _a bit better_ this morning, thank you.   ☐ a bit – good
- ☐ You could get the answer _far more easily_ with a calculator.   ☐ far – easily
1. Yesterday was _____ than it is today.   1 a lot – cold
2. This coat is _____ than is fashionable just now.   2 a bit – long
3. The corner shop is _____ than the supermarket.   3 much – expensive
4. Exports are _____ than a year ago.   4 no – high
5. Is this machine _____ than the old one?   5 any – reliable
6. I got up _____ than usual this morning.   6 slightly – early

88.2 faster and faster (B)

Complete the sentences.
- ☐ The old man seems to get _more and more confused_ every day.   ☐ confused
- ☐ The intervals between his children's visits are becoming _longer and longer_.   ☐ long
1. It's getting _____ to find cheap accommodation.   1 difficult
2. Life gets _____ all the time.   2 complicated
3. The pain in my back gets _____.   3 bad
4. The rocket climbed _____ into the sky.   4 high
5. The runners looked _____ as the race continued.   5 exhausted

88.3 the faster the better (C)

Complete each sentence using the information in brackets.
- ☐ (The rent is high.)
  The bigger a flat is, _the higher the rent is._
- ☐ (You learn quickly.)
  The younger you are, _the more quickly you learn._
1. (The roads are quiet.)
   The earlier you leave, _____
2. (The choice is wide.)
   The bigger a supermarket is, _____
3. (I get confused.)
   The more I try to work this out, _____
4. (You can speak fluently.)
   The more you practise a language, _____
5. (The beaches get crowded.)
   The hotter the weather is, _____
6. (The computer is useful.)
   The bigger the memory is, _____
7. (The problem will become serious.)
   The longer we do nothing, _____

89 Adverbs and word order

A Types of adverbs

Type	Tells us ...	Examples
Manner	how	slowly, suddenly, eagerly, anxiously, carefully, hard
Place	where	here, there, upstairs, outside, nearby
Time	when	now, then, soon, yesterday, once
Frequency	how often	sometimes, always, ever, never, usually, occasionally
Degree	how much	very, quite, almost, completely, fully, really
Sentence		certainly, probably, maybe, obviously, clearly, luckily, (un)fortunately

B Where do adverbs go?

There are three main positions for adverbs: front, mid and end.

    Front   Mid   End
    Then the man's hands **suddenly** began to shake **violently**.

<u>Front position</u> is at the beginning of a sentence:
    Sometimes I get up in the night.   **Perhaps** the letter is from Celia.

<u>Mid position</u> is after the first auxiliary (e.g. *They are **just** finishing*). If there is no auxiliary, it is before the main verb (e.g. *I **really** hate it*).

	AUXILIARY	ADVERB	MAIN VERB
The workmen	are	**just**	finishing.
James	has	**always**	liked Fiona.
We	don't	**often**	play this game.
I		**really**	hate housework.
You		**probably**	left the bag on the bus.

Note the word order in questions:
    Has James **always** liked Fiona?
    Do you **often** play this game?

When the verb is **be** on its own, the adverb comes after it:
    Sally is **often** in a bad temper.   You're **probably** right.

<u>End position</u> is at the end of a sentence:
    The crowd waited **patiently**.   The two men shook hands **warmly**.
An adverb does not usually go between the verb and direct object:
    I like classical music **very much**. NOT *I like very much classical music*.
But an adverb can go before a long object:
    Detectives examined **carefully** the contents of the dead man's pockets

C Adverbs of manner

Adverbs of manner can go in mid position or end position:
    She **eagerly** tore off the paper.   I **slowly** sank into a deep sleep.
    He spread the butter **thickly**.   We arrived **safely**.

D Adverbs of place and time

These adverbs and adverbial phrases usually go in end position:
 *Is there a phone box **nearby**?* *People didn't have cars **then**.*
 *We're meeting **by the entrance**.* *Debbie wasn't very well **last week**.*
 *Did you have a nice time **in Paris**?* *I'll see you **before very long**.*

Some short adverbs of time (e.g. **soon**, **now**) can go in mid position:
 *We were **soon** travelling through open countryside.*
For **yet**, **still** and **already** see Unit 90.

E Adverbs of frequency

Adverbs of frequency usually go in mid position:
 *You're **always** in such a hurry.* *I **sometimes** feel depressed.*
 *I've **often** wondered about that.* *Do you **usually** work so late?*

Normally, **usually**, **often**, **sometimes** and **occasionally** can also go in front position or end position, where they have more emphasis:
 ***Normally** there's no difficulty.* *I feel depressed **sometimes**.*

Phrases like **every day**, **once a week** or **most evenings** go in front or end position:
 ***Every day** we go jogging.* *I do aerobics **three times a week**.*
 *There's a news summary **every hour**.* *We watch television **most evenings**.*

F Sentence adverbs

These can come in any position, although front position is the most usual:
 ***Fortunately** the weather was fine.* ***Maybe** you'll win a free holiday.*
 *We'll **probably** have to wait hours.* *There's no lift **of course**.*

In a negative sentence, **probably** and **certainly** come before the auxiliary + **n't** (e.g. **won't**):
 *We **probably** won't be in time.* *I **certainly** didn't expect a present!*

G End position

There can be more than one adverb or adverbial phrase in end position. Usually a single-word adverb comes before a phrase:

	ADVERB	ADVERBIAL PHRASE
They landed	*safely*	*on a small airfield.*
I always eat	*here*	*at lunch time.*

When there is a close link in meaning between a verb and an adverb, then the adverb goes next to the verb. For example, a phrase of place goes next to **go**, **come**, **move** etc:
 *I usually **go to bed** early.* *My parents **moved to London** in 1985.*

But often two adverbial phrases can go in either order:
 *The concert was held **at the Arts Centre last night**.*
 *It was held **last night at the Arts Centre**.*

89 Exercises

89.1 What is an adverb? (A)

From each sentence write down the word which is an adverb.

- I feel quite ill.   *quite*
1. Luckily the glass didn't break.   _____
2. You should never leave litter.   _____
3. We must finish the job quickly.   _____
4. I hope to see you tomorrow.   _____
5. We ran inside when it started raining.   _____

89.2 Types of adverb (A)

Read this story and then say what type of adverb each underlined word is.

A tourist was <u>once</u> on a holiday cruise to Rio de Janeiro. He was looking at all the sights and <u>eagerly</u> taking photos. He had <u>completely</u> forgotten about the time. When he realized that his ship was leaving <u>soon</u>, he rushed <u>anxiously</u> to the docks. When he got <u>there</u>, he saw that the ship was moving <u>slowly</u> away from the side of the dock. He tried to jump onto the ship and <u>almost</u> succeeded. <u>Unfortunately</u> he fell into the water. <u>Luckily</u> some sailors saw what was happening and fished him out. <u>Then</u> they told him that it was the wrong ship. The right one sailed an hour later. Well, everyone makes mistakes <u>sometimes</u>!

- once   *time*
- eagerly   *manner*
1. completely   _____
2. soon   _____
3. anxiously   _____
4. there   _____
5. slowly   _____
6. almost   _____
7. unfortunately   _____
8. luckily   _____
9. then   _____
10. sometimes   _____

89.3 Adverbs in mid position (B)

Complete the sentences using the words on the right. Put the adverb (**certainly**, **usually** etc.) in the best place.

- I *would certainly recognize* the man again.   would recognize – certainly
- We *usually spend* our holidays in France.   spend – usually
1. It _____ later.   will rain – probably
2. The ball _____ the line.   crossed – clearly
3. Our neighbours _____ out.   are – always
4. The central heating _____ properly again.   was working – soon
5. The carnival _____ a great success.   is – usually
6. I _____ the place as a child.   visited – occasionally
7. Phil _____ all about it.   has forgotten – obviously
8. I _____ the directions.   didn't understand – fully

89 Adverbs and word order

89.4 Adverbs of frequency (**B,E**)

Write the sentences with the adverb (e.g. **always**) or adverbial phrase (e.g. **every morning**) in mid position or end position. Choose the best position.

☐ I shall remember your kindness to me. (always)
   I shall always remember your kindness to me.
☐ The birds wake me up. (every morning)
   The birds wake me up every morning.
1 I can open these milk cartons. (never)

2 It rains when I'm on holiday. (usually)

3 I do fitness training. (three times a week)

4 My flat mate is at home. (most evenings)

5 These toilets are inspected. (every hour)

6 Have you been to New York? (ever)

89.5 Adverbs in end position (**G**)

Complete the sentences. Put the words and phrases on the right in the best order. (Sometimes there is more than one possible order.)

☐ I just want to sit *peacefully in the garden* .   ☐ in the garden – peacefully
1 We've visited the fair _____.   1 regularly – since about 1985
2 Alex went _____.   2 last year – to Wales
3 The match is _____.   3 next Wednesday – at Wembley
4 I like York. I spent a week _____.   4 in June – there
5 You can park _____.   5 by the town hall – all day
6 We came _____.   6 here – five years ago

89.6 The position of adverbs (**A–G**)

Read this postcard and write the sentences. Put the adverbs on the right in the best place.

Dear Louise, ☐Thank you for having us. ¹We had a lovely   ☐ last weekend
time. ²We arrived home at about eight. ³You must come and   1 in London   2 safely
visit us. ⁴It's nice to see you and Mike. ⁵You'll be able to 3 before too long
come in the New Year. ⁶We hope to see you. Love, Kate   4 always   5 maybe
                                                             6 some time

☐ *Thank you for having us last weekend.*
1 _____
2 _____
3 _____
4 _____
5 _____
6 _____

90 yet, still and already

A Meanings

Look at this conversation:
> Tracy: *Have you written your report for the magazine **yet**?*
> Shane: *No, I haven't started writing it **yet**. I'm **still** interviewing people.*
> Tracy: *I haven't started my article. I **still** can't decide what to put in it.*
> Shane: *Tina has **already** finished hers. She gave it to the editor yesterday.*

Yet = we are expecting something to happen, e.g. Shane writing his report.
Still = going on longer than we expected, e.g. Shane interviewing people.
Already = before now, sooner than we expected, e.g. Tina finishing her article.

B yet

We use **yet** at the end of a negative statement or a question:
> *Colin has got a present, but he hasn't opened it **yet**.*
> *Wait a minute. I'm not ready **yet**.*
> *Has your visa arrived **yet**? ~ No, not **yet**. I should get it next week.*

C still and already

In a positive statement these words go in mid position (after **be** or an auxiliary but before the main verb – see Unit 89B for more about mid position):
> *Alice isn't home yet. She's **still** at work.*
> *I've only been at work an hour, and I'm **already** exhausted.*
> *Three weeks later we're **still** waiting for a reply.*
> *We've **already** booked our holiday for next year.*
> *There's no need to tell me. I **already** know.*
> *John is forty-five, but he **still** plays cricket.*

We can also use **still** in a negative statement before the auxiliary + **n't** (e.g. **haven't**):
> *It's nearly lunch time and you **still** haven't opened your mail.*
> *Sarah is fifteen and she **still** can't swim.*

With a negative, **still** expresses surprise at the situation going on for so long. It is more emphatic than **yet** (e.g. *You haven't opened your mail **yet***).

In a question **still** and **already** go after the auxiliary + subject:
> *Are you **still** waiting?*   *Has your sister **already** read this book?*

D no longer and any longer / any more

No longer means that something is over, finished. It goes in mid position (see Unit 89B):
> *You can't buy these bikes now. They **no longer** make them.*
> *I used to belong to the club, but I'm **no longer** a member.*

We can also use **not ... any longer** or **not ... any more**. This phrase comes at the end:
> *They do**n't** make these bikes **any longer** (OR **any more**).*
> *The Cliffords have moved. They do**n't** live here **any longer** (OR **any more**).*

90 Exercises

90.1 Meanings (**A**)

Put in **yet**, **still** or **already**.
- I'm hungry. ~ It isn't lunch time _yet_ . ~ Well, I must eat something. ~ It's only eleven o'clock. And you've _already_ had two cups of coffee since breakfast.
1. You've _____ got this library book, and it was due back ten days ago. ~ Well, I haven't finished it _____ .
2. Charles is a very slow eater, isn't he? He's _____ having his soup. ~ Yes, and everyone else has _____ started their pudding.
3. Is it time for a rest _____ ? ~ Well, we're doing very well. We've only been going fifty minutes, and we've _____ walked four miles.
4. The postman hasn't come _____ , has he? ~ Yes, he's _____ been, but he went straight past. ~ Oh, dear. That parcel _____ hasn't come.

90.2 The position of **yet**, **still** and **already** (**B,C**)

Put each word into one of the two sentences.
- I've bought some new tapes. I haven't played them.
  I haven't played them yet. — yet
- This calculator is working. I've had it for about twenty years.
  This calculator is still working. — still
- I owe Jane £10. I can't ask her for more money.
  I already owe Jane £10. — already
1. We've spent all our money. And we're only half-way through our holiday. — 1 already
2. I've cleaned this window. But it looks dirty. — 2 still
3. Our friend took some photos. We haven't seen them. — 3 yet
4. I've been doing this crossword for hours. I haven't finished it. — 4 still
5. I wasn't surprised at the news. I'd guessed. — 5 already
6. I can't understand the rules. I know you explained them to me. — 6 still
7. Have you done your Christmas shopping? It'll be Christmas soon. — 7 yet

90.3 **yet**, **still**, **already**, **no longer** and **any longer/any more** (**A–D**)

Put in the missing words.
1. It's _____ raining, look. How much longer can it go on?
2. The railway was closed down many years ago. There's _____ a railway station here.
3. They want to build a new hotel, but they haven't got permission _____ .
4. Jeff didn't want to go on doing so much overtime _____ .
5. That couple moved here only six months ago, and they're _____ leaving.

217

91 Adverbs of degree (e.g. **very**, **quite**)

A **very**, **quite** and **a bit**

Look at these examples:
> It feels **a bit** cold in here. I've got my pullover on.
> It's **quite** cold outside. You'll need a coat if you go out.
> It was **very** cold yesterday. I wore a scarf and gloves.

An adverb of degree makes the meaning stronger (+) or weaker (−):
(++) **very** cold (scarf and gloves)   (+) **quite** cold (coat)   (−) **a bit** cold (pullover)

B **very cold**, **a bit tired** etc.

An adverb of degree (e.g. **very**) goes before an adjective (e.g. **cold**) or an adverb (e.g. **quickly**):
> It's **very cold** today. (++)   The time passed **quite quickly**. (+)
> I'm feeling **a bit tired**. (−)   We have to go **fairly soon**. (+)
> That's **absolutely marvellous**. (++)   You played **extremely well**. (++)

We can use **a lot** (++) and **much** (++) with a comparative (see Unit 88A):
> These tapes are **a lot cheaper**.   The new trains go **much faster**.

Many adverbs of degree (e.g. **really**) can go with a verb. Most go in mid position (after an auxiliary but before the main verb – see Unit 89B):
> My foot is **really hurting**. (++)   Celia **quite enjoys** shopping. (+)
> I **just know** you're wrong. (++)   I **rather like** these biscuits. (+)

These adverbs go at the end of a sentence when they describe a verb: **much**, **a lot** (++); **a little**, **a bit** (−); **terribly**, **awfully** (++).
> I ride my bike **a lot**.   Let's rest **a little**.   My foot hurts **terribly**.

These words can go in mid or end position: **completely**, **absolutely**, **totally**.
> We **completely** lost our way. OR We lost our way **completely**.

In a positive statement we use **very much**, in a negative **very much** or **much**:
> I like this book **very much**. NOT *I like this book much.*
> I don't like this book **very much**. OR I don't like this book **much**.

C Summary

	WITH ADJECTIVE, ADVERB OR VERB	WITH ADJECTIVE OR ADVERB ONLY	WITH VERB OR COMPARATIVE ONLY
High degree 'very' (++)	just, completely, absolutely, totally; really; terribly, awfully	very, extremely	very much, a lot
Some degree 'rather' (+)	rather, quite	fairly, pretty	
Low degree 'a little' (−)	a little, a bit	slightly	not . . . (very) much

For more details about **quite** and **rather** see Unit 92. For **too** and **enough** see Unit 93.

91 Exercises

91.1 very, quite and a bit (A)

For each situation put in **very**, **quite** or **a bit**.
- There was a reasonable bus service. They were every half hour.
  The buses were _quite_ frequent.
1. I couldn't sleep. There was a lot of noise from the disco.
   The disco was _____ noisy.
2. There was a fair amount of traffic on the road.
   The road was _____ busy.
3. It was only a minute or two after the scheduled time when the train came in.
   The train was _____ late.
4. Someone paid a great deal of money for the house.
   The house was _____ expensive.
5. There were one or two small traces of mud on the boots.
   The boots were _____ dirty.
6. We had reasonable weather. It wasn't marvellous, but it didn't rain.
   The weather was _____ good.

91.2 very cold etc. (B)

Put the adverbs in the right place. Sometimes more than one answer is correct.
- (very) These books are old.   _These books are very old._
- (really) I hate travelling by air.   _I really hate travelling by air._
1. (a bit) That music is loud.
2. (quite) I like my new job.
3. (a little) Why don't you slow down?
4. (completely) The rain spoilt my day.
5. (rather) I agreed with the speaker.
6. (fairly) We did the job quickly.
7. (a lot) I feel better now.
8. (a bit) I'm getting hungry.
9. (very much) We enjoyed the concert.
10. (terribly) The prisoners suffered.

91.3 Adverbs of degree (B,C)

Complete the advertisement by choosing the best word for the context.

Interlux Timeshare

Why not take this opportunity to buy a wonderful Interlux Timeshare apartment in San Manila? These are □ _really_ luxurious apartments set in this ¹_____ magnificent seaside resort, a ²_____ unspoilt place that you'll ³_____ adore. The apartments are ⁴_____ good value. And we are an experienced company with a ⁵_____ good reputation. This is a ⁶_____ safe way of investing your money. But hurry! People are buying up these apartments ⁷_____ quickly.

□ rather/a bit/really
1. absolutely/slightly
2. fairly/really
3. just/rather/slightly
4. extremely/pretty/quite
5. just/rather/very
6. fairly/slightly/totally
7. a lot/very/very much

219

92 quite and rather

A quite meaning 'fairly'

Quite usually means 'fairly', 'to some degree':
*I feel **quite** tired now.*   *This puzzle is **quite** difficult.*
*The talk was **quite** interesting.*   *We were **quite** surprised at the result.*
Quite tired means 'fairly tired'. (But see D for another meaning of **quite**.)

B Stress with quite

In speech, if we stress **quite**, it means 'fairly but not very'. The meaning is negative:
The exhibition was 'quite good (but not very good). I've seen better ones.
I got up 'quite early (but not very early).

If we stress the adjective, the meaning is positive:
The exhibition was quite 'good. I enjoyed looking round it.
I got up quite 'early. I had a lot to do.

C quite or rather?

When we make a favourable comment, we usually prefer **quite** to **rather**:
*These jackets are **quite** cheap.*   *It's **quite** warm now, isn't it?*
*It was **quite** nice walking through the park.*

In unfavourable comments, we usually prefer **rather**, but **quite** is possible:
*These jackets are **rather/quite** expensive.*
*The floor was **rather/quite** dirty.*
*It was **rather/quite** awkward taking the case on the Underground.*

Rather in a favourable comment means 'to a surprising or unusual degree':
*It's **rather** warm for October. (It isn't usually so warm.)*
*I didn't know Laura could paint. Her pictures are **rather** good.*
*I expect the speech was boring. ~ Actually it was **rather** interesting.*

We can use **rather** with a comparative but not **quite**:
*The second test was **rather easier** than the first.*

For the word order of **quite** and **rather** with **a/an** see Unit 66A.

D quite meaning 'completely'

Quite can also mean 'completely', 'totally':
*I feel **quite exhausted** now.* (= completely exhausted)
*The idea is **quite absurd**.* (= totally absurd)
*The talk was **quite fascinating**.*   *The situation is **quite hopeless**.*
Here are some other adjectives where **quite** means 'completely':
brilliant, perfect; horrible, dreadful; amazing, extraordinary; ridiculous; impossible (but NOT **possible**); **useless** (but NOT **useful**); **true, false, right, wrong sure, certain; dead; alone; different.**

92 Exercises

92.1 Stress with quite (B)

Which word do we stress, **quite** or the adjective? Underline the stressed word.
- ☐ These pens are <u>quite</u> good but not as good as the ones I usually buy.
- ☐ This book is quite <u>exciting</u>. I can't put it down.
1. These fashions are quite new but not the absolutely latest thing.
2. It's quite late. We'd better be going.
3. The sums are quite easy. I can do them in my head.
4. The music was quite good, but I wasn't really impressed.
5. The sun is quite bright. You'll need your sunglasses.
6. The film was funny, wasn't it? ~ Quite funny, I suppose.

92.2 quite or rather? (C)

Put in **quite** or **rather**. (Sometimes either is possible.)
- ☐ Let's walk along by the river. It's _quite_ pleasant there.
- ☐ I don't like Greg much. He's _rather_ aggressive.
1. We have to change trains twice. It's _____ complicated.
2. We can easily put you up. Our house is _____ big.
3. I didn't expect to enjoy the show, but in fact I found it _____ amusing.
4. The crowds at the festival were _____ bigger than people had expected.
5. Luckily they were able to finish the job _____ quickly.
6. Don't move the table on your own. It's _____ heavy for one person.

92.3 quite or rather? (C)

Put in **quite** or **rather**. (Sometimes either is possible.)

A: I didn't like that meal very much.
B: The soup was ¹_____ nice, wasn't it?
A: Yes, but the chicken wasn't. On the whole I'm ²_____ disappointed.
B: It's ³_____ noisy in here, isn't it?
A: Yes, I wasn't expecting the place to be so full. It's ⁴_____ busy for a Monday evening.
B: This place is ⁵_____ popular, you know.

92.4 The meanings of quite (A,D)

Does **quite** mean 'fairly' or 'completely'?
- ☐ Try one of these sweets. I think they're <u>quite nice</u>. = _fairly_
- ☐ The driver got out unhurt. It was <u>quite amazing</u>. = _completely_
1. I simply can't do the work by tomorrow. It's <u>quite impossible</u>. = _____
2. I couldn't eat the food. It was <u>quite dreadful</u>. = _____
3. I need some help with this crossword. It's <u>quite difficult</u>. = _____
4. That isn't the same thing at all. It's <u>quite different</u>. = _____
5. I wasn't expecting to get a card. I was <u>quite surprised</u>. = _____
6. I bought this guidebook. It looks <u>quite useful</u>. = _____
7. Are you sure about this? ~ Yes, I'm <u>quite certain</u>. = _____
8. Will Fiona give up her job? ~ I think it's <u>quite likely</u>. = _____

93 too and enough

A Meanings

Too means 'more than the right amount':
*This sweater is **too** big.*
Enough means 'the right amount':
*The dress is big **enough**. It's just right.*
Not enough means 'less than the right amount':
*The jacket is**n't** big **enough**.*

B The position of too and enough

Too goes before an adjective or adverb, and **enough** goes after it:
*Don't walk on the grass. It's **too wet**.*
*The company reacted to the situation **too slowly**.*
*The water isn't **hot enough**. It needs to be boiling.*
*You didn't put the screws in **tightly enough**.* NOT *... enough tightly.*

Too many / too much and **enough** go before a noun:
*No wonder you're tired. You've had **too many** late **nights**.*
*There's **too much noise** in here.*
*There'll be fifteen people. Have we got **enough cups**?*
*Did you bring **enough money**?*

We use **many** with a plural noun and **much** with a mass noun. See Unit 73A.

We leave out the noun if the meaning is clear without it:
*Just add a little water. Not **too much**.*
*We'll need fifteen cups. Have we got **enough**?*

Compare **enough** with an adjective and with a noun.
After an adjective: *The coffee isn't **strong enough**.*
Before a noun: *You didn't put **enough coffee** in.*

C Patterns with too and enough

We can use a phrase with **for** after **too** or **enough**:
*These shoes are **too** big **for me**.*
*This coat isn't warm **enough for winter**.*
*Have we got **enough** cups **for everyone**?*

We can also use a to-infinitive:
*It's **too** wet **to walk** on the grass.*
*There are **too** many museums here **to visit** in a single day.*
*Are you tall **enough to reach** the top shelf?*
*I couldn't get close **enough to see** properly.*
*I didn't bring **enough** money **to buy** two tickets.*

93 Exercises

93.1 Meanings (A)

Put in **too** or **enough** with the word in brackets, e.g. **too tired** or **tired enough**.

☐ You aren't concentrating. ~ No, I'm _too tired_ . (tired)
1. We can't hear the music. ~ Sorry, isn't it _____ ? (loud)
2. You could take a photo now. ~ Yes, it's _____ . (light)
3. Why can't Lisa come tonight? ~ She's _____ . (busy)
4. Can't we all go in your car? ~ No, it isn't _____ . (big)
5. Why couldn't the plane take off? ~ It was _____ . (foggy)
6. I'm sure you'll succeed if you try _____ . (hard)
7. Two sugars for you? ~ Please. One isn't _____ . (sweet)
8. Can we walk to the sports field? ~ No, it's _____ . (far)

93.2 The position of **too** and **enough** (B)

Put in **too**, **too many**, **too much** or **enough** with these words: **clearly, complicated, difficult, expensive, food, hastily, long, mistakes, old, rain, traffic**.

☐ You should have thought about it first. You acted _too hastily_ .
☐ The quiz is rather easy. The questions aren't _difficult enough_ .
1. This carpet is just too short. It isn't quite _____ .
2. I can't afford a new car. It would be _____ .
3. There's a water shortage. We haven't had _____ .
4. I can't read your writing. You don't write _____ .
5. Try to be more careful. You're making _____ .
6. You can't leave school yet. You aren't _____ .
7. The roads are very crowded. There's simply _____ .
8. I can't understand these instructions. They're _____ .
9. Thousands of people are dying because they can't get _____ .

93.3 Patterns with **too** and **enough** (C)

Join each pair of sentences using **too** or **enough** and a phrase with **for** or a to-infinitive.

☐ A taxi would have been best. But we didn't have much money.
   We didn't have _enough money for a taxi_.
☐ Lorraine can't take a day off. She's very busy.
   She's _too busy to take a day off_.
1. A picnic? It's rather wet, isn't it?
   It's _____
2. Trevor wants to be a professional musician. Is he that good?
   Is he _____
3. All the guests will need chairs. But we haven't got very many.
   We haven't got _____
4. We couldn't carry the equipment. We had such a lot.
   We had _____
5. Tennis? Well, the garden is rather small.
   The garden is _____
6. Viv Richards couldn't play in the match. He was quite badly hurt.
   He was _____

94 Prepositions of place

Look at these prepositions:

The bird is **in/inside** the cage.

She's jumping **in/into** the water.

He's getting **out of** the car.

They're waiting **outside** the bank.

The jug is **on** the table.

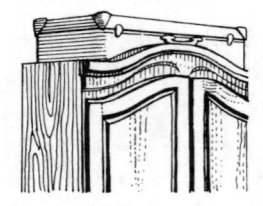

The case is **on top of** the wardrobe.

She's putting her luggage **on/onto** the trolley.

He's falling **off** the horse.

She's **at** the bus stop.

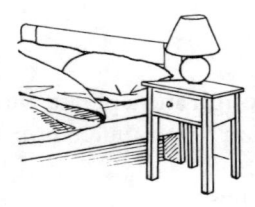

The table is **by/beside** the bed.

She's sitting **next to** Joe.

Wilmslow is **near** Manchester.

The coach is going **to** London.

The letter is **from** Chicago.

He's walking **towards** the sun.

He's running **away from** the fire.

*There's a bridge **over** the river.*

*He's **under** the car.*

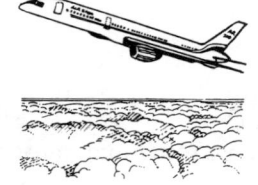

*The plane is **above** the clouds.*

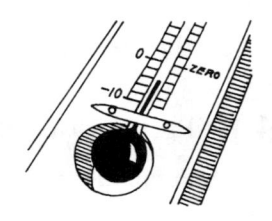

*The temperature is **below** zero.*

*The cyclist is **in front of** the bus.*

*The cyclist is **behind** the tractor.*

*He's going **up** the stairs.*

*He's coming **down** the stairs.*

*She's running **across** the road.*

*The cars are going **through** the tunnel.*

*He's walking **along** the street.*

*The car is going **past** the house.*

*The house is **among** the trees.*

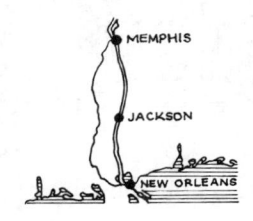

*Jackson is **between** Memphis and New Orleans.*

*She's sitting **opposite** Joe.*

*They're running **around/round** the track.*

Most of these prepositions can express either position or movement.
    Position: *The coin **was under** the sofa.*
    Movement: *The coin **rolled under** the sofa.*

Into and **onto** express movement. **In** and **on** usually express position, but they can express movement, especially in informal English:
    *My father came **in/into** the room.*   *The book fell **on/onto** the floor.*

At expresses position, and **to** expresses movement:
    *Harry **was at** the doctor's.* BUT *Harry **went to** the doctor's.*

For some differences between British and American English see p 290.

94 Exercises

94.1 Prepositions of place

Put in the prepositions. Sometimes more than one answer is correct.

☐ She's getting _out of_ the taxi.

1 He's going _____ the ladder.

2 The furniture is _____ the van.

3 They live in a flat _____ the shop.

4 Someone is coming _____ the corridor.

5 There's a garage _____ the house.

6 We walked _____ the lake.

7 There's a statue _____ the museum.

8 They're walking _____ the stadium.

94.2 Prepositions of place

Choose the correct preposition.

1 Shane drove here all the way _____ Cambridge just to see me.
2 Linda walked right _____ me and never said hello.
3 I thought someone was standing _____ me, but I didn't dare to turn round.
4 Steve wore a long coat that came down well _____ his knees.
5 We'll need a boat to get _____ the river.
6 Carol was sitting _____ me at lunch, so I couldn't help looking at her.

1 from/towards
2 along/past
3 behind/in front of
4 below/under
5 across/through
6 beside/opposite

94.3 Prepositions of place

Where did the fly go? Put in these prepositions: **around, into, on, out of, through, under, up.**

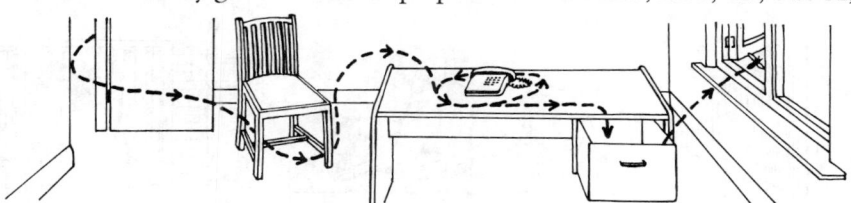

☐ The fly came in _through_ the door.
1. It flew _____ the chair.
2. It crawled _____ the chair leg.
3. It stopped _____ the desk for a moment.
4. It went _____ the telephone.
5. It flew _____ the drawer.
6. It went _____ the window.

94.4 Prepositions of place

Fill in the correct preposition.

☐ Lisa was lying _on_ the lawn reading a book.
1. It's my holiday next week. I'm going _____ Spain.
2. There was a big crowd _____ the shop waiting for it to open.
3. Some idiot pushed me _____ the swimming-pool.
4. I went _____ the chemist's just now, but I didn't notice if it was open.
5. I hurt myself. I fell _____ my bike.
6. There's a café _____ the mountain. You can have a coffee there before you walk down again.
7. The lorry had to wait _____ the traffic lights.
8. The sheep got out _____ a hole in the fence.
9. Pompeii is quite _____ Sorrento. It's only a short train ride.
10. There's such a crowd. You won't find Peter _____ all these people.

94.5 between, next to and opposite

Look at the plan and complete the sentences. Use **between, next to** or **opposite**.

Britwest Bank	The Gift Shop	Bertie's Restaurant

HIGH STREET

Baker's Sports Shop	Athena Travel Agency	Mephisto Art Gallery

☐ The bank is _next to_ the gift shop.
1. The sports shop is _____ the bank.
2. The travel agency is _____ the sports shop and the art gallery.
3. The restaurant is _____ the art gallery.
4. The gift shop is _____ the bank and the restaurant.
5. The art gallery is _____ the travel agency.

95 in, on and at (place)

A Meanings

Compare:

in

We use **in** when something is around, on all sides:
- **in** the phone box
- **in** the playpen
- **in** my pocket
- **in** the garden
- **in** the kitchen
- swimming **in** the pool

in + town/country:
- Kate lives **in** York.
- Bologna is **in** Italy.

in + street (GB):
- **in** Shirley Road

on

We use **on** for a surface:
- lying **on** the rug
- walk **on** the pavement
- a number **on** the door
- egg **on** your shirt

And we use **on** for a line:
- Bath, **on** the River Avon
- a village **on** this road
- a town **on** the border

on + floor:
- **on** the first floor

on + street (USA):
- **on** Fifth Avenue

at

We use **at** for a position, a point in space:
- someone **at** the door
- sitting **at** my desk
- **at** the crossroads

We also use **at** for events:
- See you **at** the match.
- **at** the meeting
- **at** a church service

at + house/address:
- **at** 65 Shirley Road
- **at** Mike's (house)

at + place on a journey:
- Does this train stop **at** York?

B in and at with buildings

in

We use **in** when we mean inside a building:

*There are 400 seats **in** the cinema.*

*It was raining, so we waited **in** the pub.*

at

But we use **at** when we mean an event, the normal purpose of the building:

*I was **at** the cinema last night.*
(= watching a film)
*My parents are **at** the pub.*
(= having a drink)

C Some common phrases

in prison/hospital	**on** the platform	**at** the station/airport
in the lesson	**on** the farm	**at** home/work/school
in a book/newspaper	**on** this page	
in this photo/picture	**on** the screen	
in the country	**on** the island	
	on the beach	**at** the seaside
	on the coast	
in the sky		
in the middle	drive **on** the right/left	**at** the top/bottom of a hill
in the back/front of a car	**on** the back of an envelope	**at** the back of a queue
in a queue/line/row		**at** the end of a corridor

95 Exercises

95.1 Meanings (A)

Complete the sentences with **in**, **on** or **at** and these words:
the bath, the car, the dance, the lights, the roof, the table.

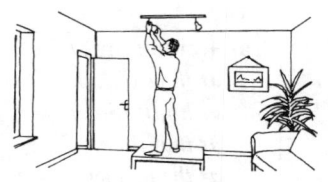

☐ He's _on the table._
1 She's _____ 
2 He's _____ 
3 She's _____ 
4 He's _____ 
5 She's _____ 

95.2 **in** and **at** with buildings (B)

Complete each sentence with **in** or **at** and these words: **the bus station, the filling-station, the restaurant, the stadium, the theatre, the zoo**.

☐ There was a huge crowd _in the stadium_ waiting for the Games to start.
1 Debbie was _____ . She was getting some petrol.
2 The children are interested in animals. They'd be delighted to spend an afternoon _____ .
3 It was so hot _____ that I didn't really enjoy the play.
4 We're a large group. There may not be enough room _____ for all of us to eat together.
5 You can get a bus timetable _____ .

95.3 **in**, **on** and **at** (A, C)

Put in the preposition: **in**, **on** or **at**.
☐ We spent the whole holiday _on_ the beach.
1 I read about this new invention _____ a magazine.
2 Mel's flat is _____ the twenty-first floor.
3 Julia was holding a small bird _____ her hands.
4 I'll meet you _____ the airport.
5 Don now lives _____ 32 The Avenue.
6 I was standing _____ the counter in the baker's shop, waiting to be served.
7 London is _____ the Thames.
8 There weren't many books _____ the shelves.
9 The passengers had to stand _____ a queue.
10 We had to change planes _____ Amsterdam.

229

96 in, on and at (time)

A Saying when

Look at these examples:
> It happened **in** 1990.   It happened **on** Friday.   It happened **at** two thirty.

Now compare:

in + year/month/season:	**on** + day/date:	**at** + clock time/meal time:
in 1990	*on* Wednesday	*at* three o'clock
in September	*on* 15th April	*at* lunch (time)
in winter	*on* that day	*at* that time
in the 20th century		*at* the moment
in + a week or more:	**on** + a single day:	**at** + two or three days:
in the Easter holiday	*on* Easter Monday	*at* Easter/Christmas
in the summer term	*on* Christmas Day	*at* the weekend
		(USA: **on** the weekend)
in + part of day:	**on** + day + part of day:	
in the morning	*on* Friday morning	
in the evenings	*on* Tuesday evenings	

Look at these examples with **night**:
> I woke up **in** the night.   It happened **on** Monday night.   I can't sleep **at** night.
> (= in the middle of the night)   (= when it is night)

But we do not use **in**, **on** or **at** before **this**, **next**, **last**, **tomorrow**, **yesterday** and **every**:
> I leave school **this year**.   I'll see you **next Friday**.
> Bob came **last Christmas**.   The group set off **yesterday morning**.
> We go there **every summer**.   The party is **tomorrow evening**.

B in time or on time?

In time means 'early enough':
> We got to the airport **in time** to have a coffee before checking in.
> We'll have to hurry if we want to be **in time** for the show.
> I was about to close the door when **just in time** I remembered my key.

On time means 'at the right time', 'on schedule':
> The plane took off **on time**.
> I hope the meeting starts **on time**.

C Other meanings of in

We can use **in** for the time it takes to complete something:
> I did the crossword **in** five minutes.   Could you walk thirty miles **in** a day?

We can also use **in** for a future time measured from the present:
> Your photos will be ready **in** an hour. (= an hour from now)
> The building will open **in** six weeks (OR **in** six weeks' time).

96 Exercises

96.1 Saying when (A)

Two business people are arranging a meeting. Use **in**, **on** or **at**.

A: I'm free ☐ _on_ the 15th March. Can we meet then?
B: That's Friday, isn't it? No, I'm afraid I can't see you ¹_____ Friday. I'll be in Brighton.
A: I'd like to have a meeting this month. I shall be very busy ²_____ April.
B: I'm having an extra couple of days' holiday ³_____ Easter, so perhaps the week after. Shall we meet ⁴_____ the 27th? That's a Wednesday.
A: Well, I've got an appointment ⁵_____ the morning but nothing ⁶_____ the afternoon. How about ⁷_____ Wednesday afternoon ⁸_____ about half past two?
B: Yes, that'll be fine.

96.2 Saying when (A)

Put in the word or phrase and use **in (the)**, **on (the)** or **at (the)** if necessary.

☐ I have to get up early _in the morning_.	☐	morning
☐ We're going on a trip _this Wednesday_.	☐	this Wednesday
1 We have a tea break _____	1	four o'clock
2 I posted the letter _____	2	Friday
3 My birthday is _____	3	June
4 Did you go away _____	4	summer holiday
5 Shirley rang _____	5	yesterday afternoon
6 I never drink alcohol _____, thanks.	6	lunch time
7 The patients get one cooked meal _____	7	every day
8 It's my photography class _____	8	Thursday evening
9 My brother often has to work _____	9	night
10 I heard a noise _____	10	night
11 My boy-friend will be here _____	11	weekend
12 It's a public holiday _____	12	New Year's Day

96.3 in time or on time? (B)

Put in the right phrase: **in time** or **on time**.
1 If the plane is late, we won't get to Paris _____ for our connection.
2 We were up very early, _____ to see the sun rise.
3 How can the buses run _____ with all these traffic jams?
4 The post goes at five. I'm hoping to get this letter written _____.
5 The coach will be here at twelve thirteen, if it's _____.

96.4 in or on? (A–C)

Put in the right word: **in** or **on**.
1 I've read that book. I read it _____ about three hours one afternoon.
2 The bank always opens absolutely _____ time.
3 The course starts _____ 15th May.
4 I can easily shower and change _____ ten minutes.
5 As the car came round the corner, we got out of the way just _____ time.
6 The holiday is almost over. We go home _____ Friday. That's _____ two days.

97 for, since, ago and before

A for

We use **for** to say how long something continues:
*I'm staying in England **for a year**.* (NOT ~~I'm staying during a year~~ ; see Unit 98)
*We swam **for quite a long time**.*
*The shop will be closed **for ten days**.*

B for and since with the present perfect

We often use **for** and **since** to talk about something continuing up to the present:

for	since
*I've been waiting **for twenty minutes**.*	*I've been waiting **since half past six**.*
*We've known about it **for two days**.*	*We've known about it **since Monday**.*
*My parents have been living in Rome **for a year** now.*	*My parents have been living in Rome **since last year**.*
*I haven't seen Phil **for a day or two**.*	*I saw Phil on Tuesday, but I haven't seen him **since then**.*
We use **for** to say how long something has continued.	We use **since** to say when something began.
HOW LONG?	WHEN?
for twenty minutes	**since** half past six
for two days	**since** Wednesday
for a year	**since** last year

C ago with the past

We can use the adverb **ago** to talk about a past time measured from the present:
*I passed my driving test **six months ago**.* (= six months before now)
*I wrote to the company **weeks ago**.*
*Have you seen Matthew? ~ Yes, I saw him **only a few minutes ago**.*
*Angela first met Steve **a long time ago**.*
We put **ago** after the phrase of time. NOT ~~... ago six months.~~

D for, since and ago

Compare these three sentences. They all describe the same action.

for	since	ago
*I've had this bike **for six months**.*	*I've had this bike **since May**.*	*I bought this bike **six months ago**.*
1 2 3 4 5 6 → NOW	MAY → NOW	6 5 4 3 2 1 ← NOW

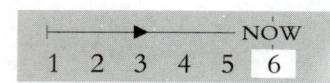

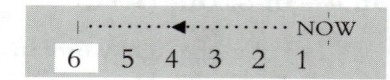

E before with the past perfect

We use **before** (not **ago**) with the past perfect (e.g. **had done**):
*I bought a car in August. I'd passed my driving test **three months before**.*
(= three months before August)
*Tom finally received a reply to the letter he had written **weeks before**.*

97 Exercises

97.1 for or since? (A, B)

Put in **for** or **since**.
A: How long have you been learning English?
B: Well, I did it ¹_____ five years at school, and I've been having evening classes ²_____ then.
A: And you're staying here ³_____ three months?
B: That's right. I've been here ⁴_____ the end of April. Then I'm going to London ⁵_____ a week afterwards.

97.2 for or since? (A, B)

Complete the sentences.
☐ You ought to wash the car. You haven't _washed it for_ ages.
☐ I'd better have a shower. I haven't _had one since_ Thursday.
1 Shall we play tennis? We haven't _____ our holiday.
2 I think I'll ring my girl-friend. I haven't _____ the weekend.
3 We're going to see some old friends. We haven't _____ five years.
4 Let's watch a video, shall we? We haven't _____ quite a while.
5 Aren't you going to write to Becky and Jim? You haven't _____ about six months.
6 We could have a barbecue. We haven't _____ last summer.

97.3 for, since or ago? (A–D)

Put in a phrase with **for**, **since** or **ago**.
☐ I got here an hour ago. ~ You mean you've been waiting _for an hour_?
1 The last visitor called at four o'clock. ~ So you've had no visitors _____?
2 I haven't been to the dentist for ten years. ~ You mean you last went _____?
3 I saw Wendy on Tuesday, I think. ~ You haven't seen her _____?
4 We've had six weeks without rain. ~ You mean it last rained _____?
5 It's five years since our wedding. ~ Oh, you've been married _____?
6 It's eight months since Graham worked. ~ So he lost his job _____?
7 Mrs Brooks was taken ill three weeks ago. ~ So she's been ill _____?

97.4 ago or before? (C, E)

Put in **ago** or **before**.
☐ The road was wet when the accident happened. It had stopped raining only half an hour _before_.
1 My telephone is working now. They repaired it a week _____.
2 The Porter family went back to live in Winchester in 1989. They had lived there ten years _____.
3 A young man threw himself off this bridge last year. His girl-friend had left him two days _____.
4 This film looks familiar. Didn't we see it at the cinema about two years _____?

98 during or while? by or until? as or like?

A during or while?

We use **during** and **while** to talk about the time in which something happens. But compare:

During is a preposition (like **in**). It comes before a noun phrase (e.g. **a meal**):
> I often read **during a meal**.
> It happened **during the night**.
> You'll have to be quiet **during the performance**.

While is a linking word (like **when**). It comes before a clause (e.g. **I'm eating**):
> I often read **while I'm eating**.
> It happened **while they were asleep**.
> Were there any phone calls **while I was out**?

B by or until?

By Thursday means 'on or before Thursday', 'not later than Thursday'.
> Could I borrow that book? ~ Yes, if you can give it me back **by** Thursday.
> You must be home **by** half past eleven.
> They hope to finish the bridge **by** next July.

Until Thursday means 'continuing up to Thursday'.
> Could I borrow that book? ~ Well, you can have it **until** Thursday.
> You can't stay out **until** midnight.
> There will be traffic hold-ups **until** next summer.

Till is more informal than **until**.
> I slept **till** (OR **until**) ten o'clock.

Before a clause we can use **by the time** or **until**:
> There was no food left **by the time** we arrived. NOT *...by we arrived.*
> I'll wait **until** you're ready.

C as, like and as if

We use **as** to talk about the job, role or function of someone or something:
> She works **as** a fashion model.
> (She **is** a model.)
> **As** a beginner, you have to learn the basics.
> I'm using this tin **as** an ashtray.

We use **like** to talk about similarity:
> She dresses **like** a fashion model.
> (Her clothes are **similar** to a model's.)
> He's a good golfer, but today he played **like** a beginner.
> You look **like** your brother.

We can also use **as** or **like** before a clause to mean 'in the same way'. **Like** is more informal than **as**.
> We drive on the left here, **as** (OR **like**) they do in Britain.
> We're having a winter holiday, **as** (OR **like**) we usually do.

We also use **as** with verbs of speaking and knowing (e.g. **say, know, expect**):
> **As I said before**, I'm sorry. (= I'm sorry, and I said so before.)
> I haven't much money, **as you know**. (= I haven't much money, and you know it.)
> Tom arrived late, **as we expected**.

We use **as if** before a clause to express similarity:
> Alec looks really awful. He looks **as if he's been up all night**.
> Pamela can be quite bossy. She sometimes behaves **as if she owns the place**.

98 Exercises

98.1 during or while? (A)

Put in **during** or **while**.
- Did you take notes _during_ the lecture?
- You're not supposed to get off the train _while_ it's still moving.
1. I caught a bad cold _____ my holiday.
2. Shall we have a coffee _____ we're waiting?
3. Try not to make any noise _____ the baby is asleep.
4. The fire alarm rang _____ yesterday's meeting.
5. Dennis decorated the sitting-room _____ his wife was in Majorca.
6. We hope to see a couple of shows _____ our stay in New York City.

98.2 by or until? (B)

Claire is talking to her teacher. Put in **by** or **until**.

Claire: I'm supposed to finish my project this week, aren't I?
Mrs Lewis: Yes, you should give it to me □ _by_ the end of the week. I'd like to have it ¹_____ Friday, ideally.
Claire: I'm afraid that's going to be difficult. I'm going on a three-day study trip tomorrow. I'll be away ²_____ Thursday. I think the project is going to take me ³_____ the middle of next week. I can't finish ⁴_____ the end of this week.
Mrs Lewis: Well, let me have it ⁵_____ Wednesday of next week.

98.3 as or like? (C)

Put in **as** or **like**. Sometimes either word is possible.
- Helen speaks Italian, so she acted _as_ our interpreter.
- My driving instructor looks _like_ Peter Ustinov.
1. Laura works in here. She uses this room _____ her study.
2. The Scotts have an enormous house. It's _____ a palace.
3. Simon is working _____ a waiter at the moment.
4. Why don't we have a quiet evening at home, _____ we did last Saturday?
5. The way your sister plays the violin sounds _____ two cats fighting.
6. Do you mind using this saucer _____ a plate?
7. The old man is employed _____ a gardener.
8. You go to college, so _____ a student you can get cheap tickets.
9. The body sank _____ a stone to the bottom of the river.
10. Pubs are allowed to open all day now, _____ they are in other countries.

98.4 as or as if? (C)

Put in **as** or **as if**.
1. That poor dog looks _____ it never gets fed.
2. Steve failed his exams, _____ I expected him to.
3. Mandy spends money _____ it grows on trees.
4. We shall deliver the goods next month _____ we promised.
5. From what Kate said, it sounds _____ she and Jeremy are going to get divorced.

99 Preposition + noun (e.g. **on holiday**)

A Some common idioms

on holiday, on business; on a journey/a trip/a tour
    I'm travelling **on business**.   We're **on a** coach **tour** of Europe.

in cash, by cheque/credit card
    It's cheaper if you pay **in cash**.   Can I pay **by credit card**?

in writing, in pen/biro/ink/pencil
    Could you confirm that **in writing**?   I'll write the names **in pencil**.

on television/the radio/the phone
    a programme **on TV/on the radio**   I was **on the phone** to my sister.

for sale, on the market
    The house next door is **for sale**.   It's the best hi-fi **on the market**.

on the whole, in general
    On the whole it's a good idea, but there are one or two problems.

in advance, out of date, up to date
    The company wants us to pay for the goods **in advance**.
    Oh no! My passport is **out of date**.   These latest figures are **up to date**.

in my opinion, from my point of view
    All sport is silly **in my opinion**.   Try to see things **from my point of view**.

on purpose, by mistake/chance/accident
    I didn't break the glass **on purpose**.   I pressed the wrong button **by mistake**.
    We didn't arrange to meet. We met **by chance** in the street.

on the way (= during the journey), **in the way** (= blocking the way)
    I'm driving into town. I'll get some petrol **on the way**.
    We couldn't walk along the path because there was a pile of stones **in the way**.

in the end (= finally, after a long time), **at the end** (= when something stops)
    It took me hours to decide. **In the end** I chose a long blue dress.
    We all left quickly **at the end** of the meeting.

B Transport

We use **by** without **a/the** when we talk about a means of transport, for example: **by bike, by car, by taxi, by bus/coach, by train/tube, by rail, by boat/ship/ferry, by sea, by plane, by air**.
    We decided to go to Scotland **by train**. NOT ~~... go by the train.~~

On foot means 'walking', e.g. We came **on foot**. NOT ~~... by foot.~~

We can also use **on my bike, in the/my/your car, in a taxi** or **on the bus/train/boat/ship/ferry/plane**.
    It'll be quicker to go **in the car**.   They came **on the train**.

99 Exercises

99.1 Some common idioms (A)

Put in **by, from, in** or **on**.

☐ There's something I want to watch _on_ television.
1. They've told me I can have time off, but I haven't got it _____ writing.
2. I found the English to be fairly friendly people, _____ the whole.
3. Why can't you look at the problem _____ my point of view?
4. Would you mind moving? You're rather _____ the way here.
5. I dialled the wrong number _____ mistake.
6. Is it OK if I write _____ pencil?
7. Are you here _____ holiday or _____ business?
8. I booked our seats a month _____ advance and paid _____ cheque.
9. Jessica fell ill while she was _____ a trip to Ireland.
10. Could you be quiet for a minute, please? I'm _____ the phone.
11. We've had a few nice days, but _____ general it's been a poor summer.
12. I was lucky. I found the solution _____ accident.
13. It's a long journey. Let's stop somewhere _____ the way and have a meal.
14. I spent ages looking for a phone box. _____ the end I found one.

99.2 Some common idioms (A)

Put in the nouns on the right with the correct prepositions (e.g. **on, in, by**). You may also need to use **the** or **my**.

☐ Do you think we ought to book seats _in advance_? ~ No, I don't think so. _On the whole_ it's better to buy a ticket on the day.   ☐ advance / whole

1. Is it all right if I pay _____? ~ Well, if you don't mind, I'd prefer it _____.   1 credit card / cash
2. A lot of this information is _____. ~ I know. We do our best to keep _____, but it's difficult.   2 date / date
3. Did the others lock you out of the house _____? ~ No, it happened quite _____.   3 purpose / chance
4. Is there anything _____ tonight? ~ No, but there's something _____ I want to listen to.   4 television / radio
5. These flats are still _____. ~ Yes, they've been _____ for over a year now.   5 sale / market
6. Was it an interesting talk? ~ _____ it was boring, but everyone clapped _____ of it.   6 opinion / end

99.3 Transport (B)

Put in **by, in** or **on**.
1. It'll be easier if I go _____ the train.
2. The quickest way to get there is _____ air, of course.
3. Shall we go _____ your car or mine?
4. They decided to go _____ foot.
5. The family arrived at the guest house _____ a taxi.
6. In summer I go to work _____ my bike.
7. Mrs Thatcher never travelled _____ train.

100 Noun + preposition

A Introduction

Some nouns can have a preposition after them:
- an **invitation to** a party
- the **cost of / price of** food
- some **damage to** the car
- a **lack of** hotels in the area
- an **application for** a job
- a **tax on** alcohol
- an **example of** what I mean
- We've got no **hope of** winning.

B trouble, method, advantage etc.

I'm having **trouble with** the car.
What's the **matter with** you?
the **answer/solution/key to** the problem

There's some **difficulty over/with** my visa.
It's a new **way/method of** storing data.
the **cause of/reason for** the delay

C connection, difference etc.

Compare:

One thing has a link **with** another.
- a **connection with** another crime
- Dave's **relationship with** Sue
- the **contrast with** yesterday's weather

There is a link **between** two things.
- a **connection between** the two crimes
- the **relationship between** Dave and Sue
- the **contrast between** rich and poor
- the **difference between** a boat and a ship

But note the prepositions in these examples:
It's a cheap **alternative to** leather.   This food is a **substitute for** meat.

D increase, rise etc.

We use **in** with words for increases and decreases, but we use **of** before a number. Compare:

- an **increase in /** a **reduction in** the price
- a **rise in** the numbers out of work

- an **increase of /** a **reduction of** fifteen per cent
- a **rise of** fifty thousand

E student, knowledge etc.

She is a **student of** chemistry.
I have some **knowledge of** Italian.
an **interest in** architecture
I have some **experience of** management.

He has some **ability in** maths.
I admire his **skill at** organizing things.
success at golf / **success in** my search
She's an **expert on/at** computers.

F need, wish etc.

These nouns all take **for**: need, demand, request; wish, desire, preference; taste, appetite.
There's a **need for** more facilities.
We made a **request for** more money.
There's no **demand for** the product.
I've got no **desire for** a fight.

G opinion etc.

What's your **opinion of / attitude to** these rumours?
I can't feel any **respect/sympathy for** a person like that.
a **belief in** God   an **attack on** the government

100 Exercises

100.1 Noun + preposition (A, B)

Complete the sentences. Use a preposition after these nouns:
answer, cause, damage, difficulty, invitation, matter, tax, way.

- I've had an _invitation to_ the barbecue.
1. The accident caused some _____ the car.
2. I'm trying to think of the best _____ getting this sofa upstairs.
3. I can't think of an _____ the problem, I'm afraid.
4. The _____ the accident is still unknown.
5. The government has introduced a new _____ luxury goods.
6. Unfortunately there was some _____ the arrangements.
7. The television won't come on. What's the _____ it?

100.2 Noun + preposition (A–D)

Complete the advertisement for a supermarket. Put in **between, for, of, in** or **with**.
Why not shop at Supersave? You'll find the cost ¹_____ your weekly shopping is much lower. There's quite a contrast ²_____ other stores. Here's one example ³_____ this: from today we have made a reduction ⁴_____ five per cent ⁵_____ all our meat prices. But this is not the only reason ⁶_____ Supersave's success. We're proud of our good relationship ⁷_____ our customers. And we believe there is simply no substitute ⁸_____ quality. That's the difference ⁹_____ us and ordinary stores. So come to Supersave and see the difference.

100.3 Noun + preposition (E)

Put in **at, in** or **of**.
A: What's the job you've applied for?
B: It's with a travel company. But the advert says that you need some experience ¹_____ work in tourism. I haven't got that. And I don't think my knowledge ²_____ foreign languages will be good enough. I'm having no success at all ³_____ my attempts to get a job.
A: What about your interest ⁴_____ computers? And your skill ⁵_____ typing? That's the sort of thing employers are looking for.
B: What skill? I can only type with two fingers.

100.4 Noun + preposition (F, G)

Put in **for, in, on** or **to**.
1. I felt some sympathy _____ the losing team.
2. We've received a request _____ help.
3. I just can't understand your negative attitude _____ the project.
4. I don't have much belief _____ modern medicine.
5. The union replied to the statement with an attack _____ the management.
6. After so much fighting there was a great desire _____ peace.
7. There is a need _____ new homes that young people can afford to buy.

101 Prepositional verbs (e.g. **wait for**)

A Introduction

A prepositional verb is a verb + preposition:
>I'm **waiting for** you.   The dog **belongs to** that woman.

The preposition always goes before the object. NOT ~~I'm waiting you for.~~

In questions the preposition usually goes at the end of the sentence:
>Who are you waiting **for**?

Some verbs can go with a number of different prepositions, like this:
>I'm **looking at** these photos.
>I'm **looking for** my keys. I can't find them anywhere.
>I'm **looking after** the children while their parents are out.
>The police are **looking into** the matter.

B Some common prepositional verbs

Here are some examples of prepositional verbs:
>Yes, I **agree with** you.   Tina **apologized for** her rudeness.
>Have you **applied for** the job?   The patient **asked for** a glass of water.
>Do you **believe in** God?   I don't **care about** your problems. I'm not interested.
>Lots of people **care for** elderly relatives. (= look after them)
>I didn't **care for** the film. (= didn't like it)
>Do **concentrate on** your work.   The USA **consists of** fifty states.
>I'll **deal with** (OR **see to**) the matter.   We finally **decided on** a holiday in Spain.
>Whether we have a picnic will **depend on** the weather.
>No one **laughed at** the silly jokes.   I was **listening to** the radio.
>Did you **pay for** the drinks?   Do you **suffer from** headaches?

But we do not use a preposition after these verbs: **enter, reach, approach, leave, request, demand, expect, control, answer**.
>The President **entered** the building by a side door.

C **about, of** and **to**

We can use **about** after many verbs, e.g. **speak, talk, hear, know, learn, think, ask, enquire, wonder, dream, protest, complain**.
>Did you **hear about** the accident?   Mike was **talking about** his holiday.

(But NOT after **discuss**, e.g. We **discussed** the matter.)

We also use **of** for some meanings:
>Who's Alan Phillips? ~ I don't know. I've never **heard of** him.
>Did you like the play? What did you **think of** it?
>I'd never tell you a lie. I wouldn't **dream of** it.

We can **talk to, write to, complain to** and **apologize to** a person:
>I'm **writing to** my sister.   We **talked to** Tony about his new job.

But we say **phone** without **to**:
>I'm **phoning** my sister.

101 Exercises

101.1 Prepositions with **look** (A)

Complete the conversation. Put in **at, for, after** or **into**.
- A: Did you say you were looking ¹_____ a baby-sitter?
- B: Yes, I'm just looking ²_____ these advertisements. It's so difficult to get anyone to look ³_____ young children.
- A: I expect it's expensive too, isn't it?
- B: I don't know. I'll have to look ⁴_____ the money side of it.

101.2 Some common prepositional verbs (B)

Look at this paragraph from a letter. Put in these verbs and add a preposition:
agree, applied, ask, care, caring, concentrate, decided, pay, suffering.

I'm working at Linbrooke Hospital now. I ⁰ _applied for_ a nurse's job last July and started in September. I don't earn much money, and I even had to ¹_____ my uniform out of my own money. Perhaps I should ²_____ a pay rise. But I don't really ³_____ the money. The work is the important thing. Of course it's very hard work ⁴_____ the patients, and at the moment I'm ⁵_____ backache. But I knew it would be like this when I ⁶_____ a career in nursing. I just try to forget all the problems and ⁷_____ the job. I think it's a worthwhile thing to do; I hope you ⁸_____ me.

101.3 Some common prepositional verbs (B)

Put in the verbs and add a preposition if necessary.

Jeff and Sarah had arranged to go to Phil's party. Jeff had to stay at work to ⁰ _deal with_ one or two problems. Sarah was sitting in the Parade Café ¹_____ the juke box. Jeff finally arrived at the café and ²_____ the delay. After a short walk they ³_____ Phil's flat. At the party Sarah met a man who kept ⁴_____ his own jokes. Phil talked to a young lady who ⁵_____ ghosts and had seen one the night before. They ⁶_____ the party early and got a taxi home.

◦ deal
1 listening
2 apologized
3 reached
4 laughing
5 believed
6 left

101.4 **about, of** and **to** (C)

Complete the conversation. Put in **about, of** or **to**.
- A: Did you hear ⁰ _about_ our experience at the Quick Burger Café?
- B: No. And I've never heard ¹_____ the Quick Burger Café.
- A: Oh, it's near Oxford. I was just talking ²_____ Sadie ³_____ it. They took at least twenty minutes to serve me a drink. I complained ⁴_____ the waitress, but she was rude to me. The manager wasn't there, so I've written ⁵_____ him to complain ⁶_____ the service. It was terrible. I wouldn't go there if I was you.
- B: I wouldn't dream ⁷_____ going there. I hate those hamburger places.

102 Verb + object + preposition

A Introduction

We can use some verbs in the pattern: verb + object + preposition.

	VERB	OBJECT	PREPOSITION
People	**admired**	Cleopatra	**for** her beauty.
The trees	**protect**	the garden	**from** the wind.

In the passive, the preposition comes after the verb:
>Cleopatra was **admired for** her beauty.
>The garden is **protected from** the wind.

B Some examples

Look at these sentences:
>The police actually **accused** me **of** the robbery.
>Can I **add** something **to** your shopping list?
>You should never **aim/point** a gun **at** someone.
>We'll have to **ask** someone **for** directions.
>The passengers **blamed** the airline **for** the delay.
>I'll have to **borrow** ten pounds **from** my parents.
>If you **compare** these results **with/to** last year, you'll see the improvement.
>I **congratulated** Jeremy **on** his excellent exam results.
>The teacher **divided/split** the class **into** four groups.
>You should **insure** the camera **against** theft. It might get stolen.
>Louise has **invited** us **to** a party.
>I **prefer** hot weather **to** cold. I hate the cold.
>The hotel **provided/supplied** us **with** a packed lunch.
>Most people **regard** Picasso **as** a great artist.
>The two men **robbed** the woman **of** all her savings. They **stole** £2,000 **from** her.
>The restaurant was full. We **shared** a table **with** a young Swedish couple.
>We don't **spend** much money **on** food.
>Don't forget to **thank** Dave **for** his help.

C about, of and to

We can use **about** with **tell** and **ask**:
>Did I **tell** you **about** my operation?   Ask your travel agent **about** cheap flights.

With **inform** and **warn** we can use **about** or **of**:
>You should **inform** everyone **about/of** the decision.
>A large sign **warned** motorists **about/of** the danger.

With **remind**, there is a difference in meaning between **about** and **of**:
>Ben **reminded** me **about** my appointment. (= told me not to forget)
>Ben **reminds** me **of** my brother. (= is like, makes me think of)

We can **write, describe** or **explain** something **to** a person:
>I've **written** several letters **to** the company.
>The woman **described** her attacker **to** the police.

102 Exercises

102.1 Verb + object + preposition (B)

Complete the sports commentator's words. Put in the correct prepositions (e.g. **on**, **to**).
'... and so Australia's Mark Brearley wins the gold medal ahead of Germany's Klaus Schliemann and Ivan Podorosky of Bulgaria. They're just congratulating him ¹_____ his victory. Brearley's speed over the first kilometre split the runners ²_____ two groups, and in the end it was a race between the three leaders. I've always regarded Brearley ³_____ a great athlete, and look how well he's done today. I would even compare him ⁴_____ the great Emil Kristo himself. There's no doubt now that Brearley will be invited ⁵_____ Oslo for next year's World Championships. So the Australian runner adds another medal ⁶_____ his collection. And Australia are doing really well in the medals table. In fact, they share fourth place ⁷_____ the United States ...'

102.2 Verb + object + preposition (B)

Complete these short conversations. Use a pattern with a preposition (e.g. **on, to**).
☐ A: I've bought a lot of books. I've spent £200.
   B: What! You've _spent £200 on books!_
1 A: I don't like wine. I prefer water.
   B: What! You prefer _____
2 A: You heard about the accident? Well, everyone's blaming me.
   B: What! They're blaming _____
3 A: I gave Linda the present, but she didn't thank me.
   B: What! She _____
4 A: The police say it's murder. They're accusing the headmaster.
   B: What! They're _____
5 A: We had no towels. The hotel didn't provide them.
   B: What! They _____
6 A: It's my sister's wedding today, but she didn't invite me.
   B: What! She _____
7 A: The team won a great victory, but no one congratulated them.
   B: What! No one _____

102.3 about, of and to (C)

Put in **about, of** or **to**.
☐ The interviewer asked the novelist _about_ his latest book.
1 I've told the police _____ people making a noise at night.
2 That man over there reminds me _____ someone I know.
3 Mr Norris explained _____ the court that he had some personal problems.
4 I'm just writing a letter _____ my friend.
5 There is a sign warning motorists _____ the danger.
6 We would like to inform our customers _____ a number of improvements in the service we offer.
7 Julia had to remind Bob _____ the money that he owed her.

103 Phrasal verbs (e.g. **go out**)

A What is a phrasal verb?

A phrasal verb is a verb + adverb (e.g. **go out, turn round, take away, put down**). There are very many phrasal verbs in English.

Some phrasal verbs have an object:

	VERB	OBJECT	ADVERB
I	let	the cat	out.
Did you	throw	the letter	away?

Others have no object:

	VERB	ADVERB
The cat	went	out.
The thief	got	away.

B Understanding phrasal verbs

Some phrasal verbs are easy to understand:
   *The man in front **turned round** and stared at me.*
   *I **left** my umbrella **behind**.*
The meanings are clear if you know the words **turn, round, leave** and **behind**.

But many phrasal verbs are idiomatic. The verb and adverb together have a special meaning:
   *Emma **turned up** half an hour late.* (= arrived)
   *Why did you **turn down** such a good offer?* (= refuse)
   *The machine often **breaks down**.* (= stops working properly)
   *I can't **make out** if it's a man or a woman over there.* (= see clearly)

Sometimes there is a one-word verb with the same meaning as the phrasal verb:
   go on = continue   **put off** = postpone   **leave out** = omit
   give out = distribute **throw away** = discard   **find out** = discover
   mix up = confuse   **make up** = invent (a story) **come off** = succeed
The phrasal verb is usually more informal than the one-word verb.

C Word order with phrasal verbs

An object can usually go either before or after the adverb:
   *I wrote **the number down**.* OR *I wrote **down the number**.*
   *Put **your hands up**, please.* OR *Put **up your hands**, please.*

A long object goes after the adverb:
   *The gang have **carried out** a number of bank raids in the last few months.*
   *Why don't you **try on** that dress in the window?*

A pronoun (e.g. **them, it**) always goes before the adverb:
   *The police know which gang **carried them out**.* NOT *... carried out them.*
   *If you like the dress, why not **try it on**?* NOT *... try on it?*

D Adverb meanings

Look at these adverbs and their meanings. (Remember that an adverb can have a number of different meanings.)

up (= completely)
  eat up these chocolates
  tear up the paper
  fill up with petrol
up (= increasing)
  prices are *going up*
  put up taxes
  speak up so we can hear
down (= completely to the ground)
  knock down a house
  cut down a tree
down (= decreasing)
  bring down inflation
  turn the sound *down*
down (= on paper)
  copy down the words
  write down the message
over (= from start to finish)
  check your work *over*
  think the problem *over*
on (= connected)
  switch on the kettle
  turn on the TV
  leave the lights *on* all night

on (= continuing)
  carry on working
  drive on a bit further
  Come on. Hurry up.
  hang on / hold on a minute
off (= away, departing)
  the thief *ran off*
  jump in the car and *drive off*
  the pain is *wearing off*
off (= disconnected)
  switch off the fire
  cut off our electricity
out (= completely)
  write out the whole text
  work out the answer
out (= away, disappearing)
  wash out the dirt
  cross out a mistake
out (= aloud)
  read out the article
  call out anxiously
out (= to different people)
  hand out free tickets
  share out the winnings

E Phrasal verbs and prepositional verbs

Compare:

PHRASAL VERB	PREPOSITIONAL VERB (See Unit 101)
Verb + adverb (e.g. **throw away**)	Verb + preposition (e.g. **pay for**)

The adverb can go before or after the object and is usually stressed:
  I'**made** '**up** the story.
  I'**made** the story '**up**.
The adverb goes after a pronoun (see C):
  I made **it up**.
  We threw **them away**.
	The preposition goes before the object and is not usually stressed:
	  I '**asked for** my key.
	  NOT *I asked my key for.*
	The preposition goes before a pronoun:
	  I asked **for it**.
	  I've looked **at them**.

Compare these adverbs and prepositions:

Some adverbs are: **about, away, back, down, in, off, on, out, over, round, through, up.**	Some prepositions are: **about, after, at, for, from, in, into, of, on, to, with.**

Notice that some words (e.g. **about, in, on**) can be either an adverb or a preposition.

103 Exercises

103.1 Understanding the meaning (A, B)

Work out the meaning of these phrasal verbs and put them in the right sentences: **come in, cut out, fall down, get in, give away, go away, let in, lie down, pay back, stay in, take back.** (Use a dictionary if you need to.)

- □ I was feeling so tired I had to _lie down_ for a while.
- □ I didn't have a key, but luckily someone was here to _let_ me _in_.
1. Can't we go out to a disco? I don't want to _____ all evening.
2. Can you lend me £10? I'll _____ you _____ on Friday.
3. The pavement is slippery. Be careful you don't _____.
4. Hello. Nice to see you. _____ and sit down.
5. There was an article in the newspaper that I wanted to _____ and keep.
6. We can't eat all the apples from the tree, so we _____ a lot of them _____.
7. The driver unlocked the coach so that we were able to _____.
8. I'll have to _____ these books _____ to the library.
9. Your brother was being a nuisance, so I told him to _____.

103.2 One-word verb and phrasal verb (B)

Put in a phrasal verb that means the same as the one-word verb on the right. Use the correct form of the phrasal verb.

A: I've □ _found out_ what the problem is with the exam.	□ discovered
B: Oh, good.	
A: When they printed the papers, they ¹_____ a page.	1 omitted
No one noticed until the papers had all been ²_____.	2 distributed
They'll have to ³_____ all the papers and ⁴_____ the exam.	3 discard
	4 postpone
B: Are you sure you haven't ⁵_____ this whole story?	5 invented
A: It's true, I tell you. And isn't it good news?	
B: I don't know. Now we'll have to ⁶_____ revising.	6 continue

103.3 Word order (C)

Complete the sentences by putting in the phrasal verbs. Some of the spaces you have to leave empty. Sometimes more than one answer is correct.

□ The sweater was full of holes, so I _threw_ it _away_.	□ threw away
□ I've _put up_ that picture you bought last week _____.	□ put up
1 There's always litter here. No one ever _____ it _____.	1 picks up
2 It's quite warm now. I think I'll _____ my coat _____.	2 take off
3 I haven't heard from my sister. I might _____ her _____.	3 ring up
4 You'll have to go into college to _____ your essay _____.	4 hand in
5 I'm trying to _____ the money I've just lost _____.	5 win back
6 If you don't know the number, you can _____ it _____ in the phone book.	6 look up
7 There was an accident which _____ all the traffic going into town _____.	7 held up
8 These two words are so similar that I keep _____ them _____.	8 mixing up

103.4 Adverb meanings (D)

Look back at D and then write the meaning of the underlined adverbs in these sentences.
- ☐ There's a film on television. Can I put it <u>on</u>? = _connected_
- ☐ I must just get these ideas <u>down</u> in writing. = _on paper_
1. We finished all the food <u>up</u>. = _____
2. I'm writing in pencil so I can rub <u>out</u> my mistakes. = _____
3. Martin didn't answer. He just went <u>on</u> reading. = _____
4. I'll just read <u>over</u> what I've written. = _____
5. A woman in the audience shouted something <u>out</u>. = _____
6. The water was <u>off</u> for an hour today. = _____
7. Ellie has an aggressive manner which frightens people <u>off</u> = _____
8. The company is trying to get its costs <u>down</u>. = _____
9. The embassy was burnt <u>down</u> by terrorists. = _____
10. I've got this form that I have to fill <u>out</u>. = _____
11. Social workers were giving <u>out</u> soup to the hungry. = _____
12. The boss is optimistic. The sales figures are moving <u>up</u> again = _____

103.5 Adverb meanings (D)

Put in the correct adverb.
1. Everything is so expensive. Prices seem to go _up_ all the time. ~ Yes, and the government is supposed to be bringing inflation _____.
2. You shouldn't leave the television _____ all night. ~ Sorry, I forgot. I usually turn it _____.
3. I've written the wrong word here. ~ Well, rub it _____. ~ I can't. It's in biro. I'll have to write it all _____ again.
4. They're going to pull _____ this beautiful old building. ~ I know. There are some protestors handing _____ leaflets about it.
5. Hold _____ a minute. I thought I heard someone call _____. ~ You imagined it. Come _____, or we'll be late.
6. Why don't you read _____ the letter so that we all know what's in it? ~ Yes, and could you speak _____ so that everyone can hear you.

103.6 Phrasal verb or prepositional verb? (E)

Complete the sentences. Use **him, her, it** or **them** with these verbs: **call for, deal with, laugh at, listen to, make up, show round, wash up, write down.**

- ☐ They say the story was untrue. Did Helen _make it up_?
- ☐ There were a few problems, but we were able to _deal with them_.
1. I'll never remember the address. I must _____.
2. Phil has never been here before. I'm going to _____.
3. I made the suggestion quite seriously. Why did everyone _____?
4. What about the breakfast things? Are we going to _____?
5. I bought a new tape, but I haven't had time to _____.
6. Judy is at home waiting for us. We're going to _____ on our way to the party.

104 Verb + adverb + preposition (e.g. **catch up with**)

A Introduction

Look at these examples:

	VERB	ADVERB	PREPOSITION	
I couldn't	**get**	**through**	**to**	Telephone Enquiries.
You'll have to	**get**	**up**	**onto**	the roof.
We	**look**	**out**	**over**	a beautiful valley.
So you've	**come**	**in**	**from**	the cold.
I'll just	**pop**	**along**	**to**	the shop.
The boy	**fell**	**down**	**on**	the pavement.
It was nice to	**go**	**out**	**into**	the fresh air.
We all	**looked**	**up**	**at**	the aeroplane.
The cat	**ran**	**away**	**from**	our dog.

B Some examples

A verb + adverb + preposition often has a special, idiomatic meaning. Look at these examples:

You go on ahead. I'll soon **catch up with** you.
I'm afraid we've **come up against** another difficulty.
Did the trip **come up to** (OR **live up to**) your expectations? (= Was it as good as you expected?)
We need to **cut down on** our spending. (= reduce)

They should **do away with** these useless traditions. (= abolish)
Martin is always **dropping in on** us without warning. (= pay a short visit)

You've got to **face up to** your responsibilities. You can't just ignore them.
If Plan A doesn't work, we've got Plan B to **fall back on**. (= use if necessary)
I'm tired. I don't really **feel up to** going out.

The thief managed to **get away with** about £2,000 in cash.
The goods are damaged. We'll have to **get on to** our suppliers. (= contact)
You haven't started packing yet. You'd better **get on with** it. (= start, continue)
Naomi doesn't really **get on with** Laura. They're always arguing.
I've got lots of little jobs to do, but I never seem to **get round to** actually doing them. (= find time for them)
I can't make a promise and then **go back on** it, can I? (= change, fail to keep)
I've decided to **go in for** the ten-mile Road Run this year. (= enter, compete in)
Most of the audience had left in the interval, but the actors decided to **go on with** the show. (= continue)

If you **hold on to** the rope, you'll be perfectly safe.
Andy was walking so fast I couldn't **keep up with** him. (= go as fast as him)
I'm **looking forward to** the trip. (= thinking ahead with pleasure)
If you're going barefoot, **look out for** (OR **watch out for**) broken glass. (= be careful about)
I got some money from the insurance company, but nothing could **make up for** losing my wedding ring. (= compensate for)
I'm not going to **put up with** this nonsense. (= tolerate)
We've **run out of** milk, I'm afraid. (= We have none left.)
This is the address you'll need if you want to **send away for** your free gift. (= write to ask for it)

104 Exercises

104.1 Simple meanings (**A**)

Put in these words:
away from, down on, in from, out at, out into, through to, up at, up onto.

☐ To reach the light bulb I had to get _up onto_ the table. ✓
1. I hurt myself when I was skating. I fell _____ the ice.
2. The journey through the tunnel took ages, and it was a relief finally to come _____ the sunshine.
3. Wondering if it was going to rain, Chris looked _____ the clouds.
4. People were running _____ the gunman as fast as they could.
5. I can't get _____ this phone number you've given me.
6. From the top of the building you can look _____ miles of open countryside stretching away to the horizon.
7. When I've come _____ from the cold, all I want to do is sit by the fire.

104.2 Idiomatic meanings (**B**)

Put in a phrasal verb + preposition which means the same as the expression on the right. Look back at the verbs in B if you need to.

☐ I'm afraid this product won't _live up to_ the claims made in the advertisement.	☐	be as good as
1 I'll just call at the filling-station. I don't want to _____ petrol.	1	have none left
2 If you want a catalogue, I'll _____ one.	2	write to ask for
3 We'd better _____ sheep in the road.	3	be careful about
4 I _____ seeing you again some time.	4	look ahead with pleasure
5 The teacher dictated the text so fast that the students couldn't _____ her.	5	go as fast as
6 Why should we have to _____ this awful noise?	6	tolerate
7 It's half past twelve. I'd better _____ our lunch.	7	start making
8 Do you think the committee are likely to _____ their previous decision?	8	change
9 There was a mistake in Barbara's bank statement, so she decided to _____ the bank immediately.	9	contact
10 I'm afraid an apology alone cannot _____ all the inconvenience we have suffered.	10	compensate for
11 Sharon likes to _____ quiz competitions.	11	enter
11 I'm trying to _____ the amount of coffee I drink.	12	reduce
13 I might lose my job. And I haven't got any savings to _____.	13	use if necessary
14 I've been meaning to reply to Paul's letter, but I haven't managed to _____ it yet.	14	find time for

105 Direct and reported speech

A Direct speech

Direct speech means the words actually spoken:

> Simon: *'I'm tired.'*
>
> Wasn't it Greta Garbo who said *'I want to be alone'*?
>
> *'I like pigs,'* replied Lord Emsworth.

(Speech bubble: We are doing well. Things will get better soon.)

We put direct speech in quotation marks (' '), for example *'I'm tired'*. These marks are also called inverted commas. We use direct speech when we want to repeat the exact words.

B Reported speech

But usually there is no need to repeat the exact words. In reported speech we only give the meaning of what was said:

> Simon says **he's tired**.
>
> Wasn't it Greta Garbo who said **that she wanted to be alone**?
>
> Lord Emsworth replied **that he liked pigs**.

> The Prime Minister said yesterday that the country was doing well. Things would get better soon.

In reported speech we often change the actual words, e.g., *'I am tired'* → *He is tired*. Sometimes the verb tense changes, e.g. *I want* → *she wanted* (see 106B).

When we report statements, we often use **that**, but we can sometimes leave it out:

> You told me **(that)** you were working today.
>
> Ben promised **(that)** he wouldn't be late.

When we leave out **that**, we sound less formal.

We can also report thoughts as well as speech:

> We **think** the meal was expensive.   Dave **knew** it was his last chance.

C **tell** or **say**?

Compare:

We use **tell** if we want to say who we are speaking to: *The boss **told them** they could leave early.* NOT *The boss told they ...* *Carl **tells me** he's ready.*	We use **say** when we do not mention the person we are speaking to: *The boss **said** they could leave early.* NOT *The boss said them ...* *Carl **says** he's ready.*
We use **tell** without an indirect object (e.g. **them, me**) only in the expressions **tell a story, tell the truth** and **tell a lie**.	We sometimes use **to** after **say**, especially when the words are not reported: *The boss wanted to **say** something **to** all of them.* *What did Pamela **say to** you?*

105 Exercises

105.1 Reported speech (B)

Why are these people at the doctor's? What do they say is wrong with them?

She says she gets pains in her leg.

1 She says _____

2 He says _____

3 She says _____

4 _____

5 _____

105.2 tell or say? (C)

Put in **tell** or **say**.

- All the doctors _say_ there's nothing wrong with me.
- Did you _tell_ Nancy how to get here?
1. Jeremy is going to _____ everyone about the meeting.
2. Why don't you _____ what the matter is?
3. They _____ they're going to build a new Disneyland here.
4. What did Fiona _____ about her holiday plans?
5. Could you _____ me the way to the bus station, please?
6. The company should _____ its employees what's going on.
7. You shouldn't _____ lies, you know.
8. Did you _____ anything to Desmond about that little problem?

106 Changes in reported speech

A Changes of person, place and time

Imagine that on Friday afternoon you and Steve are visiting Adrian at his flat. Adrian says:
  'I'm having a party here tomorrow evening. Would you like to come?'

Steve didn't hear what Adrian said, so a few moments later you tell Steve:
  *Adrian said **he's** having a party here tomorrow evening.*
(The speaker has changed, so **I** changes to **he**.)

The next day you tell someone else:
  *Adrian said he's having a party **at his flat this evening**.*
(The place is different, so **here** changes to **at his flat**. And the time has changed. It is now the day of the party, so **tomorrow evening** changes to **this evening**.)

Changes from direct speech to reported speech depend on changes in the situation – a different speaker or a different place or time. Some typical changes are:
  I → he/she, my → his/her; here → there; now → then, today → that day, tomorrow → the next day, this week → that week, last week → the week before.

B When do we change the tense?

After a past-tense verb (e.g. **said, told, was complaining**), there is often a tense change (e.g. **is → was**).
  'It's cold.' → *Tim said it **was** cold.*
  'You look pale.' → *I told Emma she **looked** pale.*

If the statement is still up to date when we report it, then we have a choice. We often leave the tense the same, but we can change it:
  Adrian said he's (OR he was) having a party next weekend.
  You said you like (OR liked) walking.
  Angela told me her father owns (OR owned) a supermarket.
  Rachel said that the room is (OR was) too small.
We can say that Adrian **is** having a party because it is still true that there will be a party.

If the statement is out of date, then we change the tense in reported speech:
  *Adrian said he **was** having a party last weekend.*
  *At half time the team thought they **had** a good chance of winning. But in the end they lost the game.*
  *Angela told me years ago that her father **owned** a supermarket.*
Adrian's party is over, so it is no longer true that he **is** having a party. The information is out of date.

We usually change the tense if we think the statement may be untrue:
  *You said you **liked** chocolate, but you aren't eating any.*
  *Rachel said that the room **was** too small, but it seemed big enough to me.*

In news reports the tense usually changes. (Some people may think the statement is untrue.)
  *The Prime Minister said that the government **had** made the right decision.*

C is → was, like → liked etc.

Look at these examples of direct and reported speech:

DIRECT SPEECH	REPORTED SPEECH
'We **like** this place.' →	The couple said they **liked** the place.
'I**'m** fit now.' →	The player said he **was** fit.
'Zoe**'s** cheating.' →	Jill thought Zoe **was** cheating.
'The letters **aren't** opened'. →	They said the letters **weren't** opened.
'I**'ve** finished my course.' →	Tom told me he**'d** finished his course.
'It**'s** been raining.' →	We noticed it **had** been raining.
'We**'ve** got plenty of time.' →	Joe insisted they **had** plenty of time.

After **said, thought, told,** etc. the verb often changes from present to past, e.g. *like* → *liked*, *am* → *was*. If the verb phrase is more than one word, then the first word changes, e.g. *is* cheating → *was* cheating, *aren't* opened → *weren't* opened, *have* finished → *had* finished, *has* been raining → *had* been raining.

If the verb is already past (e.g. **did**), then it can stay the same or change to the past perfect (e.g. **had done**):

'We **travelled** here by car.' → The couple said they **travelled** (OR **had travelled**) there by car.
'I **wasn't** expecting to see you.' → Carol said she **wasn't** (OR **hadn't been**) expecting to see me.

If the verb is past perfect, it stays the same:

'My money **had run** out.' → Steve said his money **had run** out.

D Modal verbs: can → could etc.

There can also be a tense change to some of the modal verbs.
The changes are **will/shall** → **would**, **can** → **could** and **may** → **might**.
Look at these examples:

DIRECT SPEECH	REPORTED SPEECH
'I**'ll** help if you like.' →	Alan said he **would** help.
'You **can** sit over there.' →	The steward said we **could** sit here.
'We **may** move house.' →	The family thought they **might** move house.

But **would, could, should, might** and **ought to** stay the same:

'Sue **would** love a holiday.' → Mark thought Sue **would** love a holiday.

Must can change to **had to**:

'I **must** answer this letter.' → Gavin said he **must** (OR he **had to**) answer the letter.

106 Exercises

106.1 Changes of person (**A**)

Put in the pronouns (**I, you** etc.).
1. Susan (to you): 'I feel really fed up with my job.'
   You (to Wayne): Susan says _____ feels really fed up with her job.
2. Laura (to you): 'How is Louise?'
   You (to Louise): Laura asked how _____ are.
3. Phil (to you): 'I haven't got any money.'
   You (to Gary): Phil says _____ hasn't got any money.
4. Joanna (to you): 'Kevin never speaks to me.'
   You (to Kevin): Joanna says _____ never speak to _____.

106.2 Changes of place and time (**A**)

Put in: **here, that day, the day before, the next day, the week before**.
1. Angela (a week ago): 'Terry and I are going to a concert tomorrow.'
   You (today): Angela said she and Terry were going to a concert _____.
2. Jan (two days ago): 'I've only been in England since yesterday.'
   You (today): Jan said he had only been in England since _____.
3. Neil (a week ago): 'I'm meeting my friend at the airport later today.'
   You (today): Neil said he was meeting his friend at the airport later _____.
4. Max (in the street): 'I'll see you at the coffee bar.'
   You (at the coffee bar): Max said he would see me _____.
5. Paul (a month ago): 'The festival was last week.'
   You (today): Paul told me the festival had been _____.

106.3 The choice of tense (**B**)

Put in **is** or **was**. (Sometimes both are possible.) Is the statement still true (**is**) or out of date (**was**)?
- ☐ I heard today that the block of flats where I live _is_ for sale. I wonder who is going to buy it?
- ☐ I saw Martin yesterday. He said he _was_ on his way to visit his sister.
1. This wallet is made of plastic not leather. Why did you tell me it _____ leather?
2. We had to hurry yesterday morning. Just as we arrived at the station, we heard an announcement that the train _____ about to leave.
3. What did Barbara say just now? ~ She said her tooth _____ still aching.
4. I was going to get a cup of coffee, but Mike just told me the machine _____ out of order. It's going to be fixed tomorrow.
5. I'm surprised Emma lost her match against Sheila. I thought she _____ a much better player than Sheila.
6. It said on the radio that the Queen _____ coming here next month. Isn't that exciting?
7. When he spoke to reporters yesterday, the Chairman said that the company _____ now in a much better financial position.
8. The advertisement said that the swimming-pool _____ free, but when we got here, we found we had to pay.

106 Changes in reported speech

106.4 The tense change (C)

Reply to these statements. The speakers are all saying something different to what they told you before.

☐ 'I'm going out with Ingrid.'
But you said _you weren't going out with her._

☐ 'I prefer pop music to classical music.'
You told me _you preferred classical music._

1 'I haven't finished my project.'
   I thought you said _____

2 'I'm better at tennis than golf.'
   But you told me _____

3 'I enjoy parties.'
   I remember you saying _____

4 'I've got a video recorder.'
   But you said yesterday _____

5 'I'm applying for the job.'
   I thought you told me _____

6 'I like Indian food more than Chinese.'
   But you said _____

106.5 The tense change (C, D)

A comedy show called 'Don't Look Now!' has just closed after five years at a theatre in London's West End. It was the most popular comedy for a long time. This is what the critics said when it opened five years ago.

'It's a marvellous show.' The Daily Mail
'You'll love it.' The Guardian
'The production is brilliant.' The Sunday Times
'I can't remember a funnier show.' Stephen Devine
'It made me laugh.' Ben Walsh
'You must see it.' The Evening News
'It will be a great success.' The Telegraph
'You might die laughing.' The Daily Express
'It's the funniest show I have ever seen.' Joan Proctor
'You shouldn't miss it.' Time Out

Now report what the critics said.

☐ _The Daily Mail said it was a marvellous show._
☐ _The Guardian said people would love it._

1 The Sunday Times said _____
2 _____
3 _____
4 _____
5 _____
6 _____
7 _____
8 _____

107 Reported questions

A Wh-questions and yes/no questions

We can report a question by using verbs like **ask**, **wonder** or **want to know**:

DIRECT QUESTION	REPORTED QUESTION
wh-questions:	
'**When** did you leave school?' ~ 'Last year.'	→ The interviewer **asked** Jane **when** she left school.
'**What**'s the time?' ~ 'Ten to five.'	→ I just **asked what** the time is.
'**Which** way is the post office?' ~ 'Down there.'	→ Mandy **wants to know which** way the post office is.
'**How** can we find out?'	→ I was **wondering how** we can find out.
'**Where** can we eat?'	→ They **want to know where** they can eat.
yes/no questions:	
'Has Alec arrived yet?' ~ 'No, not yet.'	→ Someone was **wondering if/whether** Alec has arrived yet.
'Can we use calculators?' ~ 'Yes, we can.'	→ The students **want to know if/whether** they can use calculators.
'Is there a café?' ~ 'No.'	→ Joe **asked if/whether** there was a café.

Reported wh-questions have a question word like **when, what, which** or **how**. Reported yes/no questions have **if** or **whether**.

In a reported question, the word order is like a statement, e.g. *she left school, Alec has arrived*.
   NOT ~~He asked Jane when did she leave school.~~
   NOT ~~Someone was wondering if has Alec arrived yet.~~

B Asking for information

We sometimes use a phrase like **Could you tell me** . . . ? or **Do you know** . . . ? to ask for information. After the phrase, the word order is like a statement:
   Could you tell me what time the performance starts?
   Do you know if there's a public phone in the building?
   Have you any idea how much these things cost?

C The tense change: **is → was** etc.

In reported speech there are often changes to the tense, to pronouns and so on. This depends on changes to the situation since the direct speech. For details see Unit 106. Here are some examples of the tense change:

'What are you doing?'	→ An official asked what we **were** doing.
'How much money have you got?'	→ I asked Sarah how much money she **had**.
'Does Susan need a lift?'	→ Tim wondered if Susan **needed** a lift.
'Why has Tina gone home?'	→ James wondered why Tina **had** gone home.
'How did you find out?'	→ We asked Paul how he **found** (OR **had found**) out.
'Can you type?'	→ They asked me if I **could** type.
'Will there be enough time?'	→ Kay wanted to know if there **would** be enough time.

107 Exercises

107.1 Wh-questions and yes/no questions (A)

What do these tourists want to know at the Tourist Information Centre?
- German student: What are the most interesting sights?
  A German student wants to know _what the most interesting sights are._
- Young man: Have you got a town plan?
  A young man wants to know _if the Centre has got a town plan._
1 Young woman: How can I find out about the town?
  A young woman wants to know _____
2 Woman: Are there guided tours?
  A woman wants to know _____
3 French couple: Where can we stay?
  A French couple want to know _____
4 Tourist: Which way is the castle?
  A tourist _____
5 Japanese man: What shows are there?
  A Japanese man _____
6 Two young men: When does the festival start?
  Two young men _____

107.2 Asking for information (B)

Ask for information using **Could you tell me** . . . ? or **Do you know** . . . ?
- 'Where are the toilets?' (tell) _Could you tell me where the toilets are?_
1 Can I park here? (know) _____
2 How long does the film last? (tell) _____
3 How often do the buses go? (know) _____
4 Are we allowed to smoke? (know) _____
5 What time is the flight? (tell) _____
6 How much does a ticket cost? (tell) _____

107.3 is → was etc. (C)

Gavin has worked for Brisco Supermarkets for thirty years. He can still remember his job interview after leaving school, and he can remember the questions that the interviewer asked him.
- 'Where do you live?' She asked him _where he lived._
- 'Have you worked before?' She asked him _if he had worked before._
1 'Why do you want the job?' She asked him _____
2 'How did you hear about it?' She asked him _____
3 'Are you fit?' She asked him _____
4 'Can you work on Saturdays?' She asked him _____
5 'How will you travel to work?' She asked him _____
6 'Have you got a bicycle?' She asked him _____
7 'How much do you expect to earn?' She asked him _____
8 'When can you start?' She asked him _____

108 Reported requests, offers etc.

A Reported orders and requests

We can use the pattern **tell/ask someone to do something**, like this:

DIRECT SPEECH	REPORTED SPEECH
'Please move this car.'	→ A policeman **told me to move** the car.
'You really must work harder.'	→ My parents are always **telling me to work** harder.
'Would you mind turning the music down?'	→ We **asked our neighbours to turn** the music down.

The negative is **tell/ask someone not to do something**:
'Please don't wear those boots in the house.' → I **asked you not to wear** those boots in the house.
'You mustn't leave the door unlocked.' → My landlady **told me not to leave** the door unlocked.

We can also use **ask** in the pattern **ask to do something**:
   The doorman **asked to see** my membership card.

We use **ask for** when someone asks to have something:
   I **asked** (the travel agent) **for** some brochures.

It is also possible to report an order or request like this:
   My parents are always telling me (that) I must work harder.
   We asked our neighbours if they would mind turning the music down.

B Reported offers, suggestions etc.

We can use **offer**, **promise**, **agree**, **refuse** and **threaten** with a to-infinitive:

DIRECT SPEECH	REPORTED SPEECH
'We'll pay for the damage.'	→ We **offered to pay** for the damage.
'I'll definitely finish it by the end of next week.'	→ You **promised to finish** the work by the end of this week.

We can use an object + to-infinitive after **remind**, **warn**, **advise** and **invite**:
'Don't forget to ring me.' → Sue **reminded Jeremy to ring** her.
'I think you should take a taxi.' → Eric **advised me to take** a taxi.

We can use an ing-form after **suggest**, **admit**, **insist on** and **apologize for**:
'Shall we go to a night club?' → Sarah **suggested going** to a night club.
'I really must have a break.' → Clive **insisted on having** a break.

C promise that, agree that etc.

We can use a clause with **that** after **promise**, **agree**, **remind**, **warn**, **advise**, **suggest**, **admit** and **insist**:
   You **promised (that)** you would finish the work by the end of this week.
   I **warned you (that)** those steps are slippery.
   Jeff **admitted (that)** he was wrong.
   The chairman **insisted (that)** we kept to the rules.

108 Exercises

108.1 tell someone to do something (A)

There are lots of books about living a healthy life. Most of the experts say the same things.
- ☐ 'You should eat more fruit.' _They tell you to eat more fruit._
- ☐ 'It's bad to have fatty foods.' _They tell you not to have fatty foods._
1. 'You must get some exercise.' _____
2. 'Don't eat sweet things.' _____
3. 'You must relax sometimes.' _____
4. 'Find time for a hobby.' _____
5. 'You mustn't smoke.' _____
6. 'Don't drink a lot of alcohol.' _____

108.2 Reported offers, suggestions etc. (B)

Complete the sentences. Report what was said.
- ☐ Peter to Nick: Would you like to stay for lunch?
  Peter invited _Nick to stay for lunch._
- ☐ Sharon: Yes, all right. I won't tell anyone.
  Sharon agreed _not to tell anyone._
1. Tim to Martin: You ought to see a doctor.
   Tim advised _____
2. Louise: I'm sorry I caused so much trouble.
   Louise apologized for _____
3. Andy: Why don't we go out for the day?
   Andy suggested _____
4. Tracy: I'll do the washing-up.
   Tracy offered _____
5. Pat to Jane: You're going to post the letter, don't forget.
   Pat reminded Jane _____
6. Travel agent: Yes, we made a mistake.
   The travel agent admitted _____
7. Steve to Mike: Don't touch the electric wires.
   Steve warned _____

108.3 promise that, agree that etc. (C)

Combine each pair of sentences using **that**.
- ☐ The roads were dangerous. The police warned us.
  The police warned us that the roads were dangerous.
1. Everything will be ready on time. The builders have promised.

2. We have to check everything carefully. The boss insists.

3. Jill's story wasn't completely true. She admitted it.

4. My train was about to leave. Ted reminded me.
   Ted _____

109 Relative clauses with **who**, **which** and **that**

A The use of relative clauses

Look at this conversation:
- Jill: *I saw Natalie Parker the other day.*
- Tessa: *Natalie? The woman **who lived in the upstairs flat**?*
- Jill: *No, that was Naomi. Natalie is the student **who failed all her exams**, the one **who never did any studying**. She's working in Davidson's now, the shop **that sells leather goods**.*
- Tessa: *Oh, Natalie. Yes, of course.*

These relative clauses identify which person or thing we are talking about. The clause **who lived in the upstairs flat** tells us which girl Tessa means. The clause **that sells leather goods** tells us which shop Jill means.

Sometimes we can use an adjective or a phrase to identify someone or something, for example: *the **tall** girl, the **new** student, the woman **with blond hair**, the shop **on the corner***. But when we need a longer explanation we can use a relative clause, for example: *the woman **who lived in the upstairs flat***.

B who, which and that

Who and **which** go after the noun and at the beginning of the relative clause.
Who refers to people and **which** to things. Look at these examples:
- *Mrs Bryant is **the woman who** owns that enormous house.*
- *I don't like **people who** tell jokes all the time.*
- *We saw **the actual spacecraft which** landed on the moon.*
- *There are **several restaurants which** do Sunday lunches.*
- *I threw away **that old tin-opener which** didn't work.*
- ***The little girl who** sat next to me on the coach ate sweets the whole way.*
- ***Burglar alarms which** ring for no reason are a real nuisance.*

We do not use another pronoun with the relative pronoun:
- NOT *... the man who he owns that enormous dog.*
- NOT *...the actual spacecraft which it landed on the moon.*

We can use **that** instead of **who** or **which**:
- *Mrs Bryant is the woman **who/that** owns that enormous house.*
- *We saw the actual spacecraft **which/that** landed on the moon.*

With people, **who** is more usual. With things, **that** is more usual, especially in conversation. **Which** can be a little formal.
- ***The woman who** lived here before us is a romantic novelist.*
- *Have you got the phone number of **the chap who** repaired your washing-machine?*
- ***The car that** won the race didn't look anything very special.*
- *They've recaptured **all the animals that** escaped from the zoo.*

In these sentences **who**, **which** and **that** are the subject of the relative clause. For **who**, **which** and **that** as object see Units 110 and 111.

109 Exercises

109.1 Identifying (A)

Write the phrases to identify which one is meant. Use the shortest way of identifying, e.g. **the tall boy**, not **the boy who is tall**.

☐ the boy (he is tall) → _the tall boy_
☐ the man (he has long hair) → _the man with long hair_
☐ the woman (she plays golf) → _the woman who plays golf_
1 the young man (he is at the door) → _____
2 the boy (he sings in a pop group) → _____
3 the woman (she is very thin) → _____
4 the girl (she has green eyes) → _____
5 the young lady (she is well dressed) → _____
6 the man (he works here) → _____

109.2 who, which and that (B)

Complete the conversation. Put in **who**, **which** or **that**. (More than one answer is possible.)
A: Shall we have something to eat?
B: Yes, but not here. I don't like cafés ☐ _which_ don't have tables. I'm not one of those people ☐ _who_ can eat standing up.
A: There's another restaurant over there.
B: It looks expensive, one of those places ¹_____ charge very high prices. The only customers ²_____ can afford to eat there are business executives ³_____ get their expenses paid. Anyway, I can't see a menu. I'm not going into a restaurant ⁴_____ doesn't display a menu.
A: We just passed a café ⁵_____ does snacks.
B: Oh, I didn't like the look of that.
A: You're one of those people ⁶_____ are never satisfied, aren't you?

109.3 Relative clauses (A, B)

Combine the information in these news items. Make the sentence in brackets into a relative clause. Use **the** at the beginning of the sentence, e.g. **The man** . . .

☐ A man has gone to prison. (He shot two policemen.)
  The man who shot two policemen has gone to prison.
1 A bomb caused a lot of damage. (It went off this morning.)
  The bomb _____
2 A scientist has won the Nobel Prize. (He discovered a new planet.)
  _____
3 A strike is over. (It closed Britain's docks.)
  _____
4 A footballer has been banned from playing again. (He took drugs.)
  _____
5 A little girl has been found safe and well. (She had been missing since Tuesday.)
  _____
6 Some oil is five miles off the Scottish coast. (It spilled from a tanker.)
  _____

110 The relative pronoun as object

A who, which and that as subject and object

A relative pronoun (**who**, **which**, **that**) can be the subject of the clause:

*The man **who has bought** the house comes from London.*
(**he** has bought the house)

*The photo **which took** first prize was of a farmhouse.*
(the **photo** took first prize)

*The letter **that came** this morning was from my sister.*
(the **letter** came this morning)

For the difference between **who**, **which** and **that**, see Unit 109.

A relative pronoun can also be the object of the clause:

*The man **who you met** yesterday is my friend Bernard.*
(you met the **man**)

*Are these the cakes **which Helen baked**?*
(Helen baked the **cakes**)

*The TV programme **that we missed** is repeated this evening.*
(we missed the TV **programme**)

We do not use another pronoun (e.g. **him**) with the relative pronoun:
NOT *... the man who you met him.*   NOT *... the cakes which Helen baked them.*

B Leaving out the relative pronoun

We can leave out the pronoun **who**, **which** or **that** when it is the object. We often do this in spoken English.

*The man **you met** yesterday is my friend Bernard.* (OR *The man **who you met** ...*)
*The TV programme **we missed** is repeated this evening.* (OR *The TV programme **that we missed** ...*)
*We don't know the name of the person **the police are questioning**.*
*The mistake **Sarah made** was fortunately not very serious.*
*That jacket **Tony always wears** is falling to pieces.*

We can also leave out **who, which** or **that** when they are the object of a preposition (e.g. **to**):
*The man **I spoke to** yesterday is my friend Bernard.* (See Unit 111.)

We do not leave out a relative pronoun when it is the subject:
*The man **who** has bought the house comes from London.*

C who and whom

In formal English, **whom** is sometimes used when the object is a person:
*The person **whom/who** the police were questioning has now been released.*

But in conversation **whom** is not very common. We normally leave out the pronoun, or we use **who**:
*I know the woman **(who)** you were talking to.*

110 Exercises

110.1 who and that as subject and object (A)

Write a sentence with **who** or **that** as <u>subject</u> of the underlined part.
- ☐ She's the secretary. ~ Who is? ~ That woman. <u>She brought the parcel.</u>
  The woman _who brought the parcel is the secretary_.
1. The dog has been shot. ~ What dog? ~ <u>It was chasing the sheep.</u>
   The dog _____
2. The story was untrue. ~ What story? ~ You know. <u>It upset everyone.</u>
   The story _____
3. He's a film producer. ~ Who is? ~ That man. <u>He rang Lola.</u>
   The man _____

Now write a sentence with **who** or **that** as <u>object</u> of the underlined part.
- ☐ The shirt doesn't fit. ~ Which shirt? ~ Dave's. <u>He bought it yesterday.</u>
  The shirt _that Dave bought yesterday doesn't fit_.
4. He's a millionaire. ~ Who is? ~ That man. <u>Angela knows him.</u>
   The man _____
5. The vase was extremely valuable. ~ What vase? ~ You know. <u>Peter broke it.</u>
   The vase _____
6. It's really nice. ~ What is? ~ The jacket. <u>You wore it last night.</u>
   The jacket _____

110.2 Leaving out the relative pronoun (B)

Complete the advertisements. Use relative clauses without a pronoun.
- ☐ Fresho soap. Beautiful people use it. It's _the soap beautiful people use_.
1. A Wellman car. You can afford it. It's _____
2. 'Polo'. People want to see this film. It's _____
3. Jupiter chocolates. You'll enjoy them. They're _____
4. Fizzo cleaner. You can trust it. It's _____
5. 'Break' magazine. Clever people read it. It's _____

110.3 Leaving out the relative pronoun (B)

Write the full sentences. Where you see ♦, you may need to put in **who**, **which** or **that**. Sometimes more than one answer is correct.
- ☐ The man ♦ paid for the meal was a friend of Mary's
  The man who paid for the meal was a friend of Mary's.
- ☐ The school ♦ I attended had only one classroom
  The school I attended had only one classroom.
1. From here you can see the mountain ♦ we climbed

2. The man ♦ services my car is a keen fisherman

3. The detective lost the man ♦ he was following

4. I thought I recognized the assistant ♦ sold me the suit

111 Prepositions in relative clauses (e.g. the letter I was looking **for**)

A Preposition at the end

A relative pronoun can be the object of a preposition:

*The restaurant **which** we normally go **to** is closed for decoration.*
(we normally go **to the restaurant**)

*I found the letter **that** I was looking **for**.*
(I was looking **for the letter**)

*These are the people **that** we went on holiday **with** last year.*
(we went on holiday **with these people**)

In informal spoken English we normally put the preposition at the end of the relative clause. Compare the word order:

STATEMENT	RELATIVE CLAUSE
We **go to** the restaurant.	the restaurant which we **go to**
I was **looking for** the letter.	the letter that I was **looking for**

We often leave out the relative pronoun (e.g. **which**):
*The restaurant we normally go **to** is closed for decoration.*
(OR *The restaurant which we normally go to ...*)
*I found the letter I was looking **for**.*
(OR *... the letter that I was looking for.*)
*These are the people we went on holiday **with**.*
*The concert you were telling me **about** is next week.*
*I can't remember the name of the hotel we stayed **at**.*
*Is this the colour you've finally decided **on**?*

We do not use a pronoun (e.g. **it, them**) after the preposition:
NOT *The restaurant we normally go to it is closed.*
NOT *These are the people we went on holiday with them.*

B Preposition at the beginning

In formal English the preposition can come at the beginning of the relative clause, before **which** or **whom**:

*Was that the restaurant **to which** you normally go?*
*Electronics is a subject **about which** I know very little.*
*What is the evidence **on which** you base this claim?*
*Mr Bell is the person **from whom** I obtained the information.*

For **whom** see also Unit 110C.

We cannot put a preposition before **that** or **who**:
*Electronics is a subject that I know little **about**.*
NOT *... a subject about that I know little.*
*Mr Bell is the person who I obtained the information **from**.*
NOT *... the person from who I obtained the information.*

111 Exercises

111.1 Preposition at the end (A)

Someone is showing their holiday photos to a friend. Write sentences with relative clauses.

- We stayed at this camp site.   *This is the camp site we stayed at.*
1. I slept in that tent.
2. We walked up that hill.
3. We had a view of this beach.
4. Alex and I went out in that boat.
5. We sailed from this harbour.
6. We landed on this island.
7. I went to this museum.
8. We got friendly with these people.

111.2 Preposition at the end (A)

Match the phrases and write the definitions.

a kitchen	a cupboard	someone travels to it
1 a sofa bed	an instrument	you can make holes with it
2 a drill	a piece of furniture	you can either sit or sleep on it
3 a destination	a passage	we keep valuable things in it
4 a corridor	the place	you cook in it
5 a microphone	a room	people walk along it
6 a safe	a tool	people speak into it

- *A kitchen is a room you cook in.*
1.
2.
3.
4.
5.
6.

111.3 Preposition at the beginning (B)

Some politicians are arguing. Rewrite their sentences using a preposition at the beginning of a relative clause. Remember that this makes the sentences sound formal.

- I cannot agree with that statement.
  That is a statement with which I cannot agree.

1. Our party believes in that idea.

2. I am strongly opposed to that policy.

3. No one cares about these people.

4. Your party should be ashamed of those mistakes.

5. The government is dealing with that problem.

112 Relative patterns with whose, what and it

A whose

Look at these examples of relative clauses with **whose**:
  *Jeremy is the boy **whose passport** was out of date.*
  *The girl **whose photo** was in the paper lives in our street.*

Here **whose** passport means his passport, Jeremy's passport, and **whose** photo means her photo, a photo of the girl.

Here are some more examples:
  *Someone **whose bicycle** had been stolen was reporting it to the police.*
  *There were two players **whose skill** impressed everyone.*

We use **whose** mainly with people. But sometimes it goes with other kinds of nouns:
  *Which is the European **country whose** economy is growing the fastest?*
  *Round the corner was a **building whose** windows were all broken.*
  *Mary was looking after a **dog whose** leg had been broken in an accident.*

B what

We use the relative pronoun **what** without a noun in front of it:
  *The shop didn't have **what** I wanted.* (= the thing(s) that I wanted)
  ***What** we saw gave us a shock.*
  ***What** we haven't done today we can finish tomorrow.*

We can also use **what** to give emphasis to a word or phrase, to make it more important. Compare:

NEUTRAL	EMPHATIC
Julia's attitude puzzled me.	***What** puzzled me was **Julia's attitude**.*
We found a box full of old magazines.	***What** we found was **a box full of old magazines**.*
I want to make a fresh start.	***What** I want to do is **make a fresh start**.*
They shared the money equally.	***What** they did was **share the money equally**.*

C The pattern with it

We also use the pattern **it** + **be** + relative clause to give emphasis to a word or phrase, to make it more important. Compare:

NEUTRAL	EMPHATIC
The doorbell rang.	***It was the doorbell** that rang (not the phone).*
Martin has finished first.	***It's Martin** who has finished first.*
I'm eating chocolate cake.	***It's chocolate cake** (that) I'm eating.*
We arrived on Friday.	***It was on Friday** that we arrived.*

We must put in a relative pronoun (e.g. **who**, **that**) when it is the subject (e.g. **who** *has finished first*). If it is the object (e.g. **that** *I'm eating*), then we can leave it out.

112 Exercises

112.1 who or whose? (A)

You are reading a crime story. One of the suspects has murdered the industrialist Max Howard. Use relative clauses with **who** or **whose**.

☐ Charles Paxton, the director – he quarrelled with Howard
   Charles is the director who quarrelled with Howard.

☐ Vera Stokes, the politician – her sister once worked for Howard
   Vera is the politician whose sister once worked for Howard.

1 Brian Reeves, the journalist – his tape-recorder was stolen

2 Steve Wilshaw, the architect – he knew Howard at school

3 Rex Carter, the farmer – Howard bought his land

4 Louise Hollins, the model – her name was in Howard's diary

5 Mark Delbray, the lawyer – he looked after Howard's interests

112.2 what (B)

Rewrite this advice for managers. Use **what** to emphasize the important part.

☐ You must pay attention to <u>the details</u>.
   What you must pay attention to is the details.

1 You have to think about <u>your profits</u>.

2 You must get <u>good financial advice</u>.

3 You should work towards <u>a realistic target</u>.

4 You need to <u>plan ahead</u>.

112.3 The pattern with it (C)

Look at the quiz questions and write sentences with **it** + **be** + relative clause.

☐ Who invented radio? ~ Marconi.
   It was Marconi who invented radio.

1 When did Columbus sail to America? ~ In 1492.
   It was in 1492 that

2 What did Jack Nicklaus play? ~ Golf.

3 Where did the Olympic Games begin? ~ In Greece.

4 What is the highest mountain in the USA? ~ Mount McKinley.

5 Which is nearest the sun, Venus or Mercury? ~ Mercury.

113 The use of relative clauses

A Introduction

Relative clauses have different uses. Compare this conversation and news item:

Sue: *Art Gluckson has died.*
Tom: *Who?*
Sue: *You know. The film star **who played the ship's captain in 'Iceberg'**.*
Tom: *I don't think I've seen that.*
Sue: *Yes, you have. It's the film **we saw on TV the other night**.*
Tom: *Oh, I remember.*

ART GLUCKSON DIES
*The actor Art Gluckson, **who starred in films such as 'Volcano' and 'Iceberg'**, has died after a long illness. He was seventy-eight. Art Gluckson's most famous role was as the scientist in the film 'Black Hole', **which broke all box-office records**.*

These clauses identify which film star and which film the speaker means. (See also Unit 109A.)

These clauses add information about Art Gluckson and about 'Black Hole'.

B Identifying clauses and adding clauses

Compare:

IDENTIFYING

*The woman **who tackled the gunman** was shot in the leg.*

*The river **which flows through Hereford** is the Wye.*

*The picture **which was stolen** is worth thousands of pounds.*

These clauses identify which one we mean. The clause **who tackled the gunman** tells us which woman. The clause **which flows through Hereford** tells us which river. Without the relative clause the sentence would be incomplete.

An identifying clause does not have commas round it.

Most relative clauses are identifying. We use them both in speech and writing.

ADDING

*Mrs Debbie Clark, **who tackled the gunman**, was shot in the leg.*

*The Wye **(which flows through Hereford)** is a beautiful river.*

*This famous picture – **which was painted in 1960** – is worth thousands of pounds.*

These clauses add extra information to something already identified. The clause, **who tackled the gunman**, adds information about Mrs Clark. We can say the sentence on its own without the relative clause.

An adding clause has commas (or brackets or dashes) round it.★

Adding clauses can be rather formal. We use them mainly in writing. They are common in news reports.

★ Note: comma = ,   brackets = ( )   dash = –

C Relative pronouns

Compare:

IDENTIFYING

In identifying clauses we can use **who**, **whom**, **whose**, **which**, or **that**:

*I'm sure I know the person **who** served us.*

*The couple **whom** we invited haven't come.*

*The man **whose** car was stolen had to stay the night.*

*Towns **which/that** attract tourists are usually crowded and expensive.*

Sometimes we can leave out the pronoun (see Unit 110B):

*The man **(who)** we saw yesterday is my neighbour.*

*Have you seen the book **(that)** I was reading?*

A preposition usually goes at the end:

*What's the name of the man you work **for**?*

*Ian couldn't find the notebook he wrote new words **in**.*

ADDING

In adding clauses we use **who**, **whom**, **whose** or **which** (but NOT **that**):

*Andrew, **who** served us, is the owner of the restaurant.*

*The Simpsons, **whom** we invited, haven't come.*

*Mr Webster, **whose** car was stolen, had to stay the night.*

*Stratford, **which** attracts many tourists, is the place where Shakespeare was born.*

We cannot leave out the pronoun (e.g. **whom**, **which**) from an adding clause:

*Jeff, **whom** we saw yesterday, is my neighbour.*

*That book 'Brighton Rock', **which** I was reading, is really good.*

A preposition can go before the pronoun or at the end of the clause:

*Mr Bone, **for** whom Liz works, is a very strange man.*
(OR ..., who Liz works **for**, ...)

*Ian had a notebook, **in** which he wrote new words.*
(OR ..., which he wrote new words **in**.)

D A special use of **which**

In an adding clause, we can use **which** to stand for a whole sentence, not just a noun phrase:

⎡It rained all night,⎤ **which did the garden good.**

Here **which** means 'the fact that it rained all night'.

Here are some more examples:

*Mike helped us clear up, **which was very good of him**.*
*Ian pushed Nigel into the swimming-pool, **which seemed to amuse everyone**.*
*I kept everyone waiting, **which made me rather unpopular**.*

113 Exercises

113.1 Identifying or adding? (A, B)

Say what the relative clause does.

The play □*that the college students put on last week* was Oscar Wilde's 'The Importance of Being Earnest', □*which was written in 1895*. The college theatre, ¹*which holds over 400 people*, was unfortunately only half full for the Friday evening performance. However, the people ²*who bothered to attend* must have been glad they did. Lucy Kellett, ³*who played Lady Bracknell*, was magnificent. Unfortunately the young man ⁴*who played John Worthing* forgot his lines, but that did not spoil the evening, ⁵*which was a great success*.

□ *It tells us which play.*
□ *It adds information about 'The Importance of Being Earnest'.*
1 _____
2 _____
3 _____
4 _____
5 _____

113.2 Relative pronouns (C)

Complete this advertisement. Put in **who**, **whom**, **whose** or **which**.

Keswick, □ *which* lies at the heart of the Lake District, is the perfect place for a holiday, and the Derwent Hotel, ¹_____ overlooks the town, is the perfect place to stay. Peter and Debbie Jackson, ²_____ bought this small hotel three years ago, have already won a reputation for excellence. Peter, ³_____ cooking attracts people from far and wide, was once Young Chef of the Year. The comfort of the guests, ⁴_____ the owners treat almost as members of the family, always comes first. Omar Sharif, ⁵_____ once stayed at the hotel, described it as 'marvellous'. And the Lake District, ⁶_____ has so much wonderful scenery, will not disappoint you.

113.3 Adding clauses (B, C)

Rewrite this part of a letter. Write the sentences in brackets as adding clauses.

□I've had a quiet week. (I certainly needed it.) ¹Bob and Cheryl (You met them last year.) were here all last week. ²They're now running a computer software business. (It's doing very well.) ³Cheryl (She studied programming at college.) writes the programs. ⁴Bob (His subject was business studies.) handles the financial side. ⁵He explained it all to Martin. (Martin isn't very interested in business.) ⁶On Saturday we went to a Chinese restaurant. (Someone had recommended it.) It was very good.

□ *I've had a quiet week, which I certainly needed.*
1 _____
2 _____
3 _____
4 _____
5 _____
6 _____

113.4 Identifying clauses and adding clauses (B, C)

Combine the two sentences using a relative clause. Some clauses need commas; some do not.

☐ Crossford has only two hundred inhabitants. It's miles from anywhere.
  Crossford, which has only two hundred inhabitants, is miles from anywhere.

☐ Someone made the arrangements. It was Karen.
  The person who made the arrangements was Karen.

1 Mr Perkins is a bit deaf. He couldn't hear the phone.
  Mr Perkins, _____

2 St Michael's Church dates from the 14th century. It's a fine building.

3 Someone's suitcase got lost. It was Colin.

4 A road leads to the farm. It isn't suitable for cars.

5 Our teacher lives ten miles away. She stayed at home during the bus strike.

6 Diamond is a very hard substance. It is used for cutting.

7 Someone got everything ready. It was Kevin.

8 Someone knows all about it. It's the secretary.

9 Mandy's name was missed off the list. She wasn't very pleased.

113.5 A special use of **which** (D)

Match the sentence pairs and join them with **which**.

☐ My phone is out of order at the moment.	It means he can't get about very easily.
1 It poured with rain all day.	It's made her very depressed.
2 My brother is disabled.	That was very rude of him.
3 Jessica's mother paid for the meal.	That left the ground very wet.
4 You left the keys in the car.	That was very kind of her.
5 Miranda has lost her job.	It's a nuisance.
6 The police blocked off the road.	That caused a traffic jam.
7 Jeremy didn't answer my letter.	That was rather careless of you.

☐ _My phone is out of order at the moment, which is a nuisance._

1 _____
2 _____
3 _____
4 _____
5 _____
6 _____
7 _____

114 people arriving early, people left behind and the first people to arrive

A people arriving early and people left behind

Read this news report about a road accident:

*Two people were killed and four injured this morning when a lorry **carrying concrete pipes** overturned in the centre of Portsmouth and hit two cars. Ambulances **called to the scene** took a long time to get through the rush-hour traffic. The accident happened in Alfred Road, where road repairs are under way. People who saw the accident say that the lorry hit the cars after it swerved to avoid a cement mixer **left in the road**. The traffic chaos **caused by the accident** has meant long delays for people **trying to get to work**.*

These clauses are relative clauses because they relate to a noun. ***Carrying concrete pipes*** tells us something about ***a lorry***.

We can form these clauses with an active participle (e.g. ***carrying***) or a passive participle (e.g. ***called***). The participles can refer to the present or the past:

ACTIVE
*a lorry **carrying** concrete pipes*
(= a lorry **which is** (OR **was**) **carrying** concrete pipes)
*people **trying** to get to work*
(= people **who are** (OR **were**) **trying** to get to work)
*the path **leading** to the church*
(= the path **which leads** (OR **led**) to the church)

We use the active participle instead of a pronoun + a continuous verb (e.g. **is/was carrying**) or + a simple verb (e.g. **want/wanted**). But we do not use it for a single action in the past:
*people **who saw** the accident*
NOT *people seeing the accident*

PASSIVE
*ambulances **called** to the scene*
(= ambulances **which are** (OR **were**) **called** to the scene)
*a cement mixer **left** in the road*
(= a cement mixer **which had been left** in the road)
*food **sold** in supermarkets*
(= food **which is sold** in supermarkets)

We use the passive participle instead of a pronoun (e.g. **which**) + a passive verb (e.g. **are/were called**).

B the first people to arrive

Look at these examples:
*New Zealand was the **first** country **to give** women the vote.*
(= the first country **which gave** women the vote)
*Who was the **last** person **to see** the young man alive?*
(= the last person **who saw** the young man alive)
*The Times was the **only** newspaper **to appear** that day.*
*The guest on our show is the **oldest** person **to fly** an aeroplane.*
*Bobby Charlton is the **most famous** footballer **to play** on this ground.*

We use a to-infinitive after these words: **first**, **second** etc; **next** and **last**; **only**; and superlatives (e.g. **oldest**, **most famous**).

114 Exercises

114.1 Relative clauses with participles (A)

Complete the definitions. Put in an active or passive participle of these verbs:
add, arrive, block, own, play, smuggle, take, tell, watch, wear.

▫ A competitor is someone _taking_ part in a competition.
▫ Your property is everything _owned_ by you.
1 Cricket is a game _____ in English-speaking countries.
2 A wrist watch is a watch _____ on your wrist.
3 A latecomer is a person _____ late.
4 An instruction is a statement _____ you what to do.
5 A spectator is someone _____ a game or a play.
6 An extension is a new part _____ to a building.
7 An obstacle is something _____ your way.
8 Contraband is something _____ into a country.

114.2 Relative clauses with participles (A)

Write each news item as one sentence. Change the part in brackets into a clause with an active participle (e.g. **costing**) or a passive participle (e.g. **found**).
▫ A new motorway is planned. (It will cost £500 million.)
   A new motorway _costing £500 million is planned._
▫ Some weapons belong to the IRA. (They were found at a flat in Bristol.)
   Some weapons _found at a flat in Bristol belong to the IRA._
1 Families have been turned out. (They were living in an empty office building.)
   Families _____
2 A chemical company has gone bankrupt. (It employed four thousand people.)
   A chemical company _____
3 A bridge has been declared unsafe. (It was built only two years ago.)
   A bridge _____
4 Food has not reached those who really need it. (It was sent from Europe.)
   Food _____
5 People have marched to London. (They are protesting against nuclear power.)
   People _____
6 Fans have been queuing all night at Wimbledon. (They hope to buy tickets.)
   Fans _____

114.3 Relative clauses with an infinitive (B)

For each situation write a sentence with the infinitive pattern.
▫ Martin offered his help. No one else did.   _Martin was the only person to offer his help._
1 Kate swam a length of the pool. No other girl as young as her did that.
   Kate was the youngest girl _____
2 The typists got a pay rise. But no one else did.
   The typists were _____
3 The captain left the ship. Everyone else had left before him.
   _____
4 Mrs Harper has become President. No other woman has been President before.
   _____

273

115 Patterns with **if**

A Introduction

Look at this conversation:
>Ben: *How are we going to London tomorrow? Are you taking your car?*
>Phil: *I don't think so. **If** we took the car, we would have the problem of where to park.*
>Ben: *We could go by train.*
>Phil: ***If** we go by coach, it'll be cheaper.*
>Ben: *The train won't be very expensive **if** we come back the same day.*
>Phil: *But it costs more **if** you get an early train.*
>Ben: *OK. Have you got a coach timetable?*
>Phil: *No, I haven't. I could have picked one up at the travel agent's this morning **if** I had thought of it. But there are always plenty of coaches.*

A sentence with **if** has an if-clause (e.g. *if we go by coach*) and a main clause (e.g. *it'll be cheaper*). The if-clause usually comes first, but it can come after the main clause:
>*If I hear any news, I'll phone you.*
>*I'll phone you if I hear any news.*

A comma is more usual when the if-clause comes first.

There are three common verb patterns:
Type 1: *If we **take** a coach, it **will** be cheaper.*
Type 2: *If we **took** a coach, it **would** be cheaper.*
Type 3: *If we **had taken** a coach, it **would have** been cheaper.*

There are also many other possible combinations of verb forms, for example:
Present simple and modal verb: *If you **go** early, you **can't** get a cheap ticket.*
be going to and modal verb: *If it's **going to** rain, we **ought to** hurry.*
Present simple in both clauses: *If you **go** early, it (usually) **costs** more.*
Present simple and imperative: *If you **need** any help, just **ask**.*

B Type 1: **if** – present tense – **will**

>*If you **post** the letter today, it'**ll** get there by Thursday.*
>*If we **don't hurry**, the others **will** go without us.*
>*If it's fine, we'**ll** be having a picnic.*
>*A porter **will** come if you **ring** the bell.*

Here the present tense in the if-clause refers to a possible future action. *If you **post** the letter* means that you may post it or you may not. It leaves open the question of whether you will really post the letter.

We can also use **will** in an if-clause when we make a request:
>*If you'**ll** just wait a moment, I'll fetch the file.*
>(= Please wait a moment . . .)
>But NOT ~~If it'll be fine, we'll have a picnic.~~

We can also use the present continuous (e.g. **are doing**) or present perfect (e.g. **have done**) in the if-clause:
>*If we'**re having** visitors, the flat will need a good clean.*
>*If you'**ve finished** with the computer, I'll put it away.*

We can use other modal verbs (e.g. **can**, **should**) in the main clause.
> *If you need a ticket for the disco tonight, I **can** get you one cheap.*
> *If you're going to a job interview, you **should** wear a tie.*

C Type 2: **if** – past tense – **would**

> *If I **had** a million pounds, I **would** probably buy a yacht.*
> *If people **didn't eat** so many sweets, their teeth **wouldn't** fall out.*
> *If we **took** the car, we **would** have the problem of where to park.*
> *It **would** be awful if you lost your passport.*

Here the past tense in the if-clause often refers to something unreal, something imaginary. *If I **had** a million pounds* means that I haven't really got a million pounds, but I am only imagining it. *If we **took** the car* means that taking the car is only a theoretical possibility. Compare the two types:
Type 1: *If we **take** the car, we'll have to park it.* (open)
Type 2: *If we **took** the car, we'd have to park it.* (theoretical, less real)

We can use **would** (OR **'d**) in an if-clause when we make a request:
> *If you**'d** like to come this way, the doctor will see you now.*
> (= Please come this way . . .)
> But NOT *If I would have a million pounds, I would buy a yacht.*

We can also use the past continuous (e.g. **was doing**) in the if-clause:
> *If I **was leaving** the house empty, I would ask someone to keep an eye on it.*

We can use **could** or **might** in the main clause:
> *If we had a calculator, we **could** work this out a lot quicker.*
> *If you rang the bell, someone **might** come.*

D Type 3: **if** – past perfect – **would have**

> *We lost. If we **had won** the match, we **would have** got through to the final.*
> *If Graham **had read** the small print, he **wouldn't have** signed the contract.*
> *If we **had taken** your advice, we **would have** saved a lot of time.*
> *I **would have** sent Celia a postcard if I **hadn't forgotten** her address.*

Here we use the past perfect to talk about what <u>didn't</u> happen. *If we **had won*** means that we didn't really win. *If he**'d read** it* means that he didn't read it.

We do not use **would have** in an if-clause. NOT *If we would have won . . .*

We can use **could have** or **might have** in the main clause:
> *If you'd rung, we **could have** arranged to meet.*
> *If I'd bought a ticket yesterday, I **might have** won a prize.*

We can use **would** in the main clause if we are talking about the present:
> *If you had planned this properly, we **wouldn't** be in this mess now.*
> *If we had saved more money last year, we **would** have enough for a holiday now.*

115 Exercises

115.1 Type 1 (B)

Write sentences with **if** – present tense – **will/can**.

☐ It might rain. If so, we'll eat inside.
If it rains, we'll eat inside.

1 Neil might fail the exam. But he can take it again.

2 The cat might die. If so, Alex will be upset.

3 The office may be closed. In that case we won't be able to get in.

4 I may arrive a bit early. I can help you get things ready.

5 The celebrations might go on a long time. If so, we can leave early.

6 It's quite possible you'll lose the cheques. If so, you'll need to phone this number.

7 The parcel may arrive today. You'll have to sign for it.

8 The picture may be valuable. In that case we can sell it.

9 Why don't you ask for a pay rise? You'll probably get one.

10 It's possible Steve will enter the competition. And if he does, I'm sure he'll win.

115.2 Type 1 (B)

Complete the conversation. Put in the correct form.

Justin: Have you heard about the pop festival?
Carla: Yes, ¹_____ good if Micromoon are playing. They're a great band.
Debbie: Will you be able to go, Dave?
Dave: If ²_____ my boss, he'll give me some time off work, I expect.
Mike: How are we going to get there?
Justin: Well, if enough people ³_____ , we can hire a minibus.
Vicky: I won't be going if ⁴_____ too expensive.
Debbie: It ⁵_____ expensive if we all ⁶_____ the cost.
Carla: If ⁷_____ the others later on tonight, ⁸_____ them if they want to go.

1 it's/it'll be
2 I ask/I'll ask
3 are going/will go
4 it's/it'll be
5 isn't/won't be
6 share/will share
7 I see/I'll see
8 I ask/I'll ask

115 Patterns with if

115.3 Type 1 and Type 2 (B, C)

What does the if-clause mean? Write a sentence with **isn't** or **might**.

☐ If this room was tidy, I could find things.   _The room isn't tidy._
☐ If we're late tonight, we can let ourselves in.   _We might be late tonight._
1 If the phone was working, I could call you.   _____
2 If it rains, can you take the washing in?   _____
3 If we met at seven, we'd have plenty of time.   _____
4 If this spoon was silver, it would be worth a lot.   _____
5 If Richard calls, can you say I'll ring back?   _____

115.4 Type 3 (D)

For each situation write a Type 3 sentence with **if**.

☐ I couldn't buy the book because I didn't have any money.
  I could have bought the book if I had had some money.
☐ Debbie didn't lock her bike and it got stolen.
  If Debbie had locked her bike, it wouldn't have got stolen.
1 Barbara went to bed late and so she overslept.
   _____
2 It wasn't warm enough, so we didn't sit outside.
   _____
3 You forgot the map, so we lost our way.
   _____
4 Gary couldn't play basketball because he was ill.
   _____
5 I noticed the mistake when I checked the figures.
   _____
6 Wayne was wearing a crash helmet, so I didn't recognize him.
   _____
7 No one watered the flowers, so they died.
   _____

115.5 Patterns with if (A–E)

Put in the correct form of the verb. Sometimes you need **will** or **would**.

Mr Day: Can't you stop playing that trumpet?
Adam: Well, if I ☐ _don't practise_, I won't pass my exams.   ☐ not practise
Mr Day: But why at night? If you ¹_____ it in the   1 play
   day time, I ²_____ you because I'm at   2 not hear
   work. If I ³_____ about this trumpet   3 know
   when you first came, I ⁴_____ you have   4 not let
   the room. If you ⁵_____ so loud, it   5 not play
   ⁶_____ so bad.   6 not be
Adam: You can't play a trumpet quietly.
Mr Day: If I had known that, I ⁷_____ you out   7 throw
   long ago. Well, if you ⁸_____ on doing   8 go
   it, I ⁹_____ to your college.   9 complain

116 if, when, unless and in case

After **if**, **when**, **unless** and **in case** we use the present tense to talk about the future:
*You'll get a prize **if** you **win**.*   *Tell me **when** the kettle **boils**.*
*I won't do it **unless** you **agree**.*   *Write it down **in case** you **forget** it.*

A **if** or **when**?

Compare:

We use **if** to say that something might possibly happen: *If you hear any news, can you let me know immediately?* (You **might** hear some news.) *I'll probably go for a walk later on **if** it stays fine.* (It **might** stay fine.)	We use **when** to talk about something that we think will definitely happen: ***When** you hear some news, can you let me know immediately?* (You **will** hear some news.) *I'll make myself an omelette **when** I get home tonight.* (I **will** get home tonight.)

We use **if** (not **when**) to talk about something impossible or imaginary:
If I was in your shoes, I'd do the same.
NOT *When I was in your shoes, I'd do the same.*

If and **when** have similar meanings in contexts where **when** means 'every time':
If you run, you use up energy. OR *When you run, you use up energy.*

B **if** and **unless**

If . . . not means the same as **unless**. Compare:

*I can't see **if** I don't wear glasses.* *The doctor will be here **if** she isn't called to an emergency.* *If you can't pay your bills now, you'll have to leave.* *I wouldn't ride a bike **if** I did**n't** have a helmet on.*	*I can't see **unless** I wear glasses.* *The doctor will be here **unless** she's called to an emergency.* ***Unless** you can pay your bills now, you'll have to leave.* *I wouldn't ride a bike **unless** I had a helmet on.*

C **in case**

Look at these examples:
*I'll write down the address **in case** I forget it.*
*Take a sandwich with you **in case** you get hungry.*
*I'd better reserve a seat today **in case** the train is full tomorrow.*
*I took two photos **in case** one of them didn't come out.*

We use **in case** to talk about doing something because something else might happen later.

Compare **if** and **in case**:

*I'll bring in the washing **if** it rains.* (I'll bring it in after it starts raining.)	*I'll bring in the washing **in case** it rains.* (I'll bring it in now because it might rain later.)

116 Exercises

116.1 if or when? (A)

Complete the sentences using **if** or **when** and a present-tense verb.

☐ I may see Danny tonight. _If I see him,_ I'll tell him the news.
☐ Mark is coming soon. _When he comes,_ can you let him in?

1 The alarm will ring soon. _____ we all have to leave the building.
2 I might feel better tomorrow. _____ I'll probably go back to work.
3 This programme finishes at ten. _____ I'll stop the video.
4 I'm taking a photo in a minute. _____ I want everyone to smile.
5 The plan may not work. _____ we'll have to think of something else.

116.2 if and unless (B)

Rewrite the if-clauses using **unless**.

☐ You won't get there in time _unless you hurry._ (if you don't hurry)
1 We can't have a picnic _____ (if it isn't a nice day)
2 Don't leave the TV on _____ (if you aren't watching it)
3 We can't do the job _____ (if we don't get help)
4 I won't wake up _____ (if I don't use an alarm clock)
5 I wouldn't buy the picture _____ (if I didn't like it)

116.3 if and unless (B)

Put in **if** or **unless**.

☐ Mike will be pleased _if_ he passes his test.
☐ The bus won't stop _unless_ you ring the bell.

1 I can't read your letters _____ you type them.
2 Ann will be upset _____ she doesn't get the job.
3 You can't go into the theatre _____ you've got a ticket.
4 Don't bother to ring me _____ it's important.
5 I'd go to the concert _____ I wasn't so busy.

116.4 in case (C)

Combine each pair of sentences using **in case**.

☐ You'd better take a sweater. It might get cold.
  You'd better take a sweater in case it gets cold.

1 We'd better book a table. The restaurant might be full.
  _____

2 You ought to insure your jewellery. It might get stolen.
  _____

3 I'm watching this saucepan. The water might boil over.
  _____

4 I'll leave you my phone number. You might want to contact me.
  _____

117 wish and if only

A wish . . . would

Wish . . . would expresses a wish for a change in how someone behaves:
  *I wish you **would** be more polite to my friends.*
  *I wish you **wouldn't** argue all the time. It gets on my nerves.*
  *Tom wishes his flat-mate **wouldn't** keep coming in so late.*

We use the same pattern to express a wish for someone to do something, or for something to happen:
  *I wish you **would** tidy up this mess.*   *I wish they**'d** tell us what's happening.*
  *I wish that dog **would** stop barking.*   *I wish you**'d** keep quiet.*

We can also use the pattern **if only . . . would**. **If only** means the same as **I wish**, but it can be stronger, more emphatic:
  *We don't know a thing. **If only** they**'d** tell us what's happening.*
  ***If only** it **would** stop raining, then we could go for a walk.*

B wish . . . past

Wish and **if only** with a past-tense verb express a wish for the present situation to be different:
  *This room isn't very big. I wish it **was** a bit bigger.*
  *I wish I **lived** in a big city. It's so boring in the country.*
  *Marion wishes she **was** getting a decent wage.*
  *We all wish we **had** more money, don't we?*
  *If only I **was** a bit taller. Then I could reach the shelf.*

We cannot use **would** in these sentences. (For **would** see A.)
  NOT ~~I wish this room would be a bit bigger.~~

But we can use **could**:
  *I wish I **could** sing (but I can't).*
  *I feel so helpless. If only I **could** speak the language.*

C wish . . . past perfect

We use **wish** and **if only** with the past perfect to express a wish about the past:
  *I wish you **had told** me about the dance. I would have gone.*
Here *I wish you **had told** me* means that you <u>didn't</u> tell me. Here are some more examples:
  *I wish I**'d got** up earlier. I'm behind with everything today.*
  *I wish you **hadn't lost** that photo. It was a really good one.*
  *If only we **hadn't had** a puncture, we would have arrived in time.*

We do not use **would have** for the past.
  NOT ~~I wish you would have told me.~~
But we can use **could have**:
  *I wish I **could have been** at the wedding, but I was in New York.*

117 Exercises

117.1 wish ... would (A)

What might you say in these situations?
- ☐ to someone who never answers the phone
  I wish you'd answer the phone.
- ☐ to someone who makes rude remarks about you
  I wish you wouldn't make rude remarks about me.
1. to someone who won't hurry up
2. to someone who never does the washing-up
3. to someone who isn't telling you the whole story
4. to someone who blows cigarette smoke in your face
5. to someone who won't tell you what he's thinking
6. to someone who always leaves the door open
7. to someone who won't leave you alone

117.2 wish ... past (B)

Add a sentence with **I wish** or **if only**.
- ☐ I can't solve my problems. *I wish I could solve my problems.*
1. Why am I so tired? _____
2. I can't sleep. _____
3. I haven't got enough energy. _____
4. Life is so dull. _____
5. My studies aren't going well. _____
6. I can't concentrate. _____
7. I haven't got any friends. _____

117.3 wish ... past perfect (C)

Complete the sentences using: **accepted, caught, found, kept, played, saved, stayed, succeeded** and **won**.
- ☐ I spent all the money. I wish now that *I had saved it.*
- ☐ Unfortunately the plan failed. We all wish *it had succeeded.*
1. I missed the train. I wish _____
2. Jerry left the party early. Fiona wishes _____
3. Helen refused the offer. But her parents wish _____
4. It's a pity we sold the table. If only _____
5. I looked everywhere for the key. I wish _____
6. The team lost narrowly. Their fans wish _____
7. The injured player could only watch the match. He wishes _____

118 but, although and in spite of

A but and although

We can join two clauses with **but**:
*The café was crowded, **but** we found a table.*
*Sadie has passed her test, **but** she never drives.*

We can also use **although**:
***Although** the café was crowded, we found a table.*
***Although** Sadie has passed her test, she never drives.*

The clause with **although** can also come after the main clause:
*We found a table, **although** the café was crowded.*

B though and even though

Though is informal. It means the same as **although**:
***Though/Although** I liked the sweater, I didn't buy it.*
***Though/Although** it was extremely cold, Debbie wasn't wearing a coat.*

We can use **though** at the end of a sentence:
*I liked the sweater. I didn't buy it, **though**. (= But I didn't buy it.)*

Even though is stronger, more emphatic than **although**:
*Jeff looked quite fresh, **even though** he'd just run a marathon.*
***Even though** I hate Gary, I shall try to be nice to him.*

C in spite of and despite

We use **in spite of** before a noun phrase or the ing-form of a verb:
*Tom felt perfectly calm **in spite of** the danger.*
*We finally succeeded **in spite of** all the difficulties.*
*I carried on working **in spite of** not feeling well.*
*They always seem to be enjoying themselves **in spite of** having no money.*

We use **despite** in exactly the same way as **in spite of** and with the same meaning:
*He was calm **despite** the danger.*   *I worked **despite** not feeling well.*

But compare **in spite of** and **although**:

in spite of	although
*I'm no better **in spite of** the pills (OR **in spite of** taking the pills).* NOT *in spite of I've taken the pills*	*I'm no better, **although** I've taken the pills.*
*Mark is making little progress **in spite of** his hard work (OR **in spite of** working hard).* NOT *in spite of he works hard*	*Mark is making little progress, **although** he works hard.*

We can use **in spite of the fact (that)** in the same way as **although**:
*I'm no better **in spite of the fact that** I've taken the pills.*
*Debbie wasn't wearing a coat **despite the fact that** it was extremely cold.*

118 Exercises

118.1 but (A)

Complete each sentence with **but** and one of these clauses:

I still don't understand it.   It didn't break. ✓   It's really quite modern.
No one laughed.   He never uses them.

☐ I dropped the dish, _but it didn't break._
1 The house looks old, _____
2 The joke was funny, _____
3 Mike has some skis, _____
4 Phil explained the system, _____

118.2 although (A)

Rewrite the sentences in Exercise 118.1 using **although**.

☐ _Although I dropped the dish, it didn't break._
1 _____
2 _____
3 _____
4 _____

118.3 although or in spite of? (A, C)

Put in **although** or **in spite of**.

☐ The match went ahead _in spite of_ the bad weather.
1 _____ I told the absolute truth, no one would believe me.
2 Our neighbour goes for long walks _____ being eighty-five years old.
3 I caught the train, _____ I had only a minute to spare.
4 The goods were never delivered _____ the promise we had.
5 _____ the threats against his life, the minister carried on as normal.
6 The chairman resigned _____ the fact that it wasn't his fault.

118.4 although, even though, in spite of and despite (A–C)

Join each pair of sentences. Be careful where you put the words in brackets.

☐ Dave smokes. He seems to be in good health. (although)
  Although Dave smokes, he seems to be in good health.
☐ I couldn't sleep. I was tired. (despite)
  I couldn't sleep despite being tired.

1 Max didn't notice the sign. It was right in front of him. (even though)

2 Kate never learnt Spanish. She lived in Spain for years. (although)

3 Joe is a millionaire. He hates spending money. (despite)

4 A few trains were running. There was a strike. (in spite of)

5 We couldn't get a seat. We arrived early. (in spite of)

119 to, in order to, so that and for

A to (purpose)

We can use the to-infinitive to say why someone does something, what the purpose of an action is:

*Alec was hurrying **to catch** his train.*
*Most people work **to earn** money.*
*I rang **to find** out the times of the trains.*
*We went to the library **to get** some books.*

B in order to and so as to

In order to and **so as to** are more formal than **to**:
*The government took these measures **in order to reduce** crime.*
*The staff are working at weekends **in order to complete** the project on time.*

We can use the negative **in order not to** or **so as not to**, but we cannot use **not to** on its own:
*Alec was hurrying **in order not to miss** his train.*
NOT *He was hurrying not to miss his train.*
*The staff are working at weekends **so as not to delay** the project any further.*

C so that

After **so that** we use a subject and a main verb (e.g. *it gets*):
*I'll post the card today **so that it gets** (OR **it'll get**) there on time.*

We often use **will** or **can** for a present purpose and **would** or **could** for a past purpose:
*I'll give you a map **so that** you **can** find the way.*
*I gave Roger a map **so that** he **could** find the way (OR so that he **would** be able to find the way).*

In informal English we can leave out **that**:
*You should put your passport in a safe place **so (that)** it doesn't get lost.*

D to or for?

We can use **for** + noun phrase to talk about the purpose of an action:
*The whole family have gone out **for** a bike ride.*
*Why don't you come over **for** coffee?*

To talk about the purpose of a thing, we use either a to-infinitive or **for** + ing-form:
*This heater is **to keep** (OR **for keeping**) the plants warm in winter.*
*The machine is used **to cut** (OR **for cutting**) plastic.*

But we use a to-infinitive (NOT **for** + ing-form) to talk about an action:
*I put the heater on **to keep** the plants warm.*

119 Exercises

119.1 to (purpose) (A)

Complete each sentence using **to** and these words: **buy a car, cash a cheque, get some petrol, go to sleep, look smart, make some tea**.

▢ Ian went to the bank _to cash a cheque_.
1. Karen sometimes takes a pill _____
2. Monica stopped at a garage _____
3. Jeremy is going to wear a suit _____
4. Dave put on the kettle _____
5. Liz is borrowing some money _____

119.2 in order to and so as to (B)

Say what Nigel intends to do. Use either **in order to** or **so as to**. (Both are correct.)

	ACTION		PURPOSE
▢	study books on business	→	be more successful
1	get to work earlier	→	impress the boss
2	work harder	→	achieve more
3	take regular exercise	→	keep fit and alert
4	think positively	→	not miss any opportunities

▢ _He's going to study books on business in order to be more successful._
1. _____
2. _____
3. _____
4. _____

119.3 to, for and so that (A, C, D)

Write each pair of sentences as one. Use the word in brackets.

▢ I'm learning English. I want to get a better job. (to)
I'm learning English to get a better job.

▢ The driver stopped. Then the children could cross the road. (so that)
The driver stopped so that the children could cross the road.

▢ I'm saving up. I want a holiday. (for)
I'm saving up for a holiday.

1. Tom put the cream in the fridge. That would keep it cool. (to)

2. Pamela wore boots. Her feet wouldn't get wet. (so that)

3. I'm going on a diet. I want to lose weight. (to)

4. We often switch off the heating. It saves money. (to)

5. We all sat down. We needed a rest. (for)

6. Mark is going to repair the roof. Then the rain won't come in. (so that)

120 Review of linking words

A Time words

Look at these sentences with **when**, **while**, **as soon as** etc:
- *My leg hurts **when** I walk.*
- *I heard the news on the radio **as/while** I was driving home.*
  (= during the time when I was driving home)
- ***When/After** the speaker had sat down, no one knew what to say.*
- ***As soon as** I'd left the house, it started to rain.*
  (= immediately after I'd left the house)
- *I must get to the post office **before** it closes.*
- *You have to wait **until** the light changes to green.*
  (= up to the time when the light changes to green)
- *There's been a lot of new building **since** I was here last.*
  (= from the time when I was here last)

We use the present simple for future time after **when**, **while**, **as soon as** etc, for example: *before it closes*, *until it changes*. See Unit 15C.

B if, unless and in case (See Unit 116)

- *It'll be quite safe **if** we're careful.*
- *You won't learn to play the piano well **unless** you practise.*
  (= if you don't practise)
- *I've brought some sandwiches **in case** I get hungry.*
  (= because I might get hungry)

C but, although and in spite of (See Unit 118)

- *The jacket was nice, **but** it was too small.*
- ***Although** the forecast said it would rain, it turned out to be a beautiful day.*
- *We still haven't got a sponsor **in spite of** writing (OR **in spite of the fact that** we've written) to dozens of companies.*

D because and so

We use **because** to express the reason for something and **so** to express the result of something:
- *I turned the heating on **because** it was cold.*
- *Karen works on Sundays **because** she gets paid extra.*
- *It was cold, **so** I turned the heating on.*
- *The lamp didn't work, **so** I took it back to the shop.*

E to, in order to and so that (See Unit 119)

- *Lots of people jog **to** keep fit.*
- *We're having to borrow money **in order to** pay our bills.*
- *I took the bread out of the freezer **so that** it would defrost.*

120 Exercises

120.1 Time words (A)

Combine each pair to make the title of a pop song. Use these words instead of the ones in brackets: **as soon as, before, since, when, while, until.**

☐ Think of me – (during the time) I'm away   _Think of me while I'm away._
1. I'll love you – (up to the day) I die   _____
2. I hear music – (at the time) I see you   _____
3. Come home – (but not after) it's too late   _____
4. I've been sad – (from the time) you left   _____
5. I fell in love – (immediately after) we met   _____

120.2 Linking words (B–E)

Put in these words: **although, because, but, if, in case, in order to, in spite of, so, so that, unless.**

1. _____ it was late, Alex didn't seem in a hurry to leave.
2. They put video cameras in shops _____ stop people stealing things.
3. I decided not to go out for a meal _____ I couldn't afford it.
4. _____ you're ready, we can start now.
5. Our room was very small, _____ we didn't mind at all.
6. No one was watching the television, _____ I switched it off.
7. You can't drive a car _____ you've got a licence.
8. _____ having absolutely no talent, the man became a popular TV personality.
9. Vicky sent us a map _____ we'd be able to find her house.
10. I think my answers are right, but can I just check them with yours _____ I've made a mistake?

120.3 Linking words (A–E)

Choose the correct linking word.

A: We hadn't any bread, ¹_____ I went to the shop. I needed some ²_____ make sandwiches. I got there just ³_____ the shop closed and luckily they had some left.

B: Does the little shop stay open ⁴_____ the supermarket has closed?

A: Yes, it stays open till ten o'clock. It's very convenient, ⁵_____ it's rather expensive. I always go there ⁶_____ I need just one or two things. I don't go to the supermarket ⁷_____ I need a lot.

B: The shop must have done much less business ⁸_____ the supermarket has been there.

A: I don't like the supermarket ⁹_____ the fact that there's a much bigger choice. I go there ¹⁰_____ it's cheaper.

1. because/so
2. so that/to
3. after/before
4. after/before
5. but/in spite of
6. if/in case
7. if/unless
8. since/until
9. although/in spite of
10. because/so

287

American English

The differences between British and American English are mainly matters of pronunciation and vocabulary. Although the grammatical differences are not very great, those points that are most relevant to learners of English are explained here.

A Present perfect and past simple (Unit 6)

The British use the present perfect for actions in a period up to the present, and especially with **just**, **already** and **yet**:

> BRITISH
> Bob **has washed** the dishes. They're clean.
>
> We've already **eaten** our lunch.
>
> I've just **seen** Elaine.
>
> **Have** you **corrected** your work yet?

The Americans can use either the present perfect or the past simple in these contexts:

> AMERICAN
> Bob **has washed** the dishes. They're clean.
> OR Bob **washed** the dishes. They're clean.
> We've already **eaten** our lunch.
> OR We already **ate** our lunch.
> I've just **seen** Elaine.
> OR I just **saw** Elaine.
> **Have** you **corrected** your work yet?
> OR **Did** you **correct** your work yet?

The British normally use the present perfect with **ever** and **never**, not the past simple:

> BRITISH
> **Have** you ever **played** cricket?
>
> The child **has** never **seen** snow before.

Americans normally use the past simple with **ever** and **never**, but the present perfect is possible:

> AMERICAN
> **Did** you ever **play** baseball?
> OR **Have** you ever **played** baseball?
> The child never **saw** snow before.
> OR The child **has** never **seen** snow before.

B shall (Unit 13D)

The British use **will** for the future, but they can also use **shall** in the first person:

> BRITISH
> I **will** (OR I **shall**) be here tomorrow.
> We **will** (OR We **shall**) contact you.

The British use **shall** in offers and suggestions:

> BRITISH
> **Shall** I make the coffee?

The Americans do not normally use **shall** for the future:

> AMERICAN
> I **will** be here tomorrow.
> We **will** contact you.

The Americans use **should** in offers and suggestions:

> AMERICAN
> **Should** I make the coffee?

C Negatives and questions with **have** (Unit 18)

In Britain there are two different patterns:

BRITISH
*I **haven't (got)** enough time.*
OR *I **don't have** enough time.*
***Has** Carol **got** a tennis racket?*
OR ***Does** Carol **have** a tennis racket?*

The Americans normally use the auxiliary **do**:

AMERICAN
*I **don't have** enough time.*

***Does** Carol **have** a tennis racket?*

In the past **did** is usual in both countries, e.g. *We **didn't have** tickets.*

D Question tags (Unit 26)

Americans use question tags much less often than the British. A question tag (e.g. *We'll have to hurry, **won't we?***) can sound strange to an American. But Americans often use the tags **right?** and **OK?**, e.g. *We'll have to hurry, **right?** Let's go on Tuesday, **OK?***

E **needn't** and **don't need to** (Unit 32)

The British can use either of these forms:

BRITISH
*You **needn't** see the inspector.*
OR *You **don't need to** see the inspector.*

The Americans do not normally use **needn't**:

AMERICAN
*You **don't need to** see the inspector.*

F Noun phrase after **seem** etc. (Unit 56B)

In British English there can be a noun phrase (e.g. ***a good pilot***) directly after **seem, appear, look, sound** and **feel**:

BRITISH
She seemed (to be) a good pilot.
It looks a lovely evening.

I felt a fool.

Americans do not use the pattern **seem** + noun phrase:

AMERICAN
*She seemed **to be** a good pilot.*
*It looks **like** a lovely evening.*
OR *It looks **to be** a lovely evening.*
*I felt **like** a fool.*
OR *I felt foolish.*

G Group nouns (Unit 61B)

In Britain a group noun can often take either a singular or a plural verb:

BRITISH
*The crowd **was/were** getting restless.*
*Sweden **plays/play** Germany tomorrow.*

In America a group noun takes a singular verb:

AMERICAN
*The crowd **was** getting restless.*
*Sweden **plays** Germany tomorrow.*

American English

H hospital (Unit 64)

The British say that a sick person is **in hospital**:

The Americans do not leave out **the** before **hospital**:

BRITISH	AMERICAN
My sister is still **in hospital**.	My sister is still **in the hospital**.

I this and that on the telephone (Unit 69B)

There is a difference in usage when you are finding out who you are speaking to on the telephone:

BRITISH	AMERICAN
Is **that** Marcia?	Is **this** Marcia?

J you and one (Unit 75C)

The British use both **you** and **one** for people in general, including the speaker:

The Americans use **you** for people in general. **One** is unusual.

BRITISH	AMERICAN
You/One can't be too careful.	**You** can't be too careful.

K Prepositions

There are some differences in prepositions. Compare:

BRITISH	AMERICAN
round/around the village	**around** the village
towards/toward the west	**toward** the west
looking **out of** the window	looking **out** the window
	OR looking **out of** the window

There is a special use of **through** in American English:

He'll be on the road **from** Tuesday **to/till** Friday (inclusive).	He'll be on the road **from** Tuesday **through** Friday.
	They will stay in Miami **through** April. (= until the end of April)

The British normally use **different from** or **different to**:

The Americans use **different from** or **different than**:

This cup is different **from/to** the others.	This cup is different **from/than** the others.

There are also some differences in idioms with prepositions:

BRITISH	AMERICAN
in Piccadilly	**on** Broadway
at the weekend, **at** weekends	**on** the weekend, **on** weekends
a player **in** the team	a player **on** the team
ten minutes **past** four	ten minutes **past/after** four
twenty **to** seven	twenty **to/of** seven
write **to** me	write me
meet someone	meet **with** someone

American English

L Irregular verbs (p 292)

Some verbs can have either an irregular **t** ending or the regular **ed** ending in the past tense and the past/passive participle. These verbs are **burn, learn, smell, spell, spill** and **spoil**.

The British prefer the **t** ending:

BRITISH
*They **burnt** the old sofa.*
*You've **spelt** this word wrong.*

The Americans prefer the **ed** ending:

AMERICAN
*They **burned** the old sofa.*
*You've **spelled** this word wrong.*

But the participle used as an adjective has the **t** ending in American English, e.g. *a slice of **burnt** toast.*

In Britain the verbs **dream, lean** and **leap** have an irregular vowel sound and a **t** ending:

BRITISH
*I **dreamt** about you.*
[dremt]

AMERICAN
*I **dreamed** about you.*
[driːmd]

The verb **dive** is regular in Britain but irregular in America:

BRITISH
*Craig **dived** into the water.*

AMERICAN
*Craig **dove** into the water.*
[dəʊv]

M got and gotten

The British do not use **gotten**. The past participle of **get** is **got**:

BRITISH
*He's **got** a lot of money.* (= He's rich.)
*He's **made** a lot of money from his business activities.*

*Your driving has **got** better.*

The Americans use **have (got)** for a state and **have gotten** for an action:

AMERICAN
*He **has** a lot of money.* (= He's rich.)
*He's **gotten/made** a lot of money from his business activities.*

Americans also use **gotten** meaning 'become':
*Your driving has **gotten** better.*

Irregular verbs

VERB	PAST TENSE	PAST/PASSIVE PARTICIPLE
arise	arose	arisen
be	was, were	been
bear	bore	borne
beat	beat	beaten
become	became	become
begin	began	begun
bend	bent	bent
bet	bet	bet
	betted	
bind	bound	bound
bite	bit	bitten
		bit
bleed	bled	bled
blow	blew	blown
break	broke	broken
breed	bred	bred
bring	brought	brought
broadcast	broadcast	broadcast
build	built	built
burn	burnt	burnt
	burned	burned
burst	burst	burst
buy	bought	bought
catch	caught	caught
choose	chose	chosen
come	came	come
cost	cost	cost
creep	crept	crept
cut	cut	cut
deal	dealt	dealt
[di:l]	[delt]	[delt]
dig	dug	dug
dive	dived	dived
	dove (USA)	
do	did	done
draw	drew	drawn
dream	dreamt	dreamt
[dri:m]	[dremt]	[dremt]
	dreamed	dreamed
drink	drank	drunk
drive	drove	driven
eat	ate	eaten
[i:t]	[et]	['i:tn]
fall	fell	fallen
feed	fed	fed
feel	felt	felt
fight	fought	fought
find	found	found
flee	fled	fled
fly	flew	flown

VERB	PAST TENSE	PAST/PASSIVE PARTICIPLE
forbid	forbad(e)	forbidden
	[fə'bæd]	
forget	forgot	forgotten
forgive	forgave	forgiven
freeze	froze	frozen
get	got	got
		gotten (USA)
give	gave	given
go	went	gone
grind	ground	ground
grow	grew	grown
hang	hung	hung
have	had	had
hear	heard	heard
[hɪə]	[hɜ:d]	[hɜ:d]
hide	hid	hidden
hit	hit	hit
hold	held	held
hurt	hurt	hurt
keep	kept	kept
kneel	knelt	knelt
know	knew	known
lay	laid	laid
lead	led	led
lean	leant	leant
[li:n]	[lent]	[lent]
	leaned	leaned
leap	leapt	leapt
[li:p]	[lept]	[lept]
	leaped	leaped
learn	learnt	learnt
	learned	learned
leave	left	left
lend	lent	lent
let	let	let
lie	lay	lain
light	lit	lit
	lighted	lighted
lose	lost	lost
make	made	made
mean	meant	meant
[mi:n]	[ment]	[ment]
meet	met	met
mow	mowed	mown
		mowed
pay	paid	paid
put	put	put

Irregular verbs

VERB	PAST TENSE	PAST/PASSIVE PARTICIPLE
read	read	read
[ri:d]	[red]	[red]
ride	rode	ridden
ring	rang	rung
rise	rose	risen
run	ran	run
say	said	said
[seɪ]	[sed]	[sed]
see	saw	seen
seek	sought	sought
sell	sold	sold
send	sent	sent
set	set	set
sew	sewed	sewn
		sewed
shake	shook	shaken
shine	shone	shone
shoot	shot	shot
show	showed	shown
		showed
shrink	shrank	shrunk
	shrunk	
shut	shut	shut
sing	sang	sung
sink	sank	sunk
sit	sat	sat
sleep	slept	slept
slide	slid	slid
smell	smelt	smelt
	smelled	smelled
speak	spoke	spoken
speed	sped	sped
	speeded	speeded
spell	spelt	spelt
	spelled	spelled
spend	spent	spent
spill	spilt	spilt
	spilled	spilled

VERB	PAST TENSE	PAST/PASSIVE PARTICIPLE
spin	spun	spun
spit	spat	spat
split	split	split
spoil	spoilt	spoilt
	spoiled	spoiled
spread	spread	spread
spring	sprang	sprung
stand	stood	stood
steal	stole	stolen
stick	stuck	stuck
sting	stung	stung
stink	stank	stunk
	stunk	
stride	strode	stridden
strike	struck	struck
swear	swore	sworn
sweep	swept	swept
swim	swam	swum
swing	swung	swung
take	took	taken
teach	taught	taught
tear	tore	torn
tell	told	told
think	thought	thought
throw	threw	thrown
tread	trod	trodden
understand	understood	understood
wake	woke	woken
	waked	waked
wear	wore	worn
weave	wove	woven
	weaved	weaved
weep	wept	wept
win	won	won
wind	wound	wound
write	wrote	written

The verbs in this list are also irregular when they have a prefix, e.g. **overtake – overtook – overtaken**, **foretell – foretold – foretold**.

A few verbs have irregular present simple forms:

VERB	PRESENT SIMPLE
be	I **am**; you/we/they **are**; he/she/it **is**
do	he/she/it **does** [dʌz]
go	he/she/it **goes** [gəʊz]
have	he/she/it **has**
say	he/she/it **says** [sez]

For **burnt/burned, dreamt/dreamed** etc. in British and American English see p 291.   For **gotten** see p 291.

Key to the exercises

The oblique stroke / means that there is more than one possible answer. 'There won't/will not be any oil left' means that these two answers are both correct: 'There won't be any oil left' and 'There will not be any oil left'.

Brackets ( ) mean that we may leave the words out. 'I know (that) I'm right' means that these two answers are both correct: 'I know that I'm right' and 'I know I'm right'.

Unit 1

1.1
1 're trying/are trying
2 Are you finding
3 is helping/'s helping
4 're getting/are getting
5 isn't taking/is not taking
6 Are you waiting
7 'm typing/am typing

1.2
1 doesn't speak/does not speak
2 walk
3 needs
4 love
5 don't look/do not look
6 doesn't work/does not work
7 don't like/do not like
8 wins

1.3
1 is
2 aren't
3 does
4 Do
5 don't
6 are
7 doesn't
8 isn't

Unit 2

2.1
1 live
2 think
3 's talking/is talking
4 know
5 are you doing
6 'm looking/am looking
7 works
8 'm wasting/am wasting

2.2
1 's snowing/is snowing; 's coming/is coming
2 start; 'm starting/am starting
3 read; buy
4 're building/are building; want
5 'm going/am going; drive
6 rises; 're travelling/are travelling
7 go; cost

2.3
1 She always leaves early.
2 You're/You are always losing your keys.
3 You're/You are always taking time off work.
4 I always go the wrong way here.
5 She always thanks me politely.
6 They're/They are always arguing.

Unit 3

3.1
1 state   4 action
2 action   5 state
3 state

3.2
1 's being
2 'm looking
3 think
4 looks
5 didn't fit
6 's having
7 's thinking
8 have
9 was weighing
10 weighed
11 see

3.3
1 And I've still got a chance to win it.
2 It's too expensive to buy.
3 It uses a lot of petrol.
4 I think it's going to suit me.
5 I've never wanted to change it.

Unit 4

4.1
1 Have you looked
2 've looked/have looked
3 haven't finished/have not finished
4 has used/'s used
5 has cleaned/'s cleaned
6 has promised/'s promised
7 hasn't started/has not started
8 've decided/have decided

4.2
1 's bought/has bought
2 've had/have had
3 hasn't cut/has not cut
4 haven't seen/have not seen
5 's rung/has rung

4.3
1 've/have just tidied it.
2 've/have just made it.
3 's/has just repaired it.
4 've/have just spent it.
5 's/has just checked them.

Key

4.4 1 gone 3 been
   2 been 4 gone

Unit 5

5.1 1 were 10 entered
   2 started 11 found
   3 saw 12 said
   4 called
   5 tried
   6 was
   7 arrived
   8 fought
   9 brought

5.2 1 didn't know/did not know
   2 didn't have/did not have
   3 left
   4 didn't sleep/did not sleep
   5 stayed
   6 didn't play/did not play
   7 came
   8 answered

5.3 1 didn't try/did not try
   2 did you go
   3 didn't know/did not know
   4 did you see
   5 didn't like/did not like
   6 did you stay
   7 did Sarah enjoy
   8 didn't want/did not want

Unit 6

6.1 1 have arrived
   2 repaired
   3 've lost/have lost
   4 has started
   5 ran
   6 earned
   7 planted
   8 have gone
   9 has turned/'s turned
   10 phoned
   11 've made/have made
   12 broke

6.2 1 has stood
   2 was
   3 stayed
   4 have lived/'ve lived
   5 have known/'ve known
   6 was

6.3 1 has travelled; travelled
   2 has made; made
   3 won; has won
   4 didn't take/did not take; has taken

6.4 1 this; last
   2 today; yesterday
   3 last; this
   4 this; yesterday

6.5 1 's happened/has happened
   2 's had/has had
   3 fell
   4 broke
   5 did this happen
   6 told
   7 knew
   8 didn't tell/did not tell
   9 didn't see/did not see
   10 haven't seen/have not seen
   11 's had/has had
   12 did

Unit 7

7.1 1 were you doing
   2 was taking
   3 was coming
   4 was going
   5 were dreaming
   6 weren't looking/were not looking
   7 were going

7.2 1 was getting
   2 came
   3 didn't miss/did not miss
   4 was coming
   5 fell
   6 were playing
   7 was working
   8 happened
   9 stopped
   10 went

7.3 1 The train was waiting when we arrived at the station.
   2 Ella had a puncture when she was driving on the motorway.
   3 When I tried the pudding, I liked it.
   4 When Karen lifted/was lifting the chair, she felt a sudden pain in her back.
   5 When the gates opened, the crowd walked in.
   6 I was reading a library book when I found a £10 note between two pages.

Key

Unit 8

8.1
1. have you been doing
2. 's been helping/has been helping
3. have you been studying
4. 've been working/have been working
5. 's been getting/has been getting

8.2
1. He's/He has been shopping.
2. They've/They have been working hard.
3. They've/They have been sunbathing.
4. She's/She has been walking in the field.
5. They've/They have been arguing.
6. It's/It has been raining.
7. He's/He has been baking (some) cakes.

8.3
1. He's/He has been swimming for ten minutes.
2. They've/They have been talking for half an hour.
3. He's/He has been reading for an hour.
4. They've/They have been travelling for three months.
5. She's/She has been working for ten hours.
6. They've/They have been camping for four weeks.

Unit 9

9.1
1. has left
2. 's been cleaning/has been cleaning
3. 've been mowing/have been mowing
4. 've seen/have seen
5. 've cut/have cut

9.2
1. have run; 've been running/have been running
2. has been doing/'s been doing; 's done/has done
3. 've been drinking/have been drinking; 've drunk/have drunk
4. has delivered/'s delivered; 's been delivering/has been delivering
5. have been playing; 've played/have played

9.3
1. 've been clearing/have been clearing
2. 've found/have found
3. 've been reading/have been reading
4. 've been watching/have been watching
5. haven't seen/have not seen
6. 's been/has been
7. 've never had/have never had

Unit 10

10.1
1. had left
2. 've finished/have finished
3. 've eaten/have eaten
4. had ordered/'d ordered
5. 've made/have made
6. had told
7. had had/'d had
8. 's started/has started
9. 've turned/have turned
10. had made/'d made

10.2
1. I paid for it.
2. the headmaster came in.
3. First we finished the work.
4. First I pressed the switch.

10.3
1. When Joe had saved enough money, he bought a motor-bike.
2. Max put all the dishes away when he'd/he had dried them.
3. Jane signed the letter when she'd/she had typed it on her word processor.
4. When we'd/we had completed the forms, we handed them in.
5. When I'd/I had looked both ways, I pulled out into the road.
6. The golfers went into the club house when they'd/they had played the last hole.

Unit 11

11.1
1. 'd been digging/had been digging
2. hadn't been doing/had not been doing
3. 'd been waiting/had been waiting
4. 'd been dealing/had been dealing

11.2
1. He'd/He had been cleaning a window.
2. She'd/She had been walking on the ice.
3. She'd/She had been hitch-hiking.
4. They'd/They had been playing on the railway line.
5. She'd/She had been walking in her sleep.
6. He'd/He had been using a faulty electric drill.

11.3
1. had been watching
2. 'd/had been playing; hadn't/had not won
3. 'd/had been walking; 'd/had walked
4. 'd/had stopped; was smoking
5. were having (Also possible: 'd/had been having); 'd/had been seeing; had known

Unit 12

12.1
1. He uses it
2. She's/She has lost it.
3. We're/We are getting them
4. He's/He is enjoying it
5. I hate it.
6. I've/I have checked them
7. They're/They are playing it
8. You haven't/have not watered them

296

Key

12.2
1 I've/I have been working
2 she left
3 You've/You have been writing
4 They moved
5 she stopped; I was waiting

12.3
1 I haven't seen
2 I've just started
3 I started
4 have you sold
5 I've been learning
6 I think
7 You had
8 I remember
9 I've had
10 I love

12.4
1 did not/didn't return
2 live
3 went
4 played
5 'd/had played
6 sat
7 left
8 was
9 was walking
10 saw
11 has seen
12 are questioning/have been questioning
13 have spoken/'ve spoken
14 want
15 was lying
16 are searching

12.5
1 'm/am speaking
2 knows
3 had heard
4 'd/had been taking
5 's/has answered
6 arrived
7 were waiting
8 has been reading

Unit 13

13.1
1 He's/He is going to read it.
2 I'm/I am going to fry them.
3 She's/She is going to sell it.
4 I'm/I am going to correct it/them.
5 She's/She is going to accept it.

13.2
1 'm/am going to take
2 's/is going to borrow
3 Is he going to mow
4 isn't/is not going to rain

13.3
1 was going to go
2 was going to pick
3 were going to see
4 was going to drive

13.4
1 have one government.
2 There won't/will not be any wars.
3 Computers will decide our future.
4 Everyone will have a personal robot.
5 There won't/will not be any oil left.
6 People will travel to other planets.

Unit 14

14.1
1 's/is going to read
2 'll/will have
3 'll/will record
4 are you going to buy
5 'll/will wait

14.2
1 'm/am going to spend
2 'll be/will be
3 'm/am going to work
4 'll be/will be (Also possible: is going to be)
5 'm/am going to do
6 'm/am going to fail
7 won't/will not fail/aren't/are not going to fail

14.3
1 're/are going to build
2 will be (Also possible: is going to be)
3 will like (Also possible: are going to like)
4 will be (Also possible: are going to be)
5 're/are going to have
6 will be (Also possible: is going to be)
7 're/are going to stop

Unit 15

15.1
1 future   4 future
2 future   5 present
3 present

15.2
1 She's/She is working (in the office) on Saturday.
2 She's/She is flying to Acapulco.
3 They're/They are playing badminton tomorrow afternoon.
4 She's/She is visiting the New World Fun Park (on June 10th).

15.3
1 At half past twelve they arrive in Stratford.
2 At one o'clock they have lunch.
3 At two o'clock they do a tour of the town.
4 At half past five they leave/the bus leaves (Stratford).

297

Key

15.4
1 gets
2 comes
3 'll/will remind
4 'll/will make
5 knows
6 post
7 'll/will receive

Unit 16

16.1
1 We'll/We will be relaxing at our villa.
2 I'll/I will be sitting by the pool.
3 The sun will be shining.
4 We'll/We will be enjoying ourselves.
5 The police will be looking for us.
6 But we'll/we will be laughing at them.

16.2
1 writing to Emma soon?
2 Will you be going to the library today?
3 Will you be using your calculator this afternoon?
4 Will you be seeing Henry tomorrow?
5 Will you be watching the late-night film?
6 Will you be phoning your sister?

16.3
1 I'll/I will have had
2 I'll/I will have been the subject of a TV programme
3 I'll/I will have become world-famous
4 I'll/I will have made millions of pounds from my pictures before I'm forty.

Unit 17

17.1
1 I'm going to move
2 It'll be
3 I'll take
4 we're going
5 It's going to crash!
6 I'll be using

17.2
1 'm/am going to get up early tomorrow.
2 arrives at 10.30/half past ten.
3 I'm/I am seeing my bank manager tomorrow.
4 I'm/I am about to leave.
5 I'll/I will be visiting my aunt on Sunday.

17.3
1 'll be speaking
2 'm going/'m going to go
3 leave/'m leaving
4 'm visiting/'m going to visit
5 'll be
6 starts/is starting/is about to start
7 'll see
8 'll tell
9 get

Unit 18

18.1
1 is
2 is
3 has
4 is
5 has
6 has
7 is
8 are
9 have
10 is
11 has
12 have

18.2
1 've got/have got/have
2 had (Also possible: 'd got/had got)
3 've got/have got/have
4 had (Also possible: 'd got/had got)
5 's got/has got/has
6 've got/have got/have

18.3
1 've got/have got/have
2 had (Also possible: 'd got/had got)
3 haven't got/don't have
4 didn't have (Also possible: hadn't got)
5 's got/has got/has
6 hasn't got/doesn't have

18.4
1 Has … got/Does … have
2 hasn't got/doesn't have
3 didn't have (Also possible: hadn't got)
4 didn't have (Also possible: hadn't got)
5 Have … got/Do … have

Unit 19

19.1
1 We've played three games of Scrabble.
2 My father drinks a glass of beer every evening.
3 We've just spent three weeks in Yugoslavia.
4 I've already eaten a sandwich.
5 James received lots of presents on his birthday.
6 The manager was smoking a cigarette in his office.

19.2
1 don't have
2 is having
3 Did … have
4 had
5 have
6 didn't have

19.3
1 have a swim
2 had an argument
3 gave a smile
4 have a bath
5 having a rest
6 pay … a visit
7 have a look

Key

Unit 20

20.1
1. That's the problem.
2. I've seen the article.
3. I'm sorry.
4. We haven't/We've not decided.

20.2
1. Where's your ticket?
2. I don't know. I haven't got it.
3. Oh, it's here.
4. It's ten past. We'll be late.
5. Don't worry. We needn't hurry.
6. I'd like to be on time.
7. We're early. We've got time.
8. We won't be late.

20.3
1. We are ready.
2. The letter has not come.
3. What will you do?
4. You have made a mistake.
5. I did not know.
6. That book is mine.
7. Here is your ticket.
8. They will not win.

20.4
1. I would like a coffee.
2. There has been an accident.
3. That is correct.
4. I had seen the film before.
5. Who has got the key?
6. We would have stopped if we had seen you.

Unit 21

21.1
1. didn't buy
2. isn't
3. will find
4. has got
5. doesn't get
6. isn't

21.2
1. don't
2. didn't
3. wasn't
4. don't
5. aren't
6. hasn't
7. isn't
8. doesn't
9. doesn't
10. haven't

21.3
1. isn't/is not a nervous person.
2. doesn't/does not want a quiet life.
3. takes risks/does take risks.
4. wasn't/was not a very clever child.
5. didn't/did not pass (all) his exams.
6. can't/cannot relax.
7. is a good talker.
8. hasn't/has not read many books/a lot of books.

21.4
1. not
2. no
3. no
4. not
5. No
6. not

Unit 22

22.1
1. offering
2. making a suggestion
3. asking permission
4. requesting
5. inviting
6. asking for information
7. asking permission
8. requesting

22.2
1. did you leave school?
2. was your best subject?
3. Did you pass your maths exam?
4. are your hobbies?
5. Where do you live?/Do you live in Middleton?
6. Have you got a car?
7. Would you like to work evenings?

22.3
1. will the programme continue?
2. How much (money) do you earn?
3. When did you start acting?
4. Are your parents proud of you?
5. Have you got a girl-friend?
6. What's her name?
7. Where does she live?
8. How long have you known her?
9. Are you going to get married?
10. Have you ever taken drugs?

22.4
1. Who
2. When
3. How many
4. What time/When
5. What
6. How far
7. Whose
8. How often
9. What kind
10. How long

22.5
1. you (often) worry about?
2. they fed up with?
3. What do you feel ashamed of?
4. What are you going to complain about?
5. What is she famous for?
6. What are you concentrating on?

Key

Unit 23

23.1
1. Lola
2. Lola
3. Elaine
4. a bus
5. a chair
6. Jason

23.2
1. Who is/Who's having a party?
2. What were you laughing at?
3. What have you learnt?
4. What should we do?
5. Who is/Who's looking for me?
6. Who are you looking for?
7. What is/What's she planning?
8. Who has/Who's moved in next door?
9. What is/What's worrying you?
10. Who do you want to meet?

23.3
1. can we use
2. has won first prize
3. do you like best
4. have you borrowed
5. has died

Unit 24

24.1
1. Which flight did you take?
2. Which hotel did you stay at?
3. What school do you go to?
4. Which car is yours?
5. What newspaper do you buy?
6. What language are you learning?

24.2
1. What
2. Which
3. Which
4. What
5. What
6. Which
7. Which

24.3
1. Which
2. Which
3. who (Also possible: which)
4. Which
5. What
6. What
7. Which
8. Who (Also possible: Which)

Unit 25

25.1
1. I can.
2. it is.
3. she didn't.
4. they aren't.
5. I do.
6. he isn't.
7. I haven't.
8. I won't.
9. I did.

25.2
1. Yes, it has.
2. No, they don't.
3. Yes, I am.
4. Yes, we do.
5. No, she doesn't.
6. No, I wasn't.
7. Yes, they did.
8. No, I won't.
9. No, I can't.

25.3
1. please
2. of course/OK
3. please
4. OK
5. of course
6. please

Unit 26

26.1
1. It was a super show, wasn't it?
2. It feels much colder, doesn't it?
3. These sweaters are lovely, aren't they?

26.2
1. isn't it?
2. are there?
3. aren't you?
4. didn't you?
5. don't they?
6. can't we?
7. haven't we?
8. was it?

26.3
1. don't you?
2. haven't I?
3. aren't you?
4. does it?
5. is there?
6. can you?

26.4
1. shall we?
2. have you?
3. can/could you?
4. could you?
5. will you?

Unit 27

27.1
1. Neither am I.
2. Neither can I.
3. So am I.
4. So do I.
5. Neither have I.
6. so would I.

27.2
1. neither does Marie.
2. so has Mike.
3. neither can Lorna.
4. neither is Paul.
5. so does Lorna.
6. so is Paul.

Key

27.3
1. I don't expect so.
2. I suppose so.
3. I hope not.
4. I don't think so.
5. I'm afraid not.

Unit 28

28.1
1. She can't see
2. He can read
3. He can't walk
4. She can look

28.2
1. been able to
2. to be able to
3. be able to
4. been able to
5. be able to

28.3
1. could hear
2. was able to get
3. couldn't understand
4. was able to find
5. were able to help

28.4
1. couldn't/wasn't able to
2. was able to
3. could
4. could/was able to
5. were able to

Unit 29

29.1 (**Can**, **could** and **may** are all possible.)
1. Can I borrow your ruler?
2. May I sit down?
3. May I join you?
4. Could I look at your notes?

29.2
1. You can turn left.
2. You can't play ball games.
3. You can't smoke.
4. You can have a picnic.
5. You can't leave litter.

29.3
1. allowed to
2. wasn't/was not allowed to
3. 're/are allowed to
4. 'll/will be allowed to

29.4
1. Am I allowed to
2. May I
3. Am I allowed to
4. Am I allowed to
5. May I

Unit 30

30.1
1. I may/might go
2. He may/might be
3. we may/might break
4. It may/might not start
5. She may/might not get
6. We/I may/might sell
7. You may/might drop

30.2
1. mightn't
2. mightn't
3. couldn't
4. couldn't
5. mightn't
6. mightn't

30.3
1. can't
2. must
3. must
4. might
5. can't
6. might
7. must

Unit 31

31.1
1. had to; did ... have to
2. have to; have to
3. Do ... have to; have to
4. had to; didn't/did not have to
5. does ... have to; has to

31.2
1. 'You must get to work on time.'
2. has to keep his dog under control.
3. 'You must listen carefully.'
4. visitors have to report to the security officer.

31.3
1. must
2. has to
3. have to
4. must
5. must
6. have to
7. must

Unit 32

32.1
1. must; mustn't; needn't
2. mustn't; must
3. mustn't; needn't
4. mustn't; must, needn't

32.2
1. didn't have to wait ages to cross the road.
2. don't have to work long hours.
3. doesn't have to work in a factory.
4. didn't have to lock our doors.
5. don't have to wash their clothes by hand.

32.3
1. needn't have left/didn't need to leave
2. didn't need to pay
3. didn't need to borrow
4. needn't have tipped/didn't need to tip

Unit 33

33.1
1. Can I have a receipt, please?
2. Can you help me, please?
3. Would you mind opening the door for me, please?
4. Could I speak to the manager, please?

Key

33.2
1. Shall I repair it for you?
2. Shall I open it for you?
3. Shall I carry them for you?
4. Shall I post it for you?

33.3
1. Shall
2. Could
3. Shall
4. could
5. Would
6. Would
7. Would

33.4
1. Shall I walk / Would you like me to walk home with you? OR I can / I'll walk home with you.
2. Can / Could you tell me the time, please?
3. Shall we have a cup of coffee?

Unit 34

34.1
1. shouldn't
2. ought
3. shouldn't
4. should
5. ought
6. oughtn't

34.2
1. 'd better wash them.
2. 'd better answer it.
3. I'd better pay them.
4. She'd better find it.
5. They'd better return it.

34.3
1. 'm supposed to take
2. aren't supposed to watch
3. are supposed to report
4. are supposed to stand

34.4
1. 'd better hurry (Also possible: should hurry / ought to hurry)
2. 'd better not be / oughtn't to be / shouldn't be
3. should arrive / ought to arrive
4. shouldn't take / oughtn't to take
5. aren't supposed to get / 're not supposed to get

Unit 35

35.1
1. mightn't have received our message.
2. could / might have had a key.
3. couldn't have pressed the wrong button.
4. Yes, he could / might have missed the train.
5. Yes / No, he / she mightn't have seen the warning sign.

35.2
1. can't have used
2. can't have put
3. must have done

35.3
1. They shouldn't have left / oughtn't to have left litter (everywhere).
2. She should have looked / ought to have looked (before crossing).
3. He should say / ought to say hello (to people).
4. She shouldn't have been / oughtn't to have been late.

35.4
1. shouldn't have left
2. might have taken
3. must have been
4. can't have rung

Unit 36

36.1
1. 'll
2. won't
3. would
4. wouldn't
5. wouldn't
6. 'll

36.2
1. will help
2. wouldn't let
3. will give
4. won't go
5. wouldn't open
6. won't stand

36.3
1. Shall we go for a walk?
2. I won't take any risks.
3. Would you like to stay at my flat?
4. Shall I park your car?
5. I'd / I would like a shower (, please).
6. You shouldn't decide in a hurry.
7. The world will end in the year 2500. / The end of the world will be in the year 2500.

Unit 37

37.1
1. is regarded
2. have been made
3. has not been changed
4. is owned
5. has been used
6. is being built

37.2
1. are going to be done
2. will … be called
3. cannot be used
4. will be produced
5. should be sold
6. could be produced

37.3
1. are getting damaged.
2. has got knocked down.
3. has got blown off.
4. are getting paid higher wages.

Key

Unit 38

38.1
1. passed
2. burst
3. were rescued
4. received
5. reached
6. were blocked
7. were brought
8. is being done
9. said

38.2
1. became President in 1789.
2. was bought from France.
3. Gold was discovered in California.
4. The Civil War was won by the North.
5. Black people wanted equal rights.
6. Kennedy was shot in 1963.

38.3
1. has/'s been stolen.
2. have/'ve bought a video camera.
3. has/'s been taken to hospital.
4. has/'s been sold.
5. It has/It's won the competition.
6. She has/She's been sacked.
7. It has/It's been run over.

38.4
1. was taken
2. was done
3. was interviewed by a young policewoman
4. fingerprints were found
5. burglar was identified by the police computer
6. has been arrested and is being questioned

38.5
1. motor car was made by an Austrian called Siegfried Marcus.
2. did not produce cars for sale.
3. production was started by a German called Carl Benz.
4. is now seen as the father of the motor car.

Unit 39

39.1
1. Most employees are offered company shares.
2. All employees are allowed six weeks' holiday.
3. Help is given to people moving house.
4. A sum of money is paid to women who leave to have children.

39.2
1. been reported
2. is believed that the Prime Minister and his wife are getting divorced.
3. It has been said that the footballer Gary Johnson earns £1 million a year.

39.3
1. has been reported/is reported
2. are believed to be
3. The footballer Gary Johnson has been said/is said to earn £1 million a year.

Unit 40

40.1
1. his tooth filled.
2. had her photo taken.
3. Adrian has had his car serviced.
4. We have our windows cleaned once a month.
5. The Watsons are having their dishwasher repaired.

40.2
1. Peter got his tooth filled.
2. The actress got her photo taken.
3. Adrian has got his car serviced.
4. We get our windows cleaned once a month.
5. The Watsons are getting their dishwasher repaired.

40.3
1. having … re-papered   3. have … laid
2. had … done   4. have … fitted

40.4
1. had her car stolen from outside her house.
2. The family had its/their electricity cut off.
3. Old people have had their pensions increased by five per cent.

Unit 41

41.1
1. being sent away.
2. He doesn't want to be misunderstood.
3. He hopes to be offered a job.
4. He doesn't mind being paid low wages.
5. He is willing to be re-trained.
6. He would like to be given a chance.

41.2
1. being used   4. to do
2. working   5. to be invited
3. to be treated   6. being heard

41.3
1. to be cleaned
2. to take
3. washing/to be washed
4. to be dry-cleaned
5. to carry
6. clearing/to be cleared

Unit 42

42.1
1. to get   5. to go
2. staying   6. driving
3. to sit   7. to go
4. touring   8. to spend

303

Key

42.2
1. to repair
2. to see
3. to give
4. to think
5. wondering
6. to buy

42.3
1. applying
2. working
3. to start
4. to operate
5. to earn
6. missing

Unit 43

43.1
1. to lock/locking
2. driving/to drive
3. to make
4. to go/going
5. to look

43.2
1. He loves swimming/loves to swim
2. I wouldn't like to work
3. I'd like to see
4. I'd prefer to come
5. I'd love to fly
6. I hate queuing/hate to queue
7. He likes walking/likes to walk
8. like to try (Also possible: like trying)

43.3
1. mentioning
2. agreeing
3. to call
4. to lock
5. to lock
6. looking
7. to read

43.4
1. stopped to buy some cigarettes.
2. didn't even try to move the piano.
3. always remember meeting Mrs Thatcher.
4. need painting.
5. Graham didn't mean to be rude to Louise.
6. Kevin regrets missing his chance of a prize.

43.5
1. to give
2. to stop
3. smoking
4. eating
5. to go
6. to tell
7. to say
8. pulling
9. doing
10. giving
11. to become
12. to have

Unit 44

44.1
1. asked the teacher to explain.
2. The doctor told the patient to stay in bed.
3. Kay reminded Joe to pay the bill.
4. The police ordered the gunman to come out with his hands up.

44.2
1. taught her to speak Italian.
2. expected the team to lose.
3. forced the hostages to lie down.
4. meant his smile to be friendly.

44.3
1. her to hitch-hike.
2. doesn't want them to stay out late.
3. She would like her to take the exam.

44.4
1. driving
2. to travel
3. buying
4. to use
5. to take

Unit 45

45.1
1. to eat chocolate.
2. persuaded her to come to lunch.
3. We've decided to have a holiday.
4. would be silly to miss our train.
5. I must have something to eat.
6. I don't know where to go.
7. She's gone to the post office to buy some stamps.

45.2
1. see
2. know
3. explode
4. cry
5. snow
6. go
7. crash

45.3
1. to stay
2. to have
3. buy
4. to read
5. feel
6. look
7. get
8. to leave
9. to change
10. forget

Unit 46

46.1
1. wondered who to invite to the party.
2. asked what to play next.
3. The trainer hadn't decided who to choose for the team.
4. Ralph didn't understand how to fill in the form.
5. The students wanted to know what to expect in the exam.

Key

46.2 1 what to expect
      2 where to go
      3 how to find
      4 what to do

46.3 1 what number to ring.
      2 whether to do it.
      3 how much (money) to give.
      4 whether to join (it).
      5 which (one) to take.
      6 how to solve it.

Unit 47

47.1 1 for children to play with matches.
      2 arranged for the taxi to come at eight o'clock.
      3 is impatient for the party to begin.
      4 It's important for people to know the truth.

47.2 1 There's a pool for guests to swim in.
      2 There are tables for you to picnic at.
      3 There's music for you to listen to.
      4 There are gift shops for tourists to buy souvenirs in.

47.3 1 It's too high for her to reach.
      2 It's too difficult for us to understand.
      3 It wasn't loud enough for everyone to hear.
      4 It wasn't warm enough for him to swim (in).

47.4 1 of   4 for
      2 of   5 for
      3 of

Unit 48

48.1 1 for breaking   3 of getting
      2 on buying   4 like arguing

48.2 1 on passing her driving test.
      2 succeeded in saving the woman's life.
      3 complained about not getting his money back.
      4 blamed the van driver for not stopping at the crossroads.
      5 Vegetarians don't approve of eating meat.
      6 The complicated rules will discourage people from playing this game.
      7 The workers have accused the management of doing nothing about the problem.
      8 The courts should punish drivers for breaking the speed limit.

48.3 1 about getting   4 for not replying
      2 on travelling   5 from doing
      3 with living   6 at looking

Unit 49

49.1 1 of losing my money.
      2 was afraid to walk home alone.
      3 was afraid to argue with the policeman.
      4 He's afraid of getting (too) sunburnt.
      5 I'm afraid to touch these wires.
      6 I was afraid of offending my hostess.

49.2 1 about flying   4 to settle
      2 of behaving   5 to tell
      3 in cooking

49.3 1 to disturb you
      2 about being so rude
      3 about losing my temper

Unit 50

50.1 1 to going   5 to ring
      2 to standing 6 to come
      3 to see   7 to hitting
      4 to pay   8 to go

50.2 1 used to like
      2 didn't use / did not use to have
      3 did you use to help
      4 used to look

50.3 1 to living   5 to drinking
      2 to stop   6 to travelling
      3 to work
      4 to be

Unit 51

51.1 1 by working all night.
      2 on waking in the morning.
      3 as a result of losing his passport.
      4 without using a calculator.
      5 for carrying the food.
      6 in spite of having it on his list.

51.2 1 before signing   4 after using
      2 after eating   5 before changing
      3 before leaving

51.3 1 before deciding to buy it.
      2 He bought the shop despite having little money of his own.
      3 He became successful by giving the customers what they want.
      4 He fell ill as a result of working too hard.
      5 He was happy when running his own business.
      6 He has made a lot of money since buying his first shop (ten years ago).

Key

Unit 52

52.1
1 She sometimes goes skiing.
2 They sometimes go dancing.
3 He sometimes goes cycling.
4 She sometimes goes riding.
5 He sometimes goes sailing.

52.2
1 Nigel did the shopping.
2 Anne did the driving.
3 Mark did the map-reading.
4 Everyone did the cleaning.

52.3
1 go swimming
2 done the washing
3 do the washing
4 gone riding
5 doing the ironing

52.4
1 She does a lot of gardening.
2 He does a lot of fishing.
3 We don't do much decorating.
4 He doesn't do much dancing.
5 She doesn't do much ironing.
6 They do a lot of swimming.

Unit 53

53.1
1 Yes, I heard him lock it.
2 Yes, I watched her take it.
3 Yes, I noticed him get on (it).
4 Yes, I saw it break.

53.2
1 I can hear it barking.
2 I can see them playing.
3 I can hear it ringing.
4 I can smell it burning.

53.3
1 I felt the building shake.
2 I heard people shouting.
3 I could hear an alarm ringing.
4 I saw the police arrive.
5 I saw a woman crying.

53.4
1 waiting
2 fall
3 watching
4 play
5 painting
6 beat

Unit 54

54.1
1 Tom broke his arm playing rugby.
2 Ella cut her hand opening a tin.
3 Helen injured her leg climbing a mountain.
4 Peter hurt his back digging this hole.

54.2
1 out a gun, the man fired a shot.
2 used the whole film, Sharon developed it.
3 Having cut the grass, Teresa put the mower away.
4 Taking out his wallet, Roger offered a £20 note.
5 Having solved the puzzle, Mike sent the answer to the magazine.

54.3
1 Having studied the map, Paul knew which way to go.
2 Feeling cold, Lorna turned on the heating.
3 Not knowing the language, Tina found it hard to communicate.
4 Having finished the book, Tony took it back to the library.

Unit 55

55.1
1 determiner
2 verb
3 preposition
4 adjective
5 linking word
6 determiner
7 verb
8 pronoun
9 adjective
10 adverb
11 linking word
12 pronoun
13 noun
14 determiner
15 noun
16 noun
17 verb
18 adverb

55.2
1 adjective   4 adjective
2 verb   5 noun
3 verb   6 verb

55.3
1 your
2 this
3 I
4 mine
5 lots of
6 we
7 many
8 I
9 this
10 a
11 all
12 his
13 who

Unit 56

56.1
1. is; might go
2. we
3. very good; OK
4. outside; tomorrow
5. at the moment; on Saturday

56.2
1. subject
2. verb
3. object
4. complement
5. adverbial
6. complement

56.3
1. I must tell you the bad news.
2. This town is an awful place.
3. It is raining.
4. Everything is very expensive.
5. I hate the food.
6. Our last day is on Friday.

56.4
1. also; with several young people
2. first; in 1986
3. naturally; without help
4. fortunately; from sponsorship

Unit 57

57.1
1. cigarettes, crisps, eggs, magazines, newspapers, pens, sweets
2. bread, milk, mineral water, soap, toilet paper, toothpaste, washing powder

57.2
1. university
2. months
3. literature
4. books
5. paperbacks
6. food
7. job
8. weekends
9. money
10. fun
11. pictures
12. friends

57.3
1. a jar of jam
2. a box of matches
3. two loaves of bread
4. a bar of chocolate
5. five kilos of potatoes
6. a packet of washing powder
7. two bottles/cartons of milk
8. a tube of toothpaste

57.4
1. some
2. some
3. a
4. some
5. some
6. a
7. some
8. a
9. an
10. some
11. some
12. a

57.5
1. some music
2. traffic
3. an idea
4. some work
5. some advice
6. a problem
7. any
8. good health

57.6
1. some nice weather
2. a meal
3. some fun
4. a day
5. some lovely scenery
6. a terrible journey

Unit 58

58.1
1. sport
2. painting
3. some potatoes
4. A noise
5. cheese
6. a conversation
7. some chicken
8. war
9. Life
10. some egg

58.2
1. a light
2. some paper
3. some time
4. some ice
5. an iron
6. a glass
7. a business

58.3
1. two cups of coffee
2. (different) kinds of French cheese
3. a glass of orange juice
4. these (different) kinds of medicine
5. an extra bottle of milk

Unit 59

59.1
1. is
2. look
3. are
4. has
5. costs
6. have
7. weren't

59.2
1. were
2. was
3. were
4. were
5. was
6. was
7. were
8. was/were

Key

59.3	1 is	6 are
	2 is	7 isn't
	3 work	8 is
	4 have	9 is
	5 are	10 has

59.4	1 is	4 are
	2 are	5 is
	3 are	

Unit 60

60.1
1 thanks
2 damages
3 pain
4 belongings
5 arm
6 saving
7 goods
8 damage
9 savings
10 pains

60.2
1 is
2 were
3 have
4 is
5 was
6 were
7 aren't
8 seems

60.3
1 outskirts
2 town
3 miles
4 centre
5 aren't
6 crossroads
7 factory
8 works
9 university
10 is
11 economics
12 headquarters
13 athletics
14 tennis
15 billiards

Unit 61

61.1	1 feel	5 look
	2 go	6 suit
	3 is	
	4 fit	

61.2
1 jeans
2 pairs of shorts
3 knife
4 some scissors
5 pair of tights
6 some pyjamas

61.3	1 has	5 are
	2 are	6 want
	3 are	7 has
	4 know	

61.4
1 club is
2 choir are
3 crew are
4 population is
5 audience is
6 police are

Unit 62

62.1
1 a; the
2 a; the; a
3 the; the
4 a; the; the; The
5 a; a; the
6 a; the
7 a; the

62.2
1 We played the game on holiday.
2 A pedestrian stepped into the road.
3 I read an article in the paper.
4 The bomb exploded at midnight.
5 The pupils didn't like the teacher.
6 The police arrested a criminal.

62.3	1 A	13 a
	2 a	14 The
	3 a	15 the
	4 a	16 the
	5 The	17 a
	6 the	18 the
	7 the	19 the
	8 a	20 an
	9 the	21 the
	10 The	22 the
	11 the	23 the
	12 the	

62.4
1 the; a
2 a; a
3 a; a; the; a
4 the; a
5 a; the; an
6 the; a; the
7 a; the; the; the; The; a

62.5 1 a DJ   5 an SRN
      2 a VIP   6 a UFO
      3 an IQ   7 an AGM
      4 a PRO   8 an LEA

62.6 1 a   4 a
      2 One   5 a
      3 One   6 one

Unit 63

63.1 1 A Dutchman invented the submarine.
      2 Galileo invented the telescope.
      3 A Frenchman developed the IQ test.
      4 Thomson discovered the electron.
      5 A Scotsman invented the bicycle.

63.2 1 A violin is a musical instrument.
      2 A queue is a line of people.
      3 An apple is a fruit.
      4 A pistol is a kind of gun.
      5 A solution is an answer to a problem.

63.3 1 children; toys; games
      2 history; the history; history; geography
      3 Pollution; industry; the pollution

63.4 1 the radio   4 the guitar
      2 television   5 the country
      3 basketball

Unit 64

64.1 1 the hospital
      2 hospital
      3 prison
      4 the prison
      5 church
      6 the church
      7 the bed
      8 bed

64.2 1 at home
      2 in bed
      3 to the hospital
      4 to church
      5 at the seaside
      6 to work
      7 to the library
      8 in prison

64.3 1 university   6 bed
      2 the cinema   7 work
      3 the railway station 8 the navy
      4 sea   9 prison
      5 home

Unit 65

65.1 1 Christmas; a white Christmas
      2 the summer; 1969
      3 Thanksgiving; November
      4 the year
      5 night; the dark; the day
      6 the weekend; Saturday

65.2 1 breakfast
      2 lunch
      3 the lunch
      4 The dinner
      5 a marvellous dinner

65.3 1 breakfast
      2 midnight
      3 Wednesday
      4 plane
      5 the morning
      6 Wednesday
      7 the bus
      8 the day
      9 Christmas
     10 January

Unit 66

66.1 1 Yes, it was a fairly good flight.
      2 Yes, it's quite a fast train.
      3 Yes, it's rather an expensive coat/a rather expensive coat.
      4 Yes, it was quite an enjoyable evening.
      5 Yes, it's a very grand hotel.

66.2 1 so   5 such
      2 so   6 so
      3 so   7 such
      4 such

66.3 1 Karen is always so busy (that) she never has time to talk.
      2 I haven't cooked for so long (that)/for such a long time (that) I've forgotten how to.
      3 Neil buys such cheap clothes (that) they never last long.
      4 You made such a noise (that) you woke everyone up.
      5 There are so many tourists (that)/such a lot of tourists (that) there's no room to sit on the beach.

66.4 1 what a   4 what a
      2 What   5 what
      3 What a   6 what a

Key

Unit 67

67.1
1. Lake Michigan
2. Italy
3. The Andes
4. The United Kingdom
5. Anglesey
6. the West Indies
7. The River Seine
8. Brussels
9. the North
10. Mount McKinley

67.2
1. the Thames
2. Hyde Park
3. Heathrow Airport
4. Trafalgar Square
5. Westminster Bridge
6. the Houses of Parliament
7. Buckingham Palace
8. north London
9. The Savoy Hotel; the Strand

67.3
1. New York City
2. the Statue of Liberty
3. Central Park
4. the Metropolitan Museum
5. Broadway
6. Macy's
7. Washington Square
8. New York University

67.4
1. Millthorpe Station
2. the Classic Theatre
3. Kingston House
4. Wood Lane
5. the High Street
6. the Norfolk Hotel

67.5
1. is in George Street.
2. The Odeon Cinema is in the/The Boulevard.
3. The Clarendon Art Gallery is in Newton Lane.
4. King Edward College is in College Road.
5. St John's Church is in South Street.
6. Webster's department store is in the High Street.
7. The Bristol Hotel is in Westville Way.

67.6
1. a day at Blenheim Palace
2. a train journey in North Wales
3. a tour of the White House
4. a beach on the Riviera
5. a shopping trip to Harrod's
6. a small town in France
7. a trip across the Severn Bridge
8. a walk around Lake Windermere
9. a visit to Tower Bridge
10. a journey across the Rockies
11. a look around the National Gallery
12. a boat trip along the River Dart

Unit 68

68.1
1. sold my bike to my brother.
2. promised the workers a pay rise.
3. passed the sugar to Dave.
4. told the joke to all his friends.
5. Jeremy gave his flat-mate some help.
6. I wrote my teacher a letter of apology.
7. Sarah threw the ball to Kirsty.

68.2
1. for   4. for
2. to   5. for
3. to   6. to

68.3
1. you a little sticker
2. the card to the garage
3. it to the cashier
4. you something
5. you a sports bag
6. you mine

Unit 69

69.1
1. Look at this shirt.
2. Look at these socks.
3. Look at that dog.
4. Look at these shoes.
5. Look at that telephone.
6. Look at this clock.

69.2
1. this
2. That
3. these
4. this
5. this
6. those
7. that
8. This
9. This; that
10. this; that

Unit 70

70.1
1. our   5. yours
2. his   6. mine
3. his   7. hers
4. their   8. her

Key

70.2 1 its   3 it's   5 its
      2 its   4 it's

70.3 1 the (Also possible: my)
      2 her
      3 the (Also possible: his)
      4 their
      5 your; your

70.4 1 a hobby of mine
      2 our own (private) swimming-pool
      3 some tapes of his
      4 an ambition of hers
      5 my own room

Unit 71

71.1 1 twins'
      2 Carl's
      3 Sandy's
      4 Debbie's
      5 children's
      6 Simpsons'
      7 Pat's
      8 Kevin's
      9 Steve's

71.2 1 Mr Hillman's Gun
      2 The Smell of Blood
      3 The Terrorist's Car
      4 The Middle of the Night
      5 The Death of Someone Very Important
      6 The Chairman of the Bank/The Bank's Chairman
      7 The Gangsters' Money
      8 The Day of the Wedding
      9 The Old Woman's Handbag
      10 The Teacher's Computer
      11 Mrs Fletcher's Plan
      12 The Price of a Meal

71.3 1 yesterday's
      2 year's
      3 minutes'
      4 month's
      5 week's

Unit 72

72.1 1 some
      2 any
      3 any
      4 some
      5 some
      6 some
      7 any

72.2 1 any; some; some
      2 some (Also possible: any); anything
      3 someone; any/some
      4 some; any; some
      5 something; someone; any
      6 anyone/someone; some
      7 anything; someone

72.3 1 any time
      2 Anything
      3 anyone
      4 any bus
      5 any colour
      6 anything
      7 anything

Unit 73

73.1 1 a lot of
      2 many (Also possible: a lot of)
      3 many
      4 a lot of
      5 much/a lot of
      6 many/a lot of
      7 much

73.2 1 plenty of money
      2 lots of cats
      3 plenty of milk
      4 lots of photos

73.3 1 few
      2 little
      3 a little
      4 a few
      5 little
      6 a few

73.4 1 much   4 many
      2 little   5 few
      3 much   6 little

Unit 74

74.1 1 some   4 all
      2 all   5 some
      3 none

74.2 1 She got some of them right.
      2 He got most of them right.
      3 She got all of them right.
      4 He got none of them right.

74.3 1 Most   4 Most of the
      2 all the   5 All
      3 All

311

Key

74.4
1. each
2. each/every
3. every
4. each/every
5. every

74.5
1. all day
2. every morning
3. all morning
4. all Saturday
5. every time

74.6
1. Both of them
2. One of them
3. Both of them
4. One of them
5. Neither of them
6. either of them

74.7
1. some
2. each
3. no
4. both
5. most
6. whole
7. every
8. none

74.8
1. both
2. Neither
3. all
4. every
5. none

Unit 75

75.1
1. the dress
2. Sarah
3. the jeans
4. Helen
5. Helen and Nicola
6. Helen
7. Sue and Neil
8. Gary

75.2
1. she
2. she
3. she
4. them
5. them
6. me/us
7. he
8. They
9. you
10. him
11. you
12. him

75.3
1. We
2. you; us
3. it; it; him; He
4. Me; it
5. she; her
6. I; them; they

75.4
1. You
2. They
3. You
4. they

Unit 76

76.1
1. There's; there'll be/there will be
2. are there; There's been/There has been
3. there'll be/there will be; there won't be/there will not be
4. Is there; There are
5. There was; There was; There were

76.2
1. It was really cheap.
2. It was a friend of yours from college.
3. It's/It is a real nuisance.
4. It's/It is getting quite hot.
5. It's/It is one o'clock.
6. It's/It is important to keep it somewhere safe.

76.3
1. it
2. There
3. It
4. There; It
5. There; It
6. It; there; It; there
7. there; it

Unit 77

77.1
1. himself
2. yourselves
3. themselves
4. itself
5. herself
6. yourself
7. myself
8. ourselves

77.2
1. hurt myself
2. get himself
3. locked ourselves
4. ('ve) bought myself
5. let herself

77.3
1. ourselves
2. you
3. him
4. himself
5. her
6. yourself

Key

77.4
1 make yourself
2 feel
3 worry
4 relax
5 enjoy ourselves

77.5
1 herself   4 himself
2 itself   5 themselves
3 yourself

77.6
1 He cleans them himself.
2 I bake it myself.
3 They grow them themselves.
4 We decorated it ourselves.
5 He types them himself.

77.7
1 each other.
2 thinking about each other.
3 They've got photos of each other.
4 They enjoy each other's company.
5 They're crazy about each other.

77.8
1 each other   4 ourselves
2 each other   5 themselves
3 themselves   6 each other

Unit 78

78.1
1 it's mine. . . . it's got my name on it.
2 it's his. . . . it's got his name on it.
3 they're hers. . . . they've got her name on them.
4 it's yours. . . . it's got your name on it.

78.2
1 Sue's birthday today. She's enjoying herself. And her boyfriend has given her a leather jacket.
2 It's my birthday today. I'm enjoying myself. And my brother has given me a personal stereo.
3 It's the twins' birthday today. They're enjoying themselves. And their parents have given them some cassettes.
4 our birthday today. We're enjoying ourselves. And our friends have bought us a cake.

78.3
1 I   11 I
2 she   12 it
3 it   13 it
4 She   14 it
5 it   15 me
6 She   16 You
7 herself   17 him
8 it   18 I
9 my   19 myself
10 mine   20 they

Unit 79

79.1
1 the big one
2 white ones
3 a second-hand one
4 a cheap one
5 (some) large ones

79.2
1 The one on the left./The small one.
2 The one in the middle./The big one.
3 The one on the right.
4 The small one.

79.3
1 got one.
2 hired one.
3 you seen this one
4 cheapest (one) is £100.
5 made every one.

79.4
1 one   4 them
2 it   5 some
3 one

Unit 80

80.1
1 somewhere; someone/somebody
2 everywhere; nothing
3 something
4 everything; someone/somebody
5 everyone/everybody; no one/nobody

80.2
1 someone   4 anywhere
2 anyone   5 anything
3 somewhere   6 something

80.3
1 their
2 his
3 likes; they
4 it
5 has; their

80.4
1 someone famous   4 something else
2 Someone's car   5 Everyone's opinions
3 Nothing exciting 6 everyone else

Unit 81

81.1 pleasant; ideal; quiet; short; popular; lovely; friendly; helpful; good; free; excellent; local

81.2
1 The only girl
2 The world is asleep.
3 My chief ambition
4 These city streets
5 My heart is content.
6 The night is alive.
7 Inner secrets
8 The outdoor life

Key

81.3
1. powerful Japanese business computer.
2. It's an excellent small electric fire.
3. It's a big new chocolate bar.
4. It's a terrific American television comedy.
5. stylish aluminium garage doors.
6. They're super modern running shoes.
7. It's an attractive blue plastic model.
8. It's a high-quality German car phone.

81.4
1. lovely 19th century glass vase
2. an attractive circular wall mirror
3. a modern office desk
4. four red metal kitchen chairs
5. a splendid old model boat
6. several valuable Australian postage stamps
7. a large mahogany dining table
8. a brown woollen rug

81.5
1. It's asleep.
2. Is it a telephone number?
3. It's an old shopping bag.
4. It's alive.
5. That's the only problem.

81.6
1. The sick
2. the young people
3. the unemployed
4. the poor
5. the old people
6. The homeless
7. the deaf

Unit 82

82.1
1. interested
2. fascinating
3. confused
4. terrified
5. depressing

82.2
1. surprised
2. disappointing
3. puzzled
4. confusing
5. bored
6. interesting

82.3
1. relaxing
2. annoyed
3. amused
4. interesting
5. fascinating
6. thrilled
7. exhausting

Unit 83

83.1
1. afraid of the dark.
2. bored with the video.
3. interested in computers.
4. surprised at/by the news.
5. proud of the/their victory.
6. annoyed with her/the children.
7. satisfied with their/the pay increase.

83.2
1. to
2. for
3. at
4. at
5. for
6. at
7. to

83.3
1. responsible for
2. ready for
3. aware of
4. similar to
5. full of
6. late for
7. famous for

Unit 84

84.1
1. to use the computer.
2. very difficult to understand the handbook.
3. fascinating to work with the computer.
4. easy to operate the keyboard.
5. important to buy the best.
6. be delighted to own a Compex computer.

84.2
1. is very easy to use.
2. handbook isn't very difficult to understand.
3. The computer is fascinating to work with.
4. The keyboard is easy to operate.

84.3
1. difficult for the town to attract new industry.
2. very generous of the Council to give the land to Sanko.
3. impossible for Sanko to refuse the offer.
4. wrong of the Middleton News to criticize the new plan.
5. interesting for (the) local workers to follow Japanese methods.
6. The company is eager for production to begin soon.

Unit 85

85.1
1. slowly
2. carefully
3. politely
4. punctually
5. immediately
6. brightly
7. secretly
8. seriously
9. perfectly
10. fluently

85.2
1. easily; clever
2. happy; sure
3. nice; nice
4. funny; sick
5. properly; dirty; quickly
6. clearly; suddenly

Key

85.3
1 angrily
2 happily
3 automatically
4 publicly
5 enthusiastically
6 reasonably
7 securely
8 simply

85.4
1 free
2 friendly
3 nearly
4 low
5 hardly
6 highly
7 late

85.5
1 well
2 bad
3 good
4 badly
5 well
6 ill

85.6
1 adjective; hair
2 adjective; Pamela
3 adjective; the manager
4 adverb; looked
5 adjective; I
6 adverb; stay
7 adverb; plays
8 adverb; loud

85.7
1 dark
2 terribly
3 badly
4 suddenly
5 unhappy
6 sadly
7 anxious
8 friendly
9 hard
10 foolishly

Unit 86

86.1
1 more intelligent
2 faster
3 more helpful
4 fresher
5 smarter
6 more restful
7 more pleasant/pleasanter

86.2
1 longest
2 most successful
3 most crowded
4 oldest
5 tallest
6 most useful
7 most famous
8 richest

86.3
1 oldest
2 bigger
3 more modern
4 more comfortable
5 most expensive
6 more popular
7 more boring
8 smaller
9 more pleasant/pleasanter
10 more helpful
11 nicer
12 noisiest
13 busiest

86.4
1 more smartly
2 longer
3 later
4 more frequently
5 more carefully
6 louder

86.5
1 further
2 worst
3 better
4 worse
5 best
6 furthest

86.6
1 more convenient
2 driest
3 nicest
4 most beautiful
5 more sensible
6 cheaper
7 better
8 worse

86.7
1 less
2 least
3 more
4 Most

Unit 87

87.1
1 The church is older than the library.
2 Wendy is taller than Tim.
3 The Montero is faster than the Presto.
4 Sadie is more intelligent than Lorraine.
5 Carl is stronger than Simon.

87.2
1 Friday is the busiest day
2 The Bristol is the nicest hotel in the town.
3 This camera is the most expensive (one) (that) you can buy.
4 The latest show is the most successful of all.
5 It's/It was the most boring song I've ever heard.

Key

87.3
1 Japan isn't as big as China.
2 Plastic isn't as strong as metal.
3 A stool isn't as comfortable as an armchair.
4 A pop song isn't as long as a symphony.
5 The moon isn't as hot as the sun.

87.4
1 him
2 I
3 me
4 he

Unit 88

88.1
1 a lot colder
2 a bit longer
3 much more expensive
4 no higher
5 any more reliable
6 slightly earlier

88.2
1 more and more difficult
2 more and more complicated
3 worse and worse
4 higher and higher
5 more and more exhausted

88.3
1 the quieter the roads are.
2 the wider the choice is.
3 the more confused I get.
4 the more fluently you can speak.
5 the more crowded the beaches get.
6 the more useful the computer is.
7 the more serious the problem will become.

Unit 89

89.1
1 luckily
2 never
3 quickly
4 tomorrow
5 inside

89.2
1 degree
2 time
3 manner
4 place
5 manner
6 degree
7 sentence
8 sentence
9 time
10 frequency

89.3
1 will probably rain
2 clearly crossed
3 are always
4 was soon working
5 is usually
6 occasionally visited
7 has obviously forgotten
8 didn't fully understand

89.4
1 I can never open these milk cartons.
2 It usually rains when I'm on holiday. (Also possibl It rains usually when I'm on holiday.)
3 I do fitness training three times a week.
4 My flat mate is at home most evenings.
5 These toilets are inspected every hour.
6 Have you ever been to New York?

89.5
1 regularly since about 1985
2 to Wales last year
3 at Wembley next Wednesday/next Wednesday at Wembley
4 there in June
5 all day by the town hall/by the town hall all day
6 here five years ago

89.6
1 We had a lovely time in London.
2 We arrived home safely at about eight.
3 You must come and visit us before too long.
4 It's always nice to see you and Mike.
5 Maybe you'll be able to come in the New Year.
6 We hope to see you some time.

Unit 90

90.1
1 still; yet
2 still; already
3 yet; already
4 yet; already; still

90.2
1 We've already spent all our money.
2 (But) it still looks dirty.
3 We haven't seen them yet.
4 I still haven't finished it.
5 I'd already guessed.
6 I still can't understand the rules.
7 Have you done your Christmas shopping yet?

90.3
1 still
2 no longer
3 yet
4 any longer/any more
5 already

Unit 91

91.1
1 very
2 quite
3 a bit
4 very
5 a bit
6 quite

Key

91.2
1. That music is a bit loud.
2. I quite like my new job.
3. Why don't you slow down a little?
4. The rain completely spoilt my day./The rain spoilt my day completely.
5. I rather agreed with the speaker.
6. We did the job fairly quickly.
7. I feel a lot better now.
8. I'm getting a bit hungry.
9. We enjoyed the concert very much.
10. The prisoners suffered terribly.

91.3
1. absolutely
2. really
3. just
4. extremely
5. very
6. totally
7. very

Unit 92

92.1
1. quite
2. late
3. easy
4. quite
5. bright
6. quite

92.2
1. rather/quite
2. quite
3. rather/quite
4. rather
5. quite
6. rather (Also possible: quite)

92.3
1. quite/rather
2. rather/quite
3. rather
4. rather
5. quite

92.4
1. completely
2. completely
3. fairly
4. completely
5. fairly
6. fairly
7. completely
8. fairly

Unit 93

93.1
1. loud enough
2. light enough
3. too busy
4. big enough
5. too foggy
6. hard enough
7. sweet enough
8. too far

93.2
1. long enough
2. too expensive
3. enough rain
4. clearly enough
5. too many mistakes
6. old enough
7. too much traffic
8. too complicated
9. enough food

93.3
1. too wet for a picnic/too wet to have a picnic.
2. good enough to be a professional musician?
3. enough chairs for all the guests.
4. too much equipment to carry.
5. too small for tennis/too small to play tennis.
6. too badly hurt to play in the match.

Unit 94

94.1
1. up
2. in/inside
3. above/over
4. along
5. by/beside/next to
6. round/around
7. in front of
8. away from/out of

94.2
1. from
2. past
3. behind
4. below
5. across
6. opposite

94.3
1. under
2. up
3. on
4. around
5. into
6. out of

94.4
1. to
2. outside
3. in/into
4. past
5. off
6. on (top of)
7. at
8. through
9. near
10. among

94.5
1. opposite
2. between
3. opposite
4. between
5. next to

317

Key

Unit 95

95.1
1 in the car.
2 on the roof.
3 at the dance.
4 in the bath.
5 at the lights.

95.2
1 at the filling-station
2 at the zoo
3 in the theatre
4 in the restaurant
5 at the bus station

95.3
1 in
2 on
3 in
4 at
5 at
6 at
7 on
8 on
9 in
10 at

Unit 96

96.1
1 on
2 in
3 at
4 on
5 in
6 in
7 on
8 at

96.2
1 at four o'clock.
2 on Friday.
3 in June.
4 in the summer holiday?
5 yesterday afternoon.
6 at lunch time
7 every day.
8 on Thursday evening.
9 at night.
10 in the night.
11 at the weekend.
12 on New Year's Day.

96.3
1 in time   4 in time
2 in time   5 on time
3 on time

96.4
1 in   4 in
2 on   5 in
3 on   6 on; in

Unit 97

97.1
1 for
2 since
3 for
4 since
5 for

97.2
1 played (it) since
2 rung her since
3 seen them for
4 watched one for
5 written to them for
6 had one since

97.3
1 since four o'clock
2 ten years ago
3 since Tuesday
4 six weeks ago
5 for five years
6 eight months ago
7 for three weeks

97.4
1 ago   3 before
2 before   4 ago

Unit 98

98.1
1 during
2 while
3 while
4 during
5 while
6 during

98.2
1 by
2 until
3 until
4 by
5 by

98.3
1 as
2 like
3 as
4 as/like
5 like
6 as
7 as
8 as
9 like
10 as/like

98.4
1 as if
2 as
3 as if
4 as
5 as if

318

Key

Unit 99

99.1
1. in
2. on
3. from
4. in
5. by
6. in
7. on; on
8. in; by
9. on
10. on
11. in
12. by
13. on
14. In

99.2
1. by credit card; in cash
2. out of date; up to date
3. on purpose; by chance
4. on television; on the radio
5. for sale; on the market
6. In my opinion; at the end

99.3
1. on
2. by
3. in
4. on
5. in
6. on
7. by

Unit 100

100.1
1. damage to
2. way of
3. answer to
4. cause of
5. tax on
6. difficulty over/with
7. matter with

100.2
1. of
2. with
3. of
4. of
5. in
6. for
7. with
8. for
9. between

100.3
1. of
2. of
3. in
4. in
5. at

100.4
1. for
2. for
3. to
4. in
5. on
6. for
7. for

Unit 101

101.1
1. for
2. at
3. after
4. into

101.2
1. pay for
2. ask for
3. care about
4. caring for
5. suffering from
6. decided on
7. concentrate on
8. agree with

101.3
1. listening to
2. apologized for
3. reached
4. laughing at
5. believed in
6. left

101.4
1. of
2. to
3. about
4. to
5. to
6. about
7. of

Unit 102

102.1
1. on
2. into
3. as
4. with/to
5. to
6. to
7. with

102.2
1. water to wine!
2. you for the accident!
3. didn't thank you for the present!
4. accusing the headmaster of murder!
5. didn't provide you with towels!
6. didn't invite you to her wedding!
7. congratulated them on their (great) victory!

102.3
1. about
2. of
3. to
4. to
5. about/of
6. about/of
7. about

Key

Unit 103

103.1
1. stay in
2. pay ... back
3. fall down
4. Come in
5. cut out
6. give ... away
7. get in
8. take ... back
9. go away

103.2
1. left out
2. given out
3. throw away
4. put off
5. made up
6. go on/carry on

103.3
1. picks ... up
2. take off/take ... off
3. ring ... up
4. hand in/hand ... in
5. win back
6. look ... up
7. held up
8. mixing ... up

103.4
1. completely
2. away/disappearing
3. continuing
4. from start to finish
5. aloud
6. disconnected
7. away/departing
8. decreasing
9. completely to the ground
10. completely
11. to different people
12. increasing

103.5
1. down
2. on; off
3. out; out
4. down; out
5. on; out; on/along
6. out; up

103.6
1. write it down
2. show him round
3. laugh at it
4. wash them up
5. listen to it
6. call for her

Unit 104

104.1
1. down on
2. out into
3. up at
4. away from
5. through to
6. out at
7. in from

104.2
1. run out of
2. send away for
3. look/watch out for
4. look forward to
5. keep up with
6. put up with
7. get on with
8. go back on
9. get on to
10. make up for
11. go in for
12. cut down on
13. fall back on
14. get round to

Unit 105

105.1
1. she can't sleep.
2. he's hurt his back.
3. she feels sick all the time.
4. He says someone punched him in the face.
5. He says he fell down and hurt himself.

105.2
1. tell   5. tell
2. say   6. tell
3. say   7. tell
4. say   8. say

Unit 106

106.1
1. she   3. he
2. you   4. you, her

106.2
1. the next day
2. the day before
3. that day
4. here
5. the week before

106.3
1. was
2. was
3. is (Also possible: was)
4. is (Also possible: was)
5. was
6. is (Also possible: was)
7. was (Also possible: is)
8. was

106.4
1. you had finished it / your project.
2. you were better at golf (than tennis).
3. you didn't enjoy parties / them.
4. you didn't have / you hadn't got a video recorder.
5. you weren't applying for it / for the job.
6. you liked Chinese food more (than Indian food).

106.5
1. the production was brilliant.
2. Stephen Devine said he couldn't remember a funnier show.
3. Ben Walsh said it (had) made him laugh.
4. The Evening News said you / people had to see it. (Also possible: . . . you / people must see it.)
5. The Telegraph said it would be a great success.
6. The Daily Express said you / people might die laughing.
7. Joan Proctor said it was the funniest show she had ever seen.
8. Time Out said you / people shouldn't miss it.

Unit 107

107.1
1. how she can find out about the town.
2. if / whether there are guided tours.
3. where they can stay.
4. wants to know which way the castle is.
5. wants to know what shows there are.
6. want to know when the festival starts.

107.2
1. Do you know if / whether I can park here?
2. Could you tell me how long the film lasts?
3. Do you know how often the buses go?
4. Do you know if / whether we're allowed to smoke?
5. Could you tell me what time the flight is?
6. Could you tell me how much a ticket costs?

107.3
1. why he wanted the job.
2. how he (had) heard about it.
3. if / whether he was fit.
4. if / whether he could work on Saturdays.
5. how he would travel to work.
6. if / whether he had (got) a bicycle.
7. how much he expected to earn.
8. when he could start.

Unit 108

108.1
1. They tell you to get some exercise.
2. They tell you not to eat sweet things.
3. They tell you to relax sometimes.
4. They tell you to find time for a hobby.
5. They tell you not to smoke.
6. They tell you not to drink a lot of alcohol.

108.2
1. Martin to see a doctor.
2. causing so much trouble.
3. going out for the day.
4. to do the washing-up.
5. to post the letter.
6. making a mistake.
7. Mike not to touch the electric wires.

108.3
1. The builders have promised that everything will be ready on time.
2. The boss insists that we have to check everything carefully.
3. Jill admitted that her story wasn't completely true.
4. Ted reminded me that my train was about to leave.

Unit 109

109.1
1. the young man at the door
2. the boy who sings in a pop group
3. the very thin woman
4. the girl with green eyes
5. the well dressed young lady
6. the man who works here

109.2
1. that / which
2. who / that
3. who / that
4. that / which
5. that / which
6. who / that

109.3
1. that / which went off this morning caused a lot of damage.
2. The scientist who discovered a new planet has won the Nobel Prize.
3. The strike that / which closed Britain's docks is over.
4. The footballer who took drugs has been banned from playing again.
5. The little girl who had been missing since Tuesday has been found safe and well.
6. The oil that / which spilled from a tanker is five miles off the Scottish coast.

Unit 110

110.1
1. that was chasing the sheep has been shot.
2. that upset everyone was untrue.
3. who rang Lola is a film producer.
4. who Angela knows is a millionaire.
5. that Peter broke was extremely valuable.
6. that you wore last night is really nice.

Key

110.2 1 the car you can afford.
       2 the film people want to see.
       3 the chocolates you'll enjoy.
       4 the cleaner you can trust.
       5 the magazine clever people read.

110.3 1 From here you can see the mountain (that/which) we climbed.
       2 The man who/that services my car is a keen fisherman.
       3 The detective lost the man (who/that) he was following.
       4 I thought I recognized the assistant who/that sold me the suit.

Unit 111

111.1 1 That's the tent (that/which) I slept in.
       2 That's the hill (that/which) we walked up.
       3 This is the beach (that/which) we had a view of.
       4 That's the boat (that/which) Alex and I went out in.
       5 This is the harbour (that/which) we sailed from.
       6 This is the island (that/which) we landed on.
       7 This is the museum (that/which) I went to.
       8 These are the people (who/that) we got friendly with.

111.2 1 A sofa bed is a piece of furniture (that/which) you can either sit or sleep on.
       2 A drill is a tool (that/which) you can make holes with.
       3 A destination is the place (that/which) someone travels to.
       4 A corridor is a passage (that/which) people walk along.
       5 A microphone is an instrument (that/which) people speak into.
       6 A safe is a cupboard (that/which) we keep valuable things in.

111.3 1 That is an idea in which our party believes.
       2 That is a policy to which I am strongly opposed.
       3 These are people about whom no one cares.
       4 Those are mistakes of which your party should be ashamed.
       5 That is a problem with which the government is dealing.

Unit 112

112.1 1 Brian is the journalist whose tape-recorder was stolen.
       2 Steve is the architect who knew Howard at school.
       3 Rex is the farmer whose land Howard bought.
       4 Louise is the model whose name was in Howard's diary.
       5 Mark is the lawyer who looked after Howard's interests.

112.2 1 What you have to think about is your profits.
       2 What you must get is good financial advice.
       3 What you should work towards is a realistic target.
       4 What you need to do is (to) plan ahead.

112.3 1 Columbus sailed to America.
       2 It was golf that Jack Nicklaus played.
       3 It was in Greece that the Olympic Games began.
       4 It's Mount McKinley that is the highest mountain in the USA.
       5 It's Mercury that is nearest the sun.

Unit 113

113.1 1 It adds information about the college theatre.
       2 It tells us which people.
       3 It adds information about Lucy Kellett.
       4 It tells us which young man.
       5 It adds information about the evening.

113.2 1 which
       2 who
       3 whose
       4 whom (Also possible: who)
       5 who
       6 which

113.3 1 Bob and Cheryl, whom/who you met last year, were here all last week.
       2 They're now running a computer software business, which is doing very well.
       3 Cheryl, who studied programming at college, writes the programs.
       4 Bob, whose subject was business studies, handles the financial side.
       5 He explained it all to Martin, who isn't very interested in business.
       6 On Saturday we went to a Chinese restaurant, which someone had recommended.

Key

113.4
1 who is a bit deaf, couldn't hear the phone.
2 St Michael's Church, which dates from the 14th century, is a fine building.
3 The person whose suitcase got lost was Colin.
4 The road that/which leads to the farm isn't suitable for cars.
5 Our teacher, who lives ten miles away, stayed at home during the bus strike.
6 Diamond, which is a very hard substance, is used for cutting.
7 The person who got everything ready was Kevin.
8 The person who knows all about it is the secretary.
9 Mandy, whose name was missed off the list, wasn't very pleased.

113.5
1 It poured with rain all day, which left the ground very wet.
2 My brother is disabled, which means he can't get about very easily.
3 Jessica's mother paid for the meal, which was very kind of her.
4 You left the keys in the car, which was rather careless of you.
5 Miranda has lost her job, which has made her very depressed.
6 The police blocked off the road, which caused a traffic jam.
7 Jeremy didn't answer my letter, which was very rude of him.

Unit 114

114.1
1 played   6 added
2 worn   7 blocking
3 arriving   8 smuggled
4 telling
5 watching

114.2
1 living in an empty office building have been turned out.
2 employing four thousand people has gone bankrupt.
3 built only two years ago has been declared unsafe.
4 sent from Europe has not reached those who really need it.
5 protesting against nuclear power have marched to London.
6 hoping to buy tickets have been queuing all night at Wimbledon.

114.3
1 to swim a length of the pool.
2 the only people/employees to get a pay rise.
3 The captain was the last person to leave the ship.
4 Mrs Harper is the first woman to become President.

Unit 115

115.1
1 If Neil fails the exam, he can take it again.
2 If the cat dies, Alex will be upset.
3 If the office is closed, we won't be able to get in.
4 If I arrive a bit early, I can help you get things ready.
5 If the celebrations go on a long time, we can leave early.
6 If you lose the cheques, you'll need to phone this number.
7 If the parcel arrives today, you'll have to sign for it.
8 If the picture is valuable, we can sell it.
9 If you ask for a pay rise, you'll probably get one.
10 If Steve enters the competition, I'm sure he'll win.

115.2
1 it'll be   5 won't be
2 I ask   6 share
3 are going   7 I see
4 it's   8 I'll ask

115.3
1 The phone isn't working.
2 It might rain.
3 We might meet at seven.
4 This spoon isn't silver.
5 Richard might call.

115.4
1 If Barbara hadn't gone to bed late, she wouldn't have overslept.
2 If it had been warm enough, we would have sat outside.
3 If you hadn't forgotten the map, we wouldn't have lost our way.
4 Gary could have played basketball if he hadn't been ill.
5 I wouldn't have noticed the mistake if I hadn't checked the figures.
6 If Wayne hadn't been wearing a crash helmet, I would have recognized him.
7 If someone had watered the flowers, they wouldn't have died.

Key

115.5
1 played
2 wouldn't hear
3 had known/'d known
4 wouldn't have let
5 didn't play
6 wouldn't be
7 would have thrown/'d have thrown
8 go
9 will complain/'ll complain

Unit 116

116.1
1 When it rings,
2 If I feel better,
3 When it finishes,
4 When I take it,
5 If it doesn't work,

116.2
1 unless it's a nice day.
2 unless you're watching it.
3 unless we get (some) help.
4 unless I use an alarm clock.
5 unless I liked it.

116.3
1 unless   4 unless
2 if   5 if
3 unless

116.4
1 We'd better book a table in case the restaurant is full.
2 You ought to insure your jewellery in case it gets stolen.
3 I'm watching this saucepan in case the water boils over.
4 I'll leave you my phone number in case you want to contact me.

Unit 117

117.1
1 I wish you'd hurry up.
2 I wish you'd do the washing-up.
3 I wish you'd tell me the whole story.
4 I wish you wouldn't blow cigarette smoke in my face.
5 I wish you'd tell me what you're thinking.
6 I wish you wouldn't (always) leave the door open.
7 I wish you'd leave me alone.

117.2
1 I wish/If only I wasn't so tired.
2 I wish/If only I could sleep.
3 I wish/If only I had enough/more energy.
4 I wish/If only it wasn't so dull.
5 I wish/If only they were going well/better.
6 I wish/If only I could concentrate.
7 I wish/If only I had a friend/some friends.

117.3
1 I had caught it.
2 he had stayed.
3 she had accepted (it).
4 we had kept it.
5 I had found it.
6 they had won.
7 he could have played.

Unit 118

118.1
1 but it's really quite modern.
2 but no one laughed.
3 but he never uses them.
4 but I still don't understand it.

118.2
1 Although the house looks old, it's really quite modern.
2 Although the joke was funny, no one laughed.
3 Although Mike has some skis, he never uses them.
4 Although Phil explained the system, I still don't understand it.

118.3
1 Although   4 in spite of
2 in spite of   5 In spite of
3 although   6 in spite of

118.4
1 Max didn't notice the sign even though it was right in front of him.
2 Kate never learnt Spanish although she lived in Spain for years.
3 Despite being a millionaire, Joe hates spending money.
4 A few trains were running in spite of the strike. (Also possible: ... in spite of there being a strike.)
5 We couldn't get a seat in spite of arriving early.

Unit 119

119.1
1 to go to sleep.   4 to make some tea.
2 to get some petrol.   5 to buy a car.
3 to look smart.

119.2
1 He's going to get to work earlier in order to/so as to impress the boss.
2 He's going to work harder in order to/so as to achieve more.
3 He's going to take regular exercise in order to/so as to keep fit and alert.
4 He's going to think positively in order not to/so as not to miss any opportunities.

119.3 1 Tom put the cream in the fridge to keep it cool.
2 Pamela wore boots so that her feet wouldn't get wet.
3 I'm going on a diet to lose weight.
4 We often switch off the heating to save money.
5 We all sat down for a rest.
6 Mark is going to repair the roof so that the rain won't come in.

Unit 120

120.1 1 I'll love you until I die.
2 I hear music when I see you.
3 Come home before it's too late.
4 I've been sad since you left.
5 I fell in love as soon as we met.

120.2 1 Although
2 (in order) to
3 because
4 If
5 but
6 so
7 unless
8 In spite of
9 so that
10 in case

120.3 1 so
2 to
3 before
4 after
5 but
6 if
7 unless
8 since
9 in spite of
10 because

Index

The numbers in this index are unit numbers, not page numbers.

a/an 62
   in general statements 63A
   a cake or **cake** 58A
   a coffee etc. 58D
   with **quite**, **such** and **what** 66
a bit 91
able to 28B, C
about (*talk about*) 101C, 102C
about to 17D
above 94
across 94
action verbs 3
   + adverb (*looked carefully*) 85B
active and passive 37, 38
adding clauses 113
adjective 81–88
   adjective or adverb 85
   adjectives ending in **ly** (*friendly*) 85D
   order of adjectives 81E
   adjective used as a noun (*the rich*) 81F
   adjective after **something** (*something nice*) 80D
   comparison (*taller, tallest*) 86
   adjective + preposition (*full of*) 83
   adjective + preposition + ing-form (*bored with sitting*) 48D, 49, 50
   adjective + to-infinitive 84
   adjective + **for** + object + to-infinitive 47
adverbial 56
   adverbial phrases 89
adverbs 85–93
   types 89
   word order 89
   adverb or adjective 85
   comparison (*more quickly, most quickly*) 86D, E
   adverbs of degree (*very, quite* etc.) 91–93
   changes in reported speech 106A
   verb + adverb (*sit down*) 103
advice (mass) 57D
a few 73C
afraid to do or **afraid of doing** 49
after
   linking word (*after I left*) 120A
   + ing-form (*after leaving*) 51B
ago 97C, D
agreement between subject and verb 59
a little 73C, 91B
all 74
   with a plural verb 59B
allow + ing-form 44E
allowed to 29C

along 94
a lot 91B
   + comparative (*a lot cheaper*) 88A
a lot of 73A,B
already 90
   with present perfect 6B
although 118
   + ing-form (*although knowing …*) 51B
always 89E
   with present continuous and simple 2D
American English page 288
among 94
amount + singular verb 59E
and with comparatives (*faster and faster*) 88B
answering questions 25
anxious to do or **anxious about doing** 49B
any
   any and **some** 72
   anyone, anything etc. 80
   anyone or **someone** 72A
   any of + singular or plural verb 59D
   any longer, any more 90D
apostrophe + **s** 71
around 94, American English K
articles 62–67 see also **a/an** and **the**
as
   preposition 98C
   in comparisons (*as tall as*) 87C
   linking word (*as I left*) 120A
as a result of 51A
as if 98C
as soon as 120A
as well as 51A
ashamed to do or **ashamed of doing** 49B
at
   place (*at the door*) 95
   time (*at half past two*) 96
   at the end 99A
   skill at 100E
away from 94

be (past tense) 5A
be able to 28B, C
be about to 17D
be allowed to 29C
be going to 13A, B, 14
be supposed to 34C
be to (*it is to take place*) 17D
be used to 50C
because 120D
been to and **gone to** 4D
before
   linking word (*before I leave*) 120A

Index

+ ing-form (*before leaving*) 51B
before and **ago** 97E
behind 94
being done 41
below 94
beside 94
besides 51A
best 86E
better 86E
   had better 34B
between 94
   connection between 100C
a bit 91
bit of with mass nouns 57D
both 74E
but 118A
by
   place (*by the window*) 94
   time (*by the weekend*) 98B
   by car 99B
   by + *ing-form* (*by shouting*) 51A
   with the passive 38B

can
   ability 28A
   permission 29
   in a requests, offers and suggestions 33
   after **so that** 119C
can't (*it can't be true*) 30C
can't have been 35C
certainly 89F
changes in reported speech 106
clothes etc. (plural nouns) 60A
collective nouns (group nouns) 61B
comparative
   forms (*faster, fastest*) 86
   patterns (*than, as* etc.) 87
   after **much** etc. 88A
   faster and faster 88B
   the faster the better 88C
complement 56
conditional clauses (if-clauses) 115
conjunction see linking word
contracted forms 20
could
   ability 28C
   possibility 30A, B
   in requests 33A
   after **so that** 119C
   after **wish** 117B, C
could have been 35B
   after **wish** 117C
count nouns and mass nouns 57, 58

deep 85E
defining relative clauses see identifying clauses
definite article see **the**
degree adverbs (*very, quite* etc.) 91–93
demonstratives (*this, that, these, those*) 69
despite 51A, 118C
determiner 55
   possessive determiner (*my, your* etc.) 70
did, didn't (past simple) 5B, 21B, 22B, 26B
didn't need to 32C
different + preposition American English K
direct and indirect objects 68
direct and indirect speech 105
do (present simple) 1B, 22B, 26B
do the shopping 52
does, doesn't (present simple) 1B, 21B, 22B, 26B
don't (present simple) 1B, 21B, 26B
don't have to 32B
don't need to 32B
down
   down the hill 94
   after a verb (*knock down*) 103D
during 98A

each 74A, C
   + singular verb 59B
each other 77E
early 85E
ed adjective and **ing** adjectives 82
either 74E
   either of + singular or plural verb 59D
elder, eldest 86E
else (*something else*) 80D
emphasis with **what** and with **it** + **be** 112B, C
emphatic pronouns (*myself* etc.) 77D
empty subject (*you, they*) 38C
enough 47C
   enough and **too** 93
even though 118B
ever (with present perfect or past simple) 6D
every 74A, C
   + singular verb 59B
everyone, everything etc. 80
exciting and **excited** 82

far, farther, farthest 86E
fast 85E
few 73C
for
   time (*for three days*) 97
   with present perfect 6C
   with present perfect continuous 8B
   in indirect-object pattern (*buy it for you*) 68

327

Index

purpose 47B, 51A, 119D
for + object + to-infinitive 47, 84C
for or **of** after an adjective 47D
after **too** and **enough** 93C
need for 100F
free and **freely** 85F
a friend of mine 70E
from 94
in front of 94
further, furthest 86E

general statements with **a/an** and **the** 63
gerund see ing-form
get
  the passive with **get** 37C
  get something done 40
give + objects 68
  passive patterns 39A
go on + to-infinitive or ing-form 43C
go shopping 52
going to (future) 13A, B, 14
gone to and **been to** 4D
good and **well** 85G
good at, good for and **good to** 83B
good of and **good for** 47D
gotten American English M
group nouns 61B, American English G

had
  possession (*I had a pen*) 18
  had done 10
  had been doing 11
  had to 31
  had better 34B
hard 85E
  hard and **hardly** 85F
have
  possession (*I have a pen*) 18, American English C
  have got 18
  action verb (*I have lunch*) 19
  have done 4
  have been doing 8
  have to 31, 32B
  have got to 31C
  have something done 40
  have something happen 40D
having done 54B
he 75
help + infinitive 44C
her
  possessive (*her book*) 70
  pronoun (*I saw her*) 75
hers 70

herself 77
high 85E
  high and **highly** 85F
him 75
himself 77
his 70
how 22C
how about + ing-form 51A

I (pronoun) 75
identifying clauses 113
idioms
  preposition + noun 99
  prepositional verbs 101, 102
  phrasal verbs 103
  verb + adverb + preposition 104
  with reflexive pronouns 77C
if 115
  if and **when** 116A
  if and **unless** 116B
  if and **in case** 116C
  if only 117A
  if in reported questions 107A
  with **any** 72A
in
  place (*in the house*) 95
  in and **into** 94
  time (*in June*) 96
  idioms with **in** 99A
  in time 96B
  in the end 99A
  increase in 100D
  interest in 100E
  after a superlative 87B
in case 116C
in favour of 51A
in front of 94
in order to 119B
in spite of 51A, 118C
indefinite article see **a/an**
indirect object 68
  with **say/tell** 105C
  as subject of a passive sentence 39A
indirect speech see reported speech
infinitive 45 see also to-infinitive
infinitive without **to** 45
  see it happen 53
information (mass noun) 57D
ing adjectives and **ed** adjectives 82
ing-form
  after a verb (*enjoy watching*) 42, 43
  after **need** 41B
  after **go** and **do** 52

328

Index

after a preposition 48–51
in a relative clause (*the people watching*) 114A
other patterns (e.g. *sit watching television*) 54
see it happening 53
passive (*being done*) 41
inside 94
instead of 51A
into 94
intonation with question tags 26A
inverted commas 105A
irregular verbs page 292, American English L
it 75, 76B
it and **there** 76C
it + **be** + adjective + to-infinitive 45A
it + **be** + relative clause 112C
it is said ... 39B
item of with mass noun 57D
its and **it's** 70B
itself 77

just
with present perfect 4C, 6B
adverb of degree (*I just know*) 91B
just as 13B

late 85E
late and **lately** 85F
less, least 86F
let + object + infinitive 45B
like
+ to-infinitive or ing-form 43B
like and **would like** 43B
like and **as** 98C
linking verbs (*be, seem* etc.) 56B, 81B, 85B, American English F
linking words 115–120
+ ing-form (*before leaving*) 51
a little 73C, 91B
live (continuous or simple) 9B
long 85E
any longer 90D
a lot 91B
+ comparative (*a lot better*) 88A
a lot of 73A, B
agreement with verb 59 C
lots of 73A, B
low 85E
ly ending 85C

make + objective + infinitive 45B
many 73A, B
too many 93B
mass nouns and count nouns 57–58

mass nouns and **the** 63B
may
permission 29
possibility 30A, B
may have been 35B
me 75
mean + to-infinitive or ing-form 43C
means (singular and plural) 60C
meet (with) American English K
might 30A, B
might have been 35A
mind in requests 33A
mine 70
modal verbs 28–36
with the perfect (*may have been*) 35
in the passive 37B
in reported speech 106D
more 86F
+ adjective (*more exciting*) 86A, B
+ adverb (*more easily*) 86D
most 74A, B, 86F
+ adjective (*most exciting*) 86A, B
+ adverb (*most easily*) 86D
much 73A, B, 91B
too much 93B
+ comparative (*much better*) 88A
must 31A, B
logical **must** 30C
must have been 35C
mustn't and **needn't** 32A
my 70
myself 77

names and **the** 67
near 85E, 94
near and **nearly** 85F
need + to-infinitive or ing-form 41B, 43C
needn't and **mustn't** 32A, American English E
needn't have 32C
negative statements 21
neither 74E
+ singular or plural verb 59D
neither do I 27A
news
mass noun 57D
+ singular verb 60B
next to 94
no
no and **not** 21C
no and **none** 74F
no longer 90D
no one 80
non-defining relative clauses see adding clauses

Index

none 74F
   + singular or plural verb 59D
nor 27A
not 21
   I hope not 27B
nothing 80
nouns
   possessive form 71
   count and mass 57, 58
   agreement with verbs 59
   with a plural form (*clothes*) 60
   pair nouns 61
   group nouns 61
   noun + preposition 100
   used as adjectives 81D
   + to-infinitive (*a book to read*) 45A
a number of + plural verb 59C

object 56
   direct and indirect object 68
   with **say/tell** 105C
   object of a phrasal verb 103A
   relative pronoun as object 110
object pronouns 75
of
   the name of the boy 71
   a friend of mine 70E
   all of, some of etc. 74
   a glass of water 57C
   after a superlative (*best of all*) 87B
   student of 100E
   increase of 100D
   hear of 101C
   inform someone of something 102C
   good of and **good for** 47D, 84C
off
   in phrasal verbs (*switch off*) 103D
offers 33B, 36B, C
   with **some** 72A
   reported offers 108B
often 89E
on
   place (*on the floor*) 95
   on and **onto** 94
   time (*on Tuesday*) 96
   idioms with **on** 99
   on foot 99B
   on time 96B
   on leaving 51A
   in phrasal verbs (*carry on*) 103D
on top of 94
one
   one and **a/an** 62E

one of + singular verb 59C
   pronoun (= people in general) 38C, 75C, American English J
   one/ones 79
one another 77E
opposite 94
order of adjectives 81E
in order to 119B
ought to 34A
ought to have been 35D
our, ours 70
ourselves 77
out (*read out*) 103D
out of 94, American English K
outside 94
over 94
   in phrasal verbs (*think it over*) 103D
own (*my own*) 70D

pair nouns 61A
participles 54
   passive participle 37
   in relative clauses 114
parts of speech 55
passive 37–41
   passive verb tenses 37
   passive with **get** 37C
   special patterns 39
   passive to-infinitive and ing-form 41
past
   past the house 94
   ten past four American English K
past continuous (*was doing*) 7
   was doing and **had been doing** 11C
past perfect (*had done*) 10
   had done and **had been doing** 11C
   in if-clauses 115D
   after **wish** 117C
past perfect continuous (*had been doing*) 11
past simple (*did*) 5, 6
   did and **have done** 6
   did and **was doing** 7B
   did and **had done** 10C
   in if-clauses 115C
   after **wish** 117B
past tense of **have** 18
people
   + plural verb 61C
   empty subject 38C
perfect ing-form (*having done*) 54B, C
perfect with modal verbs (*might have done*) 35
phonetic symbols page 7
phrasal verbs 103

Index

phrasal-prepositional verbs (*catch up with*) 104
phrases 56
phrases of time
    without **a/an** or **the** (*on Thursday*) 65
    with the possessive (*today's paper*) 71C
piece of with mass noun 57D
place names and **the** 67
plenty of 73B
plural nouns and **the** 63B
plural or singular verb 59
plural or singular noun 60
police + plural 61C
possessive form of a noun 71
possessives (*my, your; mine*) 70
prepositional phrases 56
prepositional verbs 101
prepositions 94–104
    place 94, 95
    time 96, 97, 98
    in questions 22D
    in relative clauses 111
    preposition + noun (idioms) 99
    preposition + ing-form 48–51
    verb + preposition 101
    verb + object + preposition 102
    verb + adverb + preposition 104
    adjective + preposition (*full of*) 83
    noun + preposition 100
present continuous (*are doing*) 1A, 2
    are doing and **do** 2
    for the future 15A
present perfect (*have done*) 4, 6, American English A
    have done and **did** 6
    have done and **have been doing** 9
    have done and **had done** 10B
present perfect continuous (*have been doing*) 8
    have been doing and **have done** 9
present simple (*do*) 1B, 2
    do and **are doing** 2
    for the future 15B, C
    in if-clauses 115B
present tenses for the future 15
probably 89F
pronouns
    personal pronouns (*I, you*) 75
    this etc. 69
    mine etc. 70
    reflexive 77
    emphatic pronouns 77D
    one, ones 79
    everyone etc. 80
    review of pronouns and possessives 78

purpose
    with to-infinitive 119A, D
    with **for** 47B, 51A, 119D
quantifiers 72–74
    some and **any** 72
    many etc. 73
    all, most etc. 74
    comparison (*more*) 86F
questions 22
    question words 22C
    who, what and **which** 224
    question word + infinitive (*what to do*) 46
    subject/object questions 23
    reported questions 107
question tags 26, American English D
quite 91
    quite and **rather** 92
    quite a 66A
quotation marks 105A

rather 91B
    quite and **rather** 92
reflexive pronouns 77
regret + to-infinitive or ing-form 43C
relative clauses 109–114
    use 109A, 113
    who, which and **that** 109
    with pronoun as object 110
    leaving out the pronoun 110B
    with a preposition 111
    with **whose** 112
    with **what** and **it** 112
    with participles (*people arriving early*) 114
    after a superlative (*the best I've seen*) 87B
    after **all** 74B
remember + to-infinitive or ing-form 43C
remind + **of** or **about** 102C
reported speech 105–108
    introduction 105
    tense change 106
    reported questions 107
    reported requests, offers etc. 108
    It is said ... 39B
    He is said to ... 39C
requests 33A
    with **some** 72A
    reported requests 108A
as a result of 51A
right 85E
round 94, American English K

said
    It is said ... 39B

Index

He is said to ... 39C
say and **tell** 105C
see it happen/happening 53
sentence adverbs 89F
shall
    future 13D, American English B
    offers and suggestions 33B, C, 36C, American English B
she 75
short answers 25
short forms 20
should 34A, 36C
    in first person 36A
should have been 35D
simple past see past simple
simple present see present simple
since 97
    with present perfect 6C
    with present perfect continuous 8B
    + ing-form (*since leaving*) 51B
    linking word (*since I left*) 120A
singular or plural noun 60
singular or plural verb 59
so
    so + adjective 66B
    in comparisons (*not so good as*) 87C
    so do I 27A
    I think so 27B
    linking word 120D
so as to 119B
so that 119C
some 72A, 74A, B
    some and **a/an** 62A
    some and **any** 72
someone, something etc. 80
    someone (empty subject) 38C
    someone and **anyone** 72A
sometimes 89E
sorry to do and **sorry about doing** 49C
spelling
    of comparative and superlative forms 86C
    of adverbs 85C
in spite of 51A, 118C
state verbs 3
still 90
stop + to-infinitive or ing-form 43C
straight 85E
stress
    with **quite** 92B
    with prepositional and phrasal verbs 103E
subject 56
    subject/object questions 23
    subject pronouns 75

subject-verb agreement 59
such a 66B
suggestions 33C, 36C
superlative 86
    patterns (*the oldest in the world*) 87
    + to-infinitive (*the youngest player to win*) 114B
supposed to 34C

tag questions 26, American English D
tell and **say** 105C
tense change in reported speech 106B
tenses see verb tenses
than 86A, 87A
    + pronoun (*than me / than I am*) 87D
that
    that house 69
    that on the phone American English I
    in reported speech 105B, 108C
    relative pronoun 109, 110A
    so that 119C
the 62, 63B, C
    with place names 67
    go to school etc. without **the** 64
    on **Thursday** etc. without **the** 65
    by the arm 70C
    the + adjective (*the rich*) 81F
    the + comparative (*the faster the better*) 88C
    the + superlative (*the tallest*) 87B
their, theirs 70
them 75
themselves 77
there is 76
    there is something to do/to be done 41B
these 69
they 75
    general meaning 38C
this 69
    this week etc. with present perfect and past simple 6E
    this on the phone American English I
those 69
though 118B
through 94
    = until American English K
till 98B
time phrases
    with **in, on** and **at** 96
    without **a/an** or **the** 65
    with the possessive (*today's paper*) 71C
time words 120A
to
    movement (*to the office*) 94
    time (*five to six*) American English K

Index

 in indirect-object pattern (*give it to me*) 68
 an answer to 100B
 talk to 101C
 to do see to-infinitive
 to be done 41
to-infinitive 45A
 after an adjective (*safe to use*) 84
 after **too** and **enough** 93B
 after a verb (*want to go*) 42, 43
 after verb + object (*want you to go*) 44
 after **for** + object 47, 84C
 to do and **of doing** 49
 to do and **to doing** 50
 be to (*it is to take place*) 17D
 after a question word (*what to do*) 46
 pattern with **it** (*it's nice to see you*) 76B
 in a relative clause (*the first to arrive*) 114B
 infinitive of purpose 119A
 passive (**to be done**) 41
today with present perfect and past simple 6E
too (*too big*) 93B
towards 94, American English K
travel (mass noun) 57D
try + to-infinitive or ing-form 43C

uncountable nouns see mass nouns
under 94
unless 116B
until 98B
 linking word 120A
up 94
 in phrasal verbs (*eat up*) 103D
us 75
used to do and **used to doing** 50C

verb tenses 1–20
 review of present and past 12
 review of future 17
 active and passive 37A
verb + adverb 103
verb + adverb + preposition 104
verb + **for** + object + to-infinitive 47
verb + object + preposition 102
verb + object + preposition + ing-form 48C
verb + object + infinitive without **to** 45B, 53
verb + object + ing-form 53
verb + object + to-infinitive 44
verb + preposition 101
verb + preposition + ing-form 48B
verb + to-infinitive or ing-form 42, 43
verbs of perception (*see*, *hear* etc.) 53
very 91
very much 91

want someone to do something 44D
was 5A
was able to 28C
was allowed to 29C
was doing 7
was going to 13B
we 75
well 85G
as well as 51A
were 5A
were doing 7
wh-questions 22B
what 24
 what as subject/object 23A
 what in a question phrase 22C
 what + **a/an** 66C
 relative pronoun **what** 112B
what about + ing-form 51A
when
 question word 22C
 linking word (*when they leave*) 120A
 + ing-form (*when leaving*) 51B
 when and **if** 116A
where (question word) 22C
whether
 in a reported question 107A
 + to-infinitive 46C
which 24
 which as subject/object 23B
 relative pronoun **which** 109, 110A
 which standing for a whole sentence 113D
while 98A, 120A
 + ing-form (*while driving*) 51B
who 24
 who as subject/object 23A
 relative pronoun **who** 109, 110
whole 74D
whom 110C, 111B
whose
 question word 22C
 whose as subject/object 23B
 relative pronoun **whose** 112A
why 22C
will 13C, 14
 in offers 33B, 36B
 with an if-clause 115B
 after **so that** 119C
will be able to 28B
will be allowed to 29C
will be doing 16A, B
will have done 16C
wish 117

333

Index

with
  trouble with 100B
  connection with 100C
without (*without knowing*) 51A
won't 13C
  in refusals 36B
word classes (parts of speech) 55
  type of adverbs 89A
word order
  main sentence patterns 56B
  questions 22B, 23A
  reported questions 107A
  adjectives 81
  adverbs 89
  phrasal and prepositional verbs 103C, E
  yet, still and **already** 90B,C
  quite a 66A
  enough 93B
  prepositions in questions 22D
  prepositions in relative clauses 111
work
  continuous or simple 9B
  mass noun 57D
worse, worst 86E
would 36A
  with an if-clause 115C, D
  after **wish** 117A
  after **so that** 119C
  wouldn't in refusals 36B
would like 36A
  in requests and offers 33A, B
  + to-infinitive 43B
  would like someone to do something 44D
would mind 33A
would rather 45B
write (to) American English K
wrong 85E

yes/no questions 22B
yet 90
  with present perfect 6B
you 75
  (= people in general) 38C, 75C, American English J
your, yours 70
yourself, yourselves 77